MICROCOMPUTER FUNDAMENTALS

SARAH E. HUTCHINSON

STACEY C. SAWYER

IRWIN
Advantage
Series for
Computer
Education

Homewood, IL 60430
Boston, MA 02116

We recognize that certain terms in this book are trademarks, and we have made every effort to print these throughout the text with the capitalization and punctuation used by the holder of the trademark.

Sponsoring editors:	Larry Alexander and Rick Williamson
Developmental editor:	Rebecca Johnson
Project editor:	Stacey C. Sawyer
Production:	Stacey C. Sawyer, Sawyer & Williams
Designer:	Maureen McCutcheon
Cover designer:	Michael Rogondino
Cover art:	Pat Rogondino
Artists:	Rolin Graphics and GTS Graphics
Compositor:	GTS Graphics
Typeface:	10½/12 Electra
Printer:	Webcrafters, Inc.

Library of Congress Cataloging-in-Publication Data
Hutchinson, Sarah E.
    Microcomputer fundamentals / Sarah E. Hutchinson, Stacey C. Sawyer
        p. cm. — (Irwin advantage series for computer education)
    Includes index.
ISBN 0-256-13396-4
1. Microcomputers. 2. Computer software I. Sawyer, Stacey C.
  II. Title. III. Series.
    QA76.5.H877 1993   92-36228
    004.16—dc20   CIP

Printed in the United States of America
1 2 3 4 5 6 7 8 9 0 WC 9 8 7 6 5 4 3 2

SUPPLEMENTS

FOR THE INSTRUCTOR

Instructor's Manual with Transparency Masters
Color Transparencies
Test Bank
Irwin's Computerized Testing Software

PREFACE

WHY WE WROTE THIS BOOK: MEETING THE NEEDS OF USERS

Microcomputer Fundamentals is written for future microcomputer *users*, also called *end-users*—people for whom the computer will be an everyday tool for working with reports, spreadsheets, databases, and the like. It is not intended for specialists who will write programs or design computer systems.

We wrote this book in order to provide instructors and students with the most useful information possible in a microcomputer course. Specifically, we offer the following five important features.

PRACTICALITY AND COMPLETENESS

A textbook, we feel, should above all be *practical and complete*. It should give users all the information they need to effectively use a microcomputer at work or at home. Thus, for example, we try to avoid the weaknesses we've seen elsewhere of stressing software to the detriment of hardware coverage, or of being too brief or too encyclopedic. We try to give users just what they need to know to use a microcomputer competently for business or personal purposes. Some examples:

- We present up-to-date PC and Macintosh hardware information and compatibility issues so users can understand the capabilities of the computer systems they are using.
- We provide an entire chapter on how to purchase and maintain a microcomputer system, with information on user health and safety.
- We give practical information about ethics, privacy, and security.
- We offer "bonus" information users may find useful on the job, such as the different RAM requirements of different color monitors
- We cover advanced topics such as object-oriented programming, expert systems, virtual reality, and digital convergence—subjects users are sure to encounter in the workplace in the near future.

FLEXIBLE, REASONABLY PRICED SOFTWARE LABS

We realize that students (and instructors) have a great deal of concern about the cost of textbooks. Accordingly, we offer many *reasonably priced*, separately bound software tutorials. These hands-on tutorials, now available or shortly to be available from *Irwin's Advantage Series for Computer Education*, include the following:

dBASE III Plus	DOS 3.3
dBASE IV	DOS 5.0

Excel for the Macintosh	Quattro 1.01
Excel 3.0 for Windows	Quattro Pro 3.0
Filemaker Pro for the Macintosh	QuickBASIC/QBASIC
Lotus 1-2-3 release 2.01 and 2.2	System 7.0 for the Macintosh
Lotus 1-2-3 release 2.3	VisualBASIC
Lotus 1-2-3 release 2.4	Windows 3.1
Lotus 1-2-3 release 3.1	Word for the Macintosh
Microsoft Works	Word 2.0 for Windows
Microsoft Works for Windows	WordPerfect 5.1
Paradox 3.5	

Additional tutorials will be added to the series as the need arises.

Instructors adopting any of these tutorials are entitled to receive a free copy of Irwin's class-organizing software, written by Glen Coulthard.

AVOIDANCE OF CLUTTER

Our market research finds that many instructors have become tired of the cluttered, over-illustrated look and style of many introductory texts. Thus, you will not find margin notes, cartoons, wild colors, and other such distractions here.

Also, we have attempted to use color to enhance content, not overpower it. For example, as Figure 1.2 on page 4 shows, we use four specific colors to indicate input (red), storage (blue/green), processing (brown), and output (gold).

INTERESTING, READABLE STYLE

We are gratified that reviewers have consistently found our writing style praiseworthy. Our primary goal is to reach students by making our explanations as clear, relevant, and interesting as possible.

EFFECTIVE PEDAGOGY

We have carefully developed our learning aids to maximize students' comprehension and learning:

- *Chapter outlines and previews:* Each chapter opens with an outline of the chapter's content and a section called "Why Is This Chapter Important?" which explains why the material in the chapter is important to the user.

- *Chapter summaries:* Each chapter concludes with a useful summary section to help students review.

- *Key terms:* All the important terms covered—and the numbers of the pages on which they are defined—appear in a section called Key Terms at the end of each chapter. All key terms are also listed and defined in the glossary in the back of the book.

- *Self-tests and exercises:* Fill-in-the-blank tests, short-answer exercises, and projects test students' comprehension and encourage them to learn more about microcomputers on their own.

- *Career boxes:* One-page boxes in Chapters 2 through 12 show students how computers are used in some common and uncommon ways in business and other professions.

- *Time-line chart:* This chart, which follows the last chapter, provides an overview of the historical development of information processing and related events from the beginning of recorded history to projected developments in the 21st century.

SUPPLEMENTS THAT WORK

It's not important how many supplements a book has but whether they're truly useful, accurate, and of high quality. We offer a number of supplements that you will find useful.

INSTRUCTOR'S MANUAL WITH TRANSPARENCY MASTERS

This supplement contains:

- Student profile sheet
- Course planning guidelines
- Chapter outlines
- Teaching tips
- 29 transparency masters
- Suggestions for using transparency masters and full-color overhead transparencies

COLOR TRANSPARENCIES

77 full-color overhead transparencies of key illustrations and tables are available to qualified adopters.

TEST BANK

For each lesson, this supplement, prepared by L. Anne Breene, contains:

- True/false, multiple-choice, and fill-in-the-blank questions, graded in difficulty
- Sample midterm exam
- Sample final exam of the entire text
- All answers to the test-bank questions

IRWIN'S COMPUTERIZED TESTING SOFTWARE

This computer-based test bank is available to qualified adopters.

THE DEVELOPMENTAL MODEL FOR THIS BOOK

ACQUISITION AND DEVELOPMENTAL EDITORS

Microcomputer Fundamentals is published as a companion to our *Computers: The User Perspective* and follows the excellent developmental model our publisher has devised for that book. We're grateful for the assistance of our acquisition and developmental editors, who served in an invaluable capacity to guarantee the quality control of this book. Few, if any, publishers offer this high degree of editorial assistance and attention to detail. Special appreciation goes to Larry Alexander, Tom Casson, Bill Setten, and Rebecca Johnson for assistance beyond the call of duty. In addition, we thank Micky Lawler for her careful line-by-line analysis of all our books.

We are also grateful to our many reviewers, who provided helpful comments over the course of several drafts. In addition, we are appreciative of the efforts of the photo researcher, Judy Mason, and the proofreader/copyeditors, Linda McPhee and Toni Murray, whose work significantly improved the quality of this book. The staff at GTS Graphics, typesetter and producer of the new illustrations—especially Elliott Derman, Sherrie Beyen, Daniel Casquilho, and Christina Rogers—are at the top of their field in providing electronic typesetting and graphics services in record time.

WRITE TO US

Finally, we need to know: Was this book truly useful to students? We'd like to hear from you about any improvements we might make. Write to us in care of our publisher, Richard D. Irwin.

SARAH E. HUTCHINSON
STACEY C. SAWYER

CONTENTS

CHAPTER 1

MICROCOMPUTERS: POWER TOOLS FOR AN INFORMATION AGE   1

Why Is This Chapter Important?   2

What Is a Computer System?   2

Computer Hardware   3

Computer Software   5

Types of Computer Systems: What's the Difference?   6

The Anatomy of a Microcomputer   12

Microcomputers at Work   15

Managing Documents   17

Managing Databases   17

Communications   17

Accounting and Finance   18

Microcomputers in the Future   18

Summary   19

Key Terms   20

Exercises   21

CHAPTER 2

INPUT HARDWARE   24

Why Is This Chapter Important?   26

The Keyboard   27

The Keys   28

Nonkeyboard Input Devices   29

Scanning Systems   30

Voice Input Devices   31

Pointing Devices   34

Summary   42

Key Terms   44

Exercises   44

Computers and Careers: The Arts, Sports, and Entertainment   38

CHAPTER 3

PROCESSING HARDWARE   44

Why Is This Chapter Important?   46

The Microprocessor   46

Control Unit   46

Arithmetic/Logic Unit (ALU)   48

Registers   48

Bus   50

Coprocessors   51

Read/Only Memory (ROM)   51

PROM, EPROM, EEPROM   54

Random-Access Memory (RAM)   54

Function of RAM   54

RAM Chips   55

Increasing RAM   55

Measuring the Processing Power of a Computer   59

Addressing Scheme   59

Register Size   59

Data Bus Capacity   61

Clock Speed   61

Instruction Set   61

Checklist   62

Summary   62

Key terms   64

Exercises   65

Computers and Careers: Crime Fighting   60

CHAPTER 4

STORAGE HARDWARE   68

Why Is This Chapter Important?   70

Storage Fundamentals   70

Primary and Secondary Storage   70

Data Representation: Binary Code   71

Files and Data Hierarchy   74

How Is Data Stored?   75

Diskettes   76
   Retrieving and Storing Data   76
   Diskette Storage Capacity   79
   Diskette Sizes and Shapes   81
   Sectors   81
   Access Time   82
Hard Disks   82
   Retrieving and Storing Data   85
   Disk Cartridges   88
Optical Storage   88
   CD-ROM   89
   WORM   89
   Erasable Optical Disks   89
Backing Up a Microcomputer System   91
Summary   92
Key Terms   94
Exercises   95
*Computer and Careers: Food and Beverage
Service   87*

CHAPTER 5

OUTPUT HARDWARE   98

Why Is This Chapter Important?   100
How Do We Categorize Output?   101
Hardcopy Output Devices   102
   Impact (Character) Printers   102
   Nonimpact Printers   106
   Portable Printers   108
   Plotters   111
Softcopy Output Devices   111
   Cathode-Ray Tube (CRT)   111
   Flat Screen Technologies   117
   Voice Output Systems   120
Summary   121
Key Terms   123
Exercises   124
*Computers and Careers: Politics and
Government   113*

CHAPTER 6

APPLICATIONS SOFTWARE   126

Why Is This Chapter Important?   128
Categories of Applications Software   128
Common Features of Applications Software   129

Word Processing Software   130
Desktop Publishing Software   130
Electronic Spreadsheet Software   138
Database Management System Software   140
Graphics Software   141
Integrated Software   143
Computer-Aided Design, Engineering, and
Manufacturing   143
Communications Software   144
Applications Software Utilities   146
Hypertext and Multimedia   147
Deciding What to Purchase   149
Installing Applications Software   151
Summary   151
Key Terms   153
Exercises   154
*Computers and Careers: Science and
Scholarship   142*

CHAPTER 7

SYSTEMS SOFTWARE   156

Why Is This Chapter Important?   158
Internal Command Instructions   158
External Command Instructions   159
Language Processors   159
Other Systems Software Capabilities   160
   Multitasking   160
   Multiprocessing   161
   Timesharing   162
Popular Microcomputer Systems Software   163
   MS-DOS   163
   MS-DOS and Windows   164
   OS/2   166
   UNIX   167
   Macintosh Operating System   167
   Making Your Choice   167
How Is Software Written?   170
   What Tools Are Available for Developing
   Software?   170
   Which Tools Are You Most Likely to Use?   171
Summary   176
Key Terms   177
Exercises   177
*Computers and Careers: Computers for White-Collar
Workers   169*

Chapter 8

Communications and Networking Fundamentals 180

Why Is This Chapter Important? 182

Characteristics of Data Transmission 182
  Analog and Digital Signals 183
  Asynchronous and Synchronous Transmission 184
  Simplex, Half-Duplex, and Full-Duplex Traffic 185

Data Transmission Media 186
  Telephone Lines 187
  Coaxial Cable 187
  Microwave Systems 188
  Satellite Systems 189
  Fiber Optics 191

Data Communications Hardware 192
  Modems 193
  Multiplexers, Concentrators, and Controllers 194
  Front-End Processors 194
  Protocols and Protocol Converters 195

Data Communications Software 197

Communications Networks: Connectivity 198
  Network Configurations 199

Communications Services, Systems, and Utilities 205
  Public Databanks/Information Services 205
  Electronic Shopping 207
  Electronic Bulletin Boards 209
  Electronic Mail 209
  Electronic Banking and Investing 210

Computer Viruses 210

Facsimile (Fax) 213

Digital Convergence: "The Mother of All Industries" 214

Summary 215

Key Terms 217

Exercises 217

Computers and Careers: Manufacturing 202

Chapter 9

Database Management Systems 220

Why Is This Chapter Important? 222

What Is a Database Management System? 222

Data Management Concepts 225
  File Management Systems 225

Database Management Systems 226
  Hardware: Storage Counts 227
  Software: In Control 227
  Data Dictionaries and Transaction Logs 230

Database Models 232
  Hierarchical Database Model 232
  Network Database Model 233
  Relational Database Model 234

Designing a Database 235
  Matching the Design to the Organization 235
  Logical Design 237
  Physical Design 238

Database Administration 239
  Why Administer? 239
  The Job of the Database Administrator 239

Advantages and Disadvantages of the DBMS 240

Who Owns the Database? 241

Summary 242

Key Terms 243

Exercises 244

Computers and Careers: Information 236

Chapter 10

Management Information Systems and System Development 246

Why Is This Chapter Important? 248

Information Systems: What They Are, How They Work 248

What Is Management? 249

What Is a Management Information System? 250
  Levels of Management: What Kinds of Decisions Are Made? 250
  The Role of the MIS in Business 254

How Does Management Make Decisions? 254
  Step 1—Problem Recognition and Identification 254
  Step 2—Identification and Evaluation of Alternatives 254
  Step 3—Alternative Selection 255
  Step 4—Action 256
  Step 5—Follow-Up 256

What Kind of Information Does Management Use to Make Decisions? 256

Types of Management Information Systems 257
  Transaction Processing System (TPS) 257

Management Information System (MIS)   257

Decision Support System (DSS)   258

Developing and Implementing a Management Information System   260

Information Centers   261

Systems Analysis and Design   262

The Systems Development Life Cycle (SDLC)   263

Phase 1—Analyze the Current System   267

Phase 2—Define the New Systems Requirements   270

Phase 3—Design the New System   275

Phase 4—Develop the New System   278

Phase 5—Implement the New System   279

Phase 6—Postimplementation Evaluation and Maintenance   281

What Skills Does the User Need?   282

Summary   282

Key Terms   284

Exercises   285

Computers and Careers: Transportation   266

CHAPTER 11

ADVANCED TOPICS   288

Why Is This Chapter Important?   290

Artificial Intelligence   290

What Is AI Supposed to Do?   290

Robotics   290

Natural Language Processing and Fuzzy Logic   293

Expert Systems: Human Expertise in a Computer   294

Implications for Business   297

Virtual Reality   297

Object-Oriented Programming   298

Advantages and Disadvantages   299

Why Should Users Be Familiar with Object-Oriented Programming?   300

Summary   300

Key Terms   301

Exercises   301

Computers and Careers: Health and Medicine   295

CHAPTER 12

ETHICS, PRIVACY, AND SECURITY   304

Why Is This Chapter Important?   306

Computers and Privacy   306

Databases   306

Electronic Networks   308

Major Laws on Privacy   308

Computer Hazards   309

Crime and Criminals   309

Other Hazards   310

Computer Security   311

Computers and Copyright Violation   312

Software Piracy   312

Shareware, Freeware, and Public Domain Software   313

Electronic Manipulation of Copyrighted Material   314

A Last Word   315

Summary   316

Key Terms   318

Exercises   318

Computers and Disabilities: The Future   320

CHAPTER 13

PURCHASING AND MAINTAINING A MICROCOMPUTER SYSTEM   322

Why Is This Chapter Important?   324

Purchasing a System: What to Consider   324

What Hardware and Software Will You Need?   324

PC Clones: A Good Bet?   326

Macintoshes   326

Where to Go   328

Other Practical Considerations   329

Maintaining a System   330

Temperature   330

Turning the Computer On/Off   332

Plugging in the System   332

Dust and Pollutants   333

Other Practical Considerations   334

Backing Up Your Microcomputer System   334

Ergonomics: Health Issues   336

Physical Health   336

Mental Health   339

Summary   339

Key Terms   340

Portable Checklist for Buying a Microcomputer System   341

KEY DATES IN THE HISTORY AND FUTURE OF INFORMATION PROCESSING   A1

GLOSSARY   G1

INDEX   I1

MICROCOMPUTERS: POWER TOOLS FOR AN INFORMATION AGE

Two questions that you will likely be asked in a job interview are "Have you used a computer before?" and "What types of software do you know how to use?" When you can answer "yes" to the first question and answer the second with a list of different types of software packages, you will be ready for that job interview. As a person living in what is now often called the Information Age, you know that computers are used in almost all professions and offices. You will likely use some type of computer, probably a microcomputer, in your career. Chapter 1 will start you on your way to using this powerful tool to your advantage.

PREVIEW

When you have completed this chapter, you will be able to:

■

Explain what a computer system is by focusing on hardware, software, data/information, procedures, and people

■

Distinguish the four main types of computer systems

■

Describe the basic components of a microcomputer

■

Describe the types of tasks microcomputers are used for in business today

CHAPTER OUTLINE

Why Is This Chapter Important?

What Is a Computer System?

    Computer Hardware

    Computer Software

Types of Computer Systems: What's the Difference?

    The Anatomy of a Microcomputer

Microcomputers at Work

    Managing Documents

    Managing Databases

    Communications

    Accounting and Finance

Microcomputers in the Future

Summary

Key Terms

Exercises

This text focuses on microcomputers. By 1995, more than 185 million microcomputers will be in use in companies worldwide. But what is a microcomputer? How does this computer compare to other types of computers? Why do you need to know more about microcomputers than about other types of computers?

Chapter 1 defines terms, answers some questions, and puts the microcomputer into perspective by providing an overview of all types of computers. It also prepares you to learn about computer hardware and software as you progress through the text.

This chapter may mark your first step toward becoming computer literate. The meaning of **computer literacy**—also called **computer competency**—has rapidly changed. In the early 1980s, most **computer professionals** (those people who have had formal education in the technical aspects of computers) thought of it simply as *technical knowledge*; to **users** (those people without much technical knowledge of computers but who make decisions based on reports and other results produced by computers), it usually meant only *computer awareness*. Today, however, to be considered computer literate you must have a solid understanding of what a computer is and how it can be used as a resource. In addition, to be computer literate you must know how to use a microcomputer as a business or professional tool to assist in producing the information necessary to make intelligent and timely decisions.

The change in the definition of computer literacy during the 1980s is a direct result of the greatly increased use of microcomputers in business. Because many management professionals already know how to use microcomputers, your success in the business or professional world may mean that you also must master this skill.

WHAT IS A COMPUTER SYSTEM?

The term **computer** is used to describe a device made up of a combination of electronic and electromechanical (part electronic and part mechanical) components. By itself, a computer has no intelligence and is referred to as **hardware**. A computer doesn't come to life until it is connected to other parts of a computer system. A **computer system** (Figure 1.1) is a combination of five elements:

- Hardware
- Software
- Data/information
- Procedures
- People

When one computer system is set up to communicate with another computer system, **connectivity** becomes a sixth system element. In other words, the manner in which the various individual systems are connected—for example, by phone lines, microwave transmission, or satellite—is an element of the total computer system. In the 1990s, business professionals will direct a tremendous amount of attention and financial resources toward enabling different computer systems to communicate. We talk about connectivity in more detail in Chapter 8.

Software is the term used to describe the instructions that tell the hardware how to perform a task. Without software instructions, the hardware doesn't know what to do.

The purpose of a computer system is to convert data into information. **Data** is raw, *unevaluated* facts and figures, concepts, or instructions. This raw material is processed into useful **information**. In other words, information is the product of **data processing**. This **processing** includes refining, summarizing, categorizing, and otherwise manipulating data into a useful form for decision making.

People (you), however, constitute the most important component of the computer system. People operate the computer hardware; they create the computer software instructions and respond to the **procedures** that those instructions present. People "capture" data in a variety of ways—for example, by reading, listening, or seeing. Then they may record the data on a document. For instance, Roger Shu records his name on an employee timecard by first entering the letter R. This letter, and each of the remaining letters in his name, is an element of data, as are the numbers 12/22 and 5, used to indicate the date and the number of overtime hours worked. By themselves, these data elements are useless; we must process them to make them mean something. The report produced when Roger's data is run through a computer-based employee records system gives us information—for example, the amount of money due Roger for his overtime work.

Now we'll discuss the basics about the hardware devices that convert data into information in a typical computer-based system.

COMPUTER HARDWARE

If, at a job interview, you are asked about what kind of computer equipment you've used before or what you know about hardware and you don't have an answer, your interviewer will probably perceive you as a person who doesn't take an active role in what's going on around you—a perception that could dramatically hurt your chances of getting the job you want. In today's business world, not

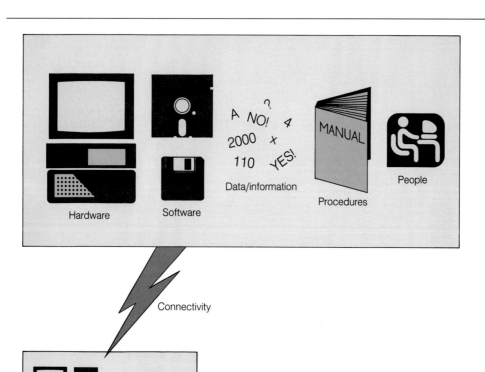

FIGURE 1.1

A computer system combines five elements: hardware, software, data/information, procedures, and people. Connectivity is a sixth element when two or more separate computer systems are set up to communicate.

knowing what computer hardware is and what typical hardware components do is similar to being a taxi driver and not knowing what a car is and that it has components such as an engine, doors, windows, and so on.

Computer hardware can be divided into four categories:

1. Input hardware
2. Processing hardware
3. Storage hardware
4. Output hardware

Figure 1.2 shows the typical configuration of computer hardware.

In this section, we provide a brief description of the components found in each of these categories so you can see how each component relates to others. In Chapters 2 through 5 we talk about input, processing, storage, and output hardware in more detail.

INPUT HARDWARE

The purpose of **input hardware** is to collect data and convert it into a form suitable for computer processing. The most common input device is a **keyboard**. It looks very much like a typewriter keyboard with rows of keys arranged in the typical typewriter layout, as well as a number of additional keys used to enter special computer-related codes. Although it isn't the only type of input device available, the computer keyboard is the one most generally used by the business community. In Chapter 2, we describe the microcomputer keyboard in detail, along with other types of popular input devices.

FIGURE 1.2

The four categories of computer hardware are input, processing, storage, and output.

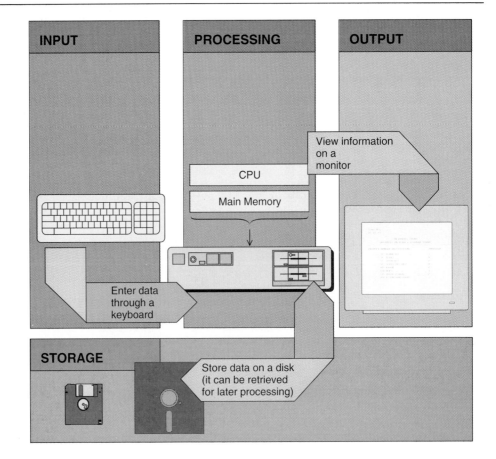

PROCESSING HARDWARE

The purpose of **processing hardware** is to retrieve, interpret, and direct the execution of software instructions provided to the computer. The most common components of processing hardware are the central processing unit and main memory.

The **central processing unit (CPU)** is the brain of the computer. It reads and interprets software instructions and coordinates the processing activities that must take place. The design of the CPU affects the processing power and the speed of the computer, as well as the amount of main memory it can use effectively. With a well-designed CPU in your computer, you can perform highly sophisticated tasks in a very short time.

Main memory (also called *random access memory* [RAM], *internal memory*, *primary storage*, or just *memory*) can be thought of as an electronic desktop. The more desk surface you have in front of you, the more you can place on it. Similarly, if your computer has a lot of memory, you can place more software instructions in it. (Some of these instructions and data are retrieved by the computer from storage on disk or tape; others are input directly by the user—for example, through the keyboard.) The amount of memory available determines whether you can run simple or sophisticated software; a computer with a large memory is more capable of holding the thousands of instructions that are contained in the more sophisticated software programs. In addition, it also allows you to work with and manipulate great amounts of data and information at one time. Quite simply, the more main memory you have in your computer, the more you can accomplish. However, the data and instructions in main memory are **volatile**—that is, they are lost when the computer's power is turned off, unless the user had saved them to a storage device. In Chapter 3, we describe processing hardware in more detail.

STORAGE HARDWARE

The purpose of **storage hardware** is to provide a means of storing computer instructions and data in a form that is relatively permanent, or **nonvolatile**—that is, the data is not lost when the power is turned off—and easy to retrieve when needed for processing. Storage hardware serves the same basic functions as do office filing systems except that it stores data as electromagnetic signals or laser-etched spots, commonly on disk or tape, rather than on paper. Storage devices are discussed in Chapter 4.

OUTPUT HARDWARE

The purpose of **output hardware** is to provide the user with the means to view information produced by the computer system. Information is output in either **hardcopy** or **softcopy** form. Hardcopy output can be held in your hand—an example is paper with text (words or numbers) or graphics printed on it. Softcopy output is displayed on a **monitor**, a television-like screen on which you can read text and graphics. We describe output devices in Chapter 5.

Communications hardware, which is used to transmit output among and receive input from different computer systems, is discussed in Chapter 8.

COMPUTER SOFTWARE

A computer is an inanimate device that has no intelligence of its own and must be supplied with instructions so that it knows what to do and how and when to do it. These instructions are called *software*. The importance of software can't be overestimated. You might have what most people consider the best computer sitting on your desk; however, without software to "feed" it, the computer will do nothing more than take up space.

Software is made up of a group of related **programs**, each of which is a group of related instructions that perform very specific processing tasks. These instructions are represented on disk or tape using a binary coding scheme. In Chapter 4, we describe in detail how instructions and data are represented on storage devices.

Software acquired to perform a general business function is often referred to as a **software package**. Software packages, which are usually created by professional software writers, are accompanied by **documentation**—users' manuals—that explains how to use the software.

Software can generally be divided into two categories:

1. Systems software
2. Applications software

SYSTEMS SOFTWARE

Programs designed to allow the computer to manage its own resources are called **systems software**. This software runs the basic operations; it tells the hardware what to do and how and when to do it. However, it does not solve specific problems relating to a business or a profession. For example, systems software will not process a prediction of what your company's tax bill will be next year, but it will tell the computer where to store the data used during processing; systems software will not process the creation of the animation strip for your next film, but it will manage how it is output.

APPLICATIONS SOFTWARE

Any instructions or collection of related programs designed to be carried out by a computer to satisfy a user's *specific* needs are **applications software**. A group of programs written to perform payroll processing is one type of applications software, as are programs written to maintain personnel records, update an inventory system, help you calculate a budget, or monitor the incubation temperatures at your poultry farm.

Applications software can be purchased off the shelf—that is, already programmed, or written—or it can be written to order by qualified programmers. If, for example, a company's payroll processing requirements are fairly routine, it can probably purchase one or more payroll applications software programs off the shelf to handle the job. However, if a company has unique payroll requirements, such as a need to handle the records of hourly employees, salaried employees, and commissioned employees, then off-the-shelf software may not be satisfactory. It may be more cost-effective to have the payroll programs written to exact specifications by a computer programmer.

Figure 1.3 shows a variety of packaged applications software available at computer stores. Many of these products are also available through vendors and mail-order sources.

Chapters 6 and 7 explore the categories of applications software and systems software.

TYPES OF COMPUTER SYSTEMS: WHAT'S THE DIFFERENCE?

Microcomputer users often come into contact with other types of computer systems. To provide a basis for comparing their capabilities, computers are generally grouped into four basic categories:

1. Supercomputers, which are the powerful giants of the computer world;
2. Mainframe computers, which are large, extremely powerful computers used by many large companies;

3. Minicomputers, which are the next most powerful;

4. Microcomputers, which are the least powerful—but which you most likely will be required to use in business.

It's hard to assign a worthwhile definition to each type of computer because definitions can get bogged down in potentially confusing technical jargon. Nevertheless, the following definitions can suffice:

- A **supercomputer** (Figure 1.4) can handle gigantic amounts of scientific computation. It's maintained in a special room or environment, may be about 50,000 times faster than a microcomputer, and may cost as much as $20 million. As a user in business, you probably would not have contact with a supercomputer. However, you might if you worked in the areas of defense and weaponry, weather forecasting, or scientific research; at one of several large universities; or for the National Aeronautics and Space Administration.

FIGURE 1.3

Need help with your budget? Want to design and print some greeting cards or your own newsletter? Want to set up a large bank of cross-referenced, business-related data? Buying software is almost like buying records, tapes, and CDs. Most computer stores offer a wide variety of applications software packages. But be sure you know what you want to accomplish before you make your selection.

- A **mainframe computer** (Figure 1.5) is a large computer, usually housed in a controlled environment, that can support the processing requirements of hundreds and often thousands of users and computer professionals. It may cost from several hundred thousand dollars up to $10 million. If you go to work for an airline, a bank, a large insurance company, a large accounting company, a large university, or the Social Security Administration, you will likely have contact—through your individual workstation—with a mainframe computer.

- A **minicomputer,** also known as a *midsized* or *low-end mainframe computer* (Figure 1.6), is similar to but less powerful than a mainframe computer. It

FIGURE 1.4

Supercomputer. This supercomputer (center), capable of performing 1.8 billion calculations a second, is the centerpiece of the National Test Bed. It was installed in mid-1988 at Colorado Springs for the U.S. Strategic Defense Initiative.

FIGURE 1.5

Mainframe. The mainframe computer is front left, between two printers. At the back left are disk-drive storage units; tape storage units are at the back and back right. These units, or peripherals, are connected to the mainframe by under-floor cables.

can support 2 to about 50 users and computer professionals. Minicomputers and mainframe computers can work much faster than microcomputers and have many more storage locations in main memory. Minicomputers cost from about $10,000 to several hundred thousand dollars. Many small and medium-sized companies today use minicomputers.

- The **microcomputer** (Figure 1.7) is the type of computer that you undoubtedly will be dealing with as a user. You may already be familiar with the microcomputer, also known as a *personal computer* (PC). Microcomputers cost between $500 and about $20,000. They vary in size from small portables, such as *notebook computers* and *laptop computers* that you can carry around like a briefcase, to powerful desktop *workstations*, such as those used by engineers and scientists. A microcomputer, which is generally used by only one person at a time but which can often support more—uses a **chip** as its CPU. This chip is referred to as the **microprocessor**. As small as one quarter of an inch square (Figure 1.8), a chip is made of silicon, a material made from sand. Silicon is referred to as a **semiconductor** because it sometimes conducts electricity and sometimes does not (*semi* means "partly"). (Silicon by itself conducts electricity poorly, but when impurities such as arsenic and indium are added, it can be used to form electrical circuits.)

Table 1.1 compares the four basic types of computers. In general, a computer's type is determined by the following seven factors:

1. *The type of CPU.* As noted, microcomputers use microprocessors. The larger computers tend to use CPUs made up of separate, high-speed, sophisticated components.

2. *The amount of main memory the CPU can use.* A computer equipped with a large amount of main memory can support more sophisticated programs and can even hold several different programs in memory at the same time.

FIGURE 1.6

Minicomputer. Four to more than 100 personal computers (workstations) can be linked to a minicomputer. (The minicomputer in this photo is on the floor to the left of the desk. The computers on the desks are linked to it.)

3. *The capacity of the storage devices.* The larger computer systems tend to be equipped with higher-capacity storage devices (covered in Chapter 4).

4. *The speed of the output devices.* The speed of microcomputer output devices tends to be rated in terms of the number of **characters per second (cps)** that can be printed—usually in tens and hundreds of cps. Larger computers' output devices are faster and are usually rated at speeds of hundreds or thousands of lines that can be printed per minute.

FIGURE 1.7

Microcomputer. This photo shows an IBM PS/2 Model 90 XP486 microcomputer; the three main components are the monitor, the system unit, and the keyboard. This unit also has a mouse.

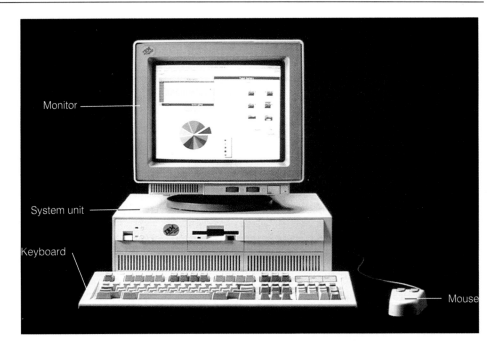

FIGURE 1.8

This photo of a microprocessor gives you an idea of how small a chip is.

5. *The processing speed in* **millions of instructions per second (mips).** The term *instruction* is used here to describe a basic task that the software asks the computer to perform while also identifying the data to be affected. The processing speed of the smaller computers ranges from 3 to 5 mips. The speed of large computers can be 70 to 100 mips or more, and supercomputers can process from 200 million up to billions of instructions per second. In other words, a mainframe computer can process your data a great deal faster than a microcomputer can.

6. *The number of users that can access the computer at one time.* Most small computers can support only a single user; some can support as many as two or three at a time. Large computers can support hundreds of users simultaneously.

7. *The cost of the computer system.* Business systems can cost as little as $1,500 (for a microcomputer) or as much as $10 million (for a mainframe)—and much more for a supercomputer.

It's difficult to say exactly what kind of computer you'll be using in the business environment. Some companies use a combination of computers. For instance, a company with branch offices around the country might use a mainframe computer to manage companywide customer data. To access information from the mainframe, the user might use a microcomputer that sits on his or her desktop. In addition to accessing information from the mainframe computer, the microcomputer can be used to perform specialized tasks such as generating invoices or drafting letters to customers. Although it is still relatively easy to find a company that doesn't use a supercomputer, a mainframe, or a minicomputer to process data, it is difficult to locate a company that doesn't use a microcomputer for some of its processing. Because microcomputers are generally versatile, increasingly powerful, and more affordable than the other types of computers, they provide a practical tool for the business that wants to computerize.

Chances are that, when you enter the business environment, you will be required to know how to use a microcomputer to perform many of your job-related functions. To use a microcomputer effectively and talk about it intelligently, you

---

TABLE 1.1   The Four Kinds of Computers*

	Microcomputer	Minicomputer	Mainframe	Supercomputer
Main memory	512,000–32,000,000 characters	8,000,000–50,000,000 characters	32,000,000–200,000,000 characters	100,000,000–2,000,000,000 characters
Storage	360,000–300,000,000 characters	120,000,000–1,000,000,000+ characters	500,000,000–? characters	No limitation
Processing speed	700,000–10,000,000 instructions per second	8–40 mips	30 mips and up	200 mips and up
Cost	$500–20,000	$10,000–$475,000	$250,000 and up	$10,000,000 and up

*The figures in this table represent average approximations. These numbers change rapidly as changing technology blurs the distinctions between categories.

must understand the typical components of a microcomputer system. The more you know about them, the more valuable you will be to an employer. In the following section, we concentrate a bit more on microcomputer components.

THE ANATOMY OF A MICROCOMPUTER

To understand the tremendous role microcomputers now play in business, it's helpful to look at how that role has developed. With the introduction of the Apple II and the Radio Shack Model I and II systems in the late 1970s, the business community began to adopt microcomputers. Then a number of additional vendors, including Atari, Commodore, Osborne, and Kaypro, entered the marketplace with computers designed to be used in the office or in the home. The interest in microcomputers grew rather slowly at first for several reasons: (1) The initial cost for some microcomputer systems was quite high, ranging up to $6,000; (2) only a limited amount of software was commercially available, and the average person was not able to write his or her own software; (3) the average person did not have sufficient background in computer-related subjects to use the computer without difficulty; and (4) there were no industrywide standards to ensure the **compatibility**—that is, the usability—of data and software on different types of microcomputer systems.

However, when IBM introduced the IBM PC in 1981, so many businesses adopted the product that an industry standard was set. Most vendors now design their products to be compatible with this standard—these products are referred to as IBM **clones**. The only other relatively successful microcomputer product lines today that have maintained their own unique standards are the Apple II and the Macintosh. The Apple II retains a loyal group of users who have supported it since its introduction in the late 1970s. Although the Apple II has been overshadowed in the business world by IBM-compatible products, the powerful and versatile Apple Macintosh line of microcomputers is now commonly used in desktop publishing operations. (We'll discuss desktop publishing in more detail in Chapter 6.)

The large number of different types of microcomputer systems in the marketplace makes it difficult to select one best system. As a result, our discussion of the microcomputer will center on the three basic hardware devices found in most desktop microcomputer systems used in business today: the keyboard, the monitor, and the system unit (Figure 1.9).

KEYBOARD
The microcomputer input device that you will use the most—the keyboard—is made up of a circuit board and related electronic components that generate a unique electronic code when each key is pressed. The code is passed along the keyboard cord to the computer system unit, where it is translated into a usable form for processing. The number of keys and their positions on the keyboard vary among machines. You should select a keyboard that is comfortable for you to use. (A mouse is also frequently used to input data, but we will describe the mouse in Chapter 2.)

MONITOR
The term *monitor* is used interchangeably with *screen, video display screen,* and *cathode-ray tube (CRT).* This output device provides your principal visual contact with the microcomputer system. When you enter commands or data from the keyboard, you see the results on the monitor. A **monochrome monitor** displays text and, in some cases, graphics in a single color—commonly green or amber—usually on a dark background. A **color monitor,** often referred to as an **RGB monitor** (for red, green, blue), can display text and graphics in various colors. Most of

the capabilities of the monitor, including image clarity and the ability to do graphics, are determined by the sophistication of the video display circuit board, if any, contained within the system unit.

System Unit

The main computer system cabinet, called the **system unit** (Figure 1.10), usually houses the power supply, the system board, and the storage devices (although

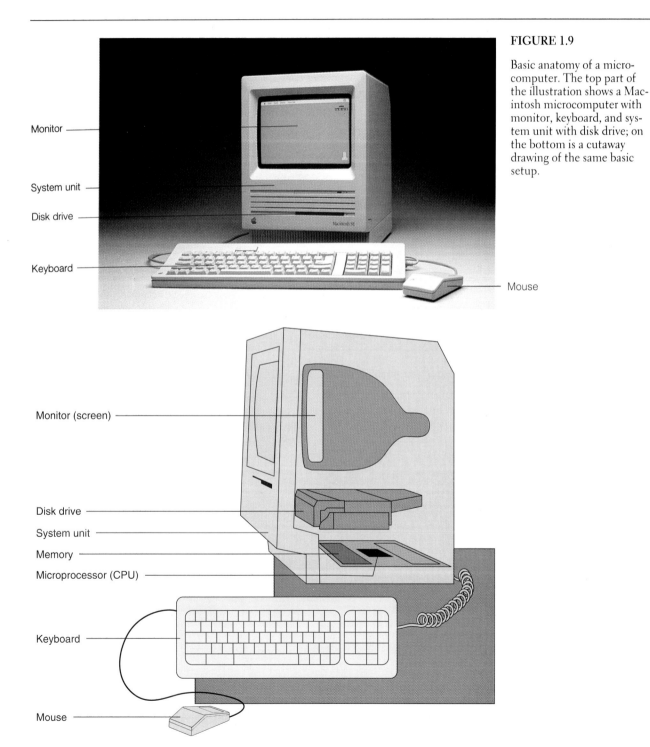

FIGURE 1.9

Basic anatomy of a microcomputer. The top part of the illustration shows a Macintosh microcomputer with monitor, keyboard, and system unit with disk drive; on the bottom is a cutaway drawing of the same basic setup.

Monitor

System unit

Disk drive

Keyboard

Mouse

Monitor (screen)

Disk drive

System unit

Memory

Microprocessor (CPU)

Keyboard

Mouse

some storage devices—disk drives, for example—are often housed in cabinets outside the system unit). These elements can be defined as follows:

1. The **power supply** provides electrical power to all components housed in the system unit. In some microcomputers—such as the Macintosh—it also provides power to the monitor.

2. The **system board,** also known as the **motherboard,** is the main circuit board of the microcomputer system. It normally includes (1) the microprocessor chip (or CPU), (2) main memory chips, (3) all related support circuitry, and (4) the expansion slots where additional components can be plugged in.

3. The **storage devices** are usually one or more floppy disk drives and usually a high-capacity hard disk drive. A **floppy disk,** or **diskette,** is a thin plastic disk enclosed in a paper or plastic covering that can be magnetically encoded with data. **Hard disks** are rigid disks capable of storing much more

---

FIGURE 1.10   This illustration shows the basic parts of the microcomputer's system unit. (The system board continues under the diskette drive.)

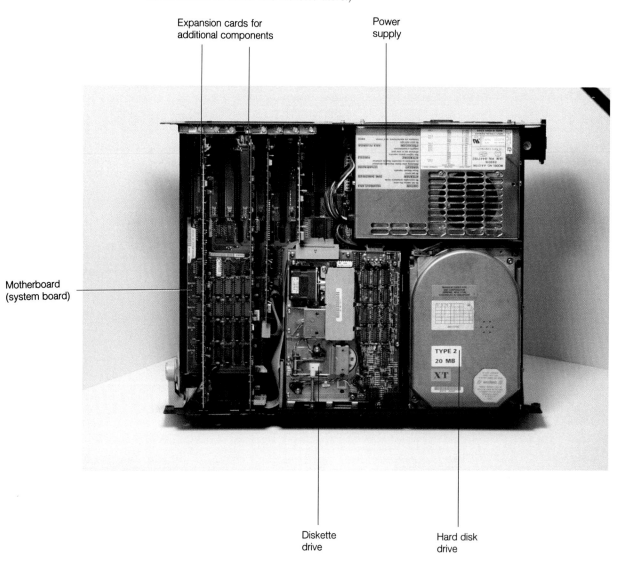

Expansion cards for additional components

Power supply

Motherboard (system board)

Diskette drive

Hard disk drive

data than a floppy disk. (And hard disk drives access data faster than do floppy disk drives.) Hard disks are more expensive than floppy disks. Since most hard disks are permanently installed in the system unit, floppy disks, which can be carried around, are often used to move data from one computer to another.

4. *Additional components:* The expansion slots on the system board allow users to add new components to their computer systems. The most popular add-on components include:
   - A memory card containing main memory chips that give you additional main memory
   - An internal modem to facilitate data communications between computers over phone lines and similar cables
   - A battery-powered clock and calendar mechanism
   - Additional printer ports (hook-ups) that allow you to communicate with several types of output devices
   - Video display boards

Don't worry about remembering what all these components are right now. They will be explained in detail later in the book. Just remember that microcomputers are likely to become an important part of your career. Pay attention to them and focus on what they can do for you.

MICROCOMPUTERS AT WORK

No longer are jobs that require computing experience the sole domain of the computer professional. Today, job applicants on any level may need personal computer experience. In most businesses, microcomputers are viewed as standard business tools for all employees, from the president of the company to the clerks in the typing pool. As the following excerpts from ads in a newspaper's Job Opportunities section demonstrate, many jobs require personal computing experience.

- Accounting—A/R (Accounts Receivable) Supervisor. "Knowledge of PC-based accounting system is a must."
- Consulting. "Prioritize work loads and manage office. Experience with word processing software required."
- Administrative Assistant. "Must have strong background in WordPerfect and Lotus."
- Banking—Loan Service Manager. "Personal computers and basic accounting skills required."
- Contracts Administrator. "Experience required in all aspects of contract administration, including contract and proposal preparation, scheduling, expediting, tracking, and closing. PC experience required."
- Data Entry Operator. "Prior experience on personal computer required."
- Copywriter. "Knowledge of word processing a must."
- Financial Operations. "Computer skills required."
- Loan Processor Trainee. "High-volume mortgage company is looking for qualified individual to train. Must have prior PC experience."
- Sales. "Growth-oriented new software engineering company seeks a results-oriented individual. PC experience preferred."
- Telemarketer. "Professional high-spirited team seeks telemarketer with microcomputer background."

- Production Editor. "Should be knowledgeable about latest desktop publishing techniques, preferably Ventura. Multimate and Lotus a plus."

For each of these jobs—and for many others—unless you have experience using a microcomputer, you probably won't even be considered (Figure 1.11)!

Microcomputing technology is being used across many nations in many different environments. Medical, education, and government sites account for approximately 42% of all installed personal computers in the United States. Other types of businesses—in the areas of banking, savings and loan, transportation, utilities, finance, insurance, process manufacturing, agriculture, data processing, publishing, wholesale and retail businesses—use microcomputers the most. As stated, no matter where you work, you will most likely use a microcomputer to perform some of your job-related tasks. Because of this likelihood, you should be asking yourself the following kinds of questions: What types of tasks are microcomputers being used for? Why are they so popular? How can a business justify the costs of hardware, software, and training? To answer these questions, the following sections

FIGURE 1.11

These job ads from real newspapers and magazines represent only a few ways computers are used in business and the professions.

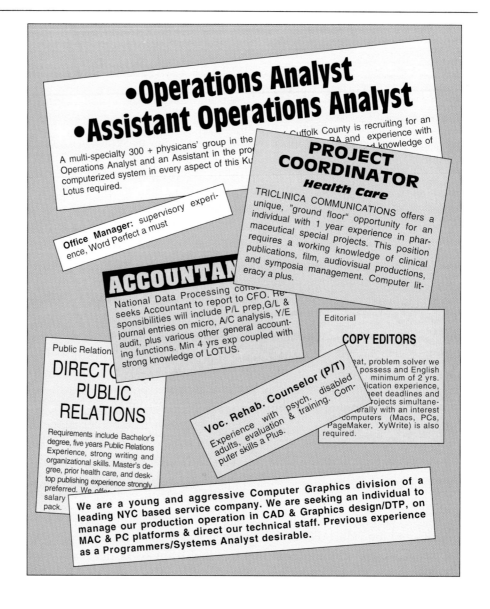

describe the types of tasks that microcomputers are typically used for in business. Most businesses perform one or more of these tasks.

Managing Documents

Word processing software—software that enables the user to electronically create, edit, store, and print documents—is one of the most popular types of microcomputer applications in business. In fact, many microcomputers are used *only* for word processing. Because word processing software makes creating, changing, "dressing up," duplicating, and printing documents much quicker and easier than it used to be, it saves the business professional a lot of time and money. Thus when a business purchases a microcomputer, it typically purchases word processing software. As a result, word processing software sales have climbed steadily over the last five years—and they continue to do so.

Managing Databases

Another major reason businesses bring microcomputers in-house is to help them manage, and draw conclusions about, huge amounts of data—their company **database**. Before dBASE II was introduced in 1982, computer-based database management activities were performed principally by mainframes and minicomputers. Because of the huge expenses associated with purchasing and operating these large systems, most businesses couldn't afford to computerize the management of company data. In addition, the computer systems weren't easy to use, and they required that experienced programmers be hired to first write the software for the system and then run the system. For most businesses, using microcomputers and dBASE II represented an astonishing alternative to managing the company database by hand. Data could now be kept up to date easily, and reports were more comprehensive and more readily available than they previously were. And the system didn't have to be run by trained programmers. Because of this new and valuable software tool, sales of microcomputers skyrocketed.

Today, database management is a common application for microcomputers in business. Sales of **database management software** continue to rise at the same rate as sales of word processing software.

Communications

One of the major reasons microcomputers are so popular in business is that they facilitate efficient communication. In more and more companies and professions, microcomputers are being "tied" together so they can share data and information. In such environments, microcomputers are used to enable people in offices around the country and around the world to communicate without playing "telephone tag." In addition, when microcomputer systems are connected, it's easy to distribute announcements and reports, thereby reducing the amount of paper shuffling that goes on. Some experts predict that soon 90% of all microcomputers in business will be part of a **network,** or connected to one or more other computers.

Microcomputers with **facsimile (fax)** capabilities—the ability to "read" text and graphics and transmit them over telephone lines to other microcomputers with fax capabilities—are being used by more and more businesses every day. Faxing documents instead of sending them via a messenger service or an overnight shipping service saves some companies thousands of dollars monthly. And, instead of having to wait one or two days to receive important documents, fax users have to wait only a few minutes.

ACCOUNTING AND FINANCE

Recently the personal computer has had a highly visible influence on how finances are managed in businesses. According to a study conducted by the National Association of Accountants, Arthur Young & Co., and Digital Equipment Corporation, most financial functions in business—including planning, forecasting, budgeting, and management reporting—are performed by microcomputers. Of 510 senior executives surveyed (from companies of more than $50 million in revenues), 83% used microcomputers routinely to receive up-to-date financial information.

From major stock exchanges around the world to individual businesses and households, computers are affecting the way huge amounts of money are being handled each day. In investment brokerage houses across the United States, microcomputers are being used to make brokers more efficient. For example, in 1987, Merrill Lynch & Co. replaced its mainframe computer with 20,000 IBM PS/2 microcomputers. The move was designed to provide brokers at the 500 offices around the world with more useful information. In 1991, Shearson Lehman had nearly 70 Sun 360 and Compaq 386 microcomputers working together on the floor of the New York Stock Exchange. Also, it is estimated that 8 out of 10 accountants use microcomputers to do their jobs. **Electronic spreadsheet software**—software that allows users to easily perform complicated calculations on large amounts of data—is used extensively to perform accounting and finance-related tasks.

MICROCOMPUTERS IN THE FUTURE

In retrospect, the development of the microcomputer into an integral part of business and North American culture seems to have progressed predictably over the past decade or so. But this is not really true. No one in the early 1980s could have foreseen what the microcomputer would look like and be able to do today. The collective effort of thousands of innovators and investors has helped to define the modern microcomputer, and it has ultimately been business that has determined what technologies stay and go and what technologies are needed.

What is the point? It is hard to foresee exactly what the microcomputer will evolve into during the next decade. However, it certainly will play an important role in your career. With each passing year, the technologies that allow all types of computers to communicate are improving so that the issue of compatibility will no longer be an issue. It won't matter whether you are using an IBM PS/2, a Macintosh, a mainframe, or some other type of computer—each one will be able to process data from the others.

You can also be sure that the microcomputers of tomorrow will be able to process data faster. It seems that, with each day, some technological advance is made that increases the speed with which microcomputers can process data into information. The faster a computer can process data, the greater the amount of work that can be done in the same amount of time—that is, if the work is being done in an appropriate manner. Even though microcomputers are becoming more and more powerful, their cost has been going down. Indeed, the microcomputer industry is one of the few industries in which the product's price goes down as the product becomes more powerful and more useful. It is predicted that by 1994, microcomputers will be as powerful as the mainframes of 10 years ago, and the cost of processing on microcomputers will be 80 times less than it was in 1984.

In short, microcomputers will continue to get better and better. When referring to the microcomputers of the 1990s, Edward M. Esber, the chairman and CEO of a prominent software company, said: "It goes without saying that the dinosaurs won't survive. It's going to be an exciting new world."

SUMMARY

- Being *computer literate*—that is, being familiar with computers and their uses— is necessary today because it is virtually inevitable that you will be using a computer in your career. As the uses of computers in business and the professions increase, graduating students will be required to have more advanced computer training.

- A computer is a device made up of electronic and electromechanical parts; by itself it has no intelligence and is referred to as *hardware.*

- A computer must be part of a system to be useful. A *computer system* has five parts:
  1. *Hardware*
  2. *Software*
  3. *Data/information*
  4. *Procedures*
  5. *People*

- *Hardware* comprises the electronic and the electromechanical parts of the computer system.

- *Software* is the instructions—electronically encoded on disk or tape—that tell the hardware what to do.

- *Data* is raw, unevaluated facts, concepts, or instructions. Through *data processing* data becomes *information*, which is data transformed into a form useful for decision making. Processing can include refining, summarizing, categorizing, and listing, as well as other forms of data manipulation.

- *Procedures* are specific sequences of steps, usually documented, that users follow to complete one or more information processing activities.

- *People*—the most important part of the computer system—operate the computer hardware, create the software instructions, and establish *procedures* for carrying out tasks.

- Computer hardware is categorized as:
  1. *Input hardware*—used to collect data and input it into the computer system in computer-usable form. The *keyboard* is the most common input device.
  2. *Processing hardware*—retrieves, interprets, and directs the execution of software instructions. The main components of processing hardware are the *central processing unit* (CPU), which is the "brain" of the computer, and *main memory*, the computer's primary storage area, where data and instructions currently being used are stored. These data and instructions are *volatile*— that is, they will be lost when the computer's power is turned off, unless they are saved to a storage device.
  3. *Storage hardware*—usually disk or tape devices for relatively permanent (*nonvolatile*) storage of data and instructions for later retrieval and processing.
  4. *Output hardware*—provides a means for the user to view information produced by the computer system—either in *hardcopy* form, such as printouts from a printer, or *softcopy* form, such as a display on a monitor, a TV-like screen that can be color (*RGB*) or *monochrome*, usually amber, green, or black and white.

- *Software*, which is usually written by professional programmers, is made up of a group of related *programs*, each of which is a group of related instructions that perform specific processing tasks. Software that runs the hardware and allows the computer to manage its resources is *systems software*; software that is written to perform a specific function for the user—such as preparing payroll or doing page-makeup for a magazine—is *applications software*. Applications software can be purchased *off the shelf* as a *software package*, or it can be *custom written* to solve the unique needs of one company or business. Software is accompanied by *documentation*, or users' manuals.

- Computers are categorized from the largest and most powerful to the smallest and least powerful:
  1. *Supercomputer*
  2. *Mainframe computer*
  3. *Minicomputer*
  4. *Microcomputer*

- A computer's type is determined by seven factors:
  1. Type of CPU
  2. Amount of main memory the CPU can use
  3. Storage capacity
  4. Speed of output devices
  5. Processing speed
  6. Number of users that can access the computer at one time
  7. Cost

- The microcomputer (*personal computer*, or *PC*) is the computer used most by business professionals. Microcomputers range in size from small *notebooks* and *laptops* to powerful desktop *workstations*, which are hooked up to a larger computer. The microcomputer has a small *semiconductor* (*silicon*) *chip*, or *microprocessor*, as its CPU.

- A microcomputer main system cabinet—the *system unit*—usually houses the *power supply*, the *system board* (*motherboard*), and some storage devices, such as one or more floppy disk drives and a high-capacity hard disk drive. The system board includes the *microprocessor chip*, *main memory chips*, *related support circuitry*, and *expansion slots*.

- Microcomputers are used for, among other things, *word processing*—creating, editing, storing, and printing documents; *database management*—creating and managing huge "banks" of data; *communications*—facilitating immediate communication and document transmission capabilities through the use of *networks*, *fax*, and *modems*; and *financial management* through the use of electronic *spreadsheets*.

KEY TERMS

applications software, p. 6
central processing unit (CPU), p. 5
characters per second (cps), p. 10
chip, p. 9
clone, p. 12
color monitor, p. 12
compatibility, p. 12
computer, p. 2
computer literacy, p. 2
computer professional, p. 2
computer system, p. 2
connectivity, p. 2

data, p. 2
data processing, p. 3
database, p. 17
database management software, p. 17
diskette, p. 14
documentation, p. 6
electronic spreadsheet software, p. 18
facsimile (fax), p. 17
floppy disk, p. 14
hardcopy, p. 5
hard disk, p. 14
hardware, p. 2
information, p. 3
input hardware, p. 4

keyboard, p. 4
mainframe computer, p. 8
main memory, p. 5
microcomputer, p. 9
microprocessor, p. 9
millions of instructions per second (mips), p. 11
minicomputer, p. 8
monitor, p. 5
monochrome monitor, p. 12
motherboard, p. 14
network, p. 17
nonvolatile, p. 5

output hardware, p. 5
power supply, p. 14
procedures, p. 3
processing, p. 3
processing hardware,
    p. 5
program, p. 6
RGB (color) monitor,
    p. 12

semiconductor, p. 9
softcopy, p. 5
software, p. 2
software package, p. 6
storage device, p. 14
storage hardware, p. 5
supercomputer, p. 7

system board, p. 14
system unit, p. 13
systems software, p. 6
user, p. 2
volatile, p. 5
word processing
    software, p. 17

EXERCISES

SELF-TEST

1. (Figure 1.12) Label the components of the microcomputer.

2. The term _____ is used to describe a device made up of electronic and electromechanical parts.

3. List four categories of hardware:
   a. _____   b. _____   c. _____   d. _____

4. Main memory is a software component. (true/false)

5. _____ _____ includes programs designed to enable the computer to manage its own resources.

6. Softcopy output can be displayed on a _____, or TV-like screen.

7. Related programs designed to be carried out by a computer to satisfy a user's *specific* needs are called _____ _____.

8. Computers are generally grouped into one of the following four basic categories:
   a. _____   b. _____   c. _____   d. _____

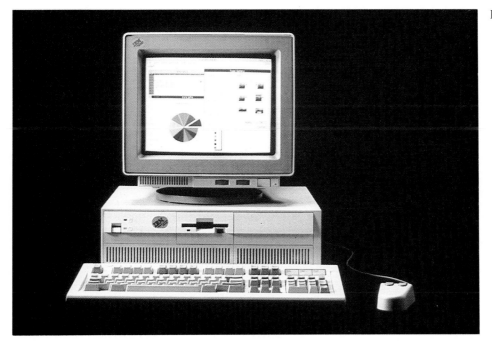

FIGURE 1.12

9. You are more likely to use a microcomputer in business than a supercomputer. (true/false)

10. The _____ _____ of a microcomputer usually houses the power supply, the system board, and the storage devices.

11. _____ monitors display images in a single color or black and white.

12. Hard disks have greater storage capacities than diskettes. (true/false)

13. _____ _____ software offers capabilities for creating, editing, storing, and printing documents.

14. Users' manuals that accompany computer hardware and software are referred to as _____.

15. Mainframe computers process faster than microcomputers. (true/false)

16. The CPU of a microcomputer is referred to as the _____.

17. Chips are made of silicon, which is referred to as a semiconductor because it sometimes conducts electricity and sometimes does not. (true/false)

18. As a result of data processing, _____ (what you put into the computer) is often processed into useful _____ (what is output by the computer).

19. List the five parts of a computer system:
    a. _____   b. _____   c. _____   d. _____   e. _____

20. To be _____ _____ you must have a solid understanding of what a computer is and how it can be used as a resource.

SOLUTIONS   (1) see Figure 1.7; (2) computer; (3) input, processing, storage, output; (4) false; (5) systems software; (6) monitor; (7) applications software; (8) supercomputer, mainframe, minicomputer, microcomputer; (9) true; (10) system unit; (11) monochrome; (12) true; (13) word processing; (14) documentation; (15) true; (16) microprocessor; (17) true; (18) data, information; (19) hardware, software, data/information, procedures, people; (20) computer literate

SHORT ANSWER

1. What is a microcomputer?

2. Describe the function of each of the five main components of a computer system.

3. What does it mean to be computer literate? Why is computer literacy, or competency, important?

4. Why do you think many companies spend a lot of money training their employees how to use computers?

5. What is the difference between systems software and applications software?

6. What is the meaning of the term *connectivity*?

7. What is a microprocessor?

8. What factors determine a computer's type (supercomputer, mainframe, minicomputer, microcomputer)?

9. What is the function of storage hardware in a computer system?

10. What is the purpose of main memory?

11. What types of tasks are microcomputers used for?

12. What is the purpose of the system unit in a microcomputer system?

13. How is a computer *user* different from a *computer specialist*?

14. What are two main differences between floppy disks and hard disks?

15. Is main memory volatile or nonvolatile? What does that mean?

16. What is word processing software? Spreadsheet software? Database management software?

PROJECTS

1. Determine what types of computers are being used where you work or go to school. Are microcomputers being used? Minicomputers? Mainframes? All types? What are they being used for? How are they connected, if at all?

2. Look in the job opportunities section of several newspapers to see if many jobs require applicants to be familiar with using microcomputers. What types of experience are required? What kinds of computer skills do you think you'll need in your chosen job or career? (Note: A school advisor in your major or field may be able to help you answer the last question.)

3. Many people are afraid of or resistant to learning about computers. Are you one of them? If so, make a list of all the factors that you think are affecting your attitude, then list reasons to refute each point. Keep your list and review it again after you have finished the course. What do you still agree with? Have you changed your mind about computers?

4. Although more new information has been produced in the last 30 years than in the previous 5,000, information isn't knowledge. In our quest for knowledge in the Information Age, we are often overloaded with information that doesn't tell us what we want to know. Richard Wurman identified this problem in his book *Information Anxiety*; Naisbitt, in his books *Megatrends* and *Megatrends 2000*, said that "uncontrolled and unorganized information is no longer a resource in an information society. Instead, it becomes the enemy of the information worker."

   Identify some of the problems of information overload in one or two departments in your school or place of employment—or in a local business, such as a real estate firm, health clinic, pharmacy, or accounting firm. What types of problems are people having? How are they trying to solve them? Are they rethinking their use of computer-related technologies?

CHAPTER 2

INPUT HARDWARE

Do you know how to type?

Perhaps it may not be necessary to learn. Methods exist for inputting data and software instructions to a microcomputer system that do not require a keyboard. We believe, however, that if you do know how to type, you are much better off. No matter what company or organization you join, it will most likely want to hire people who can handle a microcomputer keyboard— not just clerks and typists, but managers and executives as well.

PREVIEW

When you have completed this chapter, you will be able to:

■

Describe the different keys on the microcomputer keyboard

■

Name the main direct-entry (nonkeyboard) input devices used with a microcomputer and describe how they are used

CHAPTER OUTLINE

Why Is This Chapter Important?

The Keyboard

    The Keys

Nonkeyboard Input Devices

    Scanning Systems

    Voice Input Devices

    Pointing Devices

Summary

Key Terms

Exercises

WHY IS THIS CHAPTER IMPORTANT?

In most jobs, you will not be able to avoid entering data of some sort into a computer system. Thus, the more you understand about input hardware, the better you will be able to do your job. If you find keyboards somewhat cumbersome, be glad you are entering the job market now rather than back in the 60s. Then, the principal means of inputting data to a computer system was on punched cards— the so-called IBM cards that a generation of college students were admonished never to "fold, spindle, or mutilate." Although these cards are still in use in some quarters, their numbers are very few compared to the 150,000 tons of them that were used every year in the 1960s—enough, put end to end, to stretch 8 million miles.

In this chapter, we describe the input hardware components you will probably encounter in your career. One of the easiest ways to categorize input hardware is according to whether or not it uses a keyboard. We have focused special attention on the keyboard, because it will probably be your principal input device. In addition, we describe the following nonkeyboard input devices, called *direct-entry devices*: scanners, fax, mice, trackballs, light pens, touch screens, and voice recognition equipment.

FIGURE 2.1

This figure shows two common kinds of computer keyboards—(a) an IBM PC keyboard and (b) an enhanced keyboard (which has a numeric keypad separate from the cursor-movement keys).

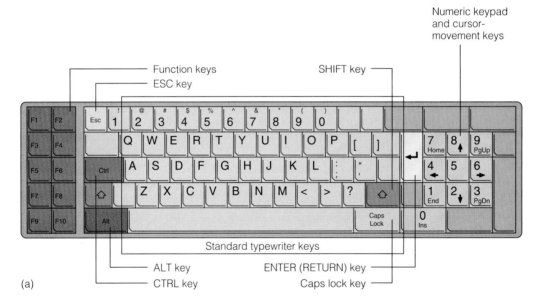

1. **ESC key:** This key can be thought of as the "undo" key. Pressing it when using many of the applications software packages in use today will move you out of a command that you didn't want to be in.

2. **CTRL key:** This key, pressed along with another key, is often used to issue commands from within applications software packages (key combinations differ according to package).

3. **ALT key:** This key, pressed along with another key, is often used to issue commands from within applications software packages.

4. **Function keys:** Software packages use these keys to perform certain commands. What each key does is determined by the software package you use.

etc.

THE KEYBOARD

A computer **keyboard** (Figure 2.1) is a sophisticated electromechanical component designed to create special standardized electronic codes when a key is pressed. The codes are transmitted along the cable that connects the keyboard to the computer system unit or the terminal (a monitor connected to a system unit in another location), where the incoming code is analyzed and converted into the appropriate computer-usable code. If you can use a typewriter keyboard, you should find it easy to work with a computer keyboard. Except for a few differences, the layout of the keys is similar.

Because a code is sent to the computer every time a key is pressed, in most cases you should only *tap* the keys on the keyboard instead of holding them down. For example, if you press the letter "A" and keep your finger pressed down on the key, you will see something like "AAAAAAAAAAAAAAAAAAA" on the screen. The same is true of issuing commands. For example, if you are trying to print a document and keep the keys pressed down that initiate the PRINT command, you may be sending multiple print instructions to the printer. As a result, with some computers, multiple copies of your document will print out on the printer.

(continued)   **FIGURE 2.1**

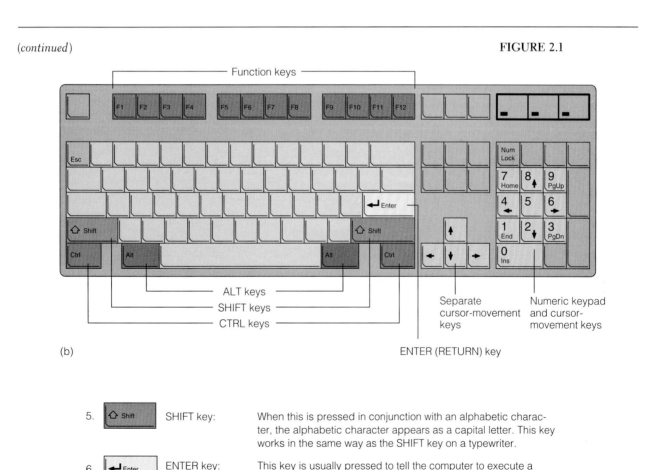

(b)   ENTER (RETURN) key

5. [⇧ Shift]	SHIFT key:	When this is pressed in conjunction with an alphabetic character, the alphabetic character appears as a capital letter. This key works in the same way as the SHIFT key on a typewriter.
6. [↵ Enter]	ENTER key:	This key is usually pressed to tell the computer to execute a command.
7. [4]	Numeric keypad and cursor-movement keys:	These keys are used to either enter numbers or to move the cursor around the screen. If the NUM LOCK key has been depressed, when you press these keys, numbers will appear on the screen. Otherwise, pressing these keys will cause your cursor to move around the screen in the direction of the arrows.

THE KEYS

Keyboards come in a variety of sizes and shapes, but most keyboards used with microcomputer systems have a certain number of features in common.

1. Standard typewriter keys
2. Function keys
3. Special-purpose keys
4. Cursor-movement keys
5. Numeric keys

You need to understand the purpose of these keys so that you can use the keyboard effectively.

The typewriter-like keys are used to type in text and special characters such as $, *, and #. In general, these keys are positioned in much the same location as the keys on a typewriter. People often refer to this layout as the **QWERTY** layout, because the first six characters on the top row of alphabetic keys spell "QWERTY."

The **function keys,** labeled F1, F2, F3, and so on, are used to issue commands (Figure 2.1). (Function keys are also called *programmable keys*.) Most keyboards are configured with from 10 to 12 function keys. The software program you are using determines how the function keys are used. For example, using one software program, you would press the F2 key to print your document. However, in a different software program, you would use the F2 key to save your work to disk. The user's manual (documentation) that comes with the software tells you how to use the function keys.

Computer keyboards also have some special-purpose keys such as Ctrl (Control), Alt (Alternate), Shift, Del (Delete), Ins (Insert), Caps Lock, and Enter. The **Ctrl key,** the **Alt key,** and the **Shift key** are modifier keys. By themselves they do nothing. But when pressed along with another key, they modify the function of the other key.

The **Ins key** and the **Del key** are used for editing what you type. Word processing software uses them frequently to insert and delete text.

The **Caps Lock key** is used to place all the alphabetic keys into an uppercase position (that is, capital letters only). This key is similar to the shift lock key on a typewriter, with one difference. The shift lock key allows you to type the upper character on any typewriter key, whereas the Caps Lock key affects *only* the alphabetic keys on the computer keyboard.

The **Enter key** is usually pressed to tell the computer to execute a command entered by first pressing other keys.

Cursor-movement keys (arrow keys) are used to move the **cursor** around the screen. (The cursor is the symbol on the video screen that shows where data will be input next; see Figure 2.2.) On the keyboards used with the early IBM PC-compatible microcomputers (which are still used in many businesses today), the keys for cursor movement were combined with the **numeric keypad**—the keys used to enter numbers (Figure 2.1a). When you turn it on, your microcomputer system "assumes" that the numeric keypad keys will be used for cursor movement. Therefore, you have to remember to press the **Num Lock key** or a Shift key before using these keys to enter numbers. On these older keyboards, it's easier to enter numerals by using the numbers across the top of the keyboard.

Most of today's keyboards have cursor-movement keys that are separate from the numeric keypad keys (Figure 2.1b). These keyboards are often referred to as *101-key enhanced keyboards*. When a microcomputer system that uses an enhanced keyboard is turned on, the assumption made by your computer system is that the Num Lock key is active—that is, the numeric keypad will be used for entering numbers.

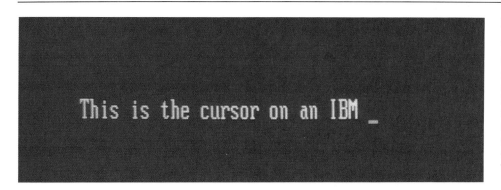

FIGURE 2.2

The cursor shows the position on the screen where the next character, space, or command instruction will be entered. The cursor-movement (arrow) keys are used to move the cursor up, down, right, and left. The cursor can also be moved with a mouse.

The Macintosh extended keyboard   **FIGURE 2.3**

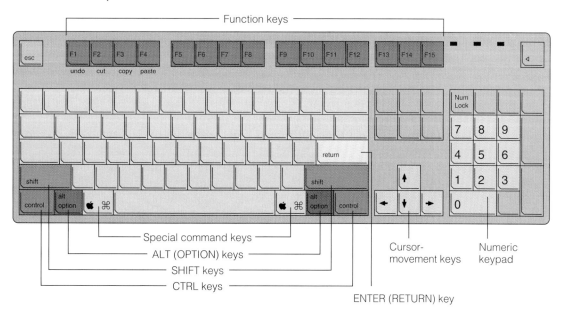

Figure 2.3 identifies the common types of keys on the Apple Macintosh keyboard.

NONKEYBOARD INPUT DEVICES

Some of the most exciting kinds of input systems don't use a keyboard. For example, did you know that you can touch a video display screen or use a "magic" wand to input data? Talk to a computer? Even use the movement of your eyes to tell the computer what to do? Nonkeyboard, or **direct entry,** data entry systems minimize the amount of human activity required to get data into a computer-usable form. The ones receiving the most attention today are

1. Scanning devices that "read" data
2. Voice input devices
3. So-called "pointing" devices

Most direct-entry input devices are used in conjunction with a keyboard because these specialized devices can't be used to input all types of data and instructions. An exception may be the Eyescan Communicator, which translates eye movements into signals for a computer. This innovation—still being refined— allows people who cannot speak or use keyboards to communicate using a computer.

SCANNING SYSTEMS

A **scanning system** consists of a microcomputer (PC), a scanner, and scanning software (Figure 2.4). These systems enable users to convert (digitize) a hardcopy picture or a photograph into a computer-usable graphics file that can be understood by a desktop publishing or graphics package (such as Aldus PageMaker or Adobe Illustrator). In addition, they enable users to convert hardcopy (printed) text into a text file that can be used by a word processing package (such as WordPerfect or Microsoft Word). Scanned images can be stored in a computer system, manipulated (changed), and/or output in a different form.

The software required to scan graphics is usually packaged with the scanner when you purchase it. The software required to scan characters, or text, called **optical character recognition (OCR) software,** isn't normally packaged with the scanner.

One factor to consider when choosing a scanner is whether you plan to scan graphics and/or text. If you typically scan graphics to be used by a desktop publishing or graphics package, you want your scanner to scan images at a high resolution—**resolution** refers to the clarity of an image. In addition, you want your scanner to support scanning as many shades of gray as possible; this is called *grayscale scanning.* The more shades of gray that a scanner is capable of scanning, the more natural the scanned image is, which is important if you're working with pho-

FIGURE 2.4

Scanning system. The scanner (left) converts the hardcopy photo into computer-usable form so it can be manipulated by desktop publishing or graphics software.

tographs. Color scanners and slide scanners are available for users who are using desktop publishing to produce sophisticated magazines and books.

Another factor to consider when purchasing a scanner is the physical format of the material you plan to scan. If you will often scan text or graphics from a bound volume, you should consider a **flatbed scanner** (Figure 2.5a). To use a flatbed scanner, the user must hold the material to be scanned in place on a piece of glass while the scanning mechanism, referred to as the **scanhead,** passes over it in a fashion similar to that of a copy machine. If you are working with loose sheets, consider a **sheet-fed scanner** (Figure 2.5b), which uses mechanical rollers to move the paper past the scanhead. Another type of scanner is the **hand-held scanner** (Figure 2.5c), which relies on the human hand to move the scanhead over the material to be scanned.

Scanners are also used for specialized purposes, such as identifying an individual by his or her fingerprints (Figure 2.6).

FAX

A **fax (facsimile) machine** uses a built-in scanner to read text and graphics and transmit them over phone lines to another fax machine or a computer with a fax board in its system unit. One factor to consider before purchasing a fax capability is your need to fax graphics, such as photos. If you do need to fax graphics, make sure the fax scanner can support displaying halftones, or shades of gray. If you are only faxing text, it doesn't matter if your computer can support shades of gray. Fax machines are described in greater detail in Chapter 8.

VOICE INPUT DEVICES

In an effort to increase worker productivity, a substantial amount of research is being done in voice recognition—programming the computer to recognize spoken commands. **Voice input devices** (Figure 2.7), or **voice recognition systems,** convert spoken words into computer-usable code by comparing the electrical patterns produced by the speaker's voice with a set of prerecorded patterns. If a matching pattern is found, the computer accepts this pattern as a part of its standard "vocabulary."

Voice input technology is used today in a number of successful business applications. NASA has developed experimental space suits that use microprocessors and storage devices to allow astronauts to view computerized displays across their helmet visors. These displays are activated and manipulated by spoken commands—convenient when both hands are busy on a repair job in space! The brokerage house of Shearson Lehman uses a voice input technology called the Voice Trader to enable brokers to communicate trades verbally rather than writing them down on scraps of paper that are often illegible or become lost. The medical industry has also been using voice recognition products to help physicians, hospitals, and clinics minimize the huge quantities of paperwork and handwritten notes they would otherwise have to deal with.

Voice technology is also used by people whose jobs do not allow them to keep their hands free and by handicapped people, such as the blind, who may not be able to use traditional input devices. A blind person, for example, can enter commands verbally rather than using the keyboard. In a system with this capability, computer output is typically communicated to the user using text-to-speech capabilities—that is, the computer responds to the user with spoken words. (A blind skipper reportedly used a voice-navigational system to successfully navigate a boat!) For the physically handicapped, the ability to control computers without using a keyboard is crucial. Voice input technology is now used by quadriplegics and people with severe arthritis to control computers, telephones, and other devices.

FIGURE 2.5   (a) Flatbed scanner; (b) sheet-fed scanner; (c) hand-held scanner. Photo (b) also shows the documentation that accompanies the software necessary to use the scanner with a computer and the expansion card that must be put in the computer's expansion slot. The computer needs the software and the circuitry on the expansion card to be able to interact with the scanner; (d) Slide scanner.

(a)

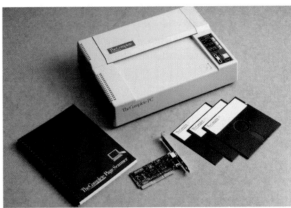

(b)

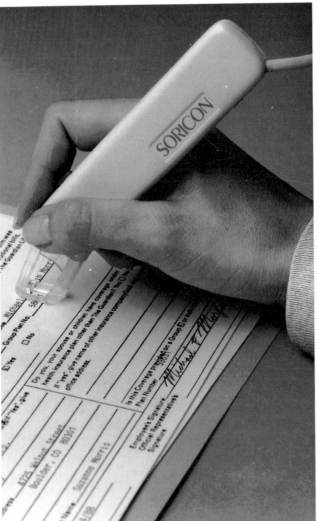

(c)

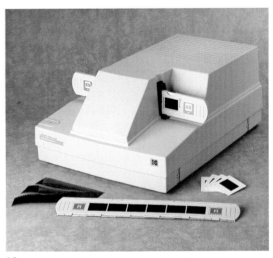

(d)

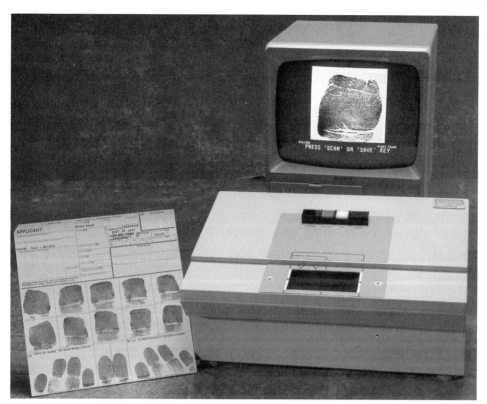

FIGURE 2.6

Fingerprint reader—a type of scanner that is used to identify an individual's fingerprint for security purposes. After a sample is scanned, access to the computer or other restricted system is granted if the user's fingerprint matches the stored sample.

FIGURE 2.7

Voice recognition. (a) This diagram gives you a basic idea of how voice input works (adapted by permission of Wide World Photos); (b) Texas Instruments voice input system.

How does it work?

Speech
A person speaks into a microphone connected to the computer.

Signal Processing
The sound wave is transformed into a sequence of codes that represent speech sounds.

1. Phonetic Models
Describe what codes may occur for a given speech sound.
In the word *how*, what is the probability of the "aw" sound appearing between an H and a D?

2. Dictionary
Defines the phonetic pronunciation (sequence of sounds) of each word
How does it work
haw   daz   it werk

3. Grammar
Defines what words may follow each other, using part of speech
How does < it > [work]
adv   vt   pron   v

Output
Computer recognizes word string and prints it on the screen.

Recognition Search
Using the data from 1, 2, and 3, the computer tries to find the best matching sequence of words as learned from a variety of examples.

(b)

To date, the biggest problems with voice technology involve limitations on the size of the computer's vocabulary, pronunciation differences among individuals, and the computer's inability to accept continuous speech. However, research continues at a fast pace. Several voice input units are currently available for use with microcomputers. For example, Covox, Inc. introduced a voice recognition system that lets IBM PC and IBM PS/2 users replace keystroke entries with spoken commands. This system requires users to use the keyboard to type in a word they want the system to listen for, type in the command keystrokes they want the system to execute when the word is spoken, and to then say the word into a microphone that is built into the Covox system. When the words are spoken at a later time, the appropriate keystrokes will automatically execute.

POINTING DEVICES

Data input also involves not only typing in text but also entering commands and selecting options. The mouse, the trackball, the light pen, the touch screen, and the digitizer tablet were all developed to make these functions easy. Each of these devices allows the user to identify and select the necessary command or option by, in effect, moving the cursor to (pointing at) a certain location on the screen or tablet and sending a signal to the computer. For this reason they are sometimes called *pointing devices*.

Systems that enable users to use their eyes to point at the screen to specify screen coordinates are being used by the handicapped (Figure 2.8). A system that has this capability is typically referred to as a **line-of-sight** system.

FIGURE 2.8

Line of sight. To track the position of the eye's pupil, a video camera is mounted beneath the monitor. These positions are then translated into screen coordinates, thus allowing the eyes to "point." This technology is being used by the handicapped to enable them to direct computer processing.

MOUSE

When using applications software, you can often select menu options by using a mouse to choose a picture, or graphic, (called an *icon*) that represents the processing option you want. The **mouse** (Figure 2.9) is a hand-held device connected to the computer by a small cable. As the mouse is rolled across the desktop, the cursor moves across the screen. When the cursor reaches the desired location, the user usually pushes a button on the mouse once or twice to signal a menu selection or a command to the computer.

Mouse technology is often used with graphics-oriented microcomputers like the Macintosh and the Macintosh portable, as well as with new graphics-oriented programs for the IBM. Indeed, graphical user interfaces such as those used on the Macintosh line of computers are becoming commonplace. As a result, the emphasis will shift from the keyboard as the principal input device to pointing devices such as the mouse to select screen objects and functions. The keyboard, however, will still be used to type in characters and to issue some commands, depending on the software.

When mice were first introduced, they functioned mainly as cursor-movement devices that enabled users to choose menu options. Although they are still used this way today, they are increasingly used to create graphics. The technology has improved so that mice can be used to move tiny *pic*ture *ele*ments—called **pixels**—on the screen one by one. In other words, the mouse can be used like a pen or a paintbrush to draw figures and create patterns directly on the video display screen. Used with a monitor capable of displaying high-quality graphics, a sophisticated mouse enables users to generate very complex and precise images. A sophisticated mouse can manipulate extremely small pixels, influencing the clarity of an image.

(a)

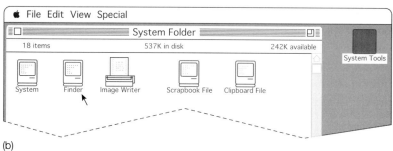

(b)

FIGURE 2.9

Nonkeyboard input control. (a) When the user rolls the mouse around the desktop, the pointer moves correspondingly on the screen. By rolling the mouse to move the pointer to an icon and clicking the mouse button once or twice, the user can select and open the file that the icon represents. By pointing at a particular place on a text line and clicking the mouse button, the user can move the cursor to the desired place. (The use of multiple mouse buttons is determined by the software; the accompanying documentation explains the uses.) (b) Examples of icons.

A type of mouse that may soon become popular is built into a pen-like body. It works in the same basic way as does the traditional mouse; however, it is shaped like a pen. It's small enough to fit into a shirt pocket and is capable of working on most surfaces. As a result, this type of mouse is well-suited for use with portable microcomputers.

TRACKBALL

Trackballs have all the functionality of a mouse but don't need to be rolled around on the desktop. The ball is held in a socket on the top of the stationary device (Figures 2.10, 2.11). Instead of moving the ball by rolling the device around on the desktop, you move the ball with your fingers. Trackballs have become especially popular in offices where crowded desktops are the norm and on airplanes, where space is limited.

FIGURE 2.10

MAC Portable with reversible numeric keypad and trackball. The positions of the numeric keypad and the trackball can be swapped to accommodate left-handed trackball users.

FIGURE 2.11

Kensington TurboMouse 4.0 trackball

*N*ot planning to make a career in computers and information processing? Think computers will have only the barest presence in your professional life? We're guessing otherwise. In every line of work, computers have become nearly as commonplace as pencil and paper, even in those fields that seem to be mostly rooted in intuition, emotions, and creativity. In this box, the first of several on computers and different career fields, we show how these instruments of logic are used in the arts, sports, and entertainment.

The casting agent is looking for an actor who can speak Spanish, owns cowboy gear, and can shoot a rifle while riding a horse. She turns to her computer and feeds her request into RoleCall, a computerized casting service for film, theater, and television. Almost instantly the computer screen produces the names of 40 actors who fit the bill.

In rehearsals, the director uses a Macintosh computer and a program called TheaterGame to go through the process of staging ("blocking") a scene. The program offers a choice of sets, props (such as furniture, trees), and costumed characters that can be moved around on the screen by using a mouse to direct the cursor. If a chair gets in the way of the action, the director can use the mouse to push it aside. Characters can be manipulated so that they turn their heads to talk, sit, fall down, and so on. Afterward, the director can play back the staging to see how it looks.

In the television studio, there are no longer headphone-wearing operators rolling three or four cameras back and forth. Rather, there are now robotic cameras linked to a central computer called the "cue computer," which prompts the cameras. The cue computer is operated by an engineer, who keeps his or her eyes on several wall monitors to keep each camera in focus. Standard shots, such as an overhead view of the set, can be programmed in advance and called up on the computer as needed.

Examples of how computers can be used in nonscientific ways are found in other artistic fields. Dancers may use computers to choreograph their movements. Musicians may use them to write out musical scores while they compose them on a piano keyboard. Computer artists don't use bristles and pigments but rather metal-tipped styluses, with which they "paint" on slate-like digitizing pads, which in turn transmit their movements and colors to a computer screen. Art dealers may use the Omnivex electronic art catalogue, which stores images of artwork on videodisk and allows dealers to view them by calling them up on high-resolution computer screens.

Viewers of televised sports have become accustomed to seeing all kinds of statistics and percentages flashed on the screen. Now, however, coaches and athletes can receive this kind of computerized analysis even for sports such as tennis, using a program called Computennis. And cyclists can use computer-generated three-dimensional maps, called Terragraphics guidebooks, which give the rider a preview of a planned route. Even people who like to fish can improve their odds with the use of a computerized sonar device, called Specie Select, which, using software based on information from over 1,000 professional anglers and guides, can home in on the fish-locating information pertinent to a particular species.

Computers are an important part of all sectors of the entertainment industry. Just one example: Computer-based animation has come of age to produce spectacular new images, from glowing, flying, spinning station call letters to cartoon characters. ∎

LIGHT PEN

The **light pen** uses a photoelectric (light-sensitive) cell to signal screen position to the computer (Figure 2.12). The pen, which is connected to the computer by a cable, is pressed to the video display screen at the desired location. The switch on the pen is pushed to close the photoelectric circuit, thereby indicating the x-y (horizontal and vertical) screen coordinates to the computer. The computer stores these coordinates in main memory (RAM). Depending on the applications software you are using, you can then edit the data stored in RAM and save it onto a disk. Light pens are frequently used by graphics designers, illustrators, and drafting engineers.

TOUCH SCREEN

Limited amounts of data can be entered into the computer via a **touch screen** (Figure 2.13). The user simply touches the screen at the desired locations, marked by labeled boxes, to "point out" choices to the computer. The software determines the kinds of choices the user has. Of course, not all microcomputers have touch screens. Some touch screens are built into the monitor and others can be snapped on to certain kinds of existing monitors.

FIGURE 2.12

Light pen. This user is employing a light pen to analyze an angiogram of certain blood vessels and arteries.

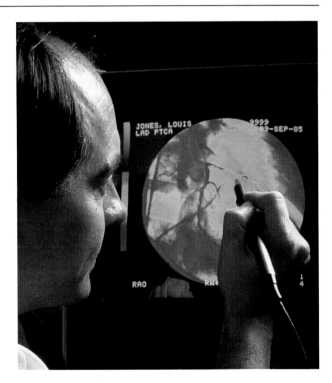

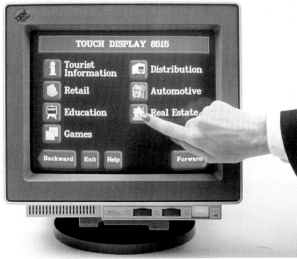

FIGURE 2.13

Touch screen

DIGITIZER

An specialized method of input that is used in drafting and mapmaking is the **digitizer,** or **digitizing tablet** (Figure 2.14). The tablets, which come in different sizes, are the working surface. Each is covered by a grid of many tiny wires that are connected to the computer by a cable. (Wacom, Inc. has produced a digitizer that is cordless.) Drawings placed over this grid can be traced and entered into the computer by the use of a special pen or a mouse-like device with cross hairs that opens and closes electrical circuits in the grid and thus identifies x-y coordinates. Original drawings also can be entered. As it progresses, the drawing is displayed on the screen; it can later be stored or printed out. Digitizers are also used in design and engineering businesses—such as those that develop aircraft or computer chips.

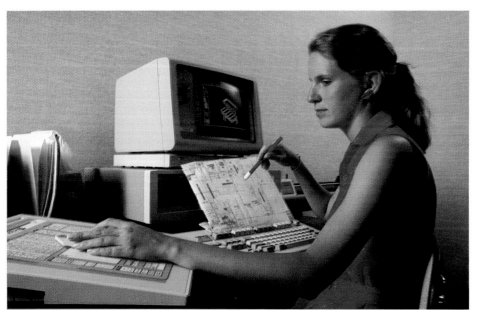

(a)

FIGURE 2.14

Digitizer. (a) This engineer is creating a blueprint using a mouse-like digitizer on a grid with electronic wires that is connected to the computer. (b) A student in the School of Visual Arts in New York City is using a 3-space Isotrack digitizer to draw a freehand 3-D project viewed on the monitor.

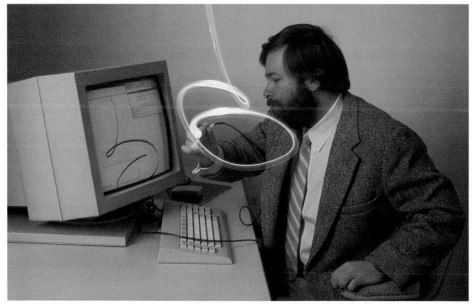

(b)

PEN-BASED COMPUTING

Pen-based computing is a recent development by which special software interprets handwriting done directly on a special type of computer screen (Figure 2.15). As the computer—such as Go Corporation's PenPoint and Tandy's Grid System—interprets the handwriting, it displays what was written on the screen in a computer typeface. Users can edit what they have entered and give commands by circling words, checking boxes, and using symbols developed by the manufacturer. This type of small computer is used by police officers to record tickets and by salespeople to record sales.

FIGURE 2.15   Pen-based computing. The chart shows 11 basic handwriting gestures used to issue commands and move around on the screen and within files.

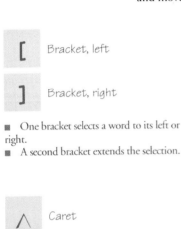

[Bracket, left

] Bracket, right

■ One bracket selects a word to its left or right.
■ A second bracket extends the selection.

∧ Caret

■ In text, pops up a small writing pad to insert a word.
■ In the Table of Contents, pops up the Create menu to create a new document.

✓ Check

Displays options for selected text, objects, icons, documents, and tools.

○ Circle

Opens an edit pad for a word or selection in text, text fields, and labels.

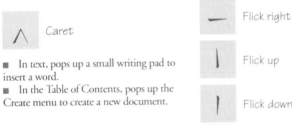

X Cross out

Deletes a word or selection in text or any object directly beneath the X.

— Flick left

— Flick right

| Flick up

| Flick down

Scrolls documents right, left, down, or up.
■ On the document title line, flick left — or right — to turn to the next or previous page.
■ On overlapped tabs, flick up | or down | to move the tab up or down. Flick left — to display all tabs at once.

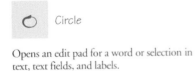

L Insert space

■ In text, adds a space.
■ In writing and edit pads, adds one or more spaces.

9 Pigtail

Deletes a character in a writing or edit pad character box, or an individual character in text.

▸ Press

■ Begins a move.
■ Begins a drag-through selection.

▸ Tap

Selects or activates what you touch with the pen.
■ In text, selects one character.

▸ Tap press

Begins a copy.

PenPoint has eleven basic gestures for commands and navigation. Most gestures have menu equivalents. See the user manuals for more details.

SUMMARY

- Input hardware is categorized either as *keyboard-based* or *direct-entry* (non-keyboard).
- The keyboard is the most widely used input device. It includes five basic types:
  1. *Standard typewriter keys*—used to type in text and special characters.
  2. *Function keys*—used to issue commands.
  3. *Special-purpose keys*—Ctrl, Alt, Ins, Del, Caps Lock, and Num Lock, used to modify the functions of other keys. The Enter key is usually pressed to tell the computer to execute a command entered by first pressing other keys.
  4. *Cursor-movement keys*—used to move the *cursor*, which marks the position of the next character to be typed, around the screen. The keys for cursor movement are sometimes combined with the *numeric keypad*.
  5. *Numeric keys*—used to enter numbers.

  The software package dictates how the function keys and special-purpose keys are used (check the documentation that comes with the package).
- Direct-entry devices, which are used in conjunction with a keyboard, include:
  1. *Scanning* devices that "read" data
  2. *Voice input* devices
  3. *Pointing* devices
- Scanners convert hardcopy text or graphics into computer-usable code. The text and/or graphics can then be displayed on the monitor and edited, modified, printed, communicated, and stored for later retrieval.
- A *fax (facsimile) machine* is a type of scanner that "reads" text and graphics and then transmits them over telephone lines to another fax machine or a computer with a fax board in its system unit.
- *Voice input devices*, or *voice recognition systems*, convert spoken words into computer-usable code by comparing the electrical patterns produced by the speaker's voice with a set of prerecorded patterns. After the computer matches the patterns, it executes the appropriate command.
- Pointing devices include:
  1. The *mouse*—a hand-held device connected to the computer by a cable and rolled around the desktop to move the cursor around the screen. When the cursor is placed at the desired location, the user pushes a button on the mouse once or twice to issue a command or select an option. The mouse can be used to move the tiny *pixels*, or *picture elements*, on the screen to create graphics.
  2. The *light pen*—a pen-shaped input device that uses a photoelectric (light-sensitive) cell to signal screen position to the computer. The pen, which is connected to the computer by a cable, is placed on the display screen at the desired location. The switch on the pen is pushed to close the photoelectric circuit, thereby signaling the location to the computer.
  3. The *touch screen*—a special display screen that is sensitive to touch. The user touches the screen at desired locations, marked by labeled boxes, to "point out" choices to the computer.
  4. The *digitizer*—a tablet covered by a grid of tiny wires that are connected to the computer by a cable. Drawings placed on the tablet can be traced with a special pen or mouse-like device to translate the image into computer-usable code. Original drawings also can be entered.
  5. *Pen-based computing* uses special software and hardware to interpret handwriting done directly on the screen.

KEY TERMS

Alt key, p. 28
Caps Lock key, p. 28
Ctrl key, p. 28
cursor, p. 28
cursor-movement keys,
    p. 28
Del key, p. 28
digitizer, p. 39
digitizing tablet, p. 39
direct entry, p. 29
Enter key, p. 28
fax (facsimile) machine,
    p. 31
flatbed scanner, p. 31

function keys, p. 28
hand-held scanner,
    p. 31
Ins key, p. 28
keyboard, p. 27
light pen, p. 38
line-of-sight, p. 34
mouse, p. 35
Num Lock key, p. 28
numeric keypad, p. 28
optical character recog-
    nition (OCR), p. 30
pen-based computing,
    p. 40

pixel, p. 35
QWERTY, p. 28
resolution, p. 30
scanhead, p. 31
scanning system, p. 30
sheet-fed scanner, p. 31
Shift key, p. 28
touch screen, p. 38
trackball, p. 36
voice input device,
    p. 31
voice recognition
    system, p. 31

EXERCISES

SELF-TEST

1. One of the easiest ways to categorize input hardware is whether or not it uses a _____.

2. Most keyboards used with microcomputers include the following types of keys:
   a. _____ b. _____ c. _____ d. _____ e. _____

3. What determines what the function keys on a keyboard do?

4. Cursor-movement keys are used to execute commands. (true/false)

5. The _____ key, the _____ key, and the _____ key are modifier keys.

6. A _____ enables users to convert hardcopy text and graphics into computer-usable code.

7. List three common categories of direct entry (nonkeyboard) input devices.
   a. _____ b. _____ c. _____

8. List four pointing devices commonly used with microcomputer systems.
   a. _____ b. _____ c. _____ d. _____

9. A picture element on the screen is called a *pixel*. (true/false)

10. An input device commonly used in mapmaking is the _____ _____

11. Light pens enable you to type text faster than do keyboards. (true/false)

12. To date, the biggest problems with voice technology are:
    a. _____ b. _____ c. _____

13. The most popular input hardware component is the _____.

14. QWERTY describes a common keyboard layout. (true/false)

15. Scanners cannot scan color images. (true/false)

16. The most common keyboard layout is called QWERTY. (true/false)

17. Function keys are used the same way with every software application. (true/false)

18. Some keyboards have cursor-movement keys that are separate from the numeric keypad. (true/false)

19. A code is sent to the computer *every* time a keyboard key is pressed. (true/false)

20. Pointing devices were developed to make the functions of entering commands and selecting options easy. (true/false)

SOLUTIONS   (1) keyboard; (2) standard typewriter keys, function keys, special-purpose keys, cursor-movement keys, numeric keys; (3) software program or applications software; (4) false; (5) Ctrl, Alt, Shift; (6) scanner; (7) scanning devices, voice input devices, pointing devices; (8) mouse, light pen, touch screen, digitizer tablet; (9) true; (10) digitizer tablet; (11) false; (12) size of the computer's vocabulary, pronunciation differences among individuals, computer's inability to accept continuous speech; (13) keyboard; (14) true; (15) false; (16) true; (17) false; (18) true; (19) true; (20) true

SHORT ANSWER

1. What are the two main categories of input hardware?

2. What is a fax machine?

3. What is a mouse and how is it used?

4. What do a mouse, a light pen, and a digitizer have in common?

5. What direct-entry devices are commonly used in conjunction with the microcomputer keyboard?

6. What is an optical character recognition system?

7. What is a digitizer?

8. What are function keys, and what determines what happens when you press one of them?

9. What is a light pen? How does the use of a light pen differ from pen-based computing?

10. What is a voice recognition system?

PROJECTS

1. A new type of keyboard, called the *Mouseboard*, puts the mouse *on* the keyboard, where most keyboards have their cursor-movement (arrow) keys. Do you think this keyboard would be easier to use than the standard keyboard plus mouse or trackball combination? Write or call the manufacturer and ask for brochures and other information about this new development; then describe this new keyboard to the class.
    Cherry Corporation
    Cherry Electrical Products
    3600 Sunset Avenue
    Waukegan, IL 60087
    708/360-3599

2. Research scanning technology. What differentiates one scanner from another? Is it the clarity of the scanned image? Price? Software? If you were going to buy a scanner, which do you think you would buy? Why? What do you need to run a color scanner?

3. Research possible copyright infringement problems arising from first scanning photos and other pictures and then modifying them.

CHAPTER 3

PROCESSING HARDWARE

When you look at a computer, you can see and even touch most of the input, output, and storage equipment—the keyboard and the mouse, the video display screen, the printer and the disk drive doors. But unless you open up the computer, you cannot see the equipment that actually does the processing—the electronic circuitry inside the cabinet of the computer. Although you have no need to puzzle through wiring diagrams and the like, you should have some understanding of the processing hardware, because the type of processing hardware used affects how much the computer can do for you and how quickly it can do it.

PREVIEW

When you have completed this chapter, you will be able to:

Identify the main parts of the microprocessor and describe their functions

Explain the importance of and distinguish between random access memory and the different types of read-only memory

Describe the factors that should be considered when evaluating the processing power of a microcomputer

CHAPTER OUTLINE

Why Is This Chapter Important?

The Microprocessor
    Control Unit
    Arithmetic/Logic Unit (ALU)
    Registers
    Bus
    Coprocessors

Read-Only Memory (ROM)
    PROM, EPROM, EEPROM

Random Access Memory (RAM)
    Function of RAM
    RAM Chips
    Increasing RAM

Measuring the Processing Power of a Computer
    Addressing Scheme
    Register Size
    Data Bus Capacity
    Clock Speed
    Instruction Set
    Checklist

Summary

Key Terms

Exercises

As a microcomputer user, you need a basic understanding of the hardware components that enable you to process data into information.

- Just as some people like to work on their own cars, you may decide it's economical for you to do some work on your microcomputer. For instance, you may find that some new software programs are too sophisticated for your computer—that your computer cannot hold enough data or instructions or process them fast enough—and that you need to add some more random access memory. This may well be something you can do yourself.

- More likely, you will some day need to make a buying decision about a microcomputer, either for yourself or for an organization. And, just as when you buy a car, you should learn something about the topic first. It is important to understand processing facts and trends to avoid purchasing a machine that will be obsolete in the near future.

Let's start our discussion of processing with the "brain" of the microcomputer—the microprocessor.

THE MICROPROCESSOR

A central processing unit (CPU) of the 1940s that weighed 5 tons, took up six rooms, processed about 10,000 instructions per second, and cost about $5 million is now 5 millimeters square, about 12 inches thick, can process about 4 million instructions per second, and costs less than $5. This revolution in computer processing was caused by the development of the **microprocessor,** the "brain," or CPU, of the microcomputer system (Figure 3.1). The microprocessor consists of the main processing circuitry on one silicon chip. Today a microcomputer priced at about $5,000 has essentially the same power as an IBM mainframe of more than 10 years ago—but that machine cost $3.4 million at the time. If the automobile industry had advanced this fast since 1982, said Edward Lucente, the head of IBM's Information Systems Group, "Today we'd have cars that go zero to 60 in three seconds, circle the globe on a tank of gas, and cost half as much as they did six years ago. Of course, they would be difficult to get into, because they would be only half the size."

Among other things, a microprocessor's configuration determines whether a microcomputer is fast or slow in relation to other microcomputers. The microprocessor is the most complex computer system component, responsible for directing most of the computer system activities based on the instructions provided. The microprocessor has two main parts: (1) the control unit and (2) the arithmetic/logic unit. The parts of the microprocessor are usually connected by an electronic component referred to as a *bus*, which acts as an electronic path between them (Figure 3.2). To temporarily store data and instructions, the microprocessor has special-purpose storage areas called *registers*.

CONTROL UNIT

The **control unit,** a maze of complex electronic circuitry, is responsible for directing and coordinating all computer system activities. It controls the movement of electronic signals, including the signals between main memory and the input/output devices. Also, it coordinates activities between main memory and the microprocessor.

The control unit (and the entire microprocessor) can deal only with instructions written in **machine language** (Figure 3.3). When programmers write programs, they use high-level (human-language-like) languages. Before the programs can be used, the programmer must convert them into machine language by using a language processor—a type of systems software (language processors are described in more detail in Chapter 7). In machine language, data and instructions are represented in binary form—that is, as 0s and 1s, which stand for the absence or the presence of an electronic pulse. Each type of computer—microcomputer, minicomputer, or mainframe—responds to a unique version of machine language. Once the instructions have been converted into this form, they can be interpreted by the control unit (sometimes referred to as *decoding*). According to each specific instruction, the control unit issues the necessary signals to other computer system components as needed to satisfy the processing requirements. This could involve,

FIGURE 3.1

Intel 80386 microprocessor chip

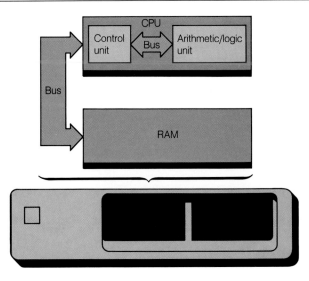

FIGURE 3.2

Buses, a kind of electronic transportation system, connect the main components of the central processing unit and memory.

for example, directing that data be retrieved from a disk storage device, telling the printer to print the letter you just wrote, or simply directing the arithmetic/logic unit to add two numbers.

ARITHMETIC/LOGIC UNIT (ALU)

Without the **arithmetic/logic unit (ALU)**, you wouldn't be able to perform any mathematical calculations. In fact, without the ALU, microcomputers would not be able to do most of the tasks that we find useful. The ALU performs all the arithmetic and logical (comparison) functions—that is, it adds, subtracts, multiplies, divides, and does comparisons. These comparisons, which are basically "less than," "greater than," or "equal to," can be combined into several common expressions, such as "greater than or equal to." The objective of most instructions that use comparisons is to determine which instructions should be executed next. The ALU also controls the speed of calculations.

REGISTERS

A **register** is a special temporary storage location within the microprocessor. Registers very quickly accept, store, and transfer data and instructions that are being used *immediately* (random access memory or main memory, to be discussed shortly, holds data that will be used *a little bit later*). To process an instruction, the control unit of the microprocessor retrieves it from main memory and places it into a register. The typical operations that take place in the processing of instructions are part of either the instruction cycle or the execution cycle.

The **instruction cycle,** or I-cycle, refers to the retrieval of an instruction from memory and its subsequent decoding (the process of alerting the circuits in the microprocessor to perform the specified operation). The time it takes to go through the instruction cycle is referred to as *I-time*. The **execution cycle,** or E-cycle, refers to the execution of the instruction and the subsequent storing of the result in a register. The time it takes to go through the execution cycle is referred to as *E-time*. The instruction cycle and the execution cycle together, as they apply to one instruction, are referred to as a **machine cycle** (Figure 3.4). The microprocessor has an internal **clock** that synchronizes all operations in the cycle. The speed is expressed in **megahertz (MHz)**; 1 MHz equals 1 million cycles per

FIGURE 3.3

Machine language. This illustration shows the Apple and the IBM instructions for adding two numbers. IBM computers are incompatible with Apple computers because their processors use different versions of machine language instructions. Software written for one machine cannot be used on the other without special conversion software.

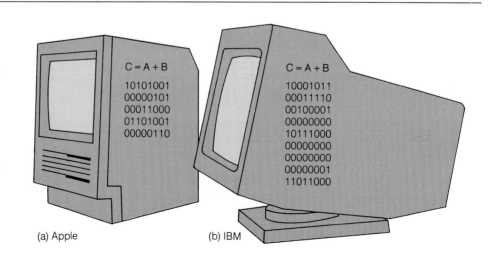

C = A + B

10101001
00000101
00011000
01101001
00000110

C = A + B

10001011
00011110
00100001
00000000
10111000
00000000
00000000
00000001
11011000

(a) Apple

(b) IBM

second. Generally, the faster the clock speed, the faster the computer can process information. An older IBM PC has a clock speed of 4.77 MHz; an IBM PS/2 Model 50 SX has a clock speed of 16 MHz; the Mac IIci's clock speed is 25 MHz; and the Compaq Deskpro 386/33 has a clock speed of 33 MHz. Some newer microprocessors have a clock speed of 50 MHz.

Typically the faster a microcomputer is (as measured in megahertz), the more expensive it is. Depending on your needs you may (or may not) need a fast computer. Therefore, before purchasing a computer, determine the computer's clock speed by either looking at the documentation that accompanies the computer or asking a salesperson.

Before we continue, we must briefly define a few terms that will help you evaluate the power of processing hardware. Just as inches, feet, and yards are used to measure certain surfaces, bits, bytes, kilobytes, and megabytes are used to measure and compare the processing power and storage capacity of microcomputers. (Each of these terms is described in more detail in Chapter 4.) Data is represented in microcomputers by using a coding scheme that uses groups of **binary digits,** or **bits,** to represent characters. Think of a bit as a light switch. One switch—1 bit— can be either on (1) or off (0)—that is, an electric or light pulse is either present or absent. In microcomputers, it takes 8 bits—known as a **byte**—to form a character. (For example, in some microcomputer coding schemes, A is represented as 01000001.) A **kilobyte (KB,** or **K)** is equal to 1,024 bytes, and a **megabyte (MB)** is equal to 1,024,000 bytes. A **gigabyte (GB)** is equal to 1,024,000,000 bytes. For simplicity, most users think of a kilobyte as one thousand bytes, a megabyte as one million bytes, and a gigabyte as one billion bytes.

The number and types of registers in a microprocessor vary according to the microprocessor's design. Their size (capacity) and number can dramatically affect the processing power of a computer system. In general, the larger the register (the more bits it can carry at once), the greater the processing power. Some personal computers have general-purpose registers that hold only 8 bits (1 byte) at a time; others hold 16 bits (2 bytes); newer microcomputers have 32-bit registers that hold 4 bytes at once. The difference in processing power due to difference in register

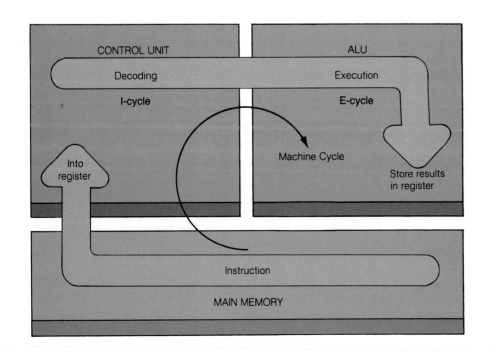

FIGURE 3.4

The machine cycle—the instruction cycle and execution cycle as they apply to the processing of one instruction

size can be illustrated by the difference between trying to put out a fire with a small drinking glass versus a 5-gallon bucket.

BUS

The term **bus** refers to an electrical pathway through which bits are transmitted between the various computer components. Depending on the design of a system, several types of buses may be present. For the user, the most important one is the **data bus,** which carries data throughout the microprocessor. The wider the data bus, the more data it can carry at one time, and thus the greater the processing speed of the computer. The data bus in the Intel 8088 microprocessor is 8 bits wide, meaning that it can carry 8 bits—or one character—at a time. In contrast, the data buses in the Motorola 68030 processor (in the Macintosh IIci microcomputer) and the Intel 80386 processor (in the IBM PS/2 Model 55 SX microcomputer) are 32 bits wide—they can move four times more data through their data buses than the Intel 8088 bus can. An 8-bit computer can do anything a 32-bit computer can, just slower. Table 3.1 shows the data bus capacity and register size of several microprocessor chips.

TABLE 3.1   Comparison of Several Microprocessors

Company	Micro-processor	Data Bus Capacity	Register Size	Clock Speed (MHz)	Microcomputers Using This Chip*
MOS Technology	6502	8	8	4	Apple IIE Atari 800 Commodore 64
Intel	8086	16	16	5–10	Some IBM-compatibles Compaq Deskpro
Intel	8088	8	16	5–8	IBM PC and XT HP 150 touch screen Compaq Portable
Intel	80286	16	32	8–16	IBM AT IBM PS/2 Model 50 Compaq Deskpro 286
Motorola	68000	16	32	8–16	Apple Macintosh SE Commodore Amiga
Motorola	68020	32	32	16–33	Macintosh II
Motorola	68030	32	32	16–50	Macintosh IIex NeXT computer
Motorola	68040	32	32	25–33	Hewlett-Packard workstations
Intel	80386SX	16	32	16–20	NEC PowerMate SC/20 Compaq Deskpro 386s/20
Intel	80386	32	32	16–33	Compaq Deskpro 386 IBM PS/2 Model 80
Intel	80486	32	32	25–50	IBM PS/2 Model 70 Compaq Systempro
Intel	i486 DX2-66	32	32	66	Compaq Deskpro 66i Dell 486P/66

*This table includes a partial list of the microcomputers using each chip.

COPROCESSORS

Additional microprocessors are often used inside a computer to handle some of the CPU's overload. These "pinch hitters," called **coprocessors,** help speed up the operation of your computer. For example, a math coprocessor chip can be installed on the motherboard to perform complex numerical calculations. This kind of a chip can speed up the processing of financial and scientific applications. It can also be used to speed up the calculations a computer uses to display complex graphics on the screen and print them out.

READ-ONLY MEMORY (ROM)

How does your microcomputer know what to do when you turn it on? How does it know to check out your hardware components (such as the keyboard or the monitor) to see that they have been connected correctly? Instructions to perform such operations, which are critical to the operation of a computer, are stored permanently on a **read-only memory (ROM)** chip (Figure 3.5) installed inside the computer by the manufacturer. This ROM chip retains instructions in a permanently accessible, nonvolatile form, which means that when the power in the computer is turned off, the instructions stored in ROM are not lost.

Having basic instructions permanently stored in ROM is both necessary and convenient. For example, if you are using a microcomputer with diskette drives, the more instructions in ROM, the fewer diskettes you may have to handle in order to load instructions into the computer. If you could have *all* the program instructions you'll ever need to use in ROM, you would have everything you need for processing data and information at your fingertips—always. Unfortunately, until recently the process of manufacturing ROM chips and recording data on them was more expensive than the process of producing other types of memory chips. As a result, manufacturers tended to record in ROM only those instructions that were crucial to the operation of the computer. However, in recent years improvements in the manufacturing process of ROM chips have lowered their cost to the point where manufacturers are beginning to include additional software instructions.

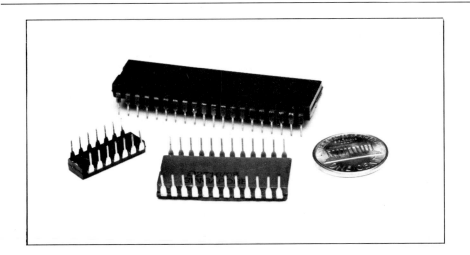

FIGURE 3.5

ROM chips, installed by the manufacturer on the computer's system board, contain instructions that are read by the computer. Since they cannot usually be rewritten, they are called *read-only memory.*

1. All fundamental circuits are designed by people using the rules of Boolean logic. After they have been designed, they reside in disk libraries in the computer system waiting to be selected by the designer.

2. The chip designer selects the appropriate circuits from the library, and the computer generates the physical circuit paths.

3. The circuit paths are refined by a designer. The final results are further inspected to ensure that all the components are aligned properly.

4. The circuitry is turned into several photomasks that will transfer the circuitry design onto chips.

Adapted from *The Computer Glossary*, Alan Freedman, © 1991, Amacom, 135 W. 50th Street, New York, NY 10020.

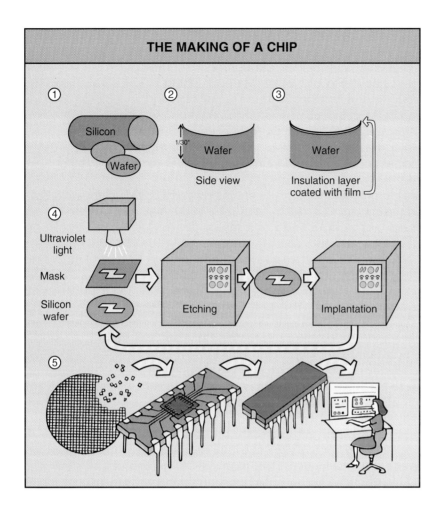

THE MAKING OF A CHIP

1./2. Silicon, the raw material of chips, is refined from quartz rocks and purified. It is fabricated into salami-like ingots from 3 to 5 inches in diameter. The ingots are sliced into wafers approximately 1/30th of an inch thick.

3. The wafer is covered with an oxide insulation layer and then coated with film.

4. A design is transferred onto the wafer by exposing it to ultraviolet light through a mask. Wherever light strikes the film, the film is hardened along with the insulation layer beneath it. The wafer is subjected to an acid that etches out the unhardened insulation layer exposing the silicon below. The next step is an implantation process that forces chemicals into the exposed silicon under pressure, creating electrically altered elements below the surface.

Through a series of masking, etching, and implantation steps, the circuitries for many chips are created on the wafer.

5. The finished wafer is tested, and the bad chips are marked for disposal. The wafer is sliced into chips, and the good ones are placed into their final spider-like package. Tiny wires bond the chip to the package's "feet." Each chip is then tested individually. The number of chips that make it through to the very end can be less than the number that don't.

PROM, EPROM, EEPROM

Three additional kinds of nonvolatile memory are used in some microcomputer systems—namely, PROMs, EPROMs, and EEPROMs. **PROM** stands for **programmable read-only memory**. This type of memory functions in the same way a regular ROM component does, with one major exception: PROM chips are custom-made for the user by the manufacturer. In other words, the user determines what data and instructions are recorded on them. The only problem with PROM chips is that, like ROM chips, once data is recorded on them, it can't be changed.

Erasable programmable read-only memory (EPROM) chips were developed as an improvement over PROM chips. EPROM functions exactly the same as PROM; however, with the help of a special device that uses ultraviolet light, in approximately 15 minutes the data or instructions on an EPROM chip can be erased. Once erased, a device generically referred to as a PROM burner is used to reprogram the chip. Unfortunately, to change instructions on an EPROM chip, the chip first must be taken out of the machine and then put back when the changes have been made. This task is one most computer users would prefer to avoid. The alternative to erasing and rerecording an EPROM chip is to replace it with a new EPROM that features the new program code. This is a task best performed by a trained computer professional.

Electrically erasable programmable read-only memory (EEPROM), the latest addition to the ROM family of chips, avoids the inconvenience of having to take chips out of the computer to change data and instructions. Unlike EPROM chips on which changes must be made optically, EEPROM chips allow changes to be made electrically under software control. In other words, they do not need to be taken out of the computer. The only disadvantage of EEPROM chips is they currently cost substantially more than regular ROM chips and disk storage devices. However, Intel and other manufacturers are planning high-volume production, which should push the prices down.

RANDOM ACCESS MEMORY (RAM)

Microprocessors, ALUs, registers, buses, ROM, instructions . . . what good are they if you have no data to work with? You wouldn't have any if it weren't for **random access memory (RAM)** (also called *primary storage, memory,* and *main memory*), the part of the processing hardware that temporarily holds data and instructions needed by the microprocessor.

FUNCTION OF RAM

The principal function of RAM is to act as a buffer between the microprocessor and the rest of the computer system components. It functions as a sort of desktop on which you place the things with which you are about to begin to work. The microprocessor can utilize only those software instructions and data that have been placed in RAM. The name *random access memory* is derived from the fact that data can be stored in and retrieved at random—from anywhere—in the electronic RAM chips in approximately the same amount of time, no matter where the data is.

RAM is an electronic state. When the computer is off, RAM is empty; when it is on, RAM is capable of receiving and holding a copy of the software instructions and data necessary for processing. Because RAM is a volatile form of storage that depends on electric power and because the power can go off during processing, users often save their work frequently onto nonvolatile storage devices such as diskettes or hard disks. In general, RAM is used for the following purposes:

- Storage of a copy of the main systems software program, which controls the general operation of the computer. This copy is loaded into RAM when the computer is turned on (you'll find out how later), and it stays there as long as the computer is on.
- Temporary storage of a copy of applications software instructions (the specific software you are using in your business) to be retrieved by the microprocessor for interpretation and execution.
- Temporary storage of data that has been input from the keyboard or other input device until instructions call for the data to be transferred into the microprocessor for processing.
- Temporary storage of data that has been produced as a result of processing until instructions call for the data to be used again in subsequent processing or to be transferred to an output device such as the screen, a printer, or a disk storage device.

The amount of RAM you have in your microcomputer directly affects the level of sophistication of the software you can use and the amount of data you can process at one time. Sophisticated, or powerful, programs take up a lot of space in RAM. Many of today's software programs require a computer to be configured with 640 K RAM to run. In general, the greater your machine's memory capacity, the better.

RAM CHIPS

RAM capacity is measured in kilobytes. Early microcomputer systems were not equipped with very much RAM by today's standards. In 1979, they were able to directly access and control only up to 64 K RAM; a microcomputer with 64 K RAM was considered satisfactory. Today a microcomputer system with less than 640 K RAM is considered underpowered. The software available for microcomputers did not require much RAM until certain new products began to appear on the market around 1984. With the introduction of software, called *spreadsheets*, to handle large financial reports, the need for increased RAM grew rapidly (because of the necessity of holding large amounts of numbers and instructions in RAM at one time). Now, for a microcomputer to effectively use many of the newer software products, it should have *at least* 640 K RAM available. In fact, today many microcomputers are configured with 4–8 MB RAM.

INCREASING RAM

What if you, like many users, are faced with the need to expand your computer's RAM capacity to be able to use some new software? For instance, what if your microcomputer isn't brand new and has a RAM capacity of only 512 K or 256 K? Unfortunately, you cannot simply pull out two of the 64 K chips and replace them with 256 K chips to increase the amount of RAM available to 640 K. The component that prevents you from doing this is the *dynamic memory access* (DMA) controller. In most older microcomputer systems, the DMA chip was designed to work with only one size of memory chip. However, in newer systems the DMA controller is designed to allow a mix of banks of 64 K, 256 K, 1 MB, 2 MB, and

4 MB memory chips. The DMA chip or module is responsible for managing the use of all RAM. It keeps track of which memory locations are in use (and by what) and which are available for use.

Two basic types of memory are used to increase memory beyond the 640 K limit (Figure 3.6). The type used is influenced by the sophistication of the microprocessor in your machine.

EXPANDED MEMORY

Expanded memory is used in 8088, 8086, 80286, and 80386 computers to increase memory beyond the conventional memory limit of 640 K. Users of early microcomputer systems couldn't increase the amount of RAM directly wired into the motherboard beyond 640 K because of limitations imposed by the systems software (programs designed to allow the computer to manage its own resources—systems software is described in Chapter 7). This situation led to the development of a wide variety of new products allowing the memory to be increased through the use of an **add-on memory board,** or **expansion card** (Figure 3.7). This board is simply pressed into an expansion slot on the motherboard. An **expansion slot** is a plug-in spot specifically meant to support add-on components (Figures 3.8

FIGURE 3.6   Types of RAM: conventional, expanded, extended. Most systems have 384 K of space called *upper memory* above the conventional memory area of 640 K. Upper memory is not considered part of the total memory of your computer because programs cannot use upper memory to store data. This memory is normally reserved for running your system's hardware.

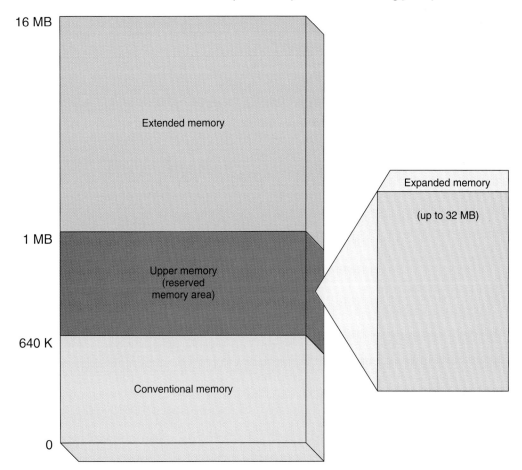

and 3.9). This slot connects the add-on board with the power supply for the computer and links the board with the buses for moving data and instructions.

In order for your computer to know you've added memory, you must also follow special software instructions that come with the board (Figure 3.10). To use expanded memory, you must run applications such as Lotus 1-2-3 (a spreadsheet) that are specifically tailored to address expanded memory.

We do need to mention here that add-on boards or cards can be inserted only in computers with **open architecture**—that is, computers built to allow users to open the system cabinet and make changes. Computers with **closed architecture,** such as the Macintosh SE, do not allow the user to add expansion cards. Thus, you can see that a computer's architecture becomes important to the user if he or she wants to upgrade the system—not only to increase RAM but also to add disk storage, graphics capabilities, some communications capabilities, or to change from a monochrome display screen to a color screen. If you are buying a microcomputer system and think you might want to upgrade it at a later time, make sure you purchase a microcomputer with open architecture.

FIGURE 3.7

This photo shows banks of RAM chips (left) on a memory expansion card that will be plugged into a slot inside the system cabinet.

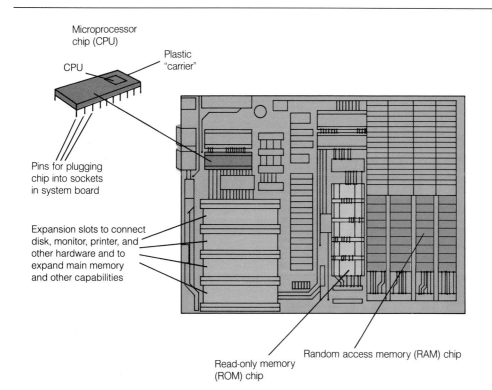

FIGURE 3.8

System board. This illustration shows the usual position of ROM and RAM chips, the CPU, and slots for expansion cards. Expansion cards are often used to increase a computer's RAM capacity.

Microprocessor chip (CPU)

CPU

Plastic "carrier"

Pins for plugging chip into sockets in system board

Expansion slots to connect disk, monitor, printer, and other hardware and to expand main memory and other capabilities

Random access memory (RAM) chip

Read-only memory (ROM) chip

EXTENDED MEMORY

Extended memory also refers to memory increased above 640 K; however, it can be used only in microcomputers with 80286, 80386, or 80486 microprocessors. Extended memory is also composed of RAM chips that either are plugged directly into the motherboard or are attached to a board that is plugged into an expansion slot. With extended memory, a machine can use up to 16 MB of memory. Like expanded memory, extended memory can be used only by software that recognizes it, such as the extended memory manager in Microsoft Windows. The applications software documentation will specify whether the software is compatible with one or both of these types of memory. Extended memory is accessed under the control of the applications software. For example, software applications that offer limited

FIGURE 3.9

Buy an add-on memory board to plug in an expansion slot and increase your RAM. (The expansion card is at the far left.)

FIGURE 3.10   Expanded memory board and the software required for a computer to use it

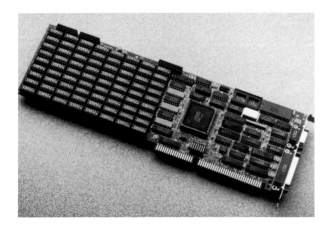

multitasking (the execution of more than one task or program at a time), such as Microsoft Windows and Desqview, can load multiple programs into 640 K (maximum) chunks of extended memory. The more memory, the greater the number of programs that can be run at once.

CACHE MEMORY

Although its definitions differ, basically **cache** (pronounced "cash") **memory** is a special high-speed memory area that the CPU can quickly access. Cache memory is often used with 386 and 486 microprocessors. Cache is a small area of RAM created in addition to the computer's main RAM. A copy of the most frequently used data and instructions is kept in the cache so the CPU can look in the cache first, which makes the computer run faster. Cache memory is usually located right on the microprocessor chip.

VIRTUAL MEMORY

Some microprocessors can also use **virtual memory,** which allows the processor—under control of special software—to use disk storage to simulate a large amount of RAM. For example, virtual memory allows an IBM AT microcomputer to use up to 1 GB (1 billion bytes) of virtual memory. Thus you can run a 4 MB program even if you have only 2 MB of RAM.

MEASURING THE PROCESSING POWER OF A COMPUTER

The proliferation of microcomputers in our society means that more and more people are becoming familiar with the processing power of computers in general. Many individuals are considering the purchase of a microcomputer on their own, with the result that more and more people are asking, "How do you determine how powerful a computer is?"

This question is fairly easy to answer. However, understanding the answer requires knowledge of a few more computer fundamentals.

ADDRESSING SCHEME

The **addressing scheme** is a computer design feature that directly determines the amount of RAM that can be controlled by the microprocessor at any one time. Early microprocessors were limited to 64 K of memory-addressing capability. The popular IBM PC-compatible computers have a memory-addressing capability of 1,024 K. The IBM PS/2 Model P70 uses the 80386 microprocessor, which allows access to approximately 4 GB of RAM—equal to the addressing capability of current minicomputers. (You'll learn in Chapter 7 that systems software prevents users from accessing the full 4 GB.)

REGISTER SIZE

Microcomputers have a number of registers that are used for a variety of purposes, including the temporary storage of results of arithmetic operations. The more of these registers you have and the larger they are, the more processing power you have. The registers in early microcomputers could hold only 8 bits each. Registers in newer computers hold 16 or 32 bits each. Each 32-bit general-purpose register can process twice as much data in each machine cycle per register as a 16-bit register can.

C rime rates have increased, but they might have increased more were it not for the presence of computer technology.

Consider home security. At one time, home-security systems were expensive and notoriously unreliable, with over 90% of alarms triggered being false. Often the alarms were caused by user error, such as a homeowner accidentally tripping a system and forgetting how to deactivate it, but they were also caused by equipment malfunction. Today's computerized home-security systems allow one to turn off some alarms (such as those inside) and turn on others (such as door and window alarms). They can also detect and isolate malfunctioning sensors, eliminating many false alarms.

Police departments, of course, have been using computers for some time, as when an officer in a patrol car calls up on a dashboard-mounted computer the license numbers of suspicious vehicles to check whether they have been stolen. More creative uses of computers have followed. Fingerprint identification, which used to require so many hours of an officer's time that it was virtually not attempted except in the most serious cases, has proved to be extraordinarily successful in those urban police departments that have moved their fingerprint files to a computerized database. The old-fashioned police artist's pad and pencil have been replaced by a software program containing more than 100,000 facial features, allowing officers with no artistic talent to create remarkably professional composite drawings of wanted suspects.

Computers have also helped increase productivity in prosecutors' offices and make the judicial system function better. For instance, a computer system may be used to log all incoming letters and phone calls; the district attorney heading the prosecutor's office can then scan the printouts and find out which callers require return calls and which assistant D.A.s must be reminded to respond to backlogged correspondence. Confidential data can be kept on various cases, and the system can be used to create appropriate legal documents to advance cases through the court system. Weekly calendars of active cases are provided to help prosecutors avoid scheduling conflicts and alert them to necessary actions they must take.

Some prosecutors' offices have a computer system that tracks cases from arrest to disposition. For example, in the Brooklyn, N.Y., district attorney's office, a system called FACTS (Facility for Accurate Case Tracking System) begins to pick up a case when the suspect is first brought to central booking at the police station, where the charges are keyed into a terminal. For misdemeanor cases, a terminal informs the judge about a suspect's prior record, outstanding charges, and the names of prosecuting attorneys. For felonies, the system is used to schedule the first grand jury hearing to determine if the evidence justifies an indictment. Other data includes names of witnesses, bail records, and the like.

Even the U.S. Supreme Court has acquired computer technology. The system is designed to transmit the court's opinion within minutes of its announcement. ■

DATA BUS CAPACITY

As you learned earlier, the data bus is like a pipeline used to move data and instructions among RAM, the microprocessor, and other microcomputer system components. The size of the data bus controls the amount of data that can travel down the pipeline at one time and thus can significantly affect a computer's performance. A data bus is constructed to carry 8, 16, or 32 bits. Hardware and software must be specifically designed for the type of bus used in a microcomputer.

Three basic bus designs, or architectures, are found in IBM and IBM-compatible microcomputer systems today. The Industry Standard Architecture (ISA) bus system is used with the Intel 8088, 80286, and 80386 microprocessors and is capable of passing 8 bits (when using the 8088) or 16 bits (when using the 80286 or 80386) through the data bus. This bus design doesn't fully utilize the 80386 microprocessor—which is capable of supporting 32-bit chunks of data in the data bus. As a result, two bus systems have been developed that enable 80386- and 80486-based machines to pass 32 bits through the data bus: (1) IBM's Micro Channel Architecture (MCA) and (2) Extended Industry Standard Architecture (EISA). There is much debate among industry observers about which of these two bus designs is better. A side-by-side comparison of the two designs reveals more similarities than differences. Unfortunately, users will have to make a choice about which bus system to adopt in their computer because the bus systems aren't compatible—that is, hardware and software must be designed specifically for the bus that will be used.

CLOCK SPEED

The clock, mentioned in the section on the instruction execution cycle, is the part of the microprocessor that synchronizes and sets the speed of all the operations in the machine cycle. The early microcomputers operated at speeds of around 1 MHz. This means that those computers had approximately 1 million processing cycles available per second to perform useful work. Today microcomputers are operating at speeds of 33–66 MHz.

INSTRUCTION SET

The early 8-bit microprocessors were extremely slow when performing mathematical operations. They were designed to handle only addition and subtraction; a more sophisticated operation (such as division or multiplication) had to be performed by a series of special program instructions, often called *subroutines*. For example, to multiply 5 times 3, a subroutine would add the number 3 together 5 times. The more powerful 32-bit microcomputers use additional instructions that handle mathematical operations in a single processing cycle. The 16-bit microprocessors also use single *blocks* of instructions (called *instruction sets*) that can cause whole blocks of data to be moved from one place to another. With the 8-bit microcomputers, this type of operation would also have to be handled by a number of subroutines (lots of "small" individual instructions).

How a microprocessor chip is designed affects how fast it can process. Most microprocessor chips today are designed using the **Complex Instruction Set Computing (CISC)** approach. A multitude of software applications, written for use with this chip design are being used in the business environment today. A new approach to chip design, called **Reduced Instruction Set Computing (RISC)**, allows microcomputers to offer very high speed performance by simplifying the internal design and reducing the number of instruction sets. The RISC design enables a computer to process about twice as fast as one based on the CISC design. The extent to which the RISC design is embraced depends on how the software industry supports it. However, industry observers do agree that the RISC design is definitely in our future.

CHECKLIST

In general, keep these points in mind when trying to determine the processing power of a microcomputer:

- *Addressing scheme:* The larger the addressing capability, the more RAM the computer can control.
- *Register size:* The larger the general-purpose registers, the more data the microprocessor can manipulate in one machine cycle.
- *Data bus:* The larger the data buses, the more efficiently and quickly data and instructions can be moved among the processing components of the computer.
- *Clock speed:* The faster the clock speed, the more machine cycles are completed per second and the faster the computer can perform processing operations.
- *Instruction set:* The more powerful the instruction set, the fewer instructions and processing cycles it takes to perform certain tasks.

SUMMARY

- The *microprocessor* is the "brain"—the CPU—of the microcomputer. It has two main parts:
  1. *Control unit*—directs and coordinates most of the computer system activities.
  2. *Arithmetic logic unit* (ALU)—performs all arithmetic and logical (comparison) functions and controls the speed of the calculations.
- The microprocessor is a ¼-inch to ⅛-inch square *semiconductor chip* that contains complicated circuitry. The power of the microprocessor chip is indicated by its number—generally, the higher the number (for example, 80286, 80386, 80486), the greater the power.
- The parts of the microprocessor and other computer components are connected by *buses*, or electronic pathways. The most important bus is the *data bus*, which carries data throughout the microprocessor.
- *Registers* temporarily store data and instructions for the microprocessor.
- The microprocessor understands only *machine language*, in which data and instructions are represented by 0s and 1s—the off and on states of electrical current or bursts of light. Each 0 or 1 is called a *bit*, short for *binary digit*. Groups of bits represent characters—it takes 8 bits, called a *byte*, to represent 1 character. 1,024 bytes equal a *kilobyte* (K); 1,024,000 bytes equal a *megabyte* (MB); and 1,024,000,000 bytes equal a *gigabyte* (GB).
- The more bits a computer's buses and registers can handle at once (8, 16, or 32), the faster the microcomputer.

- Software instructions are converted into machine language by a *language processor*. Each type of computer uses a unique machine language.

- To process an instruction, the control unit of the microprocessor retrieves it from memory and places it into a register. The *instruction cycle (I-time)* refers to the retrieval of the instruction from memory and its subsequent decoding. The *execution cycle (E-time)* refers to the processing of the instruction and subsequent storing of the result in a register. Together, the instruction cycle and the execution cycle are called the *machine cycle.*

- The microprocessor has an internal *clock* that synchronizes all operations of the machine cycle. Its speed is measured in *megahertz (MHz)*. The faster the clock speed, the faster the computer can process information.

- Many basic computer instructions are stored in *read-only memory (ROM)*, a chip installed by the manufacturer inside the computer. ROM is nonvolatile—the data and instructions are not lost when the power is turned off.

- ROM memory cannot generally be altered. However, special ROM chips exist that allow users to modify ROM.
  1. *Programmable read-only memory (PROM)* allows the user to determine what data and instructions the manufacturer records on the chip—in other words, to customize the chip. However, once the data is recorded, it cannot be changed.
  2. *Erasable programmable read-only memory (EPROM)* not only allows users to determine what data and instructions are recorded on the chip, but it also allows them to erase the data with a special ultraviolet device. Then a trained technician uses a *PROM burner* to reprogram the chip.
  3. *Electrically erasable programmable read-only memory (EEPROM)* allows users to reprogram the chip electrically, under software control.

- *Random access memory (RAM)*, also called *main memory, primary storage,* and just *memory,* refers to the part of the processing hardware that temporarily holds data and instructions needed by the microprocessor. RAM is volatile—unless the data and instructions in RAM have been saved, for example, to disk—they are lost when the power is turned off.

- RAM—sort of a "desktop"—acts as a buffer between the microprocessor and the rest of the computer system components. The microprocessor can utilize only those software instructions and data that have been placed in RAM.

- A copy of the main systems software is stored in RAM when the computer is turned on; it controls the general operation of the computer and stays there as long as the computer is on. A copy of the specific software you are using in your business (applications software) is also temporarily stored in RAM.

- The amount of RAM you have in your computer determines the level of software sophistication your computer can handle because, with more RAM:
  1. It can receive and use larger programs.
  2. It can hold more copies of more than one program in RAM to support sharing of the computer by more than one user.
  3. It can operate faster and more efficiently.
  4. It can hold images for creating graphics and animation.

- Most modern microcomputers need at least 640 K RAM to run today's software. Some software programs require even more RAM—for example, for *multitasking,* the execution of more than one task or program at a time. A user can increase his or her microcomputer's RAM by inserting *add-on memory boards,* also called *expansion cards,* into one of the computer's *expansion slots.*

- Increased memory comes in the form of either *expanded memory* or *extended memory.* The main difference between the two types of memory is the microprocessors each type can be used with. Extended memory can only be used with machines that use at least an 80286 microprocessor.

■ Memory expansion cards can be used only by those computers with *open architecture*, which allows users to open the system cabinet and make changes. Computers with *closed architecture* do not allow such changes.

■ *Cache memory* is a special high-speed area of RAM created in addition to the computer's main RAM. The CPU looks there first for frequently used data and instructions—thus making the computer run faster.

■ *Virtual memory* allows the CPU—under control of special software—to use disk space to simulate a large amount of RAM.

■ The processing power of a microcomputer can be measured in terms of:
  1. *Addressing scheme*—determines the amount of RAM that can be controlled by the microprocessor at any one time. The larger the addressing capability, the more RAM the computer can control.
  2. *Register size*—The larger the general-purpose registers, the more data the microprocessor can manipulate in one machine cycle.
  3. *Data bus*—The larger the data buses, the more efficiently and quickly data and instructions can be moved among the processing components of the computer.
  4. *Clock speed*—The faster the clock speed, the more machine cycles are completed per second and the faster the computer can perform processing operations.
  5. *Instruction set*—The more powerful the instruction set, the fewer instructions and processing cycles it takes to perform certain tasks. The design of the chip affects how instruction sets—or blocks of instructions—are processed.

KEY TERMS

add-on memory board, p. 56
addressing scheme, p. 59
arithmetic/logic unit (ALU), p. 48
binary digit, p. 49
bit, p. 49
bus, p. 50
byte, p. 49
cache memory, p. 59
clock, p. 48
closed architecture, p. 57
Complex Instruction Set Computing (CISC), p. 61
control unit, p. 46
coprocessor, p. 51
data bus, p. 50

electrically erasable programmable read-only memory (EEPROM), p. 54
erasable programmable read-only memory (EPROM), p. 54
execution cycle, p. 48
expanded memory, p. 56
expansion card, p. 56
expansion slot, p. 56
extended memory, p. 58
gigabyte (GB), p. 49
instruction cycle, p. 48
kilobyte (KB, or K), p. 49
machine cycle, p. 48

machine language, p. 47
megabyte (MB), p. 49
megahertz (MHz), p. 48
microprocessor, p. 46
multitasking, p. 59
open architecture, p. 57
programmable read-only memory (PROM), p. 54
random access memory (RAM), p. 54
read-only memory (ROM), p. 51
Reduced Instruction Set Computing (RISC), p. 61
register, p. 48
virtual memory, p. 59

EXERCISES

SELF-TEST

1. The _____ _____ performs all the microcomputer's arithmetic and logical functions.
2. In machine language, data and instructions are represented with 0s and 1s. (true/false)
3. The _____ is the CPU of a microcomputer.
4. The _____ _____ directs and coordinates most of the activities in the computer system.
5. The speed of a microprocessor is measured in _____.
6. The more bits a computer's buses and registers can handle at once, the faster the microcomputer. (true/false)
7. Read-only memory is a nonvolatile form of storage. (true/false)
8. A _____ connects the different components in the microprocessor.
9. _____ _____ _____ temporarily holds data and instructions until needed by the microprocessor.
10. Increased memory comes in two forms:
    a. _____   b. _____
11. Expansion cards, or add-on boards, can be used only in computers with _____ architecture.
12. The _____ the data bus, the more efficiently and quickly data can be moved among the processing components of the computer.
13. List three types of ROM chips:
    a. _____   b. _____   c. _____
14. Generally, the more expensive a microprocessor is, the faster it can process data. (true/false)
15. The instruction cycle and the execution cycle together are called the

    _____ _____.
16. A _____ is composed of 8 _____.
17. The retrieval of an instruction from memory and its subsequent decoding is referred to as the _____ _____.
18. Data and instructions are lost in RAM when the computer is turned off. (true/false)
19. Data and instructions are lost in ROM when the computer is turned off. (true/false)
20. The processing power of a microcomputer can be measured in terms of:
    a. _____   b. _____   c. _____   d. _____   e. _____

SOLUTIONS   (1) arithmetic/logic unit; (2) true; (3) microprocessor; (4) control unit; (5) megahertz; (6) true; (7) true; (8) bus; (9) random access memory; (10) expanded memory, extended memory; (11) open; (12) larger [or wider]; (13) PROM, EPROM, EEPROM; (14) true; (15) machine cycle; (16) byte, bits; (17) instruction cycle; (18) true; (19) false; (20) addressing scheme, register size, data bus, clock speed, instruction set

SHORT ANSWER

1. List and describe the main factors that affect the processing power of a microcomputer.
2. What is the difference between a computer with closed architecture and one with open architecture?
3. What is the function of the ALU in a microcomputer system?
4. What would be a good indication that two computers are incompatible? Why is knowing this important to you?
5. What is the function of a bus in a microcomputer system? How might one bus be better than another?
6. What does the addressing scheme in a microcomputer system affect?
7. Describe why having more RAM in your computer (as opposed to less) is useful.
8. What is a machine cycle and how does it relate to the term *megahertz*? Why would a user be interested in a computer's megahertz rate?
9. What is a coprocessor and what can it be used for?
10. What led to the development of add-on memory boards?

PROJECTS

1. Research the current uses of and the latest advances in ROM technology. How do you think ROM technology will affect the way we currently use microcomputers?
2. Advances are made almost every day in microprocessor chip technology. What are some of the most recent advances? In what computers are these chips being used? How might these advances affect the way we currently use microcomputers? Research the latest advances by reviewing the most current computer magazines and periodicals.
3. Visit a well-equipped computer store and, with the help of a salesperson, decide what microcomputer might be the best one for you to use based on your processing requirements (if necessary, pick a hypothetical job and identify some probable processing requirements). Use the checklist on page 62 to describe the microcomputer you would choose and explain why. Compare this microcomputer to the others you were shown.
4. What does it mean for a microcomputer and related equipment to be "IBM compatible"? Look through some computer magazines and identify advertised microcomputer systems that are IBM compatible. What are their clock speeds? microprocessor model numbers and manufacturers? RAM capacities? register (often called *wordsize*) and data bus capacities? Do you think there are any risks involved in buying an IBM-compatible system instead of an IBM PC?
5. Look through magazines about Apple Macintosh computers and PCs. Compare the Apple Quadra 950 microcomputer and the IBM PS/2 90 microcomputer according to:

    clock speed (MHz): _____
    RAM capacity: _____ (upgradable to: _____)
    data bus capacity: _____
    register (wordsize) capacity: _____
    cost: _____

    Which computer appears to be more powerful? Based on what you know so far, which machine would you prefer?

CHAPTER 4

STORAGE HARDWARE

A great deal of business has to do with keeping score, with record-keeping. Indeed, very few businesses can operate without keeping a running account of daily transactions: who owes what to whom, who collected what, when something is scheduled to happen, and so on. We have already described how data is converted into computer-usable form and processed. Now let us consider how this computerized data is stored and retrieved.

PREVIEW

When you have completed this chapter, you will be able to:

Explain the difference between primary and secondary storage, and how data is represented in each

Describe the secondary storage devices used the most often with microcomputers, including diskettes, hard disks, disk cartridges, and optical storage devices

Explain the importance of backup and the different methods for backing up a microcomputer system

CHAPTER OUTLINE

Why Is This Chapter Important?

Storage Fundamentals
  Primary and Secondary Storage
  Data Representation: Binary Code
  Files and Data Hierarchy
  How Is Data Stored?

Diskettes
  Retrieving and Storing Data
  Diskette Storage Capacity
  Diskette Sizes and Shapes
  Sectors
  Access Time

Hard Disks
  Retrieving and Storing Data
  Disk Cartridges

Optical Storage
  CD-ROM
  WORM
  Erasable Optical Disks

Backing Up a Microcomputer System

Summary

Key Terms

Exercises

Not understanding the concept of computer storage is like not understanding the concept of a car's gasoline tank. Without using a gasoline tank, you won't be able to get your car to go very far because, of course, without the tank, you can't use gasoline. Similarly, if you don't use a storage device with your computer, you won't have the capability to store the data that will make your computer useful.

As you learned in the previous chapter, the data you are working on—such as a document—is stored in RAM in an electrical state during processing. Because RAM is fueled by electricity, when you turn off the power to your computer, RAM is erased. Therefore, before you turn your microcomputer off, you must save your work onto a permanent storage device that stores data magnetically—such as a diskette or a hard disk—rather than electrically. When stored on a magnetic storage device, your data will remain intact even when the computer is turned off. (Optical storage, which we will cover later, is also an option.)

In general, data is stored in a computer system for three principal reasons.

1. *Current input data needs to be held for processing.* For example, daily sales data might be held in a temporary file until it is processed at the end of the day to produce invoices.

2. *Some types of data are stored on a relatively permanent basis and retrieved as required during processing.* For example, to produce a customer invoice, you need data from the customer file: customer's name, address, billing instructions, and terms.

3. *Data is stored to be periodically updated.* For example, the accounts receivable file (reflecting what customers owe) needs to be updated to reflect the latest purchases.

In addition to all this data, the computer software instructions must be stored in a computer-usable form because a copy of the software must be placed into RAM from a storage device before processing can begin.

In this chapter we describe the different storage devices you should be familiar with to use a microcomputer efficiently. We focus on how they work, as well as their speed, cost, and capacity.

STORAGE FUNDAMENTALS

You know that storage hardware provides the capability to store data and program instructions—either temporarily or permanently—for quick retrieval and use during computer processing. Before we describe the characteristics of the microcomputer storage devices you will likely use in the business environment, you must understand a number of storage fundamentals, including: (1) the difference between primary and secondary storage, (2) how data is represented in a microcomputer system, (3) what a file is, and (4) the general process of storing data on a storage device.

PRIMARY AND SECONDARY STORAGE

The term **primary storage** (main memory) refers to the RAM of a computer, where both data and instructions are temporarily held for immediate access and use by the computer's microprocessor. Although the technology is changing, most primary storage is considered a **volatile** form of storage, meaning that the data and instructions are lost when the computer is turned off. **Secondary storage** (or **aux-**

iliary storage) is any storage device designed to retain data and instructions (programs) in a more permanent form. Secondary storage is **nonvolatile,** meaning that saved data and instructions remain intact when the computer is turned off.

The easiest way to differentiate between primary and secondary storage is to consider the reason data is placed in them. Data is placed in primary storage only when it is needed for processing. Data in secondary storage remains there until overwritten with new data or deleted, and it is accessed when needed. In very general terms, a secondary storage device can be thought of as a file cabinet. We store data there until we need it. Then we open the drawer, take out the appropriate folder (file), and place it on the top of our desk (primary storage, or RAM), where we work on it—perhaps writing a few things in it or throwing away a few papers. When we are finished with the file, we take it off the desktop (out of primary storage) and return it to the cabinet (secondary storage).

DATA REPRESENTATION: BINARY CODE

When you begin to write a report, you have a large collection of symbols to choose from: the letters A–Z, both upper- and lowercase; the numbers 0–9; and numerous punctuation and other special symbols, such as ?, $, and %. People understand what these characters mean; computers cannot.

Computers deal with machine language, data converted into the simplest form that can be processed magnetically or electronically—that is, binary form. The term *binary* is used to refer to two distinct states: on or off, yes or no, present or absent (Figure 4.1). (For example, a light switch can be either on or off, so it can be viewed as a binary device.) A **binary digit (bit)** (Figure 4.2) is either the character 1 (on) or the character 0 (off)—magnetically, electrically, or optically. For example, when data is stored on magnetic tape or disk, it is represented by the presence or absence—"on" or "off"—of magnetic spots.

To store and process data in binary form, a way of representing characters, numbers, and other symbols had to be developed. In other words, *coding schemes*

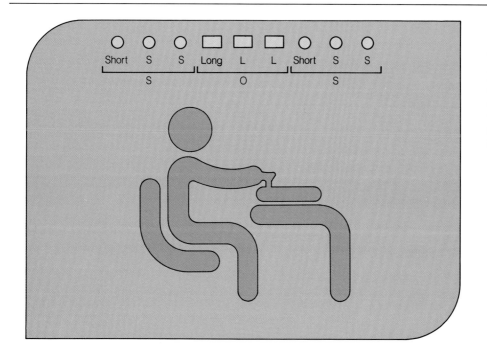

FIGURE 4.1

An early binary code. Samuel F. B. Morse, developer of the Morse code, showed that data elements (characters) could be represented by using two "states"—long and short, otherwise known as dash and dot.

had to be devised as standardized methods of encoding data for use in computer storage and processing. A scheme for encoding data using a series of binary digits is called **binary code.**

Two commonly used binary codes are ASCII (pronounced "as-key") and EBCDIC (pronounced "eb-see-dick") (Figure 4.3). The acronym **ASCII** stands for the **American Standard Code for Information Interchange,** which is widely used to represent characters in microcomputers and many minicomputers. Because microcomputers operate on 8-bit groups, ASCII uses 8 bits to represent a character. For example, the character A in ASCII is 01000001. Eight bits yield 256 possible combinations, enough to represent all the letters of the alphabet, numbers 0–9, and special symbols.

The acronym **EBCDIC** refers to **Extended Binary Coded Decimal Interchange Code,** which is the most popular code used for IBM and IBM-compatible mainframe computers. In EBCDIC, A is 11000001. As you can see in Figure 4.3, characters are coded differently in ASCII and EBCDIC. Because of these differences, transferring data between computers using different coding schemes requires special hardware and software.

PARITY BITS

The term *computer error* is often used when a mistake is caused by a person—inputting data incorrectly, for example. However, errors can be caused by other factors, such as dust, electrical disturbance, weather conditions, and improper handling of equipment. When such an error occurs, the computer may not be able to tell you exactly what and where it is, but it *can* tell you that there is an error.

How does it do this?—by using **parity bits,** or **check bits.** A parity bit is an extra (ninth) bit attached to the end of the byte (Figure 4.4). If you add the number of 1 bits in a byte, you will have either an odd number of 1s or an even

---

FIGURE 4.2

A bit (*binary digit*) is the smallest possible computer signal or impulse; it is used in combination with other signals or impulses to represent data (a character); it is a "1" or a "0"—that is, on or off. Different combinations of 0s and 1s are electronically translated into computerized codes.

A bit is the smallest possible unit of data; it is 1 or 0 — that is, on or off:

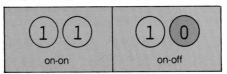

2 bits (2²) can have four possible combinations:

3 bits (2³) can have 8 possible combinations:

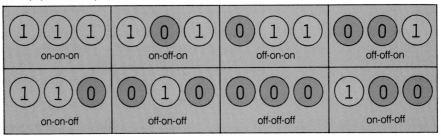

4 bits (2⁴) yield 16 possible combinations. 8 bits (2⁸) yield 256 possible combinations, enough to represent all the letters of the alphabet, numbers 0–9, and special symbols.

number of 1s (for example, ASCII A has two 1s, so it's even). Computers can be designed to use either an *odd-parity scheme* or an *even-parity scheme*. In an odd-parity scheme, a ninth bit, 0 or 1, is added to make the total number of 1s equal an odd number. If any byte turns up with an even number of 1s in an odd-parity scheme, the computer signals an error message on the screen. Similarly, if a byte turns up with an odd number of 1s in an even-parity scheme, an error message appears.

As a user, you won't have to determine whether to use an odd- or an even-parity scheme. The computer manufacturer determines this, and the systems software automatically checks the parity scheme. If your computer signals an error in the parity scheme, a message such as "Parity error" will appear on the screen. At this point, you should have your computer serviced to determine what is causing the problem.

Character	ASCII-8	EBCDIC	Character	ASCII-8	EBCDIC
A	0100 0001	1100 0001	N	0100 1110	1101 0101
B	0100 0010	1100 0010	O	0100 1111	1101 0110
C	0100 0011	1100 0011	P	0101 0000	1101 0111
D	0100 0100	1100 0100	Q	0101 0001	1101 1000
E	0100 0101	1100 0101	R	0101 0010	1101 1001
F	0100 0110	1100 0110	S	0101 0011	1110 0010
G	0100 0111	1100 0111	T	0101 0100	1110 0011
H	0100 1000	1100 1000	U	0101 0101	1110 0100
I	0100 1001	1100 1001	V	0101 0110	1110 0101
J	0100 1010	1101 0001	W	0101 0111	1110 0110
K	0100 1011	1101 0010	X	0101 1000	1110 0111
L	0100 1100	1101 0011	Y	0101 1001	1110 1000
M	0100 1101	1101 0100	Z	0101 1010	1110 1001
0	0011 0000	1111 0000	5	0011 0101	1111 0101
1	0011 0001	1111 0001	6	0011 0110	1111 0110
2	0011 0010	1111 0010	7	0011 0111	1111 0111
3	0011 0011	1111 0011	8	0011 1000	1111 1000
4	0011 0100	1111 0100	9	0011 1001	1111 1001
!	0010 0001	0101 1010	;	0011 1011	0101 1110

FIGURE 4.3

ASCII and EBCDIC. This chart shows some of the printed character codes according to the two most commonly used binary coding schemes for data representation. ASCII originally used 7 bits, but a zero was added in the left position to provide an 8-bit code (more possible combinations to form characters). The ASCII-8 code has enabled the use of many more special characters, such as Greek letters, math symbols, and foreign language symbols.

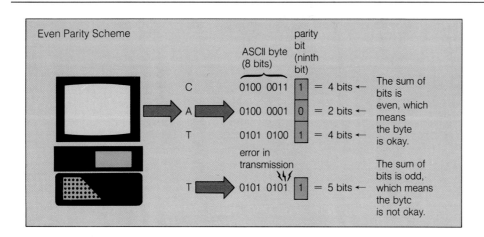

FIGURE 4.4

Parity schemes. This computer was designed to use an even-parity scheme, which means that the computer expects the total number of 1s (in the binary code) to always add up to an even number. In an even-parity scheme, a transmission error is signaled by the computer when the number of 1s adds up to an odd number. (The opposite is true when an odd-parity scheme is used.)

FILES AND DATA HIERARCHY

No matter what size or shape computer you work with, you will be working with files. But before we can put data files in their proper perspective, we need to examine the levels of data, known as the **data storage hierarchy.** If you look at Figure 4.5, at the top of the data hierarchy you'll see the term *file*. A **file** is made up of a group of related records. A **record** is defined as a collection of related fields, and a **field** is defined as a collection of related characters, or bytes, of data. Finally, a byte, or character, of data, as you have learned, is made up of 8 bits.

FIGURE 4.5

Data hierarchy. All data in an information system is stored as bits on a storage device. The data is arranged in hierarchical form: bits, bytes, fields, records, and files.

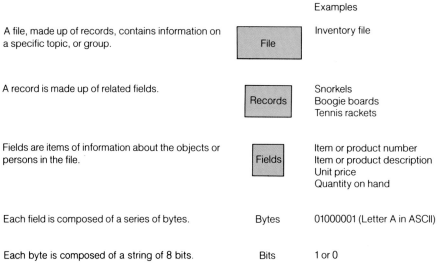

Examples

A file, made up of records, contains information on a specific topic, or group.

File — Inventory file

A record is made up of related fields.

Records — Snorkels / Boogie boards / Tennis rackets

Fields are items of information about the objects or persons in the file.

Fields — Item or product number / Item or product description / Unit price / Quantity on hand

Each field is composed of a series of bytes.

Bytes — 01000001 (Letter A in ASCII)

Each byte is composed of a string of 8 bits.

Bits — 1 or 0

FIGURE 4.6

The inventory file contains product records, such as the record for snorkels. Each record contains fields: product number, product description, unit price, and quantity on hand. Each field is made up of characters, or bytes, each of which comprises 8 bits.

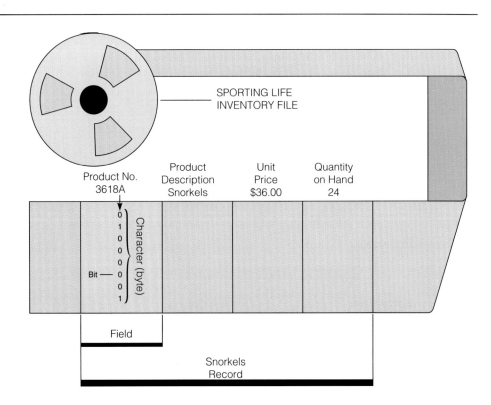

To illustrate this concept, let's look at a sample inventory file for a sporting goods store (Figure 4.6). This particular inventory *file* is made up of a group of *records*, one record for each item in inventory, such as snorkels. Each record contains the same number of *fields* such as: (1) product number, (2) product description, (3) unit price, and (4) quantity on hand. Each field contains a number of *characters*, such as the letter A in the product number. In turn, each character is made up of 8 bits, at the low end of the data hierarchy.

Files generally fall into two categories: (1) files containing data (often referred to generically as *data files*) and (2) files containing software instructions (often referred to generically as *program files*).

HOW IS DATA STORED?

To store data for later use you need two things: a storage **medium** (plural = **media**)—the type of material on which data is recorded—and a storage device. The storage device records the data onto the medium, where the data is held until needed. The process of recording data onto media, which is coordinated by software, involves four basic steps (Figure 4.7):

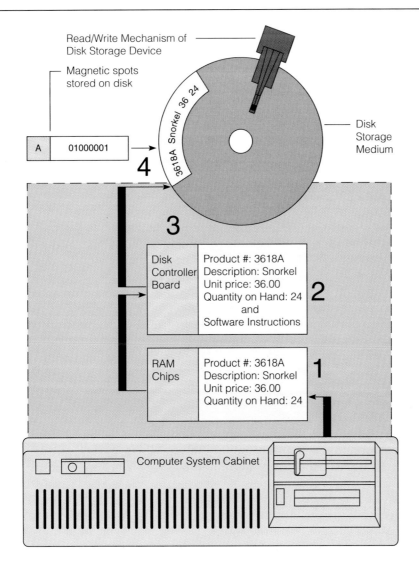

FIGURE 4.7

Data recording process. (1) Data enters RAM from an external device, such as a keyboard. (2) Software instructions determine where the data is to be recorded on the disk. (3) The data goes to the disk controller board. (4) From here it flows to the read/write head in the disk storage device and is recorded on the storage medium.

1. After input, the data to be recorded by a storage device temporarily resides in RAM.

2. Software instructions determine where the data is to be recorded on the storage medium.

3. The controller board for the storage device positions the recording mechanism over the appropriate location on the storage medium. For storage on disk, this mechanism is referred to in most cases as a **read/write head** because it can both "read" (accept) magnetic spots and convert them to electrical impulses and "write" (enter) the spots on the disk; it can also erase the spots.

4. The recording mechanism is activated and converts electrical impulses to magnetic spots placed on the surface of the medium as required to record the data according to the coding scheme being used (ASCII, for example).

DISKETTES

The **diskette,** or **floppy diskette** is a **direct access storage medium**—meaning that data can be stored and retrieved in no particular sequence. Diskettes are made of a special plastic that can be coated and easily magnetized. Diskettes are often referred to as "floppy" because they are made of flexible material. As Figure 4.8 shows, the disk is enclosed in a protective jacket—either paper or plastic—lined with a soft material specially treated to reduce friction and static. The disk jacket has four openings: (1) hub, (2) data access area, (3) write/protect notch, and (4) index hole. To store and retrieve data from a diskette, you must place it into a **disk drive** (Figure 4.9), which contains special mechanical components for storing and retrieving data.

RETRIEVING AND STORING DATA

The **hub** of the diskette is the round opening in the center. When the diskette is placed into the disk drive, the hub fits over a mount, or spindle, in the drive (Figure 4.9). In some IBM PCs, before you can access any data on the diskette, you must close the **disk drive gate,** or **door,** after you insert the diskette. The act of closing the disk drive gate moves a lever over the drive and clamps the diskette over the spindle of the drive mechanism. Many personal computers today don't have drive doors; the diskette is simply pushed into the drive until it clicks in place. An access light goes on when the disk is in use, and, in many microcomputers, the disk is ejected by pressing the eject button. (In microcomputers without eject buttons, the user simply opens the disk drive door and pulls out the diskette.)

When data is stored and retrieved, the diskette spins inside its jacket, and the read/write head on the actuator arm is clamped on the surface in the **data access area** of the disk (Figure 4.10). Most disk drives are equipped with two read/write heads so that the top and bottom surfaces of the diskette can be accessed simultaneously. The read/write heads are moved back and forth over the data access area in small increments to retrieve or record data as needed.

Just inside the disk drive unit, a small mechanism checks to determine if the user has covered the disk's **write/protect notch**. If the notch is covered, a switch is activated that prevents the read/write head from being able to touch the surface of the diskette, which means no data can be recorded (Figure 4.11). This is a security measure; covering the write/protect notch prevents accidental erasure or overwriting of data.

The **index hole** in the jacket is positioned over a photoelectric sensing mechanism in the disk drive. As the diskette spins in the jacket (when data is being recorded or retrieved), the hole (or holes—some diskettes have more than one) in the diskette repeatedly passes over the hole in the jacket, is sensed, and activates a timing switch. The timing activity is critical because this is how the mechanism determines which portion of the diskette is over or under the read/write heads. The diskette spins at a fixed speed of about 300 revolutions per minute (RPM).

As you'll learn in the next section, diskettes come in a few different sizes and with various storage capacities. The size and capacity of the diskette you use depends on the characteristics of the disk drive in your microcomputer system.

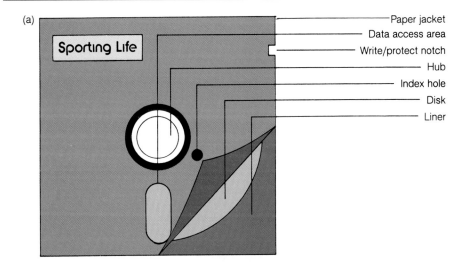

FIGURE 4.8

Diskettes were developed to replace cassette tape as a data storage medium for use with microcomputers. Diskettes provide fast direct access capabilities. IBM PCs and many IBM-compatible microcomputers use (a) the 5¼-inch diskette; the Macintosh line of microcomputers, as well as most portable IBM-compatible computers and IBM PS/2 series microcomputers, use (b) the 3½-inch diskette.

FIGURE 4.9

(a) These cutaway illustrations show the main parts of a 5¹/₄-inch disk drive and a 3¹/₂-inch disk drive for diskettes. (b) Inserting a 5¹/₄-inch diskette in a disk drive. (c) Inserting a 3¹/₂-inch diskette in a disk drive.

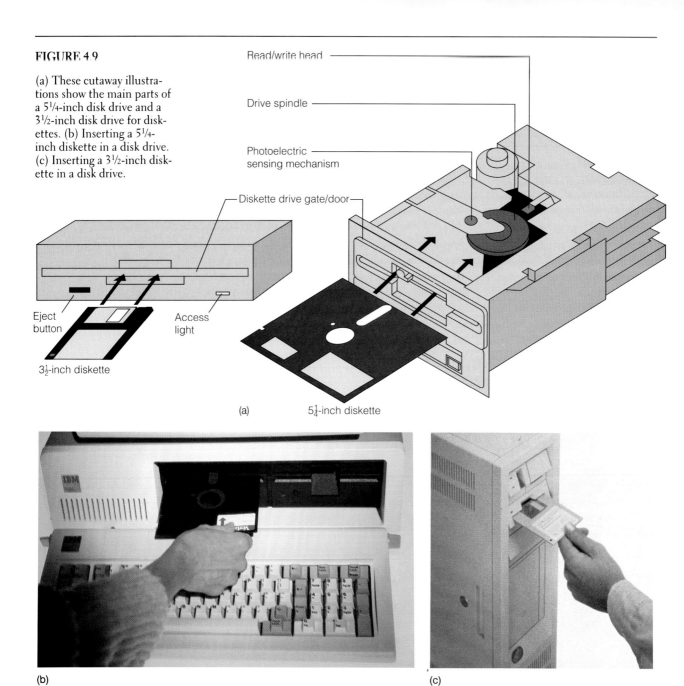

Read/write head

Drive spindle

Photoelectric sensing mechanism

Diskette drive gate/door

Eject button

Access light

3½-inch diskette

(a)   5¼-inch diskette

(b)

(c)

FIGURE 4.10

Inside the drive, the read/write head moves back and forth over the data access area in the protective jacket to read or write data on the disk.

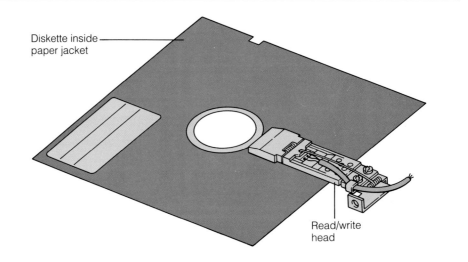

Diskette inside paper jacket

Read/write head

Some disk drives are intended to store and retrieve data from a high-capacity diskette, whereas others have been designed to be used with low-capacity diskettes. Likewise, 3½-inch disk drives are to be used only with 3½-inch diskettes. Don't try putting a 3½-inch diskette in a 5¼-inch disk drive! You could damage the read/write mechanism inside the drive. Later on in the book you will learn how to transfer data between disks of different sizes.

DISKETTE STORAGE CAPACITY

The **byte** is the unit of measure used most often to determine the capacity of a storage device used with any type of computer (Table 4.1). The capacity of a diskette does not necessarily depend on its size. A number of factors affect how much data can be stored on a disk, including:

1. Whether the diskette stores data on only one side (single-sided) or both sides (double-sided)
2. Whether the disk drive is equipped with read/write heads for both the top and the bottom surfaces of the diskette

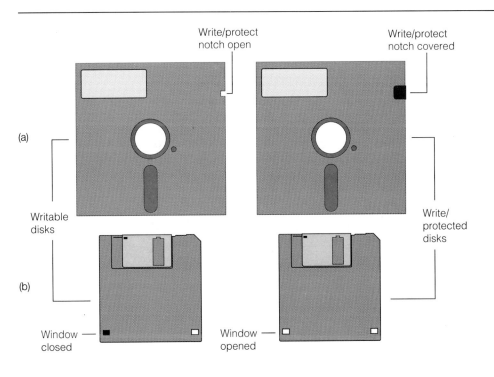

FIGURE 4.11

(a) The write/protect notch of the 5¼-inch disk on the left is open and, therefore, data can be written to the disk. The notch of the 5¼-inch disk on the right, however, is covered (the user has put tape over it). Data cannot be written to this disk. (b) Data cannot be written on the 3½-inch disk on the right because the small black piece of plastic is not covering the window in the lower left corner. Plastic covers the window of the 3½-inch disk on the left, so data can be written on this disk.

Bit	A binary digit; 0 or 1
Byte	8 bits, or 1 character
Kilobyte (K, or KB)	1,024 bytes
Megabyte (MB)	1,024,000 bytes
Gigabyte (GB)	1,024,000,000 bytes
Terabyte (TB)	1,024,000,000,000 bytes

TABLE 4.1

Units of Measurement for Disk Storage

3. What the data-recording density is (the number of bits that can be stored per inch)

4. What the track density is (the number of tracks per inch in which data is recorded)

The first diskettes were **single-sided**. But as the need to store more data became a significant concern in the business community, technology produced the **double-sided** disk, which is capable of storing twice the amount of data as a comparable single-sided disk. To take advantage of a double-sided disk, however, you must have a computer with a double-sided floppy disk drive. Double-sided disk drives are equipped with read/write heads for both the top and the bottom surfaces of a disk. This allows data to be read from or written to both surfaces simultaneously. (The heads move together on the same mechanism so that they are positioned over corresponding locations on the surfaces of the disk.) Disk capacity also depends on the recording density capabilities of the disk drive. **Recording density** refers to the number of bits per inch (bpi) of data that can be written onto the surface of the disk. Disks and drives are typically rated as having one of three recording densities:

1. **Single-density**
2. **Double-density**
3. **Quadruple-density** (often referred to as *quad-density*, or *high-density*)

The specifications for the exact number of bits per inch for each recording density vary from one manufacturer to another. Disk manufacturers use the recording density designation as a measure of the maximum bpi their diskettes can reliably be expected to store.

A double-sided, double-density 5¼-inch diskette (labeled "DS, DD," or "2S/2D") has a storage capacity of 360 K. Using a new technology called *vertical recording*, Toshiba is now producing a 3½-inch extra high-density (ED) diskette that can store 2.88 MB of data. The 3½-inch diskettes for the IBM PS/2 series of microcomputers hold from 720 K (single-density) to 1.44 MB (double-density). Table 4.2 compares the capacities of some popular diskettes.

The final factor affecting disk capacity is the track density. As pictured in Figure 4.12, data is recorded on disks in circular bands—similar to grooves on a phonograph record—referred to as **tracks**. The read/write heads are designed to move in small increments across the data access area of the disk to find the appropriate track. As the precision of positioning the read/write head increases, the widths of the tracks become thinner—that is, less dense. Common **track densities** in use today are 48 tracks per inch (tpi), 96 tpi, and 135 tpi. The recording surface of a 5¼-inch disk is slightly less than 1 inch; therefore, there are 40 or 80 usable tracks per inch in most cases.

TABLE 4.2

Capacities of Widely Used Diskettes

	Bytes	Tracks	Sectors/Track	Bytes/Sector
5¼-inch diskettes:				
Double-sided, double-density	360 K	40	9	512
Double-sided, quad-density	1.2 MB	80	15	512
3½-inch diskettes:				
Double-sided, single-density	720 K	80	9	512
Double-sided, double-density	1.44 MB	80	18	512

DISKETTE SIZES AND SHAPES

The use of 5¼-inch diskettes by IBM in their personal computer system in 1981 led to the adoption of this size as the microcomputer industry standard. However, since the Apple Macintosh introduced the 3½-inch diskette and disk drive in 1984 and IBM switched to this size in 1987 in its PS/2 microcomputer systems, the standard has been changing. Although they are smaller in size, the 3½-inch disks are capable of storing more data than 5¼-inch diskettes, and they are also less susceptible to damage because they are covered by a hard plastic jacket rather than a paper jacket. (The care of diskettes is discussed later in this chapter.)

Nearly 80% of all disk drives sold today are used with 3½-inch diskettes. "The 3½-inch is a done deal. The only momentum for 5¼-inch drives comes from clone makers who just copy old products," said James Porter, president of Disk/Trend, Inc. Laptop computers—microcomputers that typically weigh between 5 and 20 pounds and that you can carry around like a briefcase—fueled the ascension of the 3½-inch drive.

SECTORS

Typically a disk is divided into eight or nine **sectors,** or equal, wedge-shaped areas used for storage reference purposes (Figure 4.12). The point at which a sector intersects a track is used by systems software to reference the data location; the track number indicates where to position the read/write head, and the sector number indicates where to activate the read/write head as the disk spins.

Disks and drives are identified as being either hard-sectored or soft-sectored. *Hard-sectored* disks always have the same number and size of sectors, which are fixed by the manufacturer. Today most microcomputer systems use soft-sectored disks. *Soft-sectored* disks are marked magnetically by the user's computer system during a process called **formatting,** or **initializing,** which determines the size and the number of sectors on the disk. Since your diskettes must be adapted to the particular microcomputer and software you are using, you format these diskettes yourself. This is easily done using only a few simple commands on the computer.

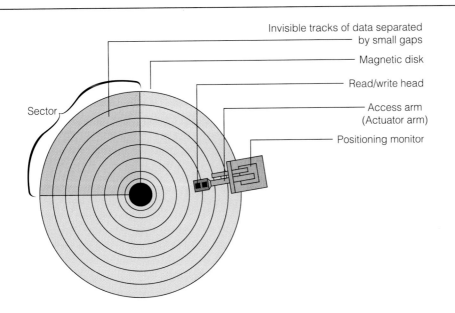

Invisible tracks of data separated by small gaps

Magnetic disk

Read/write head

Access arm (Actuator arm)

Positioning monitor

Sector

FIGURE 4.12

Tracks are circular bands on disks on which data is recorded. The tracks are separated by small gaps and are divided into equal areas called sectors. Tracks and sectors are used to determine addresses of fields of data.

ACCESS TIME

The responsiveness of your computer depends to a great extent on the time it takes to locate the instructions or data being sought and then to load a copy into RAM. The term **access time** refers to the average speed with which this is done. The access time of your computer's disk drive is determined by adding up the time it takes to perform each of the following activities:

1. Positioning the read/write heads over the proper track (the time it takes to do this is called the **seek time**)

2. Waiting for the disk to revolve until the correct sector is under or over the read/write heads (this is called **rotational delay,** or **latency**)

3. Placing the read/write head(s) in contact with the disks

4. Transferring the data from the disk into the computer's RAM (at a speed called the *data transfer rate*)

The average access time for diskettes ranges from 150 milliseconds (150 thousandths of a second) to 300 milliseconds, depending on the operating characteristics of the drive mechanism. This may not seem like very long, but access time can be a major performance factor for the following reasons: (1) Large applications software packages keep only a portion of the instructions in RAM at one time and must retrieve additional instructions from disk periodically to perform specific tasks. (2) The processing of large files is done only a few records at a time, so a substantial amount of time can be spent going back and forth to the disk to retrieve records.

Before you proceed to the next section, you need to know how to care for your diskettes—abuse means lost data. Figure 4.13 shows 5¼-inch diskettes; however, just because the 3½-inch diskettes have hard jackets does not mean that they cannot be damaged, too!

HARD DISKS

The introduction of high-capacity **hard disks**—which can store from 20 MB to more than a gigabyte, or 1,000 MB—solved two serious problems related to the limited storage capacity of diskettes. First, as a business begins to use microcomputers extensively, the amount of software it acquires and data it collects tends to grow substantially. As a result, the number of diskettes it needs to handle increases dramatically. It is not uncommon for one user alone to have a library of 100 or more diskettes. Second, the largest file that can be accessed at one time is limited to the capacity of RAM and the capacity of the storage medium. So, if the capacity of a diskette is 360 K, no file larger than that can be stored on the disk or worked with in RAM.

Hard disks can store much larger files; for example, certain businesses may need to set up an inventory system on a microcomputer that calls for working with a 45,000-item inventory master file. And the 150-page report that didn't fit on one diskette can easily fit on a hard disk. Of course, you could have stored the report in sections in separate files on different diskettes, but that would have been very inconvenient. You would have had to continually swap diskettes, inserting them and ejecting them, to work on your report. The hard disk spares you that trouble.

Just a few years ago, one 20 MB hard disk provided enough storage for most users (Figure 4.14). Today, because of storage-hungry graphical software interfaces, networking software, and more sophisticated software applications and systems software, hard disk storage capacities of 300 MB and larger are becoming increasingly commonplace and necessary. Hard disk drives can store and retrieve data much faster than can diskette drives. Whereas the average access time for diskettes is approximately 300 milliseconds, the average access time for hard disks ranges from 16–70 milliseconds.

Hard disk units have become increasingly smaller while at the same time they have achieved higher storage capacities. The most popular units today use 3½-inch disks; some units still use 5¼-inch disks. The initial 5¼-inch disk drives were approximately 3½-inches high, whereas the new disk drives are just over 1½-inches high; this means that you can put at least twice as much disk capacity in the same

FIGURE 4.13

Handle with care! This illustration shows how to avoid disk damage.

space you used before (Figure 4.15). Two diskette drives can fit where only one used to fit, and two hard disk units can occupy the space that one did. This type of configuration provides a powerful system in a small work space.

FIGURE 4.14

The use of hard disk units on microcomputers has greatly increased their ability to deal with large amounts of data at one time. For example, one 20 MB hard disk holds the same amount of data as 56 double-sided, double-density diskettes.

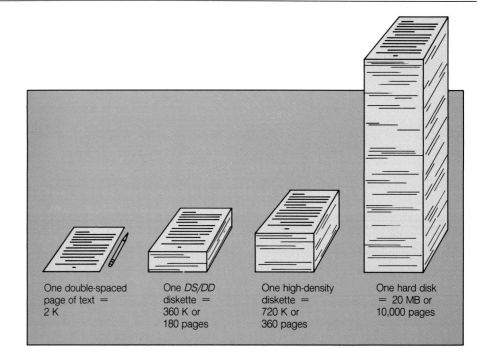

One double-spaced page of text = 2 K

One *DS/DD* diskette = 360 K or 180 pages

One high-density diskette = 720 K or 360 pages

One hard disk = 20 MB or 10,000 pages

FIGURE 4.15

This 1½-inch hard disk drive can be inserted in the computer's system unit to provide the user with high-capacity storage.

The alternative to replacing a diskette drive or taking up desk space with an external hard disk drive is to buy a **hardcard** (Figure 4.16), a circuit board with a disk that plugs into an expansion slot inside the computer. Hardcards store between 40 MB and 105 MB of data and have an average access time of from 9 to 25 milliseconds.

RETRIEVING AND STORING DATA

In hard disk systems, data is stored in the same way as it is on diskettes. A series of tracks are divided into sectors when the disk is formatted. As their name suggests, hard disks are made out of a rigid substance that is capable of storing a greater amount of data than the soft material used for diskettes. Hard disk drives for microcomputers (Figure 4.17) can be *internal* (built into the computer cabinet and nonremovable) or *external* (outside the computer cabinet and connected to it by a short cable) (Figure 4.18).

Hard disks have the following characteristics:

1. They are rigid metal platters connected to a central spindle.
2. The entire disk unit (disks and read/write heads) is placed in a permanently sealed container.
3. Air that flows through the container is filtered to prevent contamination.
4. The disks are rotated at very high speed (usually around 3,600 RPM; floppy disks rotate at about 300 RPM).

These disk drives can have four or more (often eight) disk platters in a sealed unit. In most of these disk units (which are often called *Winchester disk drives*), the read/write heads never touch the surfaces of the disks. Instead, they are designed to float from .5 to 1.25 millionths of an inch from the disk surface; because of this characteristic, the design is often referred to as a *flying head* design. Because the heads float so closely to the sensitive disks, any contamination—such as a dust particle or a hair—can cause a *head crash*, also referred to as a *disk crash*, which destroys some or all of the data on the disk. This sensitivity is the reason why hard disk units are assembled under sterile conditions.

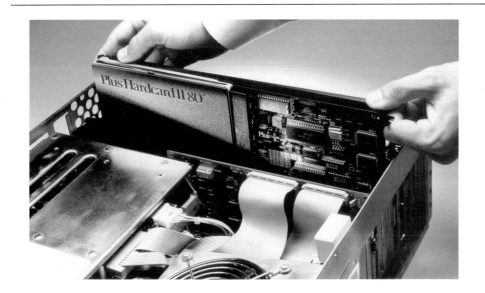

FIGURE 4.16

Hardcard. This hardcard works like a hard disk but plugs into an expansion slot inside the microcomputer cabinet. (The disk is under the cover at the left side of the card.)

FIGURE 4.17

Internal hard disk unit. (a) These illustrations show the main components of a hard disk unit. (b) As you can see from this photo of an IBM PS/2 computer, a hard disk does not have an exterior opening, because the disk(s) is sealed in a unit inside the system cabinet. (The single drive opening you see is for a diskette.)

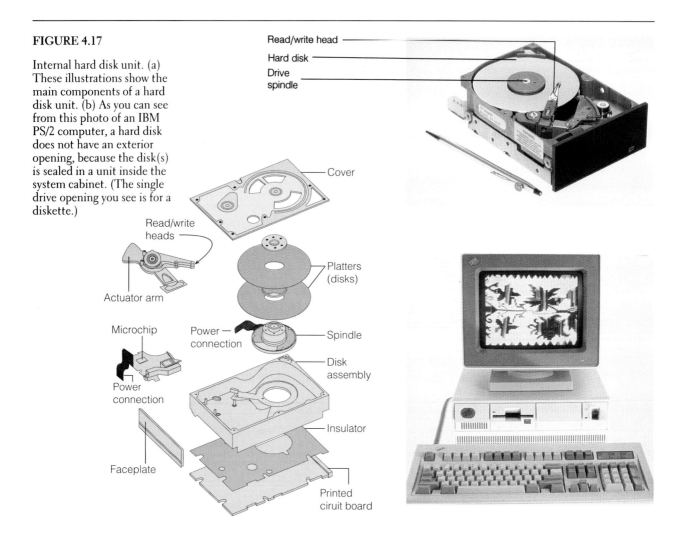

Read/write head
Hard disk
Drive spindle
Cover
Read/write heads
Actuator arm
Microchip
Power connection
Power connection
Faceplate
Platters (disks)
Spindle
Disk assembly
Insulator
Printed ciruit board

FIGURE 4.18

External hard disk drive. This shot of a Mac SE shows it hooked up to an external hard disk drive (the "box" positioned under the computer, directly behind the keyboard). You can also see the diskette drive opening on the front of the system cabinet. Some Mac systems can also include an additional internal hard disk unit and a second floppy disk drive.

All of us know how to eat. Some of us know how to cook. Numerous enterprising people go into the food and beverage business to try cooking for others. And computers have become as essential for restaurant operators as recipes and menus.

Many small eating and drinking establishments get by with just an electronic cash register, a calculator-like machine with a cash drawer that is not much different from the time-honored cash register. Larger food-service operations, however, may go to a point-of-sale (POS) system. A POS system links three areas: the eating and drinking areas, the kitchen or other food-preparation areas, and the back office.

In the eating and drinking areas—what the industry calls the "front of the house"—there may be POS registers with different cash drawers for different waiters, waitresses, and bartenders. Or, if a cash drawer is shared by several servers, separate cash accountability is maintained by the software. Special-purpose software is also available that tells the host or hostess how many customers came in and when, the size of the order, and which server took the order and when. Some software can help servers be more efficient or helpful—for example, by indicating when a particular food or beverage is out of stock or by cueing servers to ask how an order of beef should be cooked.

So-called cash-taking software is important because often the person taking the order is not the cashier. Cash-taking software consolidates bar and food charges, provides information on discounts and senior-citizen specials, and indicates whether payment is by cash or credit card. Different kinds of printers are available for printing out guest checks: dot matrix or impact printers, which are commonplace but noisy; thermal printers, which require special paper; and laser printers, the most recently developed kind, which are quiet and require no special paper.

Servers in the front of the house may use flat-membrane-type keyboards; touch-screen devices; or, sometimes, hand-held terminals. Hardware in the kitchen must be of a hardier sort, capable of working amid heat, water, and grease. If orders are transmitted electronically by servers from terminals in the front of the house via cable to the kitchen, they may appear on a printer or display screen. Software may process the information sent by the server in a way to assist the preparer. For instance, similar food items might be grouped together, cooking instructions might be put in order, special cooking instructions highlighted, and instructions given on when to begin each part of an order. Software can also indicate that a kitchen is properly stocked to meet demand, based on previous experience.

Depending on the kind of eating establishment, a POS system might be hooked up to outside payment processors for credit card charges and check clearing. Or, if the restaurant is in a hotel, it might link front-of-the-house terminals with the front desk, so that food and beverage charges may be posted to a guest's room bill.

Finally, there is the relationship of the POS system to what is called the "back office," the manager's office or the corporate headquarters. A manager may use the back-office terminal to collect information so that the restaurant can regulate the mix of products, adjust prices, and in general run things more efficiently. If the back-office machine is also a microcomputer, it can be used for other tasks, such as doing spreadsheets, word processing, and telecommunications. ■

DISK CARTRIDGES

Removable hard **disk cartridges** (Figure 4.19) are an alternative to regular hard disks as a form of secondary storage. Whereas hard disks remain inside the computer or the external disk drive, disk cartridges can be removed and replaced easily. The cartridges usually contain one or two platters enclosed in a hard plastic case that is inserted into the disk drive, much like a music cassette tape. The capacity of these cartridges ranges from 5 to 450 MB, somewhat lower than regular hard disk units but still substantially superior to diskettes. They are handy because they give microcomputer users access to amounts of data limited only by the number of cartridges used.

OPTICAL STORAGE

Because they offer practical solutions to large-scale storage requirements, optical storage technologies are increasingly becoming a rival of magnetic storage. **Optical storage technologies** involve the use of a high-power laser beam to pack information densely on a removable disk.

Optical storage technologies offer users a number of advantages. The primary advantage is storage density. You can fit a lot more data on an optical disk than you can on a comparably sized magnetic disk. Because lasers can be focused with such precision, the tracks recorded on an optical disk are much closer together than those recorded on a magnetic disk. Also, the amount of space required to

FIGURE 4.19

Hard disk cartridge. This Tandon hard disk drive has one cartridge in place; another cartridge has been placed on top of the drive.

record an optical bit is much less than that required to record a magnetic bit. As a result, removable optical disk storage capacities range from 600 MB to over 1 GB. Another advantage of optical storage is that the media on which data is stored is much less susceptible to deterioration or contamination than magnetic recording media. The reason for this durability is that nothing touches the optical disk's surface except for a beam of light. Finally, optical disks are also less susceptible to head crashes than are magnetic disks because the optical head is suspended farther from the surface of the disk. Because the heads are so close to the disk's surface in a magnetic hard disk drive, trying to remove the disk would end the life of both the magnetic disk and the drive. Optical disks, however, are easily loaded and removed without risk of damaging either the optical disk or the drive.

Most technologies come with disadvantages; optical storage isn't any different. The primary disadvantage of optical storage is that the time it takes to retrieve data, or the average access time, is much greater than it is with magnetic storage media. In other words, optical disk drives are slow.

Any microcomputer can run an optical disk drive. In the following sections, we describe three types of optical storage disks that are available for use with microcomputers today.

CD-ROM

Compact disk read-only memory (CD-ROM) is the oldest and best-defined optical storage technology. This read-only storage medium is capable of storing 540 to 748 MB of data, images, and sound—the equivalent in storage capacity to about 275,000 pages of text, 1,800 double-density floppy disks, 74 minutes of audio, or thousands of images.

CD-ROMs are imprinted by the disk manufacturer. The user cannot erase or change the data on a CD-ROM or write on the disk—the user can only read the data. The optical disk is used primarily for storing huge amounts of prerecorded information. You will find the following types of information stored on commercial CD-ROMs: (1) encyclopedias, (2) medical reference books, (3) dictionaries, (4) legal libraries, (5) engineering and drafting/design standards, (6) collections of magazine and newspaper articles on specific subjects, and (7) graphic images (called *clip art*, grouped according to subject, that can be copied—"clipped"— and used as illustrations in documents produced by desktop publishing or word processing).

WORM

Write Once, Read Many (WORM) technology goes a step beyond CD-ROM. WORM disks are also imprinted by the manufacturer, but the buyer can determine what is written on them. Once the disks have been written on, however, they can only be read from then on—again, no changes can be made. WORM disks have much greater storage capacities than CD-ROM disks. The storage capacity of a WORM disk ranges from 122 to 6,400 MB. WORM disks are ideal for storing custom data that doesn't need to be updated often.

ERASABLE OPTICAL DISKS

Although ideal for certain situations, CD-ROM and WORM drives aren't general-purpose storage devices, because—once written—the data on them can't be changed. The erasable optical disk is the first optical technology to provide to users the capability of changing data under software control.

Erasable optical disks come housed in removable cartridges (Figure 4.20) and store about 281–3,200 MB each. The data access times are between two and six times slower than those of the high-performance hard disk drives. Erasable optical disks are often used in *magneto-optical* (MO) *disk drives*, which use aspects of both magnetic disk and optical disk technologies. The new MO drives pack up to 122 MB on each removable 3½-inch disk. No matter how much data a hard disk drive can store, its capacity is limited (for example, to 60 MB or 120 MB). However, MO drives have essentially unlimited capacity—that is, limited only by the number of disks the user buys. A 3½-inch MO disk looks like a 3½-inch floppy disk but is twice as thick. MO drives are available as external or internal units.

MO drives are useful to people who need to save successive versions of large documents, handle enormous databases, work in desktop publishing or graphics, or work with sound and/or video.

FIGURE 4.20

(a) Optical disks can store much more data than magnetic diskettes, disks, or tape can. They are also cheaper. Optical storage devices are available for all sizes of computer systems. This photo shows a Maxtor erasable optical disk in a cartridge along with an optical disk drive (which may be internal or external). (b) NEC W-CDR-74 optical disks and disk drive, plus speakers for outputting sound.

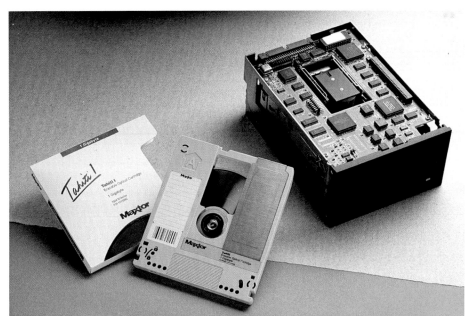

(a)

(b)

BACKING UP A MICROCOMPUTER SYSTEM

As high-capacity hard disk units increased in popularity, the problem of making backup copies of disk contents became a significant concern. *Users should make backup copies of all stored data files to ensure that they don't lose their data if the hard disk is damaged or destroyed.* Many users neglect this step and live to regret it: How would you feel if your 400-page masterpiece novel was lost forever because your hard disk crashed? Or if two weeks' worth of tax computations turned to dust because your disk storage units were electrocuted by a power surge? But it takes about twenty 3½-inch diskettes to back up the contents of one 20 MB hard disk, and 100 diskettes for a 144 MB disk! Something more efficient was needed.

This concern prompted the development and refinement of **cartridge-tape units** (also called *tape streamers* and *streaming tape*) to back up high-capacity hard disks (Figure 4.21). Tape cartridges have a capacity (per cartridge) ranging from 20 MB to 525 MB. The copying speeds of tape backup units vary; it takes approximately 12 minutes to copy the contents of a 60 MB hard disk. (In addition to tape units, hard disk cartridges are also used to back up regular hard disk units.)

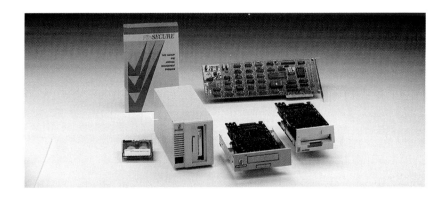

FIGURE 4.21

Cartridge tape unit. Such tape units are used with microcomputers to back up the contents of hard disk units, so that data is not lost if the hard disk units fail.

Most microcomputers have one of the following disk-drive configurations:

1. Two diskette drives
2. One diskette drive and one hard drive
3. Two diskette drives and one hard drive

When you are working with applications software and want to save the work you've done, you need to tell the software which disk drive to use to save the work. This is similar in concept to telling someone what drawer to put a folder in. To do this, you must follow certain disk-drive-naming conventions.

With DOS and IBM-type PCs, the first diskette drive is referred to as Drive A. The second diskette drive is referred to as Drive B. A hard disk is typically called Drive C. If an optical disk drive is also present, it may be called Drive D.

When you are using DOS or applications software, the drive letter is always followed by a colon (:) to represent the drive designation—that is, the colon is an essential part of the drive name.

Macintosh microcomputers do not use these disk-drive-naming conventions. Instead they use icons and labels (such as "hard disk") to represent disk drives. When you have hands-on practice in the lab or on your own computer, you will become familiar with disk-drive-naming—and file-naming—conventions.

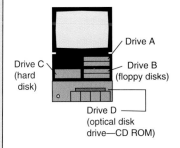

SUMMARY

- A *bit*, short for *binary digit*, is either 1 (on) or 0 (off). There are 256 possible combinations of bits used in binary *coding schemes*, the computer's language for representing data.

- Two commonly used coding schemes are the *American Standard Code for Information Interchange (ASCII)* and the *Extended Binary Coded Decimal Interchange Code (EBCDIC)*.

- Both ASCII and EBCDIC use 8 bits to represent a character. Sometimes a *parity bit*, or *check bit*, is added for the purpose of error checking. Computers are designed to use either an *odd-parity scheme* or an *even-parity scheme*. In an odd-parity scheme, if an even number of 1s turns up in a character, an error message is displayed on the screen. The reverse is true of an even-parity scheme.

- Data is stored according to a *data storage hierarchy*:
  1. *Files*—at the top of the hierarchy. A file is made up of a group of related records (example—an inventory file about sporting goods).
  2. *Records*—second in the hierarchy. A record is made up of a collection of related fields (example—the items in inventory, such as baseballs, bats, gloves, rackets, etc.).
  3. *Fields*—third in the hierarchy. A field is a collection of related characters, or bytes, of data (example—inventory item identifiers, such as product number, product description, unit price, and quantity on hand).
  4. *Bytes*—fourth in the hierarchy. A byte is made up of 8 bits (example—a character in a field, such as the first number of the product number).
  5. *Bit*—lowest in the hierarchy; 0 or 1.

- Data is stored on a storage *medium* (plural = *media*), such as disk or tape.

- The process of storing data involves four steps:
  1. After input, the data to be recorded by a storage device temporarily resides in RAM.
  2. Software instructions determine where the data is to be recorded on the storage medium.
  3. The controller board for the storage device positions the recording device over the appropriate location on the storage medium.
  4. The recording mechanism is activated and converts electrical impulses to magnetic spots placed—according to a coding scheme, such as ASCII—on the surface of the medium.

- For disk storage, the recording mechanism is called the *read-write head*.

- Modern storage devices are usually *direct access storage and retrieval devices*—that is, any record can be accessed directly, without having to read through other records.

- The *diskette*, or *floppy diskette*, is a storage medium frequently used with microcomputers. Diskettes are made of a flexible plastic that is coated with a material that is easily magnetized. The disk is enclosed in a protective paper or hard plastic jacket.

- A diskette jacket has four openings:
  1. *Hub*—the round opening in the center, which fits over the center mount, or spindle, in the disk drive.
  2. *Data access area*—where the read/write head(s) of the disk drive is positioned. The read/write head(s) moves back and forth over the data access area as the disk(s) spins.

3. *Write-protect notch*—covered, it prevents the read/write head(s) from touching the surface of the disk(s), thereby preventing accidental erasure or overwriting of data.

4. *Index hole*—repeatedly passes a photoelectric sensing mechanism in the disk drive that activates a timing switch. The timing mechanism determines which portion of the diskette is over or under the read/write head(s).

- The *byte* is used to measure the capacity of a storage device:
  1. 1,024 bytes = 1 kilobyte (K)
  2. 1,024,000 bytes = 1 megabyte (MB)
  3. 1,024,000,000 bytes = 1 gigabyte (GB)
  4. 1,024,000,000,000 bytes = 1 terabyte (TB)

- Common diskette capacities range from 360 K to 1.44 MB.

- Diskettes are *single-sided* (data is recorded only on one side) or *double-sided* (data is recorded on both sides).

- The *recording density* measures the number of bits per inch (bpi) that can be written on the surface of the disk. The higher the density, the more data that can be recorded on the diskette. Diskettes are:
  1. *Single-density*
  2. *Double-density*
  3. *Quad-density*

- Data is recorded on disks in circular bands called *tracks*. Track *density* also affects how much data can be stored on a disk. Track density is measured in tracks per inch (tpi). Common tpi's today are 48, 96, and 135.

- After you insert a diskette into the disk drive, you must close the *disk drive gate*, or *door*, if your computer has one.

- Diskettes come in two standard sizes: 5¼ inches (with paper jackets) and 3½ inches (with hard plastic jackets).

- Diskettes are divided into eight or nine *sectors*, or equal wedge-shaped areas used for storage reference purposes. The intersection of a track and a sector indicates where to position the read/write head.

- *Hard-sectored* disks have the same number and size of sectors, fixed by the manufacturer. *Soft-sectored* disks are marked magnetically by the user with software commands. This process is called *formatting*, or *initializing*. Soft-sectored disks must be formatted before they can be used.

- The average speed (usually 150 to 300 milliseconds, or thousandths of a second) with which a computer locates instructions or data and loads a copy of it into RAM is called the *access time*. Access time is determined by four factors:
  1. *Seek time*—the time it takes to position the read/write head(s) over the proper track
  2. *Rotational delay*, or *latency*—the time it takes for the correct sector to rotate over the read/write head(s)
  3. The time it takes for the read/write head(s) to contact the disk(s)
  4. *Data transfer rate*—the time it takes to transfer the data or instructions from the disk(s) to RAM

- *Hard disks*, rigid platters usually 5¼ or 3½ inches in diameter, can store more data than diskettes—from 20 MB to more than a gigabyte of data. Hard disk drives can be *internal* (inside the computer) or *external* (outside the computer, connected to it by a cable).

- The interior of a hard disk drive is sealed in order to prevent any contamination, such as dust, from coming between the disk(s) surface and the read/write head(s), which floats about .5 to 1.25 millionths of an inch above the surface. Such an occurrence could cause a *disk crash* and subsequent loss of data.

- *Hardcards*, which are inserted into an expansion slot inside the system cabinet, are an alternative to hard disk drive units.

- *Hard disk cartridges* are removable cassette-like disk units with one or two platters.

- *Optical storage technologies* use a laser beam to pack information densely on a removable disk. Although optical disks can store more data than hard disks, or diskettes, their access time is slower.

- *Compact disk read-only memory* (CD-ROM) is an optical technology capable of storing 540–748 MB of data on a disk. The data is prerecorded on the disk by the manufacturer, so the user can only read it.

- *Write once, read many* (WORM), an optical storage technology, is like CD-ROM, except that the user can determine what the manufacturer records on the disk. Once recorded, however, the data can then only be read. A WORM disk can store 122–6,400 MB of data.

- *Erasable optical disks* allow the user both to record data on an optical disk and to erase it. Each stores about 281–3,200 MB. *Magneto-optical* (MO) disk drives combine erasable optical disk technology with traditional magnetic disk drive technology.

- Users should back up their work. If they don't, and their hard disk or diskette is damaged or destroyed, all the work is lost. *Cartridge-tape units*, or *streamers*, are often used for backup. (Hard disk cartridges are also used for backup.)

KEY TERMS

access time, p. 82
American Standard Code for Information Interchange (ASCII), p. 72
auxiliary storage, p. 70
binary code, p. 72
binary digit (bit), p. 71
byte, p. 79
cartridge-tape unit, p. 91
check bits, p. 72
compact disk read-only memory (CD-ROM), p. 89
data access area, p. 76
data storage hierarchy, p. 74
direct access storage and retrieval, p. 76
disk cartridge, p. 88
disk drive, p. 76
disk drive gate (door), p. 76

diskette, p. 76
double-density, p. 80
double-sided, p. 80
erasable optical disk, p. 90
Extended Binary Coded Decimal Interchange Code (EBCDIC), p. 72
field, p. 74
file, p. 74
floppy diskette, p. 76
formatting, p. 81
gigabyte (GB), p. 79
hard disk, p. 82
hardcard, p. 85
hub, p. 76
index hole, p. 77
initializing, p. 81
kilobyte (K), p. 79
latency, p. 82
medium (media), p. 75
megabyte (MB), p. 79
nonvolatile, p. 70

optical storage technologies, p. 88
parity bit, p. 72
primary storage, p. 70
quadruple-density, p. 80
read/write head, p. 76
record, p. 74
recording density, p. 80
rotational delay, p. 82
secondary storage, p. 70
sector, p. 81
seek time, p. 82
single-density, p. 80
single-sided, p. 80
terabyte (TB), p. 79
track, p. 80
track density, p. 80
volatile, p. 70
write once, read many (WORM), p. 89
write/protect notch, p. 76

EXERCISES

SELF-TEST

1. According to the data storage hierarchy, files are composed of:
   a. _____   b. _____   c. _____   d. _____

2. Two popular coding schemes for representing data are _____ and _____.

3. The term *bit* is short for _____.

4. All computers are designed to use either an even- or an odd-parity scheme. (true/false)

5. Diskettes have the following openings:
   a. _____   b. _____   c. _____   d. _____

6. 1,024 bytes is equal to 1 _____.

7. 1,024,000 bytes is equal to 1 _____.

8. The _____ measures the number of bits per inch (bpi) that can be written on the surface of a disk.

9. Diskettes are divided into eight or nine _____, or equal wedge-shaped areas.

10. All disks must be _____ before they can store data.

11. Diskettes come in two standard sizes: _____ and _____.

12. _____ _____ _____ are removable cassette-like disk units with one or two platters.

13. _____ _____ technologies use a laser beam to store large amounts of data on a removable disk.

14. Erasable optical disks are now available that enable users to both record data and erase it. (true/false)

15. Diskettes' recording densities can be categorized as one of the following:
    a. _____   b. _____   c. _____

16. The average speed with which a computer locates instructions or data on a disk and then loads a copy of it into RAM is called _____ _____.

17. For disk storage, the recording mechanism is called the _____ _____.

18. Diskettes are often referred to as _____ disks.

19. 1,000,000,000 bytes is approximately 1 _____.

20. Modern storage devices are usually direct access storage and retrieval devices. (true/false)

SOLUTIONS   (1) records, fields, bytes, bits; (2) ASCII, EBCDIC; (3) *binary digit*; (4) true; (5) hub, data access area, write/protect notch, index hole; (6) kilobyte; (7) megabyte; (8) recording density; (9) sectors; (10) formatted [or initialized]; (11) 3½ inches, 5¼ inches; (12) hard disk cartridges; (13) optical storage; (14) true; (15) single-density, double-density, quad-density; (16) access time; (17) read/write head; (18) floppy; (19) gigabyte; (20) true

SHORT ANSWER

1. How is data represented in primary and secondary storage devices?
2. Why is it important for a microcomputer to be configured with at least one diskette drive?
3. What is the significance of the terms *track* and *sector?*
4. What are the advantages of a hard disk over a diskette?
5. What does the term *disk crash,* or *head crash,* mean?
6. What is the purpose of a parity bit?
7. How can you damage a diskette?
8. Describe the four steps involved in storing data onto a disk.
9. What are some of the uses for CD-ROM technology?
10. What happens to data saved to secondary storage when the power is turned off?

PROJECTS

1. What type(s) of storage hardware is currently being used in the computer you use at school or at work? What is the storage capacity of this hardware? Would you recommend alternate storage hardware be used? Why? Why not?
2. Computer shopping. Using newspapers or magazines, find ads for the following types of storage devices: (a) 5¼-inch double-sided, quad-density diskette; (b) 3½-inch double-sided, double-density diskette; (c) 60 MB hard disk; and (d) 120 MB hard disk. For each device, list its price, name and address of the supplier, and explain why you think the device is a good purchase. Make some price comparisons.
3. Research the latest in erasable (rewritable) optical storage technology, such as MO drives. How is the technology being applied now? How do you think it will be applied in the future?
4. Computer shopping. You want to purchase a hard disk for use with your microcomputer. Because you don't care how much money the hard disk costs, you are going to buy one with the highest storage capacity you can find. Using newspapers or magazines, find a hard disk you would like to buy. What is its storage capacity? Its average access time? How much does it cost? Who is the supplier? Is it an external or an internal drive?
5. The Bureau of Electronic Publishing's product guide lists many products and publications available on CD-ROM, such as Compton's *Multimedia Encyclopedia,* Grolier's *Electronic Encyclopedia,* National Geographic's *Mammals,* CD Fun House, U.S. History, and Birds of America. Write for a copy of the catalog and identify some business and professional uses for some of the products. What hardware and software would you need to run the programs you are interested in?

   Bureau of Electronic Publishing
   141 New Road
   Parsippany, NJ 07054
   (800) 828-4766

OUTPUT HARDWARE

What use is a computer system if you or others can't view the information you produce as a result of processing? Very little. In business, presentation is important—how you present yourself, your product, your information. Although computers may not be able to help you with your wardrobe or your public speaking skills, they *can* help you create clear and attractive informational presentations quickly. But because computers can produce beautiful, professional, seemingly error-free printouts or exciting colorful graphics on a screen, we are apt to think that the information is more believable than the same results scribbled on a yellow pad. In fact, the information that is output —the basis on which you and others will be making decisions—is no better than the quality of data that was input.

PREVIEW

When you have completed this chapter, you will be able to:

■

Describe the basic forms of output and categories of output media
and hardware

■

Explain what hardcopy output devices are available, as well as the advantages
and disadvantages of each

■

Describe what softcopy output devices are available and the advantages and
disadvantages of each

CHAPTER OUTLINE

Why Is This Chapter Important?

How Do We Categorize Output?

Hardcopy Output Devices

    Impact Printers

    Nonimpact Printers

    Portable Printers

    Plotters

Softcopy Output Devices

    Cathode-Ray Tube (CRT)

    Flat Screen Technologies

    Voice Output Systems

Summary

Key Terms

Exercises

The success of a business today can depend to a large extent on how relevant and timely the information is that the computer can produce—that is, the output. Having the right information, in the right hands, in the best form, at the right time—these are the keys to effective decision making (Figure 5.1).

To be effective, information must be produced in a usable form. To achieve this goal, you may need to use more than one output device and output medium, such as a display on a video screen as well as paper and a printer. Each type of output device has advantages and disadvantages. Is the hardware going to make a lot of noise? What is the quality of the output produced? Is the hardware slow? Is the hardware expensive? Is it compatible with the equipment you already have? Can it handle large volumes of output? Can it handle color? Not all software programs work with all types of output devices. How do you know which output hardware device to use? Many questions must be answered before output hardware can be chosen or purchased. Most important, if you are the one choosing output hardware, you must determine what *form* of output is needed to meet your needs and the needs of everyone else using your microcomputer system.

FIGURE 5.1

What form of output is best? As a computer user in the business environment, your output needs will be determined by the kind of decisions you need to make to perform your regular job duties, the type of information that will facilitate those decisions, and the frequency with which you must make decisions.

HOW DO WE CATEGORIZE OUTPUT?

There are two basic categories of computer-produced output: (1) *output for imme-diate use by people* and (2) *output that is stored in computer-usable form for later use by the computer* (and eventually, of course, by people). Output can be in either hardcopy or softcopy form. **Hardcopy,** as defined earlier, refers to information that has been recorded on a tangible medium (generally meaning that you can touch it), such as paper or microfilm. **Softcopy** generally refers to the output displayed on the computer screen (Figure 5.2).

Output hardware is categorized according to whether it produces hardcopy or softcopy. Output for immediate use can be in either hardcopy form—such as paper—or softcopy form—such as on a display screen. Output in computer-usable form for later use by the computer is in hardcopy form—such as on disk or tape. This chart shows forms of output commonly used with microcomputers.

FIGURE 5.2

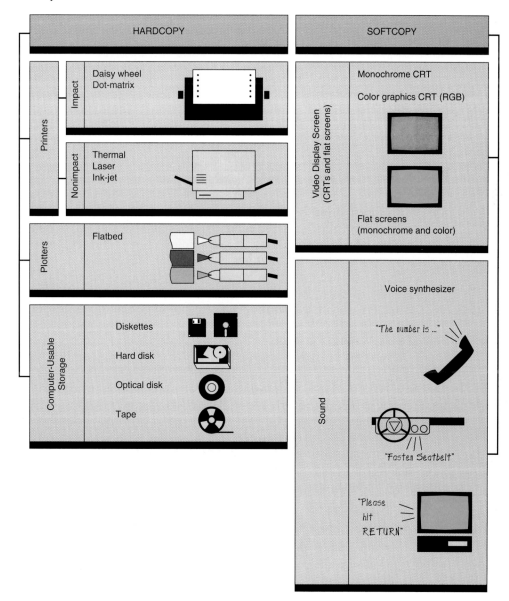

The advantages and disadvantages of each output medium must be considered to ensure that outputs are produced in the most usable form.

- When computer display devices are not readily available and information has some value over time, it is best produced as hardcopy.
- When computer display devices are readily available and information must be quickly accessible by a single user, it is best produced as softcopy.

Hardcopy output tends to have greater value over time, whereas softcopy output is best for displaying information that must be immediately accessible. The principal hardcopy output devices are printers and plotters—the different types and characteristics of these devices are described in detail in the next section. The principal softcopy output devices are cathode-ray tube video screens (CRTs), flat screens, and voice output systems.

HARDCOPY OUTPUT DEVICES

Among the wide variety of hardcopy output devices used with microcomputers, printers and plotters are used the most. A **printer** is capable of printing characters, symbols, and sometimes graphics on paper. Printers are categorized according to whether or not the image produced is formed by physical contact of the print mechanism with the paper. *Impact printers* do have contact; *nonimpact printers* do not. A **plotter** is used most often for outputting graphics because it can produce specialized and free-form drawings on paper. To suit the needs of many different users, different types of printers and plotters are available that have slightly different characteristics and capabilities—cost, quality, and speed.

IMPACT (CHARACTER) PRINTERS

An **impact printer**—also called a *character printer*—makes contact with the paper. It usually forms the print image by pressing an inked ribbon against the paper with a hammer-like mechanism. In one type of impact printer, called a *daisy wheel printer*, the hammer presses images of fully formed characters against the ribbon, just like a typewriter. The print mechanism in another type of impact printer, called a *dot-matrix* printer, is made of separate pin-like hammers that strike the ribbon against the paper in computer-determined patterns of dots.

DAISY WHEEL PRINTERS

Daisy wheel printers—often referred to as *letter-quality printers*—produce a very high-quality print image (one that is very clear and precise) because the entire character is formed with a single impact using a print "wheel" with a set of print characters on the outside tips of flat spokes (Figure 5.3). Daisy wheel printers can print around 60 characters per second (cps). This speed translates into approximately one page per minute.

The principal advantage of using daisy wheel printers is that they produce high-quality images. However, they do have some disadvantages, and their sales have declined dramatically as other types of printers have been perfected.

- They are too slow for many large-volume output situations.
- They are very noisy.
- To change the typeface style, the operator must halt the machine and change the print wheel.
- They cannot produce graphics.

DOT-MATRIX PRINTERS

Dot-matrix printers were developed with two objectives in mind: greater speed and more flexibility. Images are formed by a print head that is composed of a series of little print hammers that look like the heads of pins. These print hammers strike the ribbon individually as the print mechanism moves across the entire print line in both directions—that is, from left to right, then right to left, and so on. They can produce a variety of type styles and graphics without the operator having to stop the printer or change a print wheel. And, because they are impact printers, dot-matrix printers can be used with multipart forms.

Dot-matrix printers can print in either *draft quality* or *near-letter quality* (*nlq*) mode. The user determines which mode to operate in by pressing the appropriate button on the front of the printer. It takes longer to print in nlq mode because

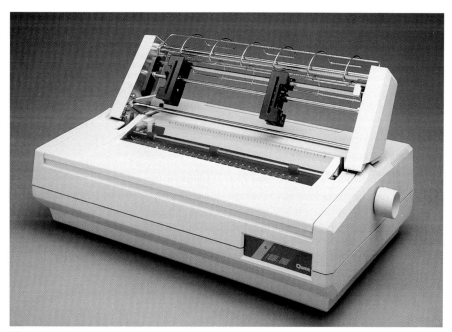

(a)

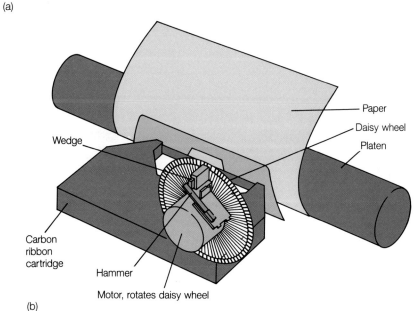

(b)

FIGURE 5.3

(a) Daisy wheel printer and (b) drawing of how a daisy wheel mechanism works. The daisy wheel spins and brings the desired letter into position. A hammer hits the wedge, which strikes the appropriate spoke against the ribbon, which hits the paper.

the print head makes more than one pass for each print line, creating a darker, thicker character (Figure 5.4). When the dot-matrix printer uses only one pass for each line, it's called *draft quality*. Nlq mode on the dot-matrix printer is used for professional correspondence and other high-quality print needs.

Figure 5.5 shows how a dot-matrix print head is constructed. The print head of a dot-matrix printer has either 9 pins or 24 pins (although other print head configurations are available, they aren't common).

Following are some of the characteristics that differentiate the two most common types of dot-matrix printers:

Nine-pin printers:

- Are less expensive
- Can print between 40 and 130 cps—between 1 and 2 pages per minute— depending on whether they're operating in draft or nlq mode
- Are best used for quick draft printing, generating forms, and jobs that don't require a high-quality image

Twenty-four-pin printers:

- Are more expensive
- Can print between 80 and 260 cps—between 1 and 4 pages per minute
- Produce a much more precise image than nine-pin printers—about 360 dpi, or dots per (square) inch
- Are best used in a heavy-volume environment where speed and quality are priorities

Table 5.1 compares daisy wheel and dot-matrix printers.

If you'd like to liven up your business reports with a little bit of color but can't afford an expensive type of color printer, a less expensive color dot-matrix printer may be the printer for you. A **color dot-matrix printer** uses the same technology as a monochrome dot-matrix printer, but it uses a color ribbon instead of a black ribbon. Color ribbons usually contain equal bands of black, yellow, red, and blue. Under software control, the colors can be blended to produce up to seven colors. Color ribbons cost up to three times as much as black ribbons.

FIGURE 5.4

To produce a near-letter-quality image with a dot-matrix printer, the character is printed twice; the second time the print head is positioned slightly to the right of the original image (a). (b) Shows a "real" (daisy wheel) letter-quality character for comparison. (c) Samples of dot-matrix output.

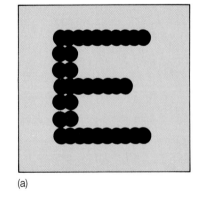

(a)

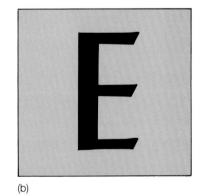

(b)

This is a sample of draft quality.

(c) This is a sample of near-letter quality.

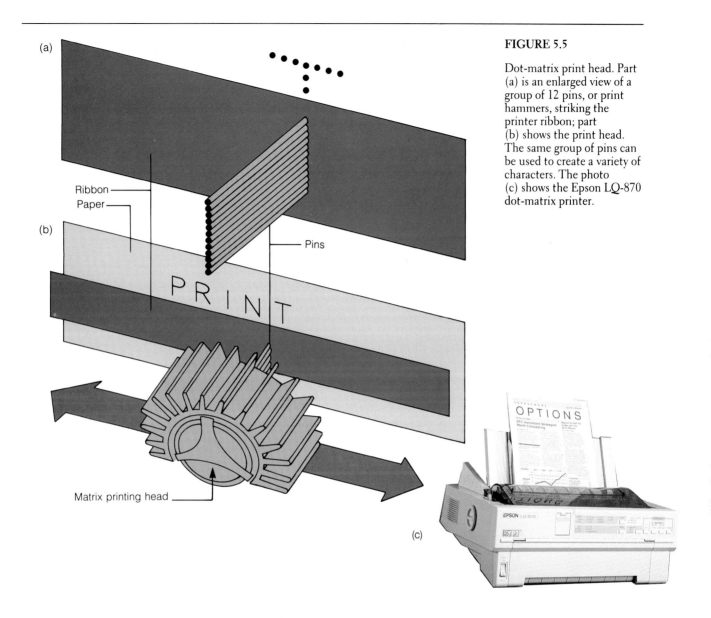

FIGURE 5.5

Dot-matrix print head. Part (a) is an enlarged view of a group of 12 pins, or print hammers, striking the printer ribbon; part (b) shows the print head. The same group of pins can be used to create a variety of characters. The photo (c) shows the Epson LQ-870 dot-matrix printer.

TABLE 5.1

Comparison of Daisy Wheel and Dot-Matrix (Impact) Printers

	Daisy Wheel	Dot-Matrix
Draft-quality speed	—	80–260 cps
Letter-quality speed	60–100 cps	40–80 cps (near-letter quality)
Image quality	Excellent	Good to very good
Cost	$500	$150–$2,000
Print mechanism	Daisy wheel	9-, 18-, or 24-pin print head
Advantages	Crisp, clear characters	Fast, can do graphics
Disadvantages	Slow, noisy, can't do graphics	Noisy, characters usually less clear
	Cannot print shades of gray	Cannot print shades of gray

NONIMPACT PRINTERS

Printers that do not strike characters against ribbon or paper when they print are **nonimpact printers**. The main categories of nonimpact printers are ink-jet printers, thermal printers, and laser printers. These printers generate much less noise than impact printers. However, if you're using a nonimpact printer, don't try to print on multiple-part carbon forms: Because no impact is being made on the paper, you'll end up with no copies!

Table 5.2 compares the various types of nonimpact printers.

INK-JET PRINTERS
Ink-jet printers (Figure 5.6) work in much the same fashion as dot-matrix printers in that they form images (text and graphics) with little dots. However, the dots are formed, not by hammer-like pins, but by tiny droplets of ink. The text these printers produce is letter quality (rather than near-letter-quality, which is produced by dot-matrix printers). These printers can match the speed of dot-matrix printers—between 1 and 4 pages per minute (ppm)—and they produce less noise. Ink-jet printers are often used to produce color proofs of posters, magazine layouts, and book covers, as well as color output for business presentations.

THERMAL PRINTERS
Thermal printers use colored waxes, heat, and special paper to produce images (Figure 5.7). No ribbon or ink is involved. For users who want the highest-quality desktop color printing available, thermal printers are the answer. However, they are also expensive, and they require special, expensive paper, so they are not generally used for high-volume output.

TABLE 5.2   Comparison of Nonimpact Printers

Type	Technology	Advantages	Disadvantages	Typical Speed	Approximate Cost
Ink-Jet	Electrostatically charged drops hit paper	Quiet; prints color, text, and graphics; less expensive; fast	Relatively slow; clogged jets; lower dpi	1–4 pages per minute	$800–$8,000
Thermal	Temperature-sensitive; paper changes color when treated; characters are formed by selectively heating print head	Quiet; high-quality color output of text and graphics; can also produce transparencies	Special paper required; expensive; slow	.5–4 pages per minute	$5,000–$22,000
Laser	Laser beam directed onto a drum, "etching" spots that attract toner, which is then transferred to paper	Quiet; excellent quality; output of text and graphics; very high speed	High cost, especially for color	4–25 pages per minute	$800–$20,000

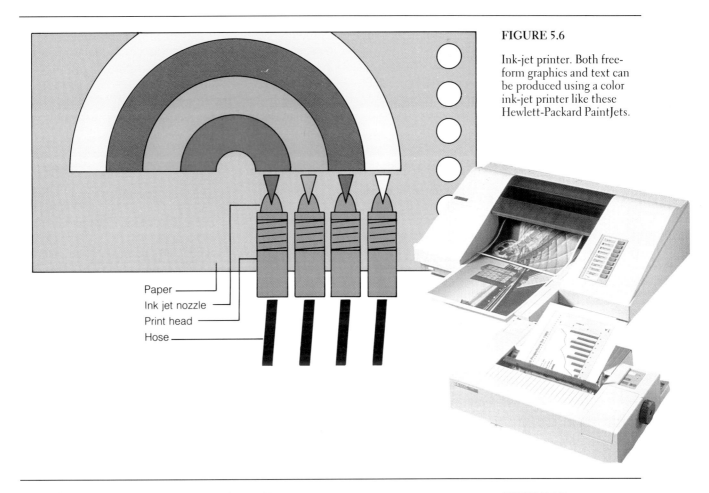

FIGURE 5.6

Ink-jet printer. Both free-form graphics and text can be produced using a color ink-jet printer like these Hewlett-Packard PaintJets.

Paper
Ink jet nozzle
Print head
Hose

FIGURE 5.7

Thermal printers produce images by using colored waxes, and heat to burn dots onto special paper. (Colored wax sheets are not required for black-and-white output because the thermal print head will register black dots on special paper.)

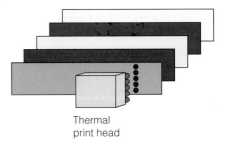

Thermal print head

LASER PRINTERS

Laser printer technology is much less mechanical than impact printing (that is, no print heads move, no print hammers hit), resulting in much higher printing speeds and quieter operation. The process resembles the operation of a photocopy machine (Figure 5.8). A laser beam is directed across the surface of a light-sensitive drum and fired as needed to record an image in the form of a pattern of tiny dots. The image is then transferred to the paper—a page at a time—in the same fashion as a copy machine transfers images, using a special toner.

The major advantages of laser printers are:

- Very high speed
- Low noise level
- Low maintenance requirements
- Very high image quality
- Excellent graphics capabilities

Laser printers can also generate text in a variety of type sizes and styles (called **fonts**), providing a business with the capability of outputting professional-looking near-typeset-quality reports and publications. Figure 5.9 shows examples of just a few of the types of fonts that can be generated using a laser printer. Most laser printers are capable of outputting a specific set of fonts. However, laser printers that include a built-in **page description language,** such as Adobe PostScript, provide greater flexibility by enabling users to generate fonts in almost any size and to produce special graphics effects. (Users can increase their font choices by purchasing "soft fonts" on diskettes and storing them on the hard disk to download—or load into RAM or the printer—whenever they want. However, their laser printer must be compatible with this technology.)

A variety of laser printers, each different in terms of cost, speed, and capabilities, are available for use with microcomputers today. In general, laser printers can be viewed as falling into three categories: (1) low end, (2) high end, and (3) color.

The laser printers that fall into the low-end category are the least expensive and can print between 4 ppm and 8 ppm. With printers in this range, 300-dpi images are common.

More expensive high-end laser printers can be purchased that are three to five times faster than low-end printers and generate clearer images (400–600 dpi). Printing between 15 and 25 ppm, these printers are appropriate in a networked environment where many users are sharing one printer.

Color laser printers are now available for less than $10,000—a recent breakthrough—and are frequently used in desktop publishing, especially in the magazine and newspaper businesses.

PORTABLE PRINTERS

Portable printers (Figure 5.10) are becoming more and more popular as portable computing using laptop computers has gained in popularity in the business environment. Many portable computer users, for example, need to print out sales reports or service estimates while on the road. So that a business traveler can carry both a 10-pound computer and a printer, **portable printers** are compact in size and typically weigh under 5 pounds. Nine-pin and 24-pin dot-matrix portable printers are available, as well as ink-jet and thermal printers.

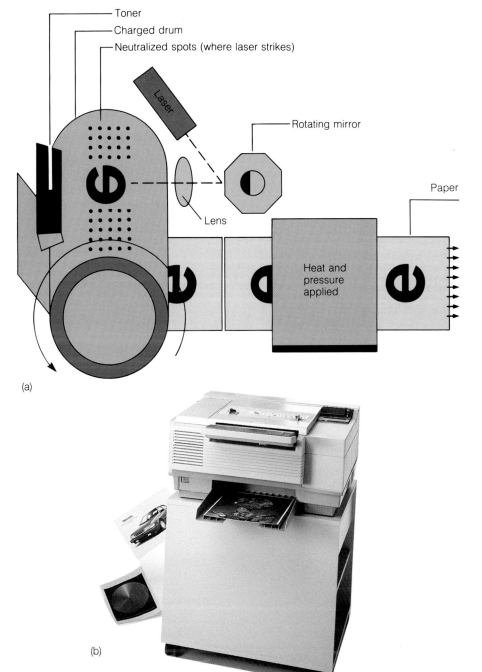

(a)

- Toner
- Charged drum
- Neutralized spots (where laser strikes)

Laser

Rotating mirror

Lens

Heat and pressure applied

Paper

(b)

FIGURE 5.8

Laser printing. (a) A microprocessor controls a small laser beam that is bounced off a mirror millions of times per second onto a positively charged drum. The spots where the laser beam hits become neutralized, enabling a special toner (containing powdered ink and powdered rosin, an adhesive) to stick to them and then print out on paper, through the use of heat and pressure. The drum is then recharged for its next cycle. Part (b) shows the Tektronix Phaser III color laser printer (on top of a supply cabinet); part (c) is actual hardcopy laser output.

"I think there is a world market for about five computers."
--- Thomas J. Watson, founder of IBM (1943)

"I think there is a world market for about five computers."
--- Thomas J. Watson, founder of IBM (1943)

(c)

FIGURE 5.9   A set of characters and symbols in a particular size and style is called a *font*. This is a partial
                          list of fonts as generated by the Hewlett-Packard LaserJet Series II.

FONT ID	NAME	POINT SIZE *	PRINT SAMPLE
S01	Dutch	10	ABCDEfghij#$@[\]^'{|}~123 ÀÂ°ÇÑ¿¡£§êéàèëöÅØåæÄÜßÁÐÒ
S02	Dutch BOLD	14	ABCDEfghij#$@[\]^'{|}~123 ÀÂ°ÇÑ¿¡£§êéàèëöÅØåæÄÜßÁÐÒ
S03	Dutch BOLD	18	ABCDEfghij#$@[\]^'{|}~ ÀÂ°ÇÑ¿¡£§êéàèëöÅØåæÄÜß
S04	Dutch BOLD	24	ABCDEfghij#$@[\] ÀÂ°ÇÑ¿¡£§êéàèëöÅØ
I00	COURIER	12	ABCDEfghij#$@[\]^'{|}~123 ÀÂ°ÇÑ¡¿£§êéàèëöÅØåæÄÜßÁÐÒ
I01	COURIER	12	ABCDEfghij#$@[\]^`{|}˜123 íó┤╢╖╕╣║╗╝┘┐└┴┬├─┼╞╟╚╔╩╦╠═╬▄█▌απΦ

*12 points = 1 pica, and 6 picas = 1 inch.

FIGURE 5.10

Portable printer. This illustration shows a Kodak Diconix 150 Plus.

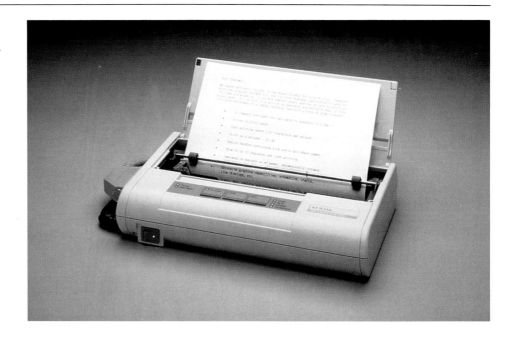

PLOTTERS

A **plotter** (Figure 5.11) is a specialized output device designed to produce high-quality graphics—especially in the areas of drafting and design—in a variety of colors using inked pens. The type of plotter used with microcomputer systems is the **flatbed plotter,** which is designed so that the paper is placed flat and one or more pens move horizontally and vertically across the paper. These plotters use from two to eight pens to generate images.

SOFTCOPY OUTPUT DEVICES

Softcopy output generally refers to the display on a monitor, the output device that many people use the most. The two main types of monitors are the cathode-ray tube (CRT) and the flat panel.

CATHODE-RAY TUBE (CRT)

The **cathode-ray tube** (**CRT**) (Figure 5.12) is probably the most popular softcopy output device used with microcomputer systems. The CRT's screen display is made up of small picture elements, called **pixels** for short. A pixel (Figure 5.13) is the smallest unit on the screen that can be turned on or off or made different shades. The smaller the pixels and the closer together they are (the more points that can be illuminated on the screen), the better the image clarity, or **resolution**. A screen resolution of 320 × 320 means the screen has horizontal and vertical rows of 320 pixels each to form images. This is medium resolution. Most users prefer higher resolutions, such as 640 × 480 or even 1,024 × 768.

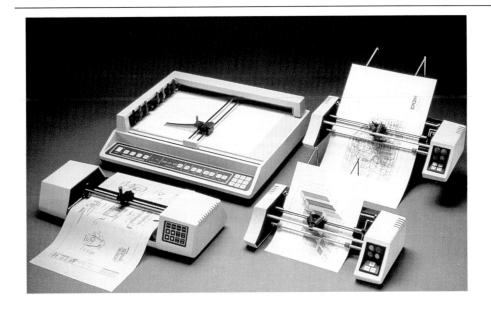

FIGURE 5.11

This illustration shows plotters from Houston instruments. The flatbed plotter is at the back, on the left.

FIGURE 5.12

The CRT's electron gun emits a beam of electrons that, under the control of the yoke's magnetic field, moves across the interior of the phosphor-coated screen. The phosphors hit by the electrons emit light, which makes up the image on the screen. The distance between the points of light is fixed by the shadow mask, a shield with holes in it that is used to prevent the dispersion of the electron beam.

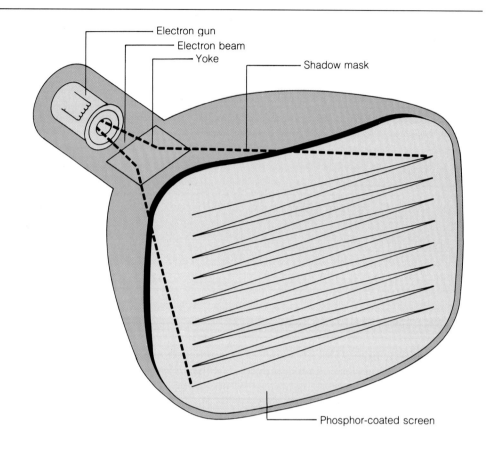

FIGURE 5.13

Each character on the screen is made up of pixels, or picture elements.

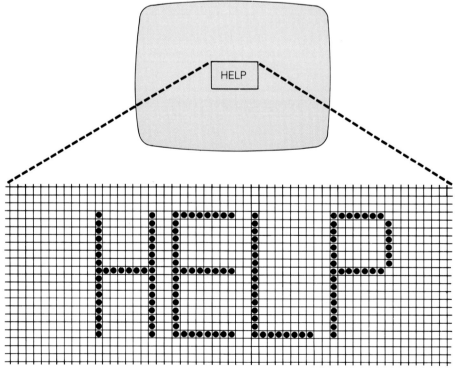

Using 70 Macintosh SE terminals located at nine campus polling places, Stanford University's student government, in April 1985, held the first totally computerized election in California history. Some 6,500 students cast ballots for the next year's Council of Presidents. Ironically, when none of the three slates won the top office, students returned to the polls a few weeks later and made their final choice using old-fashioned paper ballots.

Nevertheless, the first election was so revolutionary that it drew observers from local county registrars of voters and from the state capital. County election officials were concerned about possible fraud in electronic voting systems, but Stanford's terminals were not linked into a network, and buzzer alarms were written into the software to deter prospective hackers. To tally the results, election officials transferred the data voters recorded on the Macintosh hard disks onto floppy disks; the data was then tabulated at a single location. The biggest advantages of computerized balloting were the reduced costs of printing paper ballots (only a few were on hand for computerphobes) and the increased speed in tabulating returns.

Electronic voting may be the wave of the future, but computers are already being used extensively in politics and government. Political parties have long used computers for campaign purposes, primarily for fund-raising. Anyone who has ever contributed to a candidate or political party is sure to be in some database. Computers are also used to aim direct-mail pieces with very specific messages at selected audiences. Another use is to identify certain voter groups, such as those who tend to vote in Presidential elections but not in off-year congressional elections, in order to urge them to the polls.

Computers also came in for heavy use following the 1990 census, when state legislators used them to redraw boundaries of new election districts in ways that would most favor the party in power. For instance, in one system, a legislator could use computer graphics to call up his or her district on a screen, then shift the boundaries and get instant numbers of what the voting behavior, racial composition, and other population characteristics would be in the new district.

Census Bureau data is not available only to politicians, however. The bureau developed a computer map system called TIGER (for *Topologically Integrated Geographic Encoding and Referencing system*) that, when used with a database such as the 1990 census results or a company's own customer files, provides a detailed cartographic profile. TIGER can produce a map with 26 million street intersections and every city block, river, railroad line, or governmental entity in the country. The entire map comprises 16 billion lines. ■

COMPUTERS AND CAREERS

POLITICS AND GOVERNMENT

CRTs have some disadvantages that recent technology has been trying to overcome, most notably:

1. Large size
2. High power consumption
3. Fragility

The CRT is rather large and bulky because of the need to separate the electron gun from the screen by a particular distance, so it is unsuitable as a display screen for portable computers. The CRT also tends to use a substantial amount of electric power, again making it unsuitable for use with portable computers, which occasionally need to run on batteries. Finally, as with a television, the CRT's glass tube and screen can be damaged if not handled carefully.

MONOCHROME AND COLOR MONITORS

A **monochrome monitor** (a monitor capable of displaying only a single-color image) and an **RGB color monitor** (RGB stands for *red, green, blue*) differ in two principal ways. First, they have different numbers of electron guns. A monochrome monitor has only one electron gun; however, as shown in Figure 5.14, an RGB color monitor has three electron guns. Second, the screen in an RGB color monitor is coated with three types—or colors—of phosphors: red, green, and blue. The screen of a monochrome monitor is coated with only one type of phosphor, which is often either green or amber in color.

The operational principles of both monitors are almost exactly the same. However, each pixel in an RGB monitor is made up of three dots of phosphors, one of each color. The three electron guns direct their beams together. Each gun is aimed precisely so that it can hit a specific color dot in each pixel. A wide variety of colors can be created by controlling—through software instructions—which guns fire and how long a burst they project at each dot. As you might expect, the control circuitry and software to direct the operation of an RGB monitor are somewhat more sophisticated and expensive than the corresponding components for a monochrome monitor.

CHARACTER-MAPPED DISPLAYS

Character-mapped display screens, such as the IBM monochrome monitor, can display only characters. (Note: As described in the next section, a character-mapped display screen may be able to display graphics if a video adapter card is plugged into the motherboard.) The patterns of pixels used to represent the standard characters displayed on a monitor (the alphabetic characters, numbers, and special symbols) in character-mapped displays are drawn from prerecorded templates (guides) stored in a video display ROM chip. When the user's software sends a request to display, for example, the letter A at a specific location, the template for that pixel pattern is looked up in the video display ROM chip. The electron gun then uses this pattern when it fires at the phosphors in the appropriate **character box**. The screen of a personal computer has 25 lines with 80 characters per line; this means that there are 2,000 positions on the screen where a predefined character can be placed.

BIT-MAPPED DISPLAYS

Because most software written today requires that the monitor be capable of displaying graphics, different types of video adapter cards were developed (Table 5.3). With appropriate software, sufficient RAM, and compatible monitors, these cards are plugged into the motherboard of a microcomputer to enable monitors to display **bit-mapped graphics**. To create the variety of images necessary to produce

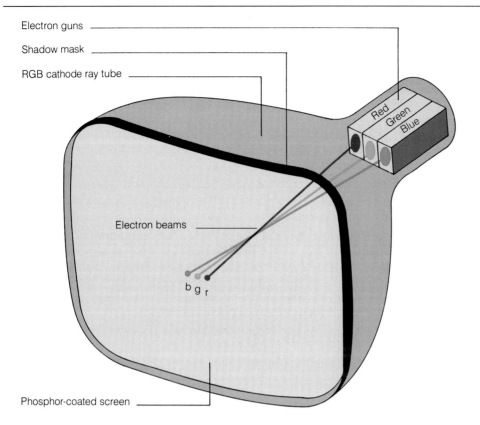

Electron guns

Shadow mask

RGB cathode ray tube

Red Green Blue

Electron beams

b g r

Phosphor-coated screen

FIGURE 5.14

RGB monitor. The workings of an RGB color monitor are similar to those of a mono-chrome CRT, except that the types of phosphors—red, green, and blue—are hit by three electron beams. Each pixel has three color dots that are activated to different degrees to produce a wide range of colors.

	Colors	Resolution (Pixels)	RAM Required
CGA (Color Graphics Adapter)	(1 bit/color) 4	320 × 200	
EGA (Enhanced Graphics Adapter)	(4 bits/color) 16	640 × 350	
VGA (Video Graphics Array)	(8 bits/color) 256 (4 bits/color) 16	320 × 200 640 × 480	 150 K
Super VGA	(8 bits/color) 256 (8 bits/color) 256	800 × 600 1,024 × 768	469 K 768 K
XGA (Extended Graphics Array)	(8 bits/color) 256 (16 bits/color) 65,536 (24 bits/color) 16,777,216	1,024 × 768 1,024 × 768 1,024 × 768	768 K 1,536 K 2,304 K

TABLE 5.3

PC Graphics Standards (Some RAM requirements for using particular color monitors at particular reso-lutions are also included.)

graphics, the computer needs to be able to direct each electron beam individually at each pixel on the screen, not just superimpose a template over a character box. This approach requires more sophisticated control circuitry, software, and RAM than is required by character-mapped displays.

Following are the common video graphics adapters (Figure 5.15):

- CGA (Color Graphics Adapter)—IBM PC video display circuit board that provides low-resolution text and graphics; CGA requires an RGB color display monitor and supports 4 colors at a resolution of 320 × 200. This standard has been superseded by EGA, VGA, Super VGA, and XGA.

- EGA (Enhanced Graphics Adapter)—IBM PC video display circuit board that provides medium-resolution (640 × 380) text and graphics and requires an RGB enhanced color display monitor to support 16 colors. This standard has been superseded by VGA, Super VGA, and XGA.

- VGA (Video Graphics Array)—IBM PC video display circuit board that is built into high-end models of IBM's PS/2 series that provides medium- to high-resolution (320 × 200 or 640 × 480) text and graphics; has 16 colors in its highest-resolution mode (640 × 480).

- Super VGA (Super Video Graphics Array)—VGA in a resolution mode of 800 × 600 or 1,024 × 768, and with 256 colors.

- XGA (Extended Graphics Array)—Video display circuit board that supports resolutions up to 1,024 × 768, with up to 16,777,216 colors.

In general, it's the circuitry that supports how many colors you can use and the monitor that determines the resolution. Macintosh computers and high-end IBM PS/2 models offer similar choices in monitor resolution modes and numbers of colors supported as do the adapter arrangements. However, these computers have the required circuitry built in on the motherboard, so they don't require extra boards (cards).

Users who work with sophisticated graphics or in desktop publishing often work in shades of gray on **gray-scale monitors**. Color monitors of high resolution that support a given number of colors can also be used at similar resolutions using the same number of gray shades. For example, a 256-color monitor will support 256 shades of gray.

FIGURE 5.15   Comparison of color adapter displays. (a) Monochrome VGA; (b) color Super VGA.

(a)

(b)

CRT SCREEN SIZE

A 1,024 × 768 resolution monitor allows you to pack 2½ times more images onto the screen than a 640 × 480 monitor does. But screen sizes are limited; if you have only a 14-inch monitor with 1,024 × 768 resolution, the images will be sharper, but they'll also be a lot smaller than on a 640 × 480 screen. Thus users who move to high-resolution monitors may also have to purchase larger ones. A 14-inch screen is fine for VGA, but 1,024 × 768 Super VGA would require a 16-inch or a 17-inch monitor for easy viewing.

Users working in graphics or desktop publishing often prefer an even larger screen: 19 inches or 20 inches, for example.

FLAT SCREEN TECHNOLOGIES

The disadvantages of the CRT—large size, high power consumption, and fragility, plus occasional flickering images—led to the development of **flat screen** technologies.

Flat screen technology is particularly useful for laptop and notebook computers, which can be used in the office and then taken home or on trips (Figure 5.16). Producing a truly lap-size, or laptop, computer—that is, one that is fully functional and weighs 15 pounds or less—has not been easy, and designing the video display has been the most difficult problem.

Interest in laptop computers encouraged researchers to explore different approaches to developing high-resolution, low-power-consumption flat screens with the same graphics capabilities as the traditional CRT. The most effective results to date have been achieved in three areas: liquid crystal display, electroluminescent display, and gas plasma display.

LIQUID CRYSTAL DISPLAY

The **liquid crystal display (LCD)** uses a clear liquid chemical trapped in tiny pockets between two pieces of glass. Each pocket of liquid is covered both front and back by very thin wires. In monochrome LCDs, when a small amount of current is applied to both wires, a chemical reaction turns the chemical a dark color—thereby blocking light. The point of blocked light is the pixel. In color LCDs, varying amounts of light pass through red, green, and blue filters.

FIGURE 5.16

CRT versus flat screen. As this photo shows, flat screen technologies have enabled manufacturers to produce personal computers small enough to be used on one's lap—the laptop computer.

LCD technology has progressed to the point that it rivals CRT technology in terms of resolution and the number of colors that can be displayed (Figure 5.17). In fact, since the screen is flat, text and graphics appear crisper than on the curved surface of the CRT, especially on the edges. In addition, images can be viewed from extreme angles with very little distortion. (Until recently, LCDs were susceptible to glare which forced the optimum viewing angle to be very narrow.)

ELECTROLUMINESCENT DISPLAY

Electroluminescent (EL) display (Figure 5.18) uses a thin film of solid, specially treated material that glows in response to electric current. To form a pixel on the screen, current is sent to the intersection of the appropriate row and column; the combined voltages from the row and the column cause the screen to glow at that point.

FIGURE 5.17

Three popular laptop computers that use a monochrome liquid crystal display: (a) NEC Prospeed 80386; (b) IBM PS/2 CL57 9X color LCD display; (c) Compaq SLT 386s/20; (d) Zenith Turbosport 386.

(a)

(b)

(c)

(d)

EL displays provide very high image resolution and excellent graphics capability. Several manufacturers are currently working on the development of electroluminescent displays with full-color capability. Most experts have predicted that this technology will soon match or even surpass all of the capabilities of the traditional CRT. Like LCD technology, the major limitation of this technology has been cost.

GAS PLASMA DISPLAY

The oldest flat screen technology is the **gas plasma display** (Figure 5.19). This technology uses predominantly neon gas and electrodes above and below the gas. When electric current passes between the electrodes, the gas glows. Depending on the mixture of gases, the color displayed ranges from orange to red.

The principal advantages of gas plasma display are:

- The images are much brighter than on a standard CRT.
- The resolution is excellent.
- Glare is not a significant problem.
- The screen does not flicker as it does on some CRTs.

The main disadvantages are:

- Only a single color is available (reddish orange).
- The technology is expensive.
- It uses a lot of power.
- It does not show sharp contrast.

FIGURE 5.18

Electroluminescent display. This Hewlett-Packard Integral computer uses an EL flat-panel display.

VOICE OUTPUT SYSTEMS

Voice output systems are relatively new and can be used in some situations in which traditional display screen softcopy output is inappropriate.

Voice output technology has had to overcome many hurdles. The most difficult has been that every individual perceives speech differently; that is, the voice patterns, pitches, and inflections we can hear and understand are different for all of us. It is not always easy to understand an unfamiliar voice pattern. At this point, two different approaches to voice output have evolved: (1) speech coding and (2) speech synthesis.

Speech coding relies on human speech as a reservoir of sounds to draw from in building the words and phrases to be output. Sounds are codified and stored on disk to be retrieved and translated back as sounds. Speech coding has been used in applications such as automobiles, toys, and games.

Speech synthesis relies on the use of a set of basic speech sounds that are created electronically without the use of a human voice.

Researchers are continuing to develop and improve voice output technologies for use with microcomputers. Many new products using voice output are expected to appear in the marketplace during the next decade. The largest application to date for the speech synthesis approach to voice output—converting text into "spoken" words—has many potential uses, including in reading machines for the blind (Figure 5.20). And, of course, sound output does not have to be in voice form; it can be music or special-effects sounds, such as the sound accompaniment for computer animation.

FIGURE 5.19

Gas plasma display. These popular laptop computers use gas plasma display: (a) GRiDCase 1500 Series; (b) Toshiba T5100; (c) IBM PS/2 P75 486.

(a)

(b)

(c)

SUMMARY

- Users must decide what *kinds* of output they require—based on the kind of information they need—before deciding which output hardware and media to use. They should also consider:
  1. How much noise the output equipment makes
  2. How fast it works
  3. How expensive it is
  4. Whether it is compatible with the equipment they already have
  5. How easily it can be upgraded
- The two basic categories of computer-produced output are:
  1. Output for immediate use by people
  2. Output stored in computer-usable form for later use by the computer (and people)
- Output is available in two forms:
  1. *Hardcopy*—refers to information that has been recorded on a tangible medium (you can touch it), such as paper or microfilm. When computer display devices are not readily available and information has some value over time, it is best produced as hardcopy.
  2. *Softcopy*—refers to the output displayed on the computer screen. When computer display devices are readily available and information must be quickly accessible, it is best produced as softcopy.
- Paper is the most widely used hardcopy output medium.
- The video display image on the computer screen is the most widely used form of softcopy output.
- Common hardcopy output devices used with microcomputers are:
  1. *Printers*—capable of printing characters, symbols, and occasionally graphics on paper. Printers are either:
     (a) *Impact printers*—the image is produced by physical contact of the print mechanism with the paper. Impact printers must be used to produce output on multipart forms with carbon layers.
     (b) *Nonimpact printers*—no contact with the paper by the print mechanism is required to form the image.

FIGURE 5.20

Xerox/Kurzweil Personal Reader, a breakthrough in technology for people who are blind, visually impaired, or dyslexic. The Personal Reader uses an optical scanner to convert typeset and typewritten material into speech. It can also be used to write and store information.

2. *Plotters*—used most often for outputting graphics because they can produce specialized free-form drawings on paper.
- Commonly used impact printers are:
  1. *Daisy wheel (letter-quality) printers*—produce a high-quality print image because the entire character is formed by a single impact by a print wheel with a set of characters on the outside tips of the wheel's spokes. Daisy wheel printers produce letter-quality output, but they are being phased out in favor of less expensive and more flexible printers.
  2. *Dot-matrix printers*—produce images with a print head composed of a series of little print hammers (usually 9 or 24) that look like the heads of pins.
- Although daisy wheel printers produce high-quality images, they also have several disadvantages:
  1. They are too slow for many large-volume output situations.
  2. They are noisy.
  3. To change the typeface style, the operator must halt the machine and change the print wheel.
  4. They cannot produce graphics or color output.
- Dot-matrix printers are more flexible, quieter, and faster than daisy wheel printers, and they can also produce graphics output. In addition, they can produce a variety of type styles without the operator having to stop the machine. However, their image quality is not as high as that produced by daisy wheel printers.
- Dot-matrix printers can print in *draft quality* (one pass of the print head for each line) or *near-letter-quality* (*nlq*) (two or more passes of the print head for each line).
- Twenty-four-pin dot-matrix printers are more expensive and faster than nine-pin printers, and they produce better-quality images. They are best used in a heavy-volume environment where speed and quality are priorities.
- *Color dot-matrix printers* use a multicolor ribbon instead of a black one.
- The main types of nonimpact printers are:
  1. *Ink-jet printers*—form images by spraying tiny droplets of ink (black or colors); text is letter quality and graphics can be output. These printers are about as fast as dot-matrix printers, and they are quiet.
  2. *Thermal printers*—use heat to produce images on special chemically treated paper. No ribbon or ink is involved. Although thermal printers are expensive, they produce excellent color output by using wax.
  3. *Laser printers*—use a laser beam to produce images in a process similar to that used by photocopiers. Laser printers are fast, quiet, have low maintenance requirements, and produce high-quality images, including graphics. They can also output text in a variety of fonts—type sizes and styles. Laser printers that have a built-in *page description language* (such as PostScript by Adobe Systems) provide greater flexibility to produce different fonts and special graphics.
- Laser printers are:
  1. *Low end*—less expensive, slower, produce lower-quality images
  2. *High end*—more expensive, faster, produce higher-quality images
  3. *Color*—expensive but effective
- *Portable printers* (9- and 24-pin dot-matrix, ink-jet, and thermal) have been developed for businesspeople to take on the road.
- *Plotters* are used for specialized output, such as blueprints of architectural designs.
- The *flatbed plotter* is the type of plotter most commonly used with microcomputers. It is designed so that the paper is placed flat and one or more pens move horizontally and vertically across the paper. Plotter output is available in color.

- The *cathode-ray tube* (CRT) is the most popular softcopy output device used with microcomputers. The CRT's screen is made up of *pixels* (*picture elements*); the smaller the pixels and the closer together they are, the better the image clarity, or *resolution*. The pixels are illuminated under software control by electron guns to form images.

- CRTs are:
  1. Large
  2. Power hungry
  3. Fragile

- CRTs can be *monochrome* or *RGB* (*red, green, blue*) *color*.

- Some CRTs, such as the IBM monochrome monitor, are *character-mapped displays*—they can display characters only and only according to template grid information stored in a video display ROM chip. Other CRTs are *bit-mapped displays*. They can display characters *and* free-form graphics because the electron beam can illuminate each individual pixel.

- *Color Graphics Adapters* (CGA), *Enhanced Graphics Adapters* (EGA), *Video Graphics Array* (VGA), *Super* VGA, and *Extended Graphics Adapter* (XGA) cards are available to upgrade a character-mapped monochrome monitor to display color bit-mapped graphics. (The card is inserted into an expansion slot in the system cabinet.) However, the resolution is determined by the monitor.

- *Flat screen technologies*, used with laptop computers, have been developed to overcome the disadvantages of the CRT: large size, high power consumption, and fragility.

- The three main types of flat screen technologies are:
  1. Liquid crystal display (LCD)
  2. Electroluminescent (EL) display
  3. Gas plasma display

- *Voice output systems*—including *speech coding* and *speech synthesis*—are a relatively new form of output used when traditional output is inappropriate.

KEY TERMS

bit-mapped graphics, p. 114
cathode-ray tube (CRT), p. 111
character box, p. 114
character-mapped display, p. 114
color dot-matrix printer, p. 104
daisy wheel printer, p. 102
dot-matrix printer, p. 103
electroluminescent (EL) display, p. 118

flat screen, p. 117
flatbed plotter, p. 111
font, p. 108
gas plasma display, p. 119
gray-scale monitor, p. 116
hardcopy, p. 101
impact printer, p. 102
ink-jet printer, p. 106
laser printer, p. 108
liquid crystal display (LCD), p. 117
monochrome monitor, p. 114

nonimpact printer, p. 106
page description language, p. 108
pixel, p. 111
plotter, p. 102, 111
portable printer, p. 108
printer, p. 102
resolution, p. 111
RGB color monitor, p. 114
softcopy, p. 101
thermal printer, p. 106
voice output system, p. 120

EXERCISES

SELF-TEXT

1. Output is available in two forms: _____ and _____.
2. _____ printers produce images with a print head composed of a series of little print hammers.
3. Printers are either _____ or _____.
4. _____ are used most often for outputting specialized graphics such as blueprints.
5. The most commonly used impact printers are _____ printers.
6. The video display image is the most widely used softcopy output. (true/false)
7. _____ _____ use heat to produce images on special chemically treated paper.
8. The _____ _____ is the most popular softcopy output device used with microcomputers.
9. Portable printers have been developed that can easily be taken on the road. (true/false)
10. Laser printers that have a built-in _____ _____ _____ provide even greater flexibility to produce different fonts and special graphics.
11. The image on a CRT is made up of _____, short for _____ _____.
12. CRTs can be _____ or _____.
13. CRTs are large, power hungry, and fragile. (true/false)
14. Three main types of flat screen technologies are:
    a. _____   b. _____   c. _____
15. Screen resolution is measured by vertical and horizontal lines of pixels. (true/false)
16. Voice output technology has advanced so far that most microcomputers are configured with voice output capabilities. (true/false)
17. The _____ plotter is the type of plotter most commonly used with microcomputers.
18. Some computer screens can display more than 16 million colors. (true/false)
19. Super VGA cards are used in Macintoshes. (true/false)
20. The more pixels that can be displayed on the screen, the better the _____ of the image.

SOLUTIONS   (1) hardcopy, softcopy; (2) dot-matrix; (3) impact, nonimpact; (4) plotters; (5) dot-matrix; (6) true; (7) thermal printers; (8) cathode-ray tube; (9) true; (10) page description language; (11) pixels, picture elements; (12) monochrome, color; (13) true; (14) liquid crystal display, electroluminescent display, gas plasma display; (15) true; (16) false; (17) flatbed; (18) true; (19) false; (20) resolution.

SHORT ANSWER

1. What advantages does the laser printer have over other printers?

2. In what ways do daisy wheel and dot-matrix printers differ? Which printer is used more?

3. What are the principal differences between how an image is formed on a monochrome monitor and on an RGB monitor?

4. What is the difference between a character-mapped display and a bit-mapped display?

5. Why has there been such interest in developing flat screen technologies?

6. What is the difference between hardcopy and softcopy? When might each be needed?

7. What must you consider before purchasing output hardware?

8. Compare ink-jet and thermal printers. How are they similar? Different?

9. What determines how many colors your monitor will display? What determines the monitor's resolution?

10. What is the main difference between a laser printer with a page description language and one without?

PROJECTS

1. Prepare an outline that indicates all the factors a user should consider when he or she is preparing to buy a printer.

2. Research the answer to the following questions: What is the state of the art in video display technology, and how is it currently being used? Is this technology being used only with microcomputers, or is it being used with all types of computers?

3. If you could buy any printer you want, what type (make, model, etc.) would you choose? Does the printer need to be small (to fit in a small space)? Does it need to print across the width of wide paper (11 × 14 inches)? In color? On multicarbon forms? Does it need to print graphics and typeset-quality text? Analyze what your needs might be and choose a printer (if necessary, make up what your needs might be). Review some of the current computer publications for articles or advertisements relating to printers. What is the approximate cost of the printer you would buy? Your needs should be able to justify the cost of the printer.

4. Visit a local computer store to compare the output quality of the different printers on display. Then obtain output samples and a brochure on each printer sold. After comparing output quality and price, what printer would you recommend to a friend who needs a printer that can output resumes, research reports, and professional-looking correspondence with a logo?

5. Explore the state of the art of computer-generated 3-D graphics. What challenges are involved in creating photo-realistic 3-D images? What hardware and software are needed to generate 3-D graphics? Who benefits from this technology?

6. At a computer store, compare the display quality of the following monitors: EGA, VGA, Super VGA, XGA, 16-bit Macintosh or Quadra, 24-bit Macintosh or Quadra. Which has the highest resolution? Displays the most colors? What size is the monitor you like best? How much does it cost and with what kind of microcomputer system is it compatible?

CHAPTER 6

APPLICATIONS SOFTWARE

Just as a hammer shouldn't be used to saw a board in half, a particular
applications software package may not be suited for your particular processing
task. Many different types of software tools are available for purchase today.
To be an effective and efficient computer user, you must be able to evaluate
your processing requirements and then choose the appropriate software tool
to use to fulfill those requirements.

PREVIEW

When you have completed this chapter, you will be able to:

List and describe the different categories of applications software

Describe the uses for different types of general-purpose applications software

List some of the factors you should consider before purchasing
applications software

Explain why applications software must be installed on your microcomputer
system before it can be used

CHAPTER OUTLINE

Why Is This Chapter Important?

Categories of Applications Software

Common Features of Applications Software

Word Processing Software

Desktop Publishing Software

Electronic Spreadsheet Software

Database Management System Software

Graphics Software

Integrated Software

Computer-Aided Design, Engineering, and Manufacturing

Communications Software

Applications Software Utilities

Hypertext and Multimedia

Deciding What to Purchase

Installing Applications Software

Summary

Key Terms

Exercises

Can you use a daisy wheel printer to print out a portrait of Abraham Lincoln? Can you use an RGB monitor to show the colors of the rainbow? With your knowledge of hardware, you know the answers to these questions. Different equipment has different uses. Likewise with software: A software program designed to handle text may not necessarily be used to draw charts and graphs or to manipulate rows and columns of numbers.

To help you begin to understand the differences among types of software, let us repeat the definitions we gave back in Chapter 1 for applications and systems software. **Applications software** is a collection of related programs designed to perform a specific task—to solve a particular problem for the user. The task or problem may require, for example, computations for payroll processing or for maintaining different types of data in different types of files. **Systems software** "underlies" applications software; it starts up the computer and functions as the principal coordinator of all hardware components and applications software programs. Without systems software loaded into the RAM of your computer, your hardware and applications software are useless. Both systems software and applications software must be purchased by the user (systems software is sometimes included in the price of a microcomputer).

This chapter focuses on applications software, and Chapter 7 covers systems software. You must understand the uses of—and the differences among—types of software so you will know what to use for a particular processing task.

CATEGORIES OF APPLICATIONS SOFTWARE

Custom software is written by programmers to meet the unique needs of an organization. However, most of the software you will be using is packaged software, also called **off-the-shelf software**, which is available at computer supply stores and by mail order. So many different types of applications software packages have come into the market that deciding which one to buy can require some investigation. Applications software is expensive. You can easily spend between $200 and $700 for a single package. In fact, individuals and companies typically spend much more on software than on hardware.

Just as the subject matter of a book determines what literary category it falls into (such as history, gardening, cooking, or fiction), the capabilities of an applications software program determine how it is categorized. Applications software falls into the following common categories:

- General business management
- Industry-specific
- Special disciplines
- Education
- Personal/home management
- General-purpose software for the user

General business management software, the largest group of applications software, includes products that cover the vast majority of business software needs, including accounting, inventory control, finance and planning, personnel, office administration, project management, and many others. However, some industries have very specialized applications software requirements; special *industry-specific software* is designed to meet these needs. Typical industries requiring specific products include specialized accounting services, advertising, agriculture and farm management, architecture, banking, construction, dentistry, engineering, legal services, leasing and rental companies, personnel agencies, property management, publishing, and others.

Special discipline software is a category set aside for such hobbies and special-interest areas as amateur radio, astrology, geography, mathematics, music, sports and leisure, visual arts, and others. *Education applications software* products focus on administration of educational institutions, computer-aided instruction (CAI), and special education. *Personal/home management software* includes products that relate to education, entertainment, finance, or home management.

This chapter highlights the types of **general-purpose applications software** you are likely to use in the business or professional environment. Specifically:

- Word processing
- Desktop publishing
- Electronic spreadsheets
- Database management systems
- Graphics
- Communications
- Integrated programs
- Computer-aided design, engineering, and manufacturing
- Applications software utilities

Don't worry if you don't know all these terms; you will by the end of the chapter. However, before we discuss the different types of general-purpose applications software, we need to go over some of the features common to most kinds of applications software packages.

COMMON FEATURES OF APPLICATIONS SOFTWARE

- **Cursor**—This is the blinking symbol that shows you where data— a character, a space, a command—will be entered next. It can be moved with the cursor-movement keys or with a mouse.

This is a cursor.

- **Scrolling**—This is the activity of moving images up or down on the display screen, so you can move to the beginning and the end of a document, for example. The portion of the file displayed on the screen is called a window. You can scroll by moving the cursor, using the PgUp and PgDn keys, by using the mouse to "click" on (select by pressing the mouse button) specified parts of the screen, or by using certain commands specified in the application package's documentation.

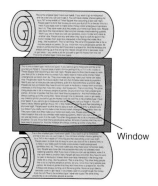

Window

- **Menu bar**—This is a row of command options displayed across the top or the bottom of the screen.

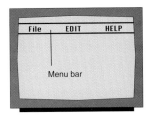

Menu bar

Pull down menu

- **Pull-down menu**—This is a list of command options, or choices, that are displayed from the top of the screen downward when its title is selected from the menu bar. Pull-down menus can be opened by keystroke commands or by "clicking" (pressing) the mouse button while pointing to the title and then dragging the mouse pointer down.

- **Help screen**—This is on-screen instruction regarding the use of the software. The Help menu or options are accessed by clicking the mouse on the Help menu bar title or by using a specified function key (usually F1). The user then chooses the option he or she needs help with—such as printing a document.

WORD PROCESSING SOFTWARE

Word processing software offers capabilities that greatly enhance the user's ability to create and edit documents. It enables the user to easily insert, delete, and move words, sentences, and paragraphs—without ever using an eraser. Word processing programs also offer a number of features for "dressing up" documents with variable margins, type sizes, and styles. The user can do all these manipulations on screen, before printing out hardcopy.

Table 6.1 provides a list of some of the common features of word processing software packages. Figure 6.1 shows screens from the WordPerfect word processing program and Microsoft Word for the Macintosh. Besides WordPerfect and Microsoft Word, some popular word processing packages are WordStar, MultiMate Advantage, PC-Write, OfficeWriter, XyWrite III Plus, and Ami Professional.

Some word processing packages, including WordPerfect, Microsoft Word, and Ami Professional, provide desktop publishing features that enable users to integrate, or combine, graphics and text on a professional-looking page (Figure 6.2). Compared to dedicated desktop publishing packages (described shortly), word processing packages lack the ease with which different elements in a document can be placed and rearranged. However, the line that differentiates word processing packages and desktop publishing packages is blurring.

DESKTOP PUBLISHING SOFTWARE

Desktop publishing (DTP) is a combination of hardware—usually microcomputer, hard disk, laser printer, and scanner—and software that together provide near-typeset-quality output in a variety of sizes, styles, and type fonts (Figure 6.3). This technology can integrate graphics and text on a professional-looking page (Figure 6.4). Well-known desktop publishing software packages are Aldus PageMaker, Ready-Set-Go, Ventura, and Quark XPress. Desktop publishing software allows the user to combine into one file or output report, the elements from different files that have been generated using different software programs (Figure 6.5).

Desktop publishing software takes advantage of both the increased processing power and storage capacities of today's microcomputers and the flexibility in terms of output that a laser printer provides. For a laser printer to effectively combine text and graphics on a single page, a *page description language*, such as Adobe's PostScript, must be stored in the printer's memory and be usable by the software.

Desktop publishing software, often referred to as **page description software,** enables users to combine text and graphics in an organized format on a single page. Page description software falls into two categories—code-oriented and "what-you-see-is-what-you-get" (WYSIWYG). With a **code-oriented page description software** (Figure 6.6), formatting instructions are embedded (keyed) into a document in the form of codes. Code-oriented packages provide the user with more sophisticated desktop publishing options, compared to the WYSIWYG packages, and are based on traditional typesetting techniques, which also use formatting codes. There are two disadvantages to using this type of package. First, because of its high degree of sophistication, the user should have some typesetting experience before attempting to use the package. Second, the user can't see the final output until it's printed out. A user who is unfamiliar with how certain codes

TABLE 6.1   Some Common Word Processing Software Features

Correcting	Deleting and inserting. You simply place the cursor where you want to correct a mistake and press either the Delete key or the Backspace key to delete characters. You can then type in new characters. (Many packages offer shortcuts to deleting and inserting—for example, deleting many lines of text at one time by hitting a special sequence of keys.)
Block and move (or cut and paste)	Marking and changing the position of a large block of text; this can be done even between different documents, not just within the same document.
Check spelling	Many packages come with a spelling checker program that, when executed, will alert you to misspelled words and offer correct versions.
Thesaurus	Thesaurus programs allow the user to pick word substitutions. For example, if you are writing a letter and want to use a more exciting word than *impressive*, you can activate your thesaurus program and ask for alternatives to that word.
Mail merge	Most word processing programs allow the user to combine different parts of different documents (files) to make the production of form letters much easier, faster, and less tedious than doing the same thing using a typewriter. For example, you can combine address files with a letter file that contains special codes where the address information is supposed to be. The program will insert the different addresses in copies of the letter and print them out.
Scrolling	This feature allows the user to "roll" text up or down the screen; you can't see your long document all at once, but you can scroll the text to reach the point you are interested in. Most packages allow you to "jump" over many pages at a time—for example, from the beginning of a document straight to the end.
Search and replace	You can easily search through a document for a particular word—for example, a misspelled name—and replace it with another word.
Footnote placement	This feature allows the user to build a footnote file at the same time he or she is writing a document; the program then automatically places the footnotes at appropriate page bottoms when the document is printed.
Outlining	Some packages automatically outline the document for you; you can use the outline as a table of contents.
Split screen	This feature allows you to work on two documents at once—one at the top of the screen and one at the bottom. You can scroll each document independently.
Word wrap	Words automatically break to the next line; the user does not have to press Return or Enter.
Font choice	Many packages allow you to change the typeface and the size of the characters to improve the document's appearance.
Justify/unjustify	This feature allows you to print text aligned on both right and left margins (justified, like the main text in this book) or let the words break without aligning (unjustified, or ragged, like the text at the right side of this table).
Boldface/italic/underline	Word processing software makes it easy to emphasize text by using **bold**, *italic*, or underlining.

will affect the report may have to perform countless revisions. However, these programs usually require less RAM, less processing power, and fewer storage requirements than the WYSIWYG programs. Among the code-oriented packages being used today are SC-LaserPlus, from Graham Software Corporation, and Deskset, from G.O. Graphics.

FIGURE 6.1

Most word processing packages provide a number of different menus to use for editing your documents. Shown here is a PC Word-Perfect Edit menu and a Macintosh Microsoft Word screen showing the Fonts pull-down menu (different type sizes are listed at the top of the pull-down menu, and different type styles are listed at the bottom).

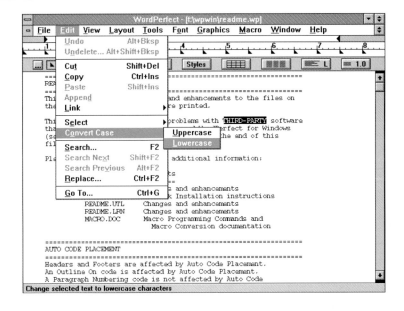

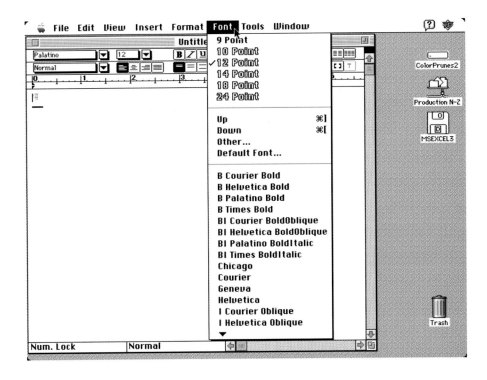

This figure illustrates the use of word processing software to integrate text and graphics on a professional-looking page.   **FIGURE 6.2**

LASER PRINTERS

Laser printer technology is much less mechanical than impact printing (that is, no print heads move, no print hammers hit), resulting in much higher speeds and quieter operation. The process resembles the operation of a photocopy machine: A laser beam is directed across the surface of a light-sensitive drum and fired as needed to record an image in the form of a pattern of tiny dots. The image is then transferred to the paper—a page at a time—in the same fashion as a copy machine, using a special toner.

Laser printers can also generate text in a variety of type sizes and styles (also called **fonts**) providing a business with the capability of outputting professional-looking typeset-quality reports. Most laser printers are capable of outputting a specific set of fonts and sizes. Laser printers that include a built-in **page description language** on a board inside the printer provide greater flexibility by enabling users to generate fonts in any size and to produce special graphics effects. The most popular page description language available is Adobe Systems' Postscript. Postscript printers are generally $1000–$2000 more than non-Postscript printers.

A variety of laser printers, each different in terms of cost, speed, and capabilities, is available for use with microcomputers today. In general, laser printers can be viewed as falling into three categories: (1) low-end, (2) high-end, and (3) color.

The laser printers that fall into the low-end category are priced between $1000 and $3000 and can print between 4 ppm and 8 ppm. With printers in this range, 300 dpi images are common. Laser printers that are priced around $1000 are providing businesses with a low-cost alternative to the high-end 24-pin dot matrix printers.

For $10,000–$20,000 a high-end laser printer can be purchased that is three to five times faster than a low-end printer and generates clearer images (400–600 dpi). Printing between 15 and 25 ppm, these printers are appropriate in a networked environment where many users are sharing one printer.

FIGURE 6.3

Desktop publishing system. These newspaper professionals are using desktop publishing software to make up pages and insert art. Such systems usually comprise large color monitors, a laser printer, a scanner, and several hard disks, along with a microcomputer with mouse and DTP software.

FIGURE 6.4

Do it yourself! This ad was done in a short time using a microcomputer-based desktop publishing system.

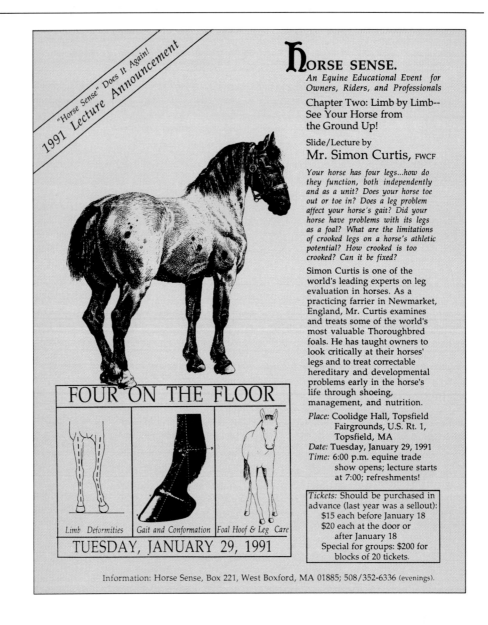

"Horse Sense" Does It Again!
1991 Lecture Announcement

Horse Sense.

An Equine Educational Event for Owners, Riders, and Professionals

Chapter Two: Limb by Limb--
See Your Horse from
the Ground Up!

Slide/Lecture by
Mr. Simon Curtis, FWCF

Your horse has four legs...how do they function, both independently and as a unit? Does your horse toe out or toe in? Does a leg problem affect your horse's gait? Did your horse have problems with its legs as a foal? What are the limitations of crooked legs on a horse's athletic potential? How crooked is too crooked? Can it be fixed?

Simon Curtis is one of the world's leading experts on leg evaluation in horses. As a practicing farrier in Newmarket, England, Mr. Curtis examines and treats some of the world's most valuable Thoroughbred foals. He has taught owners to look critically at their horses' legs and to treat correctable hereditary and developmental problems early in the horse's life through shoeing, management, and nutrition.

Place: Coolidge Hall, Topsfield
Fairgrounds, U.S. Rt. 1,
Topsfield, MA
Date: Tuesday, January 29, 1991
Time: 6:00 p.m. equine trade
show opens; lecture starts
at 7:00; refreshments!

Tickets: Should be purchased in advance (last year was a sellout):
$15 each before January 18
$20 each at the door or
after January 18
Special for groups: $200 for
blocks of 20 tickets.

FOUR ON THE FLOOR

Limb Deformities | Gait and Conformation | Foal Hoof & Leg Care

TUESDAY, JANUARY 29, 1991

Information: Horse Sense, Box 221, West Boxford, MA 01885; 508/352-6336 (evenings).

WYSIWYG programs (PageMaker from Aldus Corporation and Ventura Publisher from Xerox Corporation) allow the user to see the report on the screen as it will appear when it is printed out (Figure 6.7). For this reason, many people prefer the WYSIWYG programs over the code-oriented programs; users don't have to wait until they print to see what a document will look like. With a WYSIWYG program, the user chooses from lists of menu options to format the text. This type of desktop publishing software is more power-, memory-, and storage-hungry than code-oriented software.

Because it can lead to tremendous savings, desktop publishing can significantly affect any user who currently sends text or graphics out to a professional typesetter. Instead of hiring a typesetter to format documents and graphics into reports, which can be costly, with a desktop publishing system you can design the document yourself—once you have been trained to do it properly. Desktop publishing can offer the advantages listed on page 137.

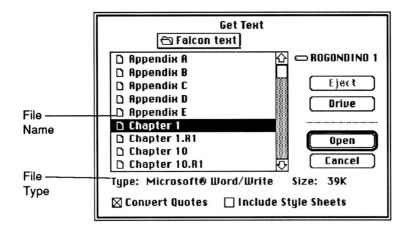

File Name

File Type

FIGURE 6.5

(a) Aldus PageMaker desk-top publishing screens. The top screen shows that a text file is being imported into the desktop publishing program from a word-processing program (Microsoft Word). The bottom screen indicates that a graphics file is being brought in to be put on a page (TIFF = tagged image file format, a common bit-mapped format for storing graphic images). (b) This diagram shows how DTP software uses files from other applications to produce documents with text and graphics.

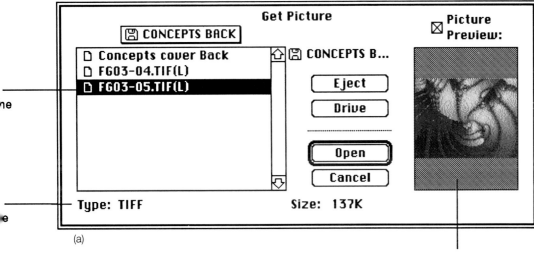

Preview of Illustration

(a)

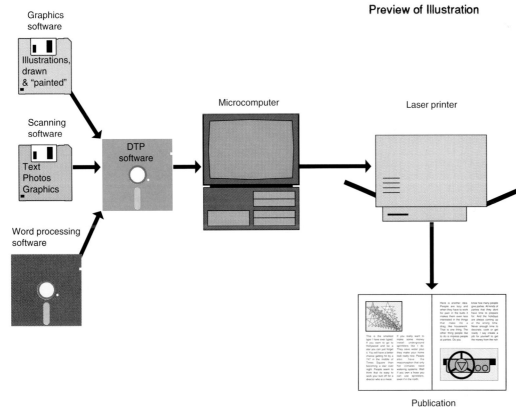

(b)

FIGURE 6.6   Code-oriented page description software. The top two lines (a bumper sticker) were printed according to the codes shown below it, which is what the user would have seen on the screen. The output was not displayed before it was printed.

DR. SCIENCE

He's not a real comedian

```
%!
/paperheight 11 72 mul def
/paperwidth 8.5 72 mul def
/width paperheight def
/height paperwidth 2 div def
/margin .375 72 mul def
/xcenter paperwidth 2 div def
/ycenter paperheight 2 div def

%xcenter ycenter translate
%.25 .25 scale
%xcenter neg ycenter neg translate

90 rotate
0 0 moveto paperheight 0 rlineto 0 paperwidth neg rlineto
paperheight neg 0 rlineto closepath 0 setlinewidth stroke

/bumpersticker
{
    /AvantGarde-Demi findfont setfont
    (ASS, DR. SCIENCE) dup stringwidth pop
    width margin sub margin sub exch div /points exch def
    /AvantGarde-Demi findfont
    [points 0 0 points 1.5 mul 0 0 ] makefont setfont
    margin margin 135 add moveto show

    /AvantGarde-DemiOblique findfont setfont
    (He's not a real comedian) dup stringwidth pop
    width margin sub margin sub exch div /points exch def
    /AvantGarde-DemiOblique findfont
    [points 0 0 points 1.5 mul 0 0 ] makefont setfont
    margin margin 20 add moveto show
} def

0 height neg translate
0 0 moveto width 0 rlineto stroke
bumpersticker
0 height neg translate
bumpersticker

showpage
```

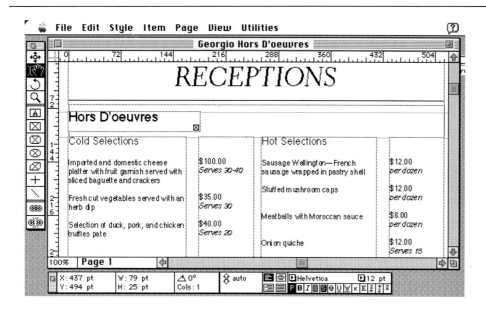

RECEPTIONS

Hors D'oeuvres

Cold Selections

		### Hot Selections	
Imported and domestic cheese platter with fruit garnish served with sliced baguette and crackers	$100.00 *Serves 30-40*	Sausage Wellington—French sausage wrapped in pastry shell	$12.00 *per dozen*
Fresh cut vegetables served with an herb dip	$35.00 *Serves 30*	Stuffed mushroom caps	$12.00 *per dozen*
Selection of duck, pork, and chicken truffles pate	$40.00 *Serves 20*	Meatballs with Moroccan sauce	$8.00 *per dozen*
		Onion quiche	$12.00 *Serves 15*

FIGURE 6.7

WYSIWYG document. The printed restaurant menu shown at the bottom was displayed on the computer screen (top) before it was printed out. The software documentation explains what the option symbols on the left and bottom sides of the screen mean.

- *You save money.* Sending a report, a newsletter, or a brochure out to a professional typesetter can easily cost a few hundred dollars.

- *You save time.* Using a desktop publishing system can cut the time spent on preparing documents by nearly 50%. Because you are preparing the report yourself electronically using a desktop publishing system, you can make any needed revisions immediately. The turnaround time necessary to make revisions when you are using a typesetter can easily add days onto a production schedule.

- *You maintain control.* You are in charge of the final output and production schedule.

A typical desktop publishing system, including a microcomputer with mouse, a laser printer, and page description software, costs around $10,000. This may sound like a lot of money, but when you consider that you might easily spend that much having just a few projects professionally designed and typeset, the cost doesn't look so bad. The cost of a desktop publishing system increases when certain other peripherals are included in the overall system; for example, an optical scanner for inserting drawings and photos into a report and a mouse and graphics tablet for drawing specialized images. Just remember—if you have the opportunity to choose a desktop publishing system, examine the features of the software programs you are most interested in first and then determine what microcomputers and peripheral devices the software is compatible with.

ELECTRONIC SPREADSHEET SOFTWARE

With **spreadsheet software,** based on the traditional accounting worksheet, the user can develop personalized reports involving the use of extensive mathematical, financial, statistical, and logical processing. Its automatic calculation abilities can save the user almost a lifetime of tedious arithmetic. The spreadsheet shown in Figure 6.8 was created by a beginner in less than an hour. This spreadsheet is designed to calculate expense totals and percentages.

Some of the terms you will encounter when using spreadsheets are listed in Table 6.2. Figure 6.9 shows a window (screen-size working area) of a Lotus 1-2-3 spreadsheet.

One of the most useful functions of spreadsheet software is the performance of "What if" analyses. The user can say: "What if we changed this number? How would future income be affected?"—and can get an immediate answer by having the spreadsheet software automatically recalculate *all* numbers based on the one change. Some spreadsheet packages, including versions 2.2 and 3.0 of Lotus 1-2-3, enable you to *link* spreadsheets together—this is called dynamic file linking. If a number, such as an expense amount, is changed in one spreadsheet, the change

FIGURE 6.8

Electronic spreadsheets (b) look much like spreadsheets created manually (a). However, when a number is changed in an electronic spreadsheet, all totals are automatically updated—certainly not the case when you work with a spreadsheet by hand!

(a)

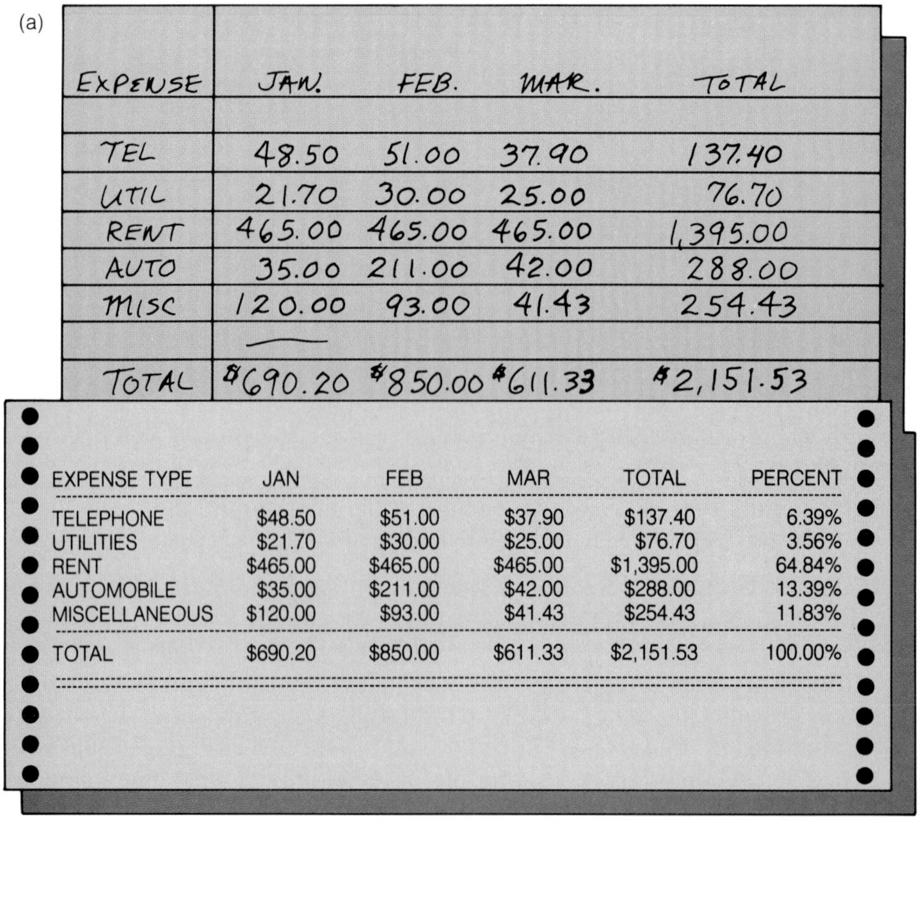

EXPENSE	JAN.	FEB.	MAR.	TOTAL
TEL	48.50	51.00	37.90	137.40
UTIL	21.70	30.00	25.00	76.70
RENT	465.00	465.00	465.00	1,395.00
AUTO	35.00	211.00	42.00	288.00
MISC	120.00	93.00	41.43	254.43
TOTAL	$690.20	$850.00	$611.33	$2,151.53

(b)

EXPENSE TYPE	JAN	FEB	MAR	TOTAL	PERCENT
TELEPHONE	$48.50	$51.00	$37.90	$137.40	6.39%
UTILITIES	$21.70	$30.00	$25.00	$76.70	3.56%
RENT	$465.00	$465.00	$465.00	$1,395.00	64.84%
AUTOMOBILE	$35.00	$211.00	$42.00	$288.00	13.39%
MISCELLANEOUS	$120.00	$93.00	$41.43	$254.43	11.83%
TOTAL	$690.20	$850.00	$611.33	$2,151.53	100.00%

Column labels	The column headings across the top of the worksheet area.	TABLE 6.2
Row labels	The row headings that go down the left side of the worksheet area.	Common Spreadsheet Terminology
Cell	The intersection of a column and a row; a cell holds a single unit of information.	
Value	The number within a cell.	
Cell address	The location of a cell. For example, B3 is the address of the cell at the intersection of column B and row 3.	
Cell pointer (cursor)	Indicates the position where data is to be entered or changed; the user moves the cursor around the spreadsheet, using the particular software package's commands.	
Window	The screen-size area of the spreadsheet that the user can view at one time (about 8 columns and 20 rows). Most spreadsheets can have up to 8,192 columns and 256 rows; some have as many as 10,000 columns and more than 300 rows (AppleWorks).	
Formula	Instructions for calculations; these calculations are executed by the software based on commands issued by the user.	
Recalculation	Automatic reworking of all the formulas and data according to changes the user makes in the spreadsheet.	
Scrolling	"Rolling" the spreadsheet area up and down, and right and left, on the screen to see different parts of the spreadsheet.	
Graphics	Most spreadsheets allow users to display data in graphic form, such as bar, line, and pie charts.	

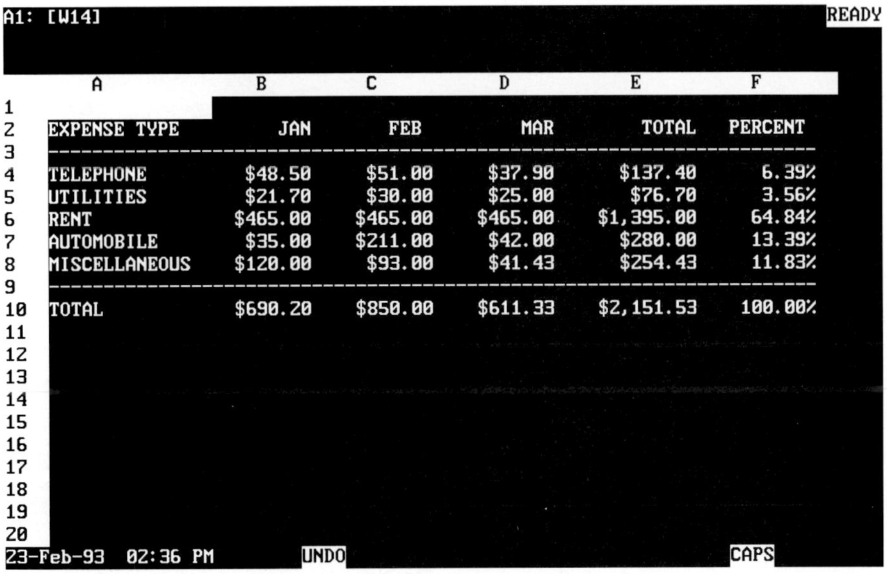

FIGURE 6.9

Window of a Lotus 1-2-3 spreadsheet

is automatically reflected in other spreadsheet files that might be affected by the change.

Along with Lotus 1-2-3, popular spreadsheet packages are Microsoft Excel, Quattro, and Quattro Pro.

DATABASE MANAGEMENT SYSTEM SOFTWARE

Database management system (DBMS) software allows the user to store large amounts of data that can be easily retrieved and manipulated with great flexibility to produce meaningful management reports. With database management system software, also called a *database manager*, you can compile huge lists of data and manipulate, store, and retrieve it without having to touch a single filing cabinet or folder. Table 6.3 lists some common functions of database management software.

Two main categories of DBMS software exist:

- Flat-file systems
- Relational systems

Flat-file database management systems (also called **file management systems**) can deal with information in only one file at a time. They can't establish relationships among data stored in different files. **Relational DBMSs** can establish links by referring to fields (database hierarchy terms were described in Chapter 4, Figure 4.5) that store the same type of data in different databases. These links enable users to update several files at once or generate a report using data from different database files. Although flat-file DBMSs are perfectly suited for generating mailing labels, most business applications require the use of a DBMS with relational capabilities.

Popular DBMS packages include dBASE III Plus, dBASE IV, Paradox, Q&A, and Filepro.

TABLE 6.3

Common Functions of Database Management System Software

Create records	Group related data concerning one unit of interest—for example, one employee. A company's database would have one record for each employee.
Create fields	Group units of data within a record. A field might contain one employee's name, for example.
Retrieve and display	When the user issues database commands (determined by the particular DBMS program) and specifies the record and field needed, the DBMS program retrieves the record and displays the appropriate section of it on the screen. The user can then change data as necessary.
Sort	Data is entered into the database in a random fashion; however, the user can use the sort function of the DBMS program to output records in a file in several different ways—for example, alphabetically by employee last name, chronologically according to date hired, or by ZIP code. The field according to which the records are ordered is the *key field.*
Calculate	Some DBMS programs include formulas that allow the user to calculate, for example, averages or highest and lowest values.
Interact	Many DBMS programs can be integrated with other types of applications software—for example, with a spreadsheet program. In other words, the data in the DBMS program can be displayed and manipulated within the spreadsheet program.

GRAPHICS SOFTWARE

One picture is often worth a thousand words. Thus reports and presentations that include graphics can be much more effective than those that don't. **Graphics software** enables users to produce many types of graphic creations.

In general, **analytical graphics** are basic graphical forms used to make numerical data easier to understand. The most common analytical graphic forms are bar graphs, line charts, and pie charts—or a combination of these forms (Figure 6.10). The user can view such graphics on the screen (color or monochrome) or print them out. Most analytical graphics programs come as part of spreadsheet packages.

Presentation graphics are fancier and more dramatic than analytical graphics, and so the software that produces them is more sophisticated (Figure 6.11). Presentation graphics allow the user to function as an artist and combine free-form shapes and text to produce exciting output on the screen, on paper, and on transparencies and film (for slides and photos). Of course, the user can also produce output using bar graphs, line charts, and pie charts. Popular presentation graphics programs are Harvard Graphics, PC Paintbrush, Adobe Illustrator, CorelDRAW, Hollywood, and Persuasion.

Analytical graphics. Bar, line, and pie charts are commonly used to display spreadsheet data in graphical form.   **FIGURE 6.10**

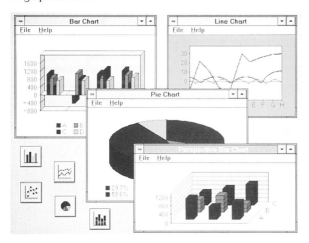
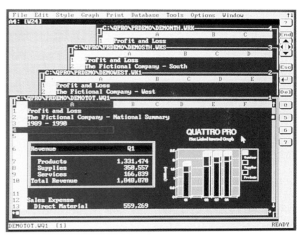

Presentation graphics software and software drawing tools provide the user with the means of producing sophisticated graphics.   **FIGURE 6.11**

COMPUTERS AND CAREERS

SCIENCE AND SCHOLARSHIP

You like the outdoors and you're looking forward to a career in environmental science or wildlife management. It's a good thing, then, that we live in an age of computer technology.

Scientists in Idaho, looking for ways to preserve the nation's diversity of plants and animals, have combined satellite images of topography and vegetation with electronic data on land ownership. The result is a mapping system that identifies habitats rich in wild species that have been poorly managed by state and federal governments. The computerized maps help natural resource administrators save money by determining which tracts of land are highest in biological richness and should be acquired before they become targets of development.

At the University of Rhode Island and Brown University, researchers have used computers to recreate the flying patterns of birds. The work has caught the interest of Federal Aviation Administration officials, who are looking into whether the research might help produce a more efficient air traffic control system.

Using computers and aerial photographs taken over five-year intervals since the 1960s, scientists are attempting to track the past movement of coastal erosion and predict yearly movements of shorelines. With this data, suggests a panel of the National Academy of Sciences, government officials could delineate beach areas with imminent, intermediate, and long-term erosion risk and limit building in those areas.

Long used to help with research in the sciences, computers have also become tools of scholarship in other fields. A few years ago, a computer researcher at New Jersey's Bell Laboratories made a discovery that may be one of the most important in the history of art. Lillian Schwartz juxtaposed a self-portrait painted by Leonardo da Vinci with his world-famous painting of the Mona Lisa and found that the eyes, hairline, cheeks, and nose were identical. From this some scholars concluded that the Mona Lisa was in fact a self-portrait by da Vinci.

An exhibition at the IBM Gallery of Science and Art in New York showed that computer technology could be used to reveal new archeological insights from old ruins and artifacts. The ancient Roman port of Pompeii was buried in A.D. 79 in the volcanic eruption of Mount Vesuvius, preserving many details of everyday life. Recently, computer enhancement techniques were used to resurrect texts from charred papyrus documents found in Pompeii. Computers were also used to restore colors and background images to partially destroyed paintings. From a huge database, experts constructed a large computer-generated map of Pompeii that includes positions and shapes of buildings, baths, and other features.

Finally, computer research has been used to bring the maddeningly complex Chinese writing system into the modern world. With more than 50,000 characters, each composed of at least 1 of 214 root parts plus additional strokes, Chinese ideograms have not been adaptable to typewriters and other office technology. In the last decade, however, researchers have succeeded in designing systems that allow word processors to accommodate characters at speeds averaging 60 per minute. ■

INTEGRATED SOFTWARE

Integrated software represents the industry's effort to combine all the software capabilities that the typical user may need into a single package with a common set of commands and rules for its use. The objective is to allow the user to perform a variety of tasks without having to switch software programs and learn different commands and procedures to run each one. Integrated software combines the capabilities of word processing, electronic spreadsheets, database management systems, graphics, and data communications (using telephone lines, satellites, and other communications technology to transmit data and information) into one program.

Microsoft Works is a well-known integrated software package in business today; others are Framework III and Framework IV (Figure 6.12), Enable, and PFS: 1st Choice. SmartSuite for Windows integrates Lotus 1-2-3 spreadsheet software with Ami Pro word processing software, Freelance Graphics software, and cc:Mail messaging software.

COMPUTER-AIDED DESIGN, ENGINEERING, AND MANUFACTURING

Industry, especially manufacturing, has probably experienced the greatest economic impact of computer graphics. Mechanical drawings that used to take days or weeks to complete can now be done in less than a day. Among other things, the drawings can be three-dimensional, rotated, shown in detailed sections or as a whole, automatically rendered on a different scale, and easily corrected and revised. But the use of computer graphics has evolved beyond the rendering of drawings; it is now used to help design, engineer, and manufacture products of all kinds, from nuts and bolts to computer chips to boats and airplanes.

FIGURE 6.12

Using integrated software. Because integrated software combines capabilities of several types of software programs, users are able to create a graphic presentation in one section of the screen while referring to data in a spreadsheet or a database—and perhaps later send the information to someone in another part of the country or the world. This Framework III Help screen lists what you can do to get started.

Computer-aided design (CAD) shortens the design cycle by allowing manufacturers to shape new products on the screen without having to first build expensive models (Figure 6.13). The final design data and images can be sent to a **computer-aided engineering (CAE)** system, which subjects the design to extensive analysis and testing that might be too expensive to do in the real world (Figure 6.14). From there, the product design may be sent to a **computer-aided manufacturing (CAM)** system, which makes use of the stored computer images in automating the machines (unintelligent robots) that manufacture the finished products (Figure 6.15). Computer simulation in industry has increased productivity enormously and made previously expensive procedures affordable.

COMMUNICATIONS SOFTWARE

Communications software allows users to access software and data from a computer in a remote location and to transmit data to a computer in a remote location—in other words, to establish *connectivity*. For example, the traveling business professional in Seattle, Wash., who needs to access client information daily from the company's main computer in San Diego, Calif., needs some communications software and a modem to enable his or her laptop computer to communicate long-distance. Popular microcomputer communications programs are ProComm, Smartcom II, Smartcom III, and Crosstalk XVI.

Communications software and hardware have become important to the computer user. Through systems connectivity the microcomputer is now able to share resources and services previously available only to users of large computer systems. Chapter 8 goes into the topic of communications in more detail.

FIGURE 6.13

CAD. This designer is using CAD software to design a valve to control missiles.

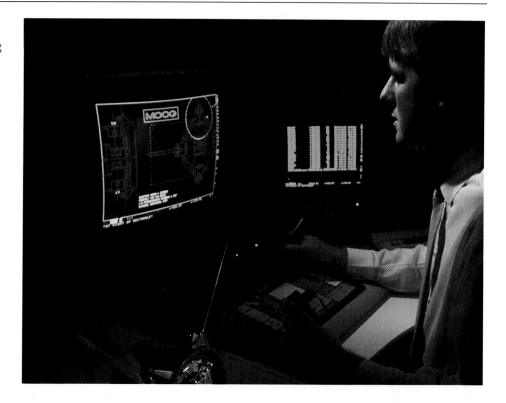

FIGURE 6.14

CAE. This national test facility is using a computer system to simulate and test space technology.

FIGURE 6.15

CAM. This computerized manufacturing plant produces high-quality cerium used in auto-exhaust catalysts, to help keep the air clean.

APPLICATIONS SOFTWARE UTILITIES

Many different types of **applications software utilities**—inexpensive programs that perform some basic "office management" functions—are available for purchase. These programs can be categorized as follows:

- Desktop management utilities
- Add-on utilities
- Disk utilities
- Keyboard and screen utilities

Depending on their function, the instructions in utility programs reside either in RAM or on disk. A **RAM-resident utility** is designed to be available at any time to the user because it resides in RAM at all times while the computer is on, even when the utility is not being used. In other words, once such a program is loaded into your computer (for example, from a diskette), a copy stays in RAM, "underneath" any applications software programs you may be using, until you turn the power off. As long as the power is on, you do not have to put the software disk back in the drive to use the utility program—you simply access it from RAM with certain keystrokes.

A **desktop management utility,** which is usually RAM-resident, allows the user to computerize many routine activities, including using a calculator, organizing an appointment calendar (Figure 6.16), taking notes, looking up words in a dictionary to make sure they are spelled correctly, and many more. The bottom line is that desktop manager software can save the user time. Sidekick and Pop-Up Windows are two popular desktop management packages.

Add-on utilities are usually RAM-resident and are used in conjunction with popular applications software packages. For example, to print wide electronic spreadsheets lengthwise on continuous-form paper (instead of across the width of the paper), many users use a program called Sideways. Allways, from Funk Software, is an add-on utility that is now sold with versions 2.2 and 3.0 of Lotus 1-2-3. This utility greatly enhances the way a spreadsheet appears in printed form through the use of stylized fonts in different sizes.

Disk utilities are usually purchased on floppy disks and then stored on hard disk. They provide users with a number of special capabilities, including:

- Recovering files that have been accidentally erased
- Retrieving damaged files
- Making automatic backup copies of a hard disk
- Organizing a hard disk by means of a menu system
- Compressing existing files on hard disk in order to free up room for additional files
- "Parking" the internal hard disk drive's actuator arm with the read/write heads in preparation for moving the computer; this way, disk damage can be avoided (not all computers need to have their disks parked before they are moved)

Keyboard utilities, such as Cursorific, are usually RAM-resident and enable you to change the way the cursor appears on the screen—usually by making it larger—so it is easier to see.

Screen utilities are used to increase the life of your screen. If your microcomputer is turned on and you don't use it for a period of a few minutes, a screen utility will automatically make the screen go blank. This saves your screen from having an image permanently burned onto the screen. When you press a key, the screen will again display the image that was showing previously.

We have mentioned only a few of the many utilities available. If your applications software package can't do something you want it to, there may be a utility that can. You can find out by phoning a computer software store.

Hypertext and Multimedia

Two new kinds of sophisticated applications software that do not easily fit into any of the preceding categories are hypertext and multimedia. **Hypertext** software—such as HyperCard, used on the Macintosh microcomputer, and Linkway, used on IBM PCs and PS/2 microcomputers—links basic file units comprising text and/or graphics with one another in creative ways. In HyperCard (Figure 6.17), a screen of information forms a record called a *card*; related groups of cards are organized into files called *stacks*. The user can work with the cards and stacks provided by the software program (for example, all the information in an encyclopedia) or create cards and stacks of text and graphics at will and combine them in all sorts of ways by using a mouse to click on "buttons" on the screen that move the user from card to card, and stack to stack. The user can program the sequences used to connect and combine cards and stacks, thereby discovering, sorting through, using, and presenting information in convenient or unusual ways.

Stackware, software packages that are collections of information created and used with HyperCard, is available at computer stores. For example, users can purchase "Research Stacks" consisting of five 800 K disks on selected subject areas—such as "Scientific Stacks," which include card stacks on amino acids, vitamin structures, galaxies, the ear, DNA structures, and the moons of Jupiter.

Multimedia is even more sophisticated than hypertext because it combines not only text and graphics but animation, video, music, and voice as well. In creating and presenting a multimedia product, one might, for example, use a Macintosh and HyperCard to create software programs that could integrate input data. The data could be input in the form of text and graphics through a scanner, animation through a special video camera, and sound through the use of a sound digitizer. The integrated data could be stored on a CD-ROM disk and then presented later on a television monitor and speaker that can run an optical disk or stored on tape and then run on a VCR. Text could also be printed out or stored on diskette or tape.

Multimedia sounds are available on disk for users with a Macintosh microcomputer, 2 MB of RAM, HyperCard, and applications software for sound management (such as HyperComposer). For example, Desktop Sounds v.1 includes the following sound effects: aircraft, animals, automotive, combat, comedy, crowds, household—and more.

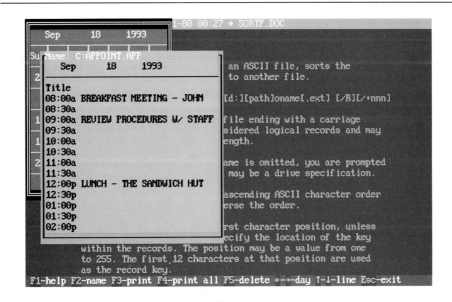

FIGURE 6.16

This desktop manager software utility allows the user to computerize many routine activities, such as keeping track of appointments.

FIGURE 6.17

HyperCard software provides a new kind of "information environment" for the Apple Macintosh computer. It stores information about any subject in the form of words, charts, sounds, pictures, and digitized photographs. Any "card" (piece of information) in any "stack" (related cards) can connect to any other card. (a) The Home card is the starting place for moving around in Hyper-Card. The various icons represent stacks for the user to click on, using a mouse. (b) An example of how HyperCard works.

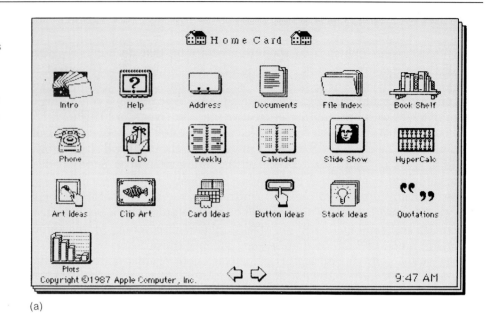

(a)

(b)

DECIDING WHAT TO PURCHASE

Computer software has become a multibillion-dollar industry. More than a thousand companies have entered the applications software industry, and they have developed a wide variety of products. As a result, the number of sources of applications software has grown. Applications software can be acquired directly from a software manufacturer or from the growing number of businesses that specialize in the sale and support of microcomputer hardware and software. Most independent and chain computer stores devote a substantial amount of shelf space to applications software programs; some businesses specialize in selling only software.

If you can't find off-the-shelf software—software that can be purchased off the shelf in a computer store—to meet your needs, you can develop your own. If you don't know how to do it yourself, you can have the computer professionals within your own organization develop custom software—software that is written to a particular organization's specifications—or you can hire outside consultants to do it. Unfortunately, hiring a professional to write software for you usually costs much more than off-the-shelf software.

Many software developers sell different versions of the same software application. Each version is usually designated by a different number—generally, the higher the number, the more current the version and the more features included with the package. For example, Lotus 1-2-3 is available in versions 2.2 and 3.0; WordPerfect for the PC in 4.2, 5.0, 5.1, and 6.0; Microsoft Windows in 3.0 and 3.1—and so on. In some cases, different versions are written to be used with particular microcomputer systems such as IBM compatibles or Macintosh microcomputers. If you buy a software package, make sure you have the version that goes with your microcomputer.

A user who buys a certain version of a software application may after a few months find that a later version of the same application is now available. This user has two choices: Either stay with the purchased version or upgrade (usually for a fee) to the later version. Because many users want the "latest," they will spend the extra amount for the most recent version of a software package, even if their current version satisfies all of their processing requirements.

Because there is so much to choose from, deciding what applications program—and then what version—to use requires very careful analysis. You should evaluate software applications by focusing on the following:

- *Quality of the documentation.* Using documentation that isn't written clearly and thoroughly can be very frustrating. Before purchasing an application, leaf through the documentation manual that accompanies the program to see if the instructions and reference information are clearly written and presented.

- *Ease of learning.* Just because the documentation for a particular application is good, it doesn't mean that the program is easy to learn. Because training can cost thousands of dollars, companies should evaluate how easy an application is to learn before purchasing it. A good way for a potential user to determine how easy a program is to learn is to ask friends or colleagues who are currently using it or to take a course at a community college or other training location.

- *Ease of use.* Some programs aren't easy to use on an ongoing basis. Before purchasing a package, ask people who are using the program if they enjoy using it. Are some procedures difficult to perform using this application?

- *Error handling.* It's human nature to make mistakes, and we don't want to go through tortuous procedures to correct them. When we make mistakes using applications software, we want the software to provide some helpful information on the screen that tells us what we did wrong. Ideally, the software should also tell us how to correct our mistakes. The documentation should tell you what "help" procedures are available.

- *Support.* Is there a phone number you can call if you have questions that relate to the software you are using? Most software development companies provide an 800 number that you can use.

If you want to try to keep track of all the software available, you can read software catalogs and directories. For example, magazines such as *Compute, PC World, Macworld, MacUser,* and *PC Computing* provide general users with reviews of many different kinds of software. *PC Magazine* and *InfoWorld* (Figure 6.18) also provide valuable guides to computer hardware, software, services, and related topics of interest.

FIGURE 6.18

(a) *PC Magazine.* This publication provides "Fact File," concise reviews of hardware and software in each issue. (b) *InfoWorld* software review. *InfoWorld* magazine publishes reviews like this in every issue.

FACT FILE

Publisher's Powerpak, Version 1.2
Atech Software, 5964 La Place Court, #125, Carlsbad, CA 92008; 800-748-5657, 619-438-6883.
List Price: With 3 type families in 10 variations each, $79.95; Font Packs (with 2 type families in 10 variations each), $29.95; Super Font Pack (11 type families in 10 variations each), $79.95; foreign alphabets (2 typefaces each), $79.95; Monotype Font Packs (4 typefaces each), $79.95.
Requires: 286-based PC or better, 1MB RAM, graphics adapter (EGA or VGA recommended), DOS 3.0 or later; *Microsoft Windows* 3.0 required for on-the-fly font scaling. Mouse recommended.
In Short: *Publisher's Powerpak* offers a multitude of fonts at low prices, and is a good source if you need non-Latin typefaces for *Windows,* but it produces the least attractive type of any *Windows* font manager, and its handling of italics is poor.

CIRCLE **426** ON READER SERVICE CARD

APRIL 16, 1991 PC MAGAZINE **187**

REPORT CARD **INFO WORLD**

GRAPHICAL WORD PROCESSOR
WordPerfect for Macintosh
VERSION 2.0

Criterion	(Weighting)	Score
Performance		
Basic editing	(60)	Very Good
Spelling checker/ thesaurus	(60)	Good
Mail merge	(20)	Very Good
Layout	(60)	Excellent
Graphics	(50)	Excellent
Outlining	(20)	Satisfactory
TOC and indexing	(20)	Good
Style sheets	(20)	Very Good
Font support	(60)	Excellent
Footnoting	(25)	Excellent
Macros	(25)	Excellent
Printer support	(60)	Very Good
Compatibility	(60)	Very Good
Speed	(50)	Good
Documentation	(75)	Very Good
Ease of learning	(75)	Good
Ease of use	(130)	Good
Error handling	(40)	Good
Support		
Support policies	(20)	Excellent
Technical support	(20)	Good
Value	(50)	Good
Final score		**7.4**

PRODUCT SUMMARY

Company: WordPerfect Corp., 1555 N. Technology Way, Orem, UT 84057; (801) 225-5000.
List price: $495.
Requires: Macintosh Plus, SE, or II computer; 1 megabyte of RAM; hard disk; System 6.0.3 or later.
Pros: Includes a robust drawing utility and an improved user interface.
Cons: None significant, except the bug in the Styles function.
Summary: A feature-filled program capable of handling a wide range of sophisticated word processing duties.

INSTALLING APPLICATIONS SOFTWARE

Once you have bought your applications software package, you must install it to work with your microcomputer system. **Software installation** usually involves telling the software the characteristics of the hardware you will be using so that the software will run smoothly. When you purchase a software application, check to see that the documentation tells you how to install the software.

To install software, you first insert the applications software diskette as indicated by the package documentation. Then the installation program usually asks a number of different questions about your hardware. For example, the installation program will usually display on your monitor a list of the popular printers on the market. You will be instructed to choose the name of the printer that corresponds to the one you are using. If the printer you are using doesn't appear on the list, and you are given no generic choice, you must contact the support staff at the company who developed your software and tell them what printer you are using. (Use the 800 number given in the documentation.) They will respond in one of the following ways:

- Send you the printer driver for the printer you are using. A **printer driver** is a file stored on a disk containing instructions that enable your software program to communicate with or print with the printer you are using.
- Tell you to choose a different printer from the list. If the printer you are using operates similarly to one on the list, your printer can use the printer driver of the other printer. This is often referred to as *emulating* the characteristics of another printer. (To **emulate** means to imitate.)

You may also be asked other questions during the installation procedure:

- What is the make and model of the microcomputer you are using?
- Are you using a color monitor? If so, what kind?
- Are you using a monochrome monitor? If so, what kind?
- Are you using 5¼-inch or 3½-inch diskettes?
- Are you using a hard disk?
- Where will you want the working copy of your applications software to be stored? On a diskette? On the hard disk?

Think about the answers to these questions *before* initiating the installation process. Once you have completed the installation procedure, your program will store most of your responses in a special file on the disk, which is referred to by your applications program when you load the software. In addition, if you will be using a hard disk, many installation programs automatically copy the program files to the hard disk for you. (*Note:* If you are using a hard disk, the installation process involves transferring *copies* of the programs that came on the diskettes in the applications package. Keep the original diskettes as backup in case your hard disk crashes. If you are using diskettes, make copies of the original package diskettes and use the copies as your working diskettes. The originals will serve as backups.)

Once the installation procedure is completed, you are ready to roll!

SUMMARY

- *Applications software* is a collection of related programs designed to perform a specific task, such as word processing or payroll management. Applications software is either purchased by the user *off the shelf* at a computer store or from a software outlet, or it is custom written for the user.

- *Systems software* "underlies" applications software; it starts up the computer and coordinates the hardware components and the applications software programs. Systems software usually comes with the microcomputer.
- Many categories of applications software exist. The most common are:
  1. *General business management*—covers the majority of business software needs—for example, accounting, inventory control, finance and planning, personnel, office administration, and project management.
  2. *Industry-specific*—meets needs of specialized businesses—for example, agriculture and farm management, architecture, banking, construction, dentistry.
  3. *Special disciplines*—covers hobbies and special-interest areas such as amateur radio, astrology, music, sports, and visual arts.
  4. *Education*—focuses on administration, computer-aided instruction (CAI), and special education.
  5. *Personal/home management*—covers uses at home relating to entertainment, instruction, finance, and home management.
  6. *General-purpose software* for the user—covers the basic types of software that general users are likely to encounter in business and professional life.
- The following are common general-purpose software types:
  1. *Word processing software*—which enables the user to easily create and edit documents, including inserting, deleting, and moving words, sentences, and paragraphs, and to easily alter the appearance of documents through the use of different type sizes and styles and through different text arrangements.
  2. *Spreadsheet software*—with which users can easily develop reports involving the use of extensive mathematical, financial, statistical, and logical processing. When a few numbers are changed, such reports can be automatically recalculated to provide "What if?" analyses.
  3. *Database management system (DBMS) software*—which allows the user to input, store, and manipulate large amounts of data to produce reports. The data can be manipulated in different ways, depending on the relationships of the data, which are determined by the software system. *Flat-file management systems (file management systems)* can't establish relationships among data stored in different files. They can deal with only one file at a time. *Relational database management systems* can establish relationships among data in different files by using *key fields* or common identifying characteristics.
  4. *Graphics software*—which gives the user the ability to make reports and other presentations more effective through the use of *analytical graphics*, common graph forms that make numerical information easier to understand, and presentation graphics, fancy free-form drawings.
  5. *Integrated software* enables the user to perform a wide variety of tasks that typically include creating documents, spreadsheets, databases, and graphs. Most integrated software packages also include communications capabilities.
  6. *Desktop publishing (DTP)* uses a combination of hardware and software to enable the user to combine text and graphics on the same page in a professional-looking, publishable format. The hardware used in a typical desktop publishing system typically includes a microcomputer, a hard disk, a laser printer, and a scanner. A *WYSIWYG* desktop publishing package lets you view on the screen what your document will look like when printed. To use a *code-oriented* desktop publishing package, the user must embed codes in the document. The effect of these codes can be viewed *after* the document is printed.
  7. *Computer-aided design (CAD) software* enables manufacturers to save much time and money because they can design products on the screen without having to construct expensive models. After the designs have been developed, they are sent to a *computer-aided engineering (CAE)* system, which subjects the design to extensive analysis and testing. From there, the product might be created using a *computer-aided manufacturing (CAM)* system, which uses unintelligent robots to manufacture the final product.

8. *Communications software* allows users to access software and data from and transmit data to a computer in a remote location.

9. *Applications software utilities* are inexpensive programs that perform some basic "office management" functions. These utilities are considered *RAM-resident utilities*, because they reside in RAM at all times while the computer is on, even when they aren't being used. These programs can be categorized as *desktop management, add-on, disk, screen,* and *keyboard utilities.*

■ When users buy applications software, they should evaluate the following:

1. *Quality of the documentation*—the instructions and presentations in the accompanying users' manual should be clear and easy to follow.

2. *Ease of learning*—the program should not be too difficult to learn how to use; ask others who have learned how to use the program.

3. *Error handling*—the program should offer on-screen help that tells the user when errors have occurred, and, ideally, how to correct them.

4. *Support*—the documentation should include an 800 number and other information about how to get professional assistance to solve software problems.

■ Applications software must be *installed* by the user before he or she can use it. Installation involves telling the software—through use of one of the software disks that came with the applications package—the characteristics of the hardware that the software will be running. The documentation includes instructions about how to install the software.

■ While installing software, you will see a list of printers on the screen from which you must indicate the one you will be using. If your printer is not on the list, call the 800 number. The software company may send you a *printer driver* on a disk, which will enable you to use your printer with the applications software, or it may tell you which printer on the list to choose.

■ Other on-screen questions often posed during installation are:

1. Make of microcomputer
2. Color or monochrome monitor
3. Brand of monitor
4. Size of diskettes being used ($3\frac{1}{2}$-inch or $5\frac{1}{4}$-inch)
5. Use of hard disk
6. Where copy of the applications software is to be stored

KEY TERMS

add-on utility, p. 146
analytical graphics, p. 141
applications software, p. 128
applications software utility, p. 146
code-oriented page description software, p. 131
communications software, p. 144
computer-aided design (CAD), p. 144
computer-aided engineering (CAE), p. 144
computer-aided manufacturing (CAM), p. 144
cursor, p. 129

custom software, p. 128
database management system (DBMS) software, p. 140
desktop management utility, p. 146
desktop publishing, p. 130
disk utility, p. 146
emulate, p. 151
file management system, p. 140
flat-file database management system, p. 140
general-purpose applications software, p. 129
graphics software, p. 141

Help screen, p. 130
hypertext, p. 147
integrated software, p. 143
keyboard utility, p. 146
menu bar, p. 129
multimedia, p. 147
off-the-shelf software, p. 128
page description software, p. 131
presentation graphics, p. 141
printer driver, p. 151
pull-down menu, p. 130
RAM-resident utility, p. 146
relational DBMS, p. 140

screen utility, p. 146   spreadsheet software,   software, p. 130
scrolling, p. 129   p. 138   WYSIWYG page
software installation,   systems software, p. 128   description software,
    p. 151   word processing   p. 134

EXERCISES

SELF-TEST

1. _____ _____ is a collection of related programs designed to perform a specific task for the user.
2. List four categories of applications software utilities:
   a. _____   b. _____   c. _____   d. _____
3. _____ _____ _____ offers capabilities that enable the user to
   easily create and edit documents.
4. Applications software starts up the computer and functions as the principal
   coordinator of all hardware components. (true/false)
5. _____ _____ enables a computer in one location to share data
   with another computer in a remote location.
6. Programs that reside in RAM at all times are referred to as RAM-resident
   utilities. (true/false)
7. When evaluating an applications software package, you should focus on the
   following five characteristics:
   a. _____   b. _____   c. _____   d. _____   e. _____
8. The type of software that enables users to input, store, and manipulate
   large amounts of data so that reports can be produced is _____

   _____ _____ _____.
9. If you need to develop a report that involves the use of extensive mathematical, financial, or statistical problems, what type of software application
   should you use? _____ _____ _____
10. Relational database management systems can't establish links among data
    stored in different files. (true/false)
11. List five questions that you may be asked during the process of installing
    software.
    a. _____   b. _____   c. _____   d. _____   e. _____
12. New applications software must be _____ by the user before it can be
    used.
13. List four tasks typically performed by disk utilities:
    a. _____   b. _____   c. _____   d. _____
14. _____ _____ software enables you to combine near-typeset-quality
    text and graphics on the same page in a professional-looking document.
15. Applications software utilities usually reside in RAM at all times. (true/false)
16. Users often spend more on software than they do on hardware. (true/false)
17. A _____ _____ is a file stored on a disk containing instructions
    that enable your software program to communicate with or print with the
    printer you are using.
18. Software installation usually involves telling the software what the charac-
    teristics are of the hardware you will be using, so that the software will run
    smoothly. (true/false)

19. Keyboard utilities enable you to change the way the cursor appears on the screen. (true/false)

20. _____ _____ gets its name from the fact that it can be purchased off the shelf in a computer store.

SOLUTIONS   (1) applications software; (2) desktop management utilities, add-on utilities, disk utilities, keyboard and screen utilities; (3) word processing software; (4) false; (5) communications software; (6) true; (7) quality of the documentation, ease of learning, ease of use, error handling, support; (8) database management system software; (9) electronic spreadsheet software; (10) false; (11) What is the make and model of the computer? Are you using a color or monochrome monitor? A hard disk? Where will you store your work?; (12) installed; (13) recovering files, making backup copies of a hard disk, organizing a hard disk, compressing files on disk to create more room; (14) desktop publishing; (15) true; (16) true; (17) printer driver; (18) true; (19) true; (20) off-the-shelf software

SHORT ANSWER

1. What should you consider before purchasing a particular applications software package?
2. What does spreadsheet software do?
3. What is the purpose of communications software?
4. What are applications software utilities?
5. What would a good use be for database management system software?
6. What do users need to install software?
7. Why do some people prefer using integrated software over other types of applications software?
8. What do the abbreviations CAD, CAE, and CAM mean?
9. What advantages can desktop publishing software provide?
10. What is the difference between applications software and systems software?
11. What is the list of options displayed across the top or bottom of the screen called? What is it used for?
12. What is an icon? What is it used for?
13. What is a Help screen, and how can the user display it?
14. What is scrolling?

PROJECTS

1. Locate an individual or a company who is using some custom-written software. What does this software do? Who uses it? Why couldn't it have been purchased off the shelf? How much did it cost? Do you think there is an off-the-shelf program that can be used instead? Why/why not?
2. Attend a meeting of a computer users' group in your area. What is the overall purpose of the group? Software support? Hardware support? In what ways? Does it cost money to be a member? How many members are there? How does the group get new members? If you were looking to join a user group, would you be interested in joining this group? Why/why not?
3. Make a list of all the ways a student could use word processing software to make life easier. Look at Table 6.1 to get some ideas, read some reviews of word processing software in computer magazines, and read the copy on word processing packages in a computer store.

CHAPTER 7

SYSTEMS SOFTWARE

Some users underestimate the importance of knowing about systems software because they don't deal directly with it on a daily basis—instead, they deal directly with applications software. But understanding the fundamentals of systems software and its purpose in the microcomputer system prepares you to get the most out of your microcomputer and avoid some common problems. This chapter provides an overview of microcomputer systems software.

PREVIEW

When you have completed this chapter, you will be able to:

List and describe the three main components of systems software and give reasons why they are necessary

Explain what is meant by the terms *multitasking, multiprocessing,* and *timesharing*

Describe some of the capabilities of MS-DOS, Windows, OS/2, UNIX, and the Macintosh operating system

Explain how software is written

CHAPTER OUTLINE

Why Is This Chapter Important?

Internal Command Instructions

External Command Instructions

Language Processors

Other Systems Software Capabilities

    Multitasking

    Multiprocessing

    Timesharing

Popular Microcomputer Systems Software

    MS-DOS

    MS-DOS and Windows

    OS/2

    UNIX

    Macintosh Operating System

    Making Your Choice

How Is Software Written?

    What Tools Are Available for Developing Software?

    Which Tools Are You Most Likely to Use?

Summary

Key Terms

Exercises

Without systems software you won't be able to use any of the software described in Chapter 6. Systems software tells the computer how to interpret data and instructions; how to run peripheral equipment like printers, keyboards, and disk drives; and how to use the hardware in general. Also, it allows you, the user, to interact with the computer. Systems software comprises a large number of instructions that can be grouped into the following categories:

1. Internal command instructions
2. External command instructions
3. Language processors

Internal and external command instructions are often referred to collectively as the **operating system,** or operating systems software.

As a microcomputer user, you will have to use systems software, so it is important to understand the role it plays in the microcomputer system.

INTERNAL COMMAND INSTRUCTIONS

Internal command instructions, often called *resident commands*, can be thought of as the innermost layer of systems software. These instructions direct and coordinate other types of software and the computer hardware. They are automatically loaded into RAM from disk when you turn on the microcomputer—called **booting**—and they reside in RAM until the computer is turned off (Figure 7.1). Without these instructions in RAM, a computer can be likened to a race car without fuel for the engine and without a driver to decide where to go and how fast. That is why the primary purpose of the procedures followed in starting up a computer is to load a copy of these operating system instructions into RAM. These instructions are referred to as *internal command instructions* because, in order to be usable, they must be stored on an internal storage device (namely, RAM). Operating instructions stored on an external storage device (such as a diskette or a hard disk) are referred to as *external command instructions* (discussed in the next section). Internal command instructions are so important to the functioning of your

FIGURE 7.1

Certain systems software instructions must be stored in RAM at all times for the user to be able to use applications software.

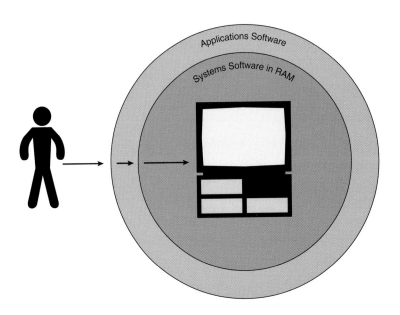

computer that they must be directly accessible to the microprocessor in RAM at all times.

The "captain" of the portion of the operating system that is stored in RAM is often referred to as the **supervisor,** or the **control program.** The supervisor calls in other parts of the operating system (external command instructions) and language processors as needed from secondary storage. The supervisor controls all other programs in the computer. For example, it:

- Coordinates processing
- Manages the use of RAM
- Allocates use of peripheral devices
- Checks equipment malfunction and displays error messages
- Manages files stored on disk

As we mentioned previously, microcomputer operating systems often come with the microcomputer (usually on diskettes). *If you have decided to use certain applications software packages, you must make sure to choose a computer whose systems software is compatible with those software packages*—or be prepared to buy special hardware and software to make them compatible. We'll describe the most popular types of systems software used on microcomputers at the end of this chapter.

EXTERNAL COMMAND INSTRUCTIONS

External command instructions are general-purpose operating system instructions that take care of what many people call "housekeeping tasks." External command instructions are not needed to run applications software; for this reason, they reside in secondary storage, instead of in RAM, until needed. These instructions are generally provided by the computer manufacturer when you purchase a microcomputer.

LANGUAGE PROCESSORS

You will recall that computers understand only one language—machine language "written" using the digits 1 and 0. Because it is too time-consuming to write programs in machine language, **high-level programming languages** were developed that are easier to learn and use. With high-level languages, programmers don't have to use 1s and 0s to represent computer instructions. Instead, they use everyday text and mathematical formulas, which enable them to use fewer instructions in a program. Programs written using high-level languages—called **source code**—still have to be converted into a machine-language version—called **object code**—before the computer "understands" them (Figure 7.2).

Programmers use a type of systems software called a **language processor,** or a **translator,** to convert high-level instructions into machine language—for example, the one used by an IBM microcomputer. You will need to use a language processor only if you create a program using a high-level language such as BASIC (*B*eginner's *A*ll-purpose *S*ymbolic *I*nstruction *C*ode), which is commonly taught in university-level courses.

When you purchase an applications software package, the software instructions have already been converted by a language processor into machine language so that you can use the package. Programmers use two types of language processors: *compilers* and *interpreters*.

FIGURE 7.2

A language processor translates the high-level language
program (source code) into a
machine-language version of
the program (object code)
before the computer can
execute the program.

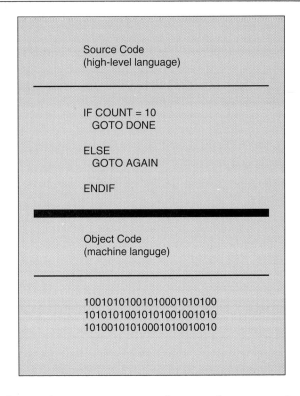

The **compiler** is a language processor that translates an *entire* high-level language program into a machine-language version of the program in a single process.
If no programming errors exist in the source code, the program becomes operative.

The **interpreter** is a language processor that converts and executes high-level
language instructions one instruction statement at a time. If an error is detected
in the source code, the interpreter displays immediate feedback on the screen. For
this reason, interpreters are commonly used with small and simple programs and
in educational settings because the user receives immediate feedback.

The most important difference between using compiled or interpreted software is speed. Programs that are compiled tend to execute up to five times faster
than programs that are interpreted (such as BASIC). However, if you are working
with microcomputers at home or in the office, you won't have to worry about
compiling or interpreting—the software packages have already been compiled, and
you will not even be able to look at the machine-level language the computer uses.

OTHER SYSTEMS SOFTWARE CAPABILITIES

Since the appearance of the first business computer, advances in hardware technology have increased the power of computers a hundred-thousandfold or more.
These hardware advances have made even more powerful systems software capabilities available to users. In the business environment, you are likely to be using
systems software that supports one or more of the following capabilities.

MULTITASKING

As we have mentioned, the first operating systems were designed for computers
with limited processing speed and limited RAM and storage capacity. These early
operating systems were referred to as *single-user operating systems* because they

could accept commands from only a single terminal or other input source and could manage only a single program in RAM at one time. Although most operating systems for microcomputers are considered single-user/single-program operating systems, some microcomputer operating systems are single-user but can also do **multitasking**—that is, they can execute more than one task or program at a time. Multitasking is also known as **multiprogramming**.

In multitasking, a copy of each program to be executed is placed in a reserved portion of RAM, usually called a *partition* (Figure 7.3). The supervisor is more sophisticated in an operating system with multitasking capabilities because it coordinates the execution of each program. It directs the microprocessor to spend a predetermined amount of time (according to programmed priorities) executing the instructions for each program, one at a time. In essence, a small amount of each program is processed, and then the microprocessor moves to the remaining programs, one at a time, processing small parts of each. This cycle is repeated until processing is complete. The processing speed of the microprocessor is usually so fast that it may seem as if all the programs are being executed at the same time. However, the microprocessor is still executing only one instruction at a time, no matter how it may appear to users.

MULTIPROCESSING

A multitasking operating system works with only one microprocessor. However, the computer is so fast that, if it spends a little bit of time working on each of several programs in turn, it can allow a number of programs to run at the same time. The key is that the operating system can keep track of the status of each program so that it knows where it left off and where to continue processing. The **multipro-**

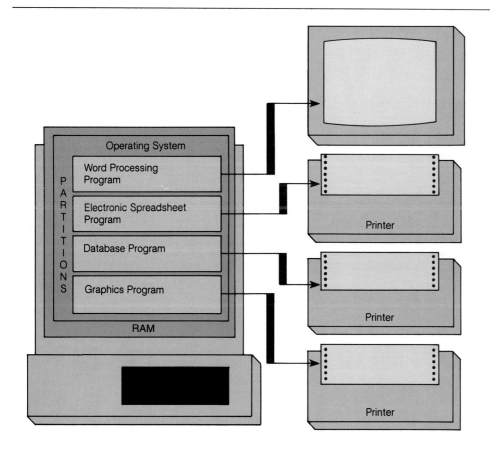

FIGURE 7.3

Multitasking. An operating system that can execute more than one program at a time (concurrently) is capable of multitasking—in other words, the user can run several different application programs at the same time. Although it may seem as if the programs are being processed at exactly the same time, they are actually being processed one after the other, extremely quickly.

cessing operating system is much more sophisticated; it manages the *simultaneous* execution of programs with two or more microprocessors (Figure 7.4). This can entail processing instructions from different programs or different instructions from the same program. Multiprocessing configurations are very popular in large computing systems and are becoming practical on UNIX-based microcomputers. (We'll discuss the UNIX operating system shortly.)

TIMESHARING

A **timesharing** computer system supports many user stations or terminals simultaneously; in other words, the users share time on the computer, based on assigned *time slices*. Timesharing is like multitasking, except that multitasking computers shift tasks based on program *priorities*, whereas timesharing systems assign each program a slice of time and then process the programs in small increments one after the other. The processing requirements of an operating system with timesharing capabilities are great.

In most cases, a computer system that includes timesharing capabilities uses a computer called a **front-end processor,** which is usually a microcomputer or minicomputer, to schedule and communicate to the main computer all the user requests and data entering the system from the terminals. The use of a front-end processor allows the main computer to concentrate solely on processing applications as quickly as possible (Figure 7.5). The UNIX operating system includes timesharing capabilities.

From the user's perspective, timesharing isn't much different from multitasking except that, with timesharing systems, usually more than one user is sharing the processing power of a central microcomputer (main computer) by using terminals connected to it. Multitasking systems are generally used by a single user who often needs to perform different tasks simultaneously.

FIGURE 7.4

Multiprocessing. Some computers use two or more microprocessors and sophisticated systems software to process different programs simultaneously.

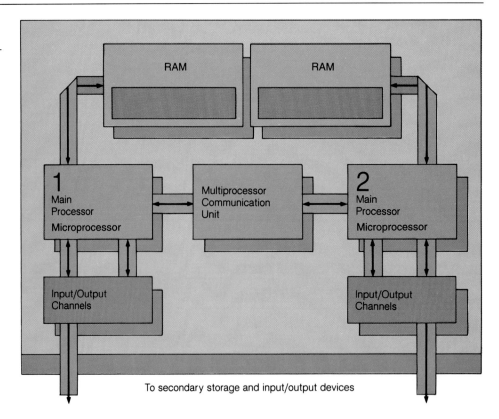

To secondary storage and input/output devices

POPULAR MICROCOMPUTER SYSTEMS SOFTWARE

In the late 1970s and early 1980s, a number of microcomputer hardware vendors introduced machines that included their own individual, machine-specific operating systems. This individualization created a software compatibility problem because each software applications package was written for a specific operating system and machine—if it worked with one type, it couldn't be used with another. A few operating systems became more popular than others because more software applications were written to be used with them. Software vendors decided to concentrate on developing software for these operating systems—namely, MS-DOS, OS/2, UNIX, and the Macintosh operating system.

MS-DOS

The development of this microcomputer **disk operating system (DOS)** (pronounced "doss") began in 1978, when Intel Corporation announced the development of a new and much more powerful microprocessor, the Intel 8088 chip. The new processor could use much more RAM and was substantially faster than the older 8080 series of processors.

Because of some differences between the old and the new processors, it became apparent that a new operating system would have to be developed to take advantage of the power of the 8088. In 1979, Tim Paterson of Seattle Computer Products began developing a new operating system called 80-DOS. The rights to distribute 80-DOS were acquired by Microsoft Corporation; Microsoft then entered into an agreement with IBM to make 80-DOS the operating system for the new personal computer IBM had under development. IBM added further pro-

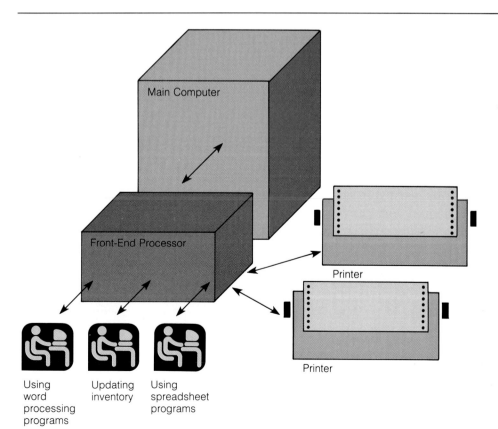

FIGURE 7.5

In a timesharing environment, the front-end processor schedules and controls users' processing requests. The main computer is thus freed up for processing.

gram enhancements to 80-DOS and released the product in 1981 as IBM **PC-DOS** (IBM Personal Computer Disk Operating System). The effect of IBM's entry into the microcomputer marketplace was so strong that users and vendors began to indicate a preference for PC-DOS and its generic equivalent, **MS-DOS** (Microsoft Disk Operating System). The main reason for the popularity was that so many quality software applications were being written to be used with PC-DOS. Today, many of the microcomputers manufactured by IBM still use PC-DOS (some IBM microcomputers use OS/2, which is described shortly). Indeed, DOS is installed on approximately 85% of all the microcomputers in the world.

Many hardware manufacturers package systems software with their microcomputer systems. To package MS-DOS, the hardware manufacturer must enter into an agreement with Microsoft. Microsoft owns the source code for MS-DOS and licenses it to hardware manufacturers for a large fee (many thousands of dollars). The hardware manufacturers make slight adaptations to the code so it will run on their systems, give it a new name, and then supply the documentation for the code. (Microsoft doesn't supply the documentation.) Compaq computer licenses MS-DOS from Microsoft and names it COMPAQ DOS. AT&T, Zenith, AST, Toshiba, and NEC also license MS-DOS from Microsoft and call their versions AT&T DOS, Zenith DOS, AST DOS, Toshiba DOS, and NEC DOS, respectively. The modifications these manufacturers make to MS-DOS are very slight so that software written for MS-DOS will run on any of these manufacturers' machines.

Every year or so, Microsoft releases an updated version of MS-DOS, which includes the same capabilities of the previous version plus a few new ones. Version 4.0 was a major improvement over previous versions in terms of ease of use because it allows users to issue commands by choosing options from a menu (Figure 7.6). Previous versions required the user to know more of the rules associated with using each command. The latest version of MS-DOS is 5.0.

When Microsoft releases an updated version, the hardware manufacturers usually upgrade the version of MS-DOS they are selling with their microcomputers. *When you purchase an applications software package, you must make sure it is compatible with the version of DOS you are using.* Some software applications are compatible only with later versions of DOS. The versions of MS-DOS that the application is compatible with are usually listed on the front of the package that the applications software is sold in. For example, the following text is displayed on the box of the popular disk management program called XTREE, from XTREE Company: "Requires IBM PC, XT, AT, PS/2, or compatible. DOS version 2.0 or higher."

MS-DOS AND WINDOWS

Despite its popularity, the MS-DOS operating system has its limitations. MS-DOS was designed principally to perform a single task for a single user—that is, it can switch back and forth between different applications, but it can't run two or more applications simultaneously. Although it is well suited for microprocessors that have been around for a while (Intel 8088, 8086), it can't fully utilize the capabilities of the more sophisticated microprocessors (Intel 80286, 80386, 80486). In addition, although the 80286 chip is capable of addressing, or using, up to 16 MB of RAM, MS-DOS can use only 640 K. And finally, users often complain that MS-DOS is difficult to use. As a result, Microsoft developed **Microsoft Windows**, which is used in conjunction with MS-DOS to make it easier to use and more powerful.

Windows creates an operating environment that extends the capabilities of DOS. It supports multitasking, which enables users to run more than one application at a time, to easily switch between applications, and to move data between them. Windows also has a memory manager that enables users to use 640 K of conventional RAM and up to 16 MB of extended memory (described in Chapter 3). Windows also provides users with a **graphic(al) user interface (GUI,** pronounced "goo-ey"), which makes IBM-type PCs easier to use (Figure 7.7). These interfaces enable users to select menu options by choosing pictures, called **icons,** that correspond to the appropriate processing option. To use software that

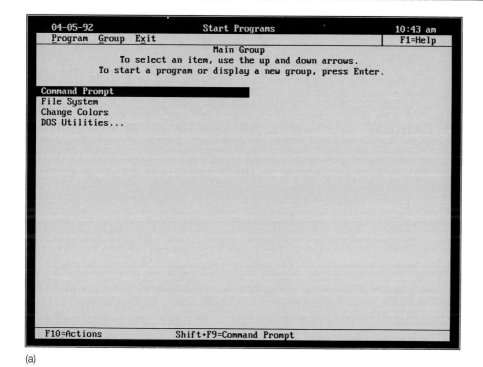

(a)

FIGURE 7.6

(a) DOS 4.0 opening menu; four choices are listed on the left. (In addition, four choices, including Help, are displayed in the menu bar across the top of the screen.) (b) DOS 5.0 screen with a list of directories (categories under which appropriate files are stored). The directories are listed at left ("Directory Tree"), and the DOS directory is highlighted. At right is the beginning of the list of files stored in the DOS directory (which is located on drive C, the hard disk drive).

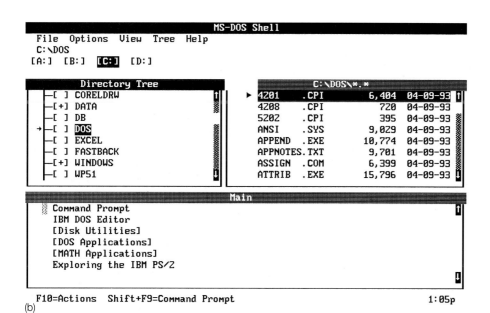

(b)

includes a graphic user interface, users typically use a mouse rather than a keyboard to choose menu options.

To use Windows, you need an 80286 or 80386 PC, a minimum of 640 K of RAM, and 4 MB to 6 MB of free hard disk space. All applications written for Windows have a similar graphic user interface, which makes it easier to learn how to use an application—that is, they all provide the user with a similar structure for choosing commands. Windows systems software is becoming very popular; however, it can extend DOS capabilities only up to a certain limit. Some people are waiting for the perfection of a more powerful systems software—such as OS/2.

OS/2

In 1988, IBM and Microsoft introduced **Operating System/2 (OS/2),** which, like Microsoft Windows, is designed to get around some of the limitations imposed by MS-DOS and to take advantage of today's more sophisticated microprocessors (Intel 80286, 80386, 80486). OS/2 supports multitasking and will allow new software applications to directly address up to 16 MB of RAM. OS/2 is packaged with a graphic user interface that is similar to the GUI used in Microsoft Windows. (Microsoft was, but is no longer, involved in the development of the GUI for OS/2.)

Compared to MS-DOS and Windows, OS/2 is much more powerful. Because of the many instructions that make up OS/2 (over 1.5 million bytes' worth), the hardware requirements to support it are greater than those required to support MS-DOS/Windows. To run efficiently, the typical OS/2 machine should use an 80386 microprocessor, run at a minimum of 20 MHz, and be configured with at least 4 MB of RAM and a 60 MB hard disk. OS/2 support can be found in large

---

FIGURE 7.7

Windows' graphic user interface. Most software developed now and in the future will incorporate a graphic user interface that uses many of the components labeled here.

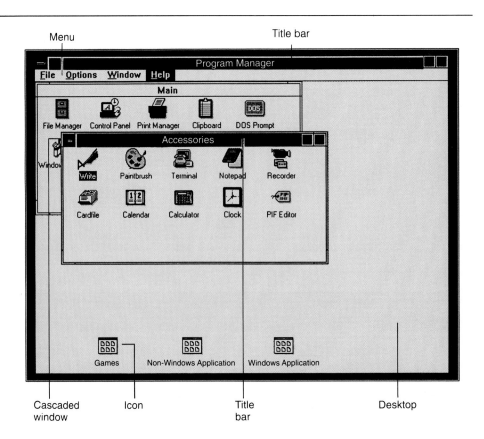

companies that need to support processing tasks with powerful applications written for OS/2. OS/2, with competition from UNIX, is expected to eventually replace MS-DOS as the standard microcomputer operating system. However, there are still very few applications available for the microcomputer user that take advantage of OS/2 systems software.

UNIX

The **UNIX** operating system was developed by Kenneth Thompson at Bell Laboratories, where the earliest version was released in 1971. This operating system was initially created for minicomputers and provides a wide range of capabilities, including virtual memory, multiprogramming, and timesharing. In 1973, the system was rewritten in a high-level language called C, which allowed it to be used on a wider variety of computers, ranging from the largest mainframe computers to some of the more powerful microcomputers. UNIX is a popular operating system in universities where a multiuser (networked) environment is needed to support computer science students, programmers, and researchers.

One of the main advantages of UNIX is that it is a *portable* operating system. That means that it can be used on almost any computer. (DOS cannot be used, for example, on a Macintosh; thus DOS is *machine dependent*, and not portable.) However, there is no UNIX standard, as there is with DOS, so there are several different variations of UNIX and different versions of its graphical user interface. Thus few applications are available for the microcomputer user who wants to use UNIX systems software. However, experts are working on identifying UNIX standards, and software companies are developing UNIX software applications. UNIX may very well be the microcomputer operating system of the future.

MACINTOSH OPERATING SYSTEM

Apple Computer Corporation introduced its popular Apple II personal computer system in the late 1970s. Because the Apple machines were based on entirely different microprocessors than those used in the IBM microcomputers, their operating systems were incompatible and unable to share data and instructions. The disk operating system used on many Apple computers is called *Apple DOS* and is designed to perform a single task for a single user.

A more powerful disk operating system—referred to as the **Macintosh operating system** (Figure 7.8)—was designed to be used on the Apple Macintosh computer (based on the 68030 microprocessor), which supports multitasking. The latest Macintosh operating system is System 7, which supports virtual memory, as well as multitasking; it also includes the Apple File Exchange (AFE) software utility, which allows file transfer between the Macintosh and DOS-based PCs. The Macintosh operating system has a refined, easy-to-use graphic user interface that the Windows environment tries to emulate (copy) for the IBM PC.

Special hardware and software must be purchased to allow Apple computers using the Macintosh operating system to share data with PC-DOS/MS-DOS-based microcomputers and OS/2-based microcomputers.

MAKING YOUR CHOICE

If you ever have to choose a microcomputer, consider carefully the systems software choices available in light of your specific processing needs. There is no right choice for everyone. The choice you make should be determined by:

- Type and quantity of compatible applications software you are interested in
- Ease of use by both users and programmers
- Speed of operation
- Capability to support multitasking and multiuser needs
- Types of compatible hardware you will need
- Availability of trained technical support personnel and manufacturer's hot-line support to help you solve problems using your equipment and software

Table 7.1 reviews the main systems software used with microcomputers.

FIGURE 7.8

This Macintosh operating system screen shows you the directories of files stored on the hard disk ("Mongo-Disk"). Some of the directories are represented by special applications icons, such as the ones for Microsoft Word and PageMaker. Other directories are represented by "file folders," such as the ones for Michael's Work and a Cover Design Class. ["Trash" is used to discard (erase) unwanted files.]

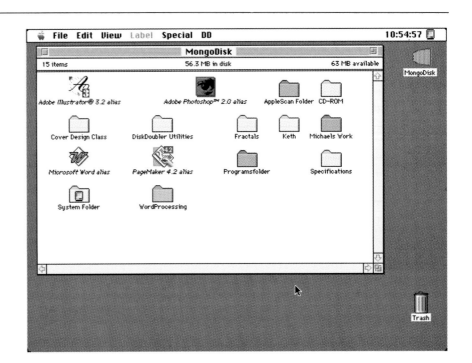

TABLE 7.1

Microcomputer Operating Systems

Processor	Apple DOS	Macintosh Operating System	MS-/PC-DOS	MS-DOS/Windows	OS/2	UNIX
M6502	X					
M68030		X				
Intel 8088			X	X		
8086			X	X		X
80286			X	X	X	X
80386			X	X	X	X
80486			X	X	X	X
Single-user	X		X	X		
Multitasking		X		X	X	X
Multiuser						X
Virtual memory		X		X	X	

If you're a white-collar worker who sits behind a desk—or even sits behind a steering wheel making sales calls on your mobile phone—it's fairly certain you'll be using computer technology.

Consider real estate sales. Century 21, an international organization of independent real estate agents, developed a system called Century Net that helps agents move away from slips of paper and lists in notebooks. Listing agents enter names and properties for sale from several directories. Sales agents list likely prospects. This database can then be used to generate lists of prospective buyers and generate personalized form letters. It can also be used to make telephone contacts: The sales agent enters a name, the computer dials the contact's telephone, and the date and time of the call are displayed on the screen. The system can also be used to generate reminders for important dates or follow-up calls. The use of modem-equipped laptops only expands the possibilities. When calling on prospective clients, agents can use the machines to do investment analysis for customers, comparing loan interest rates and showing how buying a home compares with other forms of investment.

Small investors themselves have also turned to computers for assistance. The old-time way of playing the stock market was to get stock prices from the newspapers, read investment newsletters, and place orders by phone to one's stockbroker. Now, using a computer in his or her home office, an investor can obtain up-to-the-minute stock quotes and, through modem and telephone links, press a button to transmit buy and sell orders to a broker. Some investors use their computers to do complex stock analysis. For instance, AIQ systems distilled the knowledge of several investment experts to devise a series of rules that rate up to 500 stocks on a 1–100, up-or-down scale. When there is a 100 rating on the up side, an investor should definitely buy a stock; the same number on the down side indicates one should sell.

Making money means paying taxes, of course. Many taxpayers turn to tax professionals to prepare their tax returns. Most accountants, however, turn to outside computer services for help with calculations and paperwork. Each year, about 20 service bureaus across the country, such as Computax and Accutax, process millions of tax forms. Accountants collect information from their clients, work out the tax strategy, and then send the numbers to the service bureau, which eliminates a lot of the accountant's most labor-intensive work.

Outside auditors—those analysts who go over company accounts to make sure that accounting principles are being followed, that supplies arrive when ordered, and that vendors' bills are accurate—have found that they are no longer "bean counters." With portable computers they become helpful business advisors, able to spot areas for cutting costs, gathering financial data in hours instead of days, and making essential business decisions by supplying important financial projections, such as those spotting deadbeat customers. For instance, a Peat Marwick auditor performing an annual look at the books for a chain store operator was able to use microcomputers to print out 15 different financing scenarios in one day, thus providing a means for ensuring future operations. ■

COMPUTERS AND CAREERS

COMPUTERS FOR WHITE-COLLAR WORKERS

HOW IS SOFTWARE WRITTEN?

One day at work while tinkering with your database management program on your microcomputer, you suddenly realize you can't make it produce a sales report in just the right format. Or perhaps your spreadsheet won't automatically extract all the right data for a particularly useful analysis of an investment strategy. As new computer users gain more experience, they find it easier to identify areas where software can be modified or created to provide more useful and sophisticated processing capabilities above and beyond those of a purchased package. To obtain custom-made software the user can (1) hire an outside computer specialist to develop it; (2) ask the firm's computer specialists to do it; or (3) go it alone. Regardless of the approach you take, you need to understand the process by which software is developed and be familiar with the tools available for you to use.

In addition, users need to understand the programming process so that they can effectively communicate with the programmers who are creating software for them. If users can't specify their requirements effectively, they may end up with software they are not happy with.

Because the topics of software programming and software languages are the subjects of entire courses, the following sections can offer only the basic principles that users should be familiar with.

WHAT TOOLS ARE AVAILABLE FOR DEVELOPING SOFTWARE?

Just as many tools exist for building a house, many tools are available for creating, or writing, software. These tools comprise different types of programming languages—high-level languages—each of which consists of a number of different commands that are used to describe the type of processing to be done, such as multiplying two numbers together. In short, programming languages are used to write detailed sets of instructions that enable the user to process data into information in an appropriate manner.

Software development tools can best be categorized as falling into one of five generations of programming languages (Figure 7.9). The languages in each successive generation represent an improvement over those of the prior generation—just as the electric saw was an improvement over the manual one. Languages of later generations are easier to learn than earlier ones, and they can produce results (software) more quickly and more reliably. But just as a builder might need to use a manual saw occasionally to cut a tricky corner, professional programmers still need to use some early-generation languages to create software.

Compared with later generations, the early-generation programming languages (first, second, and third) require the use of more complex vocabulary and syntax to write software; they are therefore used primarily by computer professionals. The term **syntax** refers to the precise rules and patterns required for the formation of the programming language sentences, or statements, that tell the computer what to do and how to do it. Programmers must use a language's syntax—just as you would use the rules of German grammar, not French, to communicate in German—to write a program in that language. Because more efficient software development tools are available, programmers don't create software using machine language anymore, and few use assembly language, except for programs with special processing requirements. However, third-generation languages are still in wide use today.

Fourth-generation languages still require the user to employ a specific syntax, but the syntax is easy to learn. In fact, fourth-generation programming languages are so much easier to use than those of prior generations that the noncomputer professional can create software after about a day of training.

Natural languages—currently under development—constitute the fifth generation of languages. With this type of language, the user will be able to specify processing procedures using statements similar to idiomatic human speech—simple statements in English (or French, German, Japanese, and so on). The use of natural language will not require the user to learn a specific syntax.

In addition to the five generations of programming languages, some microcomputer software packages (such as electronic spreadsheet and database management software) are widely used for creating software. Although these packages generally cannot be categorized into one of the five generations, many people consider some of the database management systems software used on microcomputers, such as dBASE IV, as belonging to the fourth-generation category.

WHICH TOOLS ARE YOU MOST LIKELY TO USE?

The decision about which software development tool to use depends on what processing procedures you need to perform. Developing software is like building a house: The work will go much faster if you have a plan and the right tools. However, the tools have little value if you don't know how to use them; consequently, one of the most important steps toward effective and efficient software development is the selection of the right development tool.

If you become a computer specialist, you will need to learn to use the most popular of the third-generation programming languages because much of the available applications software is based on them. In other words, the software that you

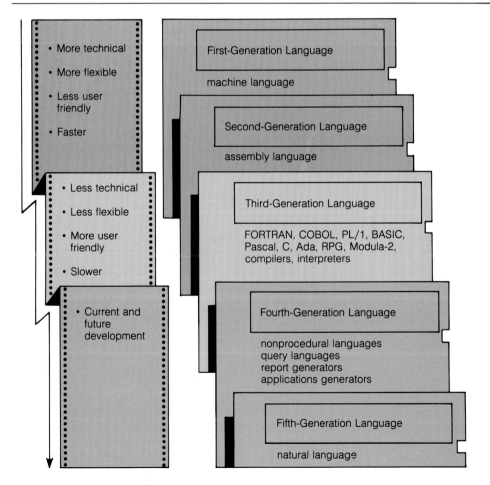

FIGURE 7.9

The five generations of programming languages

buy off the shelf of a computer store has been created by a computer specialist using one of these languages. Also, computer specialists need to know how to use these languages in order to update, or maintain, this existing software to accommodate new processing and output requirements.

For the user who is not a computer specialist, the most popular tools for developing software will be the fourth-generation programming languages and existing off-the-shelf software packages such as electronic spreadsheets and database management systems software, because one does not have to be an experienced computer professional to use them. The user who is working with these tools can create specialized software applications—for example, to keep track of a company's expenses by department (a good application for a spreadsheet package) or to maintain a customer file used in a clothing store for billing, marketing, and checking customer credit status (a good application for a database package).

FIRST AND SECOND GENERATIONS

All higher-level language instructions are converted into machine-language form—*first-generation language*—before they can be carried out by the computer. *Machine-language* instructions and data are represented by binary digits (a series of 1s and 0s corresponding to on and off electrical states). Because the specific format and content of the instructions vary according to the architecture of each type of computer, machine-language programs can be run only on the type of computer for which they were designed; that is, they are machine dependent.

The first step in making software development easier and more efficient was the creation of *assembly languages*, also known as *second-generation languages*. (Some people consider them to be the first low-level languages and place machine language in a separate category.) Assembly languages use symbols as abbreviations for major instructions instead of a long combination of binary digits. This means a programmer can use abbreviations instead of having to remember lengthy binary instruction codes. For example, it is much easier to remember L for Load, A for Add, B for Branch, and C for Compare than the binary equivalents—strings of different combinations of 0s and 1s.

Although assembly languages represented an improvement, they had obvious limitations. They can be used only by those computer specialists familiar with the architecture of the computer being used. And because they are also machine-dependent, assembly languages are not easily converted to run on other types of computers.

THIRD GENERATION

Third-generation languages, also known as **high-level programming languages**, are very much like everyday text and mathematical formulas in appearance. They are designed to run on a number of different computers with few or no changes. Unlike machine and assembly languages, then, many high-level languages are *machine-independent*. Among the most commonly used high-level programming languages are COBOL, FORTRAN, and BASIC. A large number of additional languages have been developed, each with its own strengths. The objectives of high-level languages are

- To relieve the programmer of the detailed and tedious task of writing programs in machine language and assembly language
- To provide programs that can be used on more than one type of machine with very few changes
- To allow the programmer more time to focus on understanding the user's needs and designing the software required to meet those needs

Most high-level languages are considered to be procedure-oriented languages, or **procedural languages,** because the program instructions comprise lists of steps, or procedures, that tell the computer not only *what* to do but *how* to do it. High-level language statements generate, when translated, a comparatively greater number of assembly-language instructions and even more machine-language instructions (Figure 7.10). The programmer spends less time developing software with a high-level language than with assembly or machine language because fewer instructions have to be created.

A language processor is required to convert (translate) a high-level language program into machine language.

The importance of high-level languages was quickly recognized by the computer industry, and substantial human and financial resources were dedicated to their development. By the early 1960s, most computer manufacturers were working on a version of FORTRAN, the first widely used high-level language, for their computers. Various manufacturers' versions of FORTRAN were similar; however, their efforts to make one package better than the others resulted in a number of small differences. The problems associated with resolving these differences led to the realization that industry standards were needed to ensure complete compatibility of high-level language programs with different computers. The task of establishing such standards was turned over to the American Standards Association, and in 1966 the association released the first FORTRAN standards.

Since the late 1960s, the association—now known as the *American National Standards Institute (ANSI)*—worked with the *International Standards Organization (ISO)* to develop, among other things, standards for all high-level programming languages. All versions of programming languages that developers wish to have designated as meeting the standards must accommodate all the commands, syntax, and processing requirements formulated by the ANSI and the ISO.

Following is a list of the most important high-level programming languages.

- FORTRAN (FORmula TRANslator)—designed by IBM for technical and scientific applications

- COBOL (COmmon Business Oriented Language)—designed by the U.S. Department of Defense for business applications and easier to understand than FORTRAN

- PL/1—designed to handle heavy-duty file handling and computation; harder to learn than COBOL

- BASIC (Beginner's All-purpose Symbolic Instruction Code)—designed at

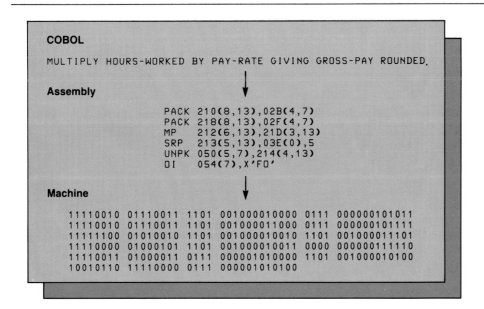

FIGURE 7.10

An example of a statement in COBOL, part of which is first converted to assembly language and then to machine language. As you can see, the high-level (third-generation) language requires few statements to create a large number of machine-language (first-generation) instructions. (T. J. O'Leary and B. K. Williams, *Computers and Information Systems*, 2nd ed. [Redwood City, CA: Benjamin/Cummings, 1989].)

Dartmouth College primarily to teach people how to program; relatively easy to learn but has limited capabilities

- RPG (Report Program Generator)—designed by IBM to help small businesses generate reports and update files easily; programmers fill out predesigned coding forms instead of writing programs entirely from scratch
- C—developed by Bell Laboratories in the early 1970s for use in writing systems software; was used to create most of the UNIX operating system
- Pascal—developed by a Swiss scientist to teach programming according to a predefined structure; is more sophisticated than BASIC
- Modula 2—developed as an improvement of Pascal; may become a popular business applications programming language
- Ada—designed by the U.S. Department of Defense to write and maintain large programs that could be used for any type of application; often used in weapons systems

FOURTH GENERATION

Also known as very-high-level languages, *fourth-generation languages* (4GLs) are as yet difficult to define, because they are defined differently by different vendors; sometimes these languages are tied to a software package produced by the vendor, such as a database management system. Basically 4GLs are easier for programmers—and users—to handle than third-generation languages. Fourth-generation languages are **nonprocedural languages,** so named because they allow programmers and users to specify *what* the computer is supposed to do without having to specify *how* the computer is supposed to do it, which, as you recall, must be done with third-generation, high-level (procedural) languages. Consequently, fourth-generation languages need approximately one tenth the number of statements that a high-level language needs to achieve the same result.

Because they are so much easier to use than third-generation languages, fourth-generation languages allow users, or noncomputer professionals, to develop certain types of applications software. It is likely that, in the business environment, you will at some time use a fourth-generation language. Five basic types of language tools fall into the fourth-generation language category: (1) query languages, (2) report generators, (3) applications generators, (4) decision support systems and financial planning languages, and (5) some microcomputer applications software.

Query languages allow the user to ask questions about, or retrieve information from, database files by forming requests in human-language statements (such as English). Query languages have a specific grammar, vocabulary, and syntax that must be mastered (like third-generation languages), but doing so is usually a simple task for both users and programmers. For example, a manager in charge of inventory may key in the following question to get information from a database:

```
How many items in inventory have a quantity-on-hand that is less than
the reorder point?
```

The query language will do the following to retrieve the information:

1. Copy the data for items with quantity-on-hand that is less than the reorder point into a temporary location in main memory
2. Sort the data into order by inventory number
3. Present the information on the video display screen (or printer)

The manager now has the information necessary to proceed with reordering certain low-stock items. The important thing to note is that the manager didn't have to specify *how* to get the job done, only *what* needed to be done. In other words, in our example, the user needed only to specify the question for the system to automatically perform each of the three steps listed above.

Report generators are similar to query languages in that they allow users to ask questions of a database and retrieve information from it for a report (the output); however, in the case of a report generator, the user is unable to alter the contents of the database file. And with a report generator, the user has much greater control over what the output (or the result of a query) will look like. The user of a report generator can specify that the software automatically determine how the output should look or can create his or her own customized output reports using special report-generator command instructions.

Applications generators—as opposed to query languages and report generators, which allow the user to specify only output-related processing tasks (and some input-related tasks, in the case of query languages)—allow the user to reduce the time it takes to *design* an entire software application that accepts input, ensures data has been input accurately, performs complex calculations and processing logic, and outputs information in the form of reports. Applications generators basically consist of prewritten modules—or program "building blocks"—that comprise fundamental routines that most programs use—such as blocks to read, write, compare records, and so on. These modules, usually written in a high-level language, constitute a "library" of routines to choose from. The user must key into computer-usable form the specifications for *what* the program is supposed to do. The resulting specification file is input to the applications generator, which determines *how* to perform the tasks and which then produces the necessary instructions for the software program.

Decision support systems and *financial planning languages* combine special interactive computer programs and some special hardware to allow high-level managers to bring data and information together from different sources and manipulate it in new ways—for example, to make projections, do "what if" analyses, and make long-term planning decisions.

Some *microcomputer applications software* can also be used to create specialized applications—in other words, to create new software. Microcomputer software packages that fall into this category include many spreadsheet programs (such as Lotus 1-2-3), database managers (such as dBASE IV), and integrated packages (such as Framework). For example, in a business without computers, to "age" accounts receivable (to penalize people with overdue account balances), someone has to manually calculate how many days have passed between the invoice date and the current date and then calculate the appropriate penalty based on the balance due. This can take hours of work. However, with an electronic spreadsheet package, in less than half an hour the user can create an application that will calculate accounts receivable automatically. And the application can be used over and over.

Another example of microcomputer software that is used to create new programs is HyperCard for the Macintosh (Chapter 6). In general, this package is a database management program that allows users to store, organize, and manipulate text and graphics, but it is also a "programmable program" that uses the programming language called *HyperTalk* to allow ordinary users to create customized software by following the "authoring" instructions that come with the package.

FIFTH GENERATION
Natural languages represent the next step in the development of programming languages—*fifth-generation languages*. Natural language is similar to query language, with one difference: It eliminates the need for the user or programmer to learn a specific vocabulary, grammar, or syntax. The text of a natural-language statement very closely resembles human speech. In fact, one could word a statement in several ways—perhaps even misspelling some words or changing the order of the words—and get the same result. Natural language takes the user one step farther away from having to deal directly and in detail with computer hardware and software. These languages are also designed to make the computer

"smarter"—that is, to simulate the human learning process. Natural languages already available for microcomputers include Clout, Q&A, and Savvy Retriever (for use with databases) and HAL (Human Access Language) for use with Lotus 1-2-3.

The use of natural language touches on *expert systems*, computerized collections of the knowledge of many human experts in a given field, and *artificial intelligence*, independently smart computer systems—two topics that are receiving much attention and development and will continue to do so in the future. (These topics are covered in detail in Chapter 11).

SUMMARY

- Systems software tells the computer how to use the hardware in general, and it allows you to interact with the computer.

- Systems software comprises a large number of instructions, which include internal command instructions, external command instructions, and language processors.

- *Internal command instructions* are loaded into RAM when you turn on your computer. They direct and coordinate other types of software and the computer hardware.

- *External command instructions* are general-purpose operating system instructions that aren't needed to run applications software; instead, they are often used to perform "housekeeping tasks," such as backing up data that is stored on a disk.

- The *supervisor* portion of the *operating system* (that is, internal and external command instructions) controls all the programs in the computer, including managing the use of RAM and managing files stored on disk.

- Programmers often write programs using *high-level programming languages* because it is too time-consuming to write programs in machine language. Because microprocessors can understand only programs written in machine language, *language processors* are used to convert high-level instructions into machine language before the software can be used.

- Popular high-level (third-generation) programming languages include:
FORTRAN	BASIC	Pascal
COBOL	RPG	Modula-2
PL/1	C	Ada

- A *compiler* is a language processor that translates an entire high-level language program, referred to as *source code*, into a machine-language version of the program, called the *object code*.

- An *interpreter* is a language translator that converts and executes high-level language instructions, one instruction statement at a time. Programs that have been compiled tend to execute up to five times faster than programs that are interpreted.

- Operating systems that can execute more than one task or program at a time are considered *multitasking*, or *multiprogramming*, operating systems.

- Operating systems that can manage the simultaneous execution of programs are considered *multiprocessing* operating systems.

- The processing requirements of an operating system with *timesharing* capabilities are great. A timesharing computer system supports many user stations or terminals simultaneously.

- The operating systems for microcomputers that are given the most attention are MS-DOS, MS-DOS/Windows, OS/2, UNIX, and the Macintosh operating system.

- *MS-DOS* was designed for a single user to perform one task at a time. It is a very popular operating system because so many applications programs have been written to be used with it.

- *Microsoft Windows* was developed to be used with MS-DOS to take advantage of more sophisticated microprocessors, including the 80286 and the 80386 chips. Microsoft Windows provides users with a *graphic user interface*, allows users to multitask, and allows users to address up to 16 MB of extended memory.

- *Operating System/2 (OS/2)* is designed to get around some of the limitations imposed by MS-DOS. It supports multitasking and will allow new software applications to directly address up to 16 MB of RAM. OS/2 also includes a graphic user interface. OS/2, with competition from UNIX, is expected to eventually replace MS-DOS as the standard microcomputer operating system.

- The *UNIX* operating system provides a wide range of capabilities, including virtual memory, multiprogramming, and timesharing. It is a popular operating system in universities where a multiuser environment is often needed. However, until UNIX standards are developed, few microcomputer applications using UNIX will be introduced.

- The *Macintosh operating system* was designed to be used on the Apple Macintosh computer. This operating system supports multitasking.

- Determining what operating system to use on your microcomputer depends on a number of factors, which include:
  1. Type and quantity of compatible applications software you are interested in
  2. Ease of use
  3. Speed of operation
  4. Capability of supporting multitasking and multiuser needs
  5. Capability of being used with other hardware (compatibility)
  6. Availability of technical and hotline support

KEY TERMS

booting, p. 158
compiler, p. 160
control program,
  p. 159
disk operating system
  (DOS), p. 163
external command
  instructions, p. 159
front-end processor,
  p. 162
graphic(al) user
  interface, p. 165
high-level
  programming
  language, p. 159, 172
icon, p. 165

internal command
  instructions, p. 158
interpreter, p. 160
language processor,
  p. 159
Macintosh operating
  system, p. 167
Microsoft Windows,
  p. 164
MS-DOS, p. 164
multiprocessing, p. 162
multiprogramming,
  p. 161
multitasking, p. 161
nonprocedural language,
  p. 174

object code, p. 159
operating system,
  p. 158
Operating System/2
  (OS/2), p. 166
PC-DOS, p. 164
procedural language,
  p. 172
source code, p. 159
supervisor, p. 159
syntax, p. 170
timesharing, p. 162
translator, p. 159
UNIX, p. 167

EXERCISES

SELF-TEST

1. _____ command instructions are automatically loaded into RAM from disk when you turn on the microcomputer.

2. The supervisor portion of the operating system is always stored on disk. (true/false)

3. _____ _____ are used to convert high-level language instructions into machine language.

4. _____ command instructions take care of what many people refer to as "housekeeping tasks."

5. The Macintosh operating system and Windows for the PC both use pictures called _____ to represent processing functions.

6. A computer system that includes timesharing capabilities uses a computer called a _____ _____ to schedule and communicate to the main computer all the user requests and data entering the system from the terminals.

7. _____ programs tend to execute much faster than programs that have been interpreted.

8. The graphic user interface used with MS-DOS is called _____ _____.

9. All programs must be converted into machine language before they can be used by a computer. (true/false)

10. MS-DOS is a multiprocessing operating system. (true/false)

11. List four points you should consider before choosing an operating system to use on your computer.
    a. _____   b. _____   c. _____   d. _____

12. UNIX, initially created for minicomputers, provides a wide range of capabilities, including virtual memory, multiprogramming, and timesharing. (true/false)

13. MS-DOS was developed to be used by a single user performing one task at a time. (true/false)

14. The _____ is a language processor that converts and executes high-level language instructions, one instruction statement at a time.

15. COBOL is a high-level language used to write business applications software. (true/false)

16. A _____ computer system supports many user stations or terminals simultaneously; in other words, the users share time on the computer based on assigned time slices.

17. The operating system used on Macintosh computers is identical to that used on IBM microcomputers. (true/false)

18. List three tasks that the supervisor of the operating system might perform.
    a. _____   b. _____   c. _____

19. A _____ operating system can execute more than one task or program at a time.

20. Microsoft Windows makes using MS-DOS easier to use by means of a _____ user interface.

SOLUTIONS   (1) internal; (2) false; (3) language processors; (4) external; (5) icons; (6) front-end processor; (7) compiled; (8) Microsoft Windows; (9) true; (10) false; (11) ease of use, speed of operation, type and quantity of compatible applications software, capability to support multitasking and compatible hardware, technical and hotline support; (12) true; (13) true; (14) interpreter; (15) true; (16) timesharing; (17) false; (18) coordinate processing, manage RAM, manage files stored on disk, allocate use of peripheral devices, check equipment malfunction; (19) multitasking or multiprogramming; (20) graphic

SHORT ANSWER

1. Why does a microcomputer user need systems software?
2. What is an icon, and why is it relevant when discussing operating systems?
3. Why are language processors used?
4. What does the term *booting* mean?
5. What is the high-level programming language often used in colleges to teach programming?
6. What are some differences between MS-DOS and OS/2?
7. What is the operating system most commonly used on microcomputers today? Which type of microcomputer uses it?
8. What is the difference between multitasking and multiprocessing?
9. What types of tasks does the operating system supervisor typically perform?
10. What is the difference between internal and external command instructions?

PROJECTS

1. Use current computer publications to research the use of OS/2 in the business environment. On what types of computers is it being used? What types of businesses are using it? Is it easy to use? What do you think the future is for OS/2? How does the use of OS/2 compare to that of UNIX?
2. Use current computer publications to research the use of UNIX in the business environment. On what types of computers is it being used? What types of businesses are using it? Is it easy to use? What do you think the future is for UNIX? How does the use of UNIX compare to that of OS/2?
3. Go to a large computer store and find out how many microcomputers (and what types) run on which operating systems—MS-DOS, MS-DOS/Windows, OS/2, UNIX, Macintosh operating system, System 7. Ask the salesperson for his or her opinion about which disk operating system is the most powerful and flexible. Ask why.
4. Pen-based computing (Chapter 2) uses its own particular type of systems software. Check some articles in computer magazines to find out what makes this type of systems software different from regular microcomputer systems software. Is pen-based systems software compatible with DOS? How would pen-based systems software limit a traditional microcomputer user?
5. Apple Computer, Inc., has recently introduced At Ease, a software package intended to make the Mac easier to use. This software acts as an extension to System 7, the newest Macintosh operating system software. Obtain a brochure and other information from Apple or from a computer supply store and give a short report on exactly how At Ease makes the Mac easier to use.
6. Apple Computer, Inc., has assembled a secret team of at least 100 programmers on a software product code-named "Pink." This new systems software—still uncompleted—is being designed to run on everything from a laptop to a mainframe and on all types of microcomputers. Research this topic and write a short report on the expected completion date of Pink. What implications would this type of systems software have for microcomputer manufacturers? for applications software package developers? Would users be able to run existing applications software using Pink?

CHAPTER 8

COMMUNICATIONS AND NETWORKING FUNDAMENTALS

Getting from here to there has always fascinated human beings—going farther and doing it faster. Aside from the thrills associated with speed, going places quickly means being able to stay connected with other people, to spread news and information and receive them in return—in other words, to *communicate*. Obviously, technology reached the point some time ago of allowing communication to occur without having to transport people from one place to another. But what about more recent developments? And what do they have to do with computers in business and the management of data and information? This chapter will explain how electronic data communications affects the business user.

PREVIEW

When you have completed this chapter, you will be able to:

Identify the basic characteristics of data transmission

Describe basic communications hardware in general terms

Explain what a communications network is, and describe the typical network configurations

List some of the communications services available to microcomputer users

Describe the basic operation and uses of a fax machine

Briefly explain what computer viruses are and what can be done about them

CHAPTER OUTLINE

Why Is This Chapter Important?

Characteristics of Data Transmission
    Analog and Digital Signals
    Asynchronous and Synchronous Transmission
    Simplex, Half-Duplex, and Full-Duplex Traffic

Data Transmission Media
    Telephone Lines
    Coaxial Cable
    Microwave Systems
    Satellite Systems
    Fiber Optics

Data Communications Hardware
    Modems
    Multiplexers, Concentrators, and Controllers
    Front-End Processors
    Protocols and Protocol Converters

Data Communications Software

Communications Networks: Connectivity
    Network Configurations

Communications Services, Systems, and Utilities
    Public Databanks/Information Services
    Electronic Shopping
    Electronic Bulletin Boards
    Electronic Mail
    Electronic Banking and Investing

Computer Viruses

Facsimile (Fax)

Summary

Key Terms

Exercises

No longer should microcomputers be thought of as stand-alone machines—that is, independent systems working each on its own. Indeed, industry observers predict that more than 60% of all microcomputers in business will be connected to a local area network in the next five years. **Networking**—or the connecting of computers and other hardware peripherals so they can share hardware, software, and data resources—has for the past few years been a popular topic in computer magazines. In fact, just about the hottest new topic these days is **digital convergence**—the merger of the computer, communications, and the consumer electronics and entertainment industries so that all manner of devices exchange data and information in the digital format understood by computers.

Microcomputers can communicate with, or be networked to, other computers located in the same proximity (locality) or in a remote location. The communication requirements in terms of hardware and software depend on where the computers are located. For example, if you want to communicate between computers at the same location, you need a length of cable to establish a link between computers. However, if you want to communicate between computers at remote locations, you need to have access to a telephone line or other transmission capability and special communications software on line at both the sending and receiving locations.

You will encounter innumerable situations in the business environment that require data to be sent to, retrieved from, or shared among different locations. For example, you might:

- Send electronic "mail" to another user in the company or to a business contact anywhere in the world—and receive electronic mail on your own computer.
- Send your computer files over telephone lines to another user.
- Share the same database management software and database with other users.
- Share hardware such as printers and secondary storage devices with other users.
- Share processing power—such as a company mainframe—with other users.
- Access data in a huge commercial subscription database on almost any subject, using your own computer equipment and telephone lines.
- Participate in teleconferences or multimedia conferences with people scattered around the world.
- Order equipment or travel services simply by using your computer.
- Schedule meetings automatically by instructing your computer to consult with other users' computers.

When a company establishes an in-house network or expands an existing network, user input is vital. It is therefore an advantage to have an understanding of networks and communication technology so that your needs are met.

CHARACTERISTICS OF DATA TRANSMISSION

When you are talking on the phone with another person who is a few houses away, you can probably hear that person clearly and do not need to speak loudly. However, sometimes the farther away you are from the person, the harder it is to hear clearly what is being said on the phone because of static and other noise. A lot of noise increases the chance that parts of your message will be garbled or misheard. This same problem can exist when data is transmitted over phone lines from computer to computer. Although alternative transmission methods and media have been developed that lessen noise problems, including satellite and microwave, they are not without their own limitations, as you will see later on. But before we discuss the various methods of data communications, we need to discuss their common characteristics.

ANALOG AND DIGITAL SIGNALS

When we speak, we transmit continuous sound waves, or **analog signals** (Figure 8.1), that form what we call the voice. Analog signals could be compared to a fairly steady stream of water coming out of a garden hose. These signals form a single, continuous wave that fluctuates a certain number of times over a certain time period—called the **frequency,** which is measured in cycles per second, or *hertz.* Sometimes our voices sound high (composed of high-frequency sound waves: many wave fluctuations per second), and sometimes our voices sound low (composed of low-frequency sound waves: fewer wave fluctuations per second). Analog signals can also differ in **amplitude,** or loudness; a soft voice is at low amplitude. Most telephone lines are currently an analog communications medium.

In contrast to human voices, computer communication uses **digital signals,** which can be compared to the short bursts of water that shoot out of a timed garden sprinkler. These signals are discontinuous (discrete) pulses over a transmission medium (Figure 8.1). Computers communicate with each other in streams of binary digits (bits) transmitted in patterns of digital signals—series of on and off electrical (or light) pulses. For data to travel from one computer to another across the phone lines, the sending computer's digital data must first be converted into analog form and then reconverted into digital form at the receiving end. This process is called *modulation* and *demodulation.*

Modulation converts digital signals into analog form so that data can be sent over the phone lines. **Demodulation** converts the analog signals back into digital form so that they can be processed by the receiving computer. The hardware that

---

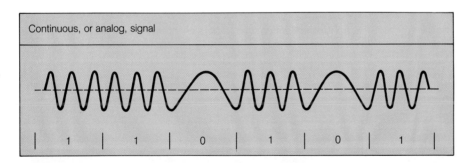

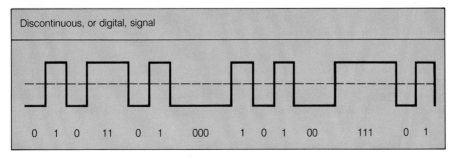

FIGURE 8.1

Analog and digital signals. Analog signals are continuous waves whose patterns vary to represent the message being transmitted; digital signals are discontinuous, or discrete, bursts that form a transmission pattern. In this figure, the horizontal axis represents time and the vertical axis represents amplitude.

performs modulation and demodulation is called a **modem** (*modulate/demodulate*). The sending computer must be connected to a modem that modulates the transmitted data, while the receiving computer must be connected to a modem to demodulate the data (Figure 8.2). Both modems are connected to the telephone line.

ASYNCHRONOUS AND SYNCHRONOUS TRANSMISSION

When signals are transmitted through modems from one computer to another, patterns of bits coded to represent data are sent one bit at a time. How does the receiving device know where one character ends and another starts? In **asynchronous transmission,** also called *start-stop transmission,* each string of bits that make up a character is bracketed by control bits (start and stop bits) (Figure 8.3a). In effect, each group of digital or analog signals making up the code for one character is individually "wrapped" in an electronic "envelope" made of a start bit (often symbolized by a 0), an error check bit (or parity bit), and one or two stop bits (often symbolized by a 1). The error check bit is set according to a parity scheme that can be odd or even.

For example, using an even parity scheme, an ASCII G would be represented as 00100011101, per Figure 8.3. The first 0 is the start bit and the last 1 is the stop bit. The nine bits in between are used to represent the code for the character and the parity scheme. In this case, the tenth bit (the parity bit) has been set to 0 to denote an even parity scheme. If an odd parity scheme is being used, then the parity bit (the tenth bit) would be set so that the number of characters between the start and stop bits in the on position would be odd—00100011111.

Users of both the sending and receiving computers must agree on the parity scheme. The scheme chosen is set within a communications software program. For example, if computer A is transmitting to computer B, the users of both computers must first agree on a parity scheme (perhaps by having a telephone conversation), then load the communications software, and choose the agreed-on parity scheme by choosing the appropriate software option. It doesn't matter which scheme is chosen as long as both computers are using the same one—odd or even.

Because asynchronous communication is inexpensive, it is widely used with microcomputers; however, it is also relatively slow, because of the number of parity

---

FIGURE 8.2

Modems are hardware devices that translate digital signals into analog waves for transmission over phone lines and then back into digital signals again for processing.

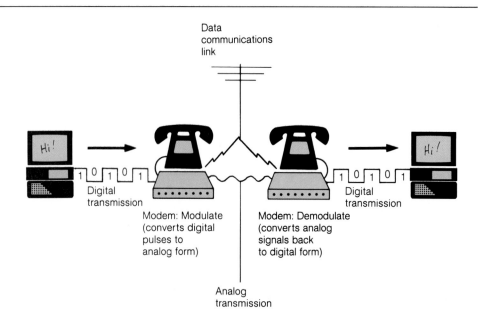

Data communications link

Digital transmission

Modem: Modulate (converts digital pulses to analog form)

Modem: Demodulate (converts analog signals back to digital form)

Digital transmission

Analog transmission

and error check bits that must be transmitted with the data bits.

In **synchronous transmission** (Figure 8.3b), characters can be sent much faster because they are sent as blocks, or "packets." Header and trailer bytes are inserted as identifiers at the beginnings and the ends of blocks. In addition, error check bits are transmitted before the trailer bytes. Synchronous transmission is used by large computers to transmit huge volumes of data at high speeds. Expensive and complex timing devices must be used to keep the transmission activities synchronized. Synchronous transmission is rarely used in microcomputer-based communications lines.

SIMPLEX, HALF-DUPLEX, AND FULL-DUPLEX TRAFFIC

Besides signal type (analog or digital) and manner of data transmission (synchronous or asynchronous), data communications technology must also consider the *direction* of data traffic flow supported by communications links such as modems. In the **simplex** mode, data can travel in only one direction at all times (Figure 8.4). For example, in some museum settings, environmental devices send information about temperature, humidity, and other conditions to a computer that monitors and adjusts office environmental settings automatically. However, the computer does not send information back to the devices. The simplex mode is used occasionally in some local area networks, which we will discuss later.

A **half-duplex** communications link can support two-way traffic, but data can travel in only one direction at one time (Figure 8.4). This mode of transmission is similar to using a walkie-talkie. When you press the transmit button you can talk, but you cannot receive. After you release the transmit button, you can receive, but you cannot transmit. Transmission of data in this mode over long distances can greatly increase the time it takes to communicate data. This delay

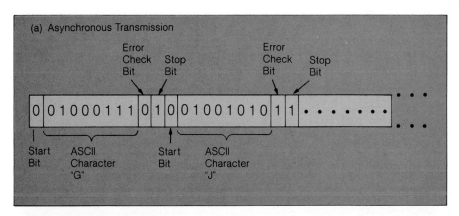

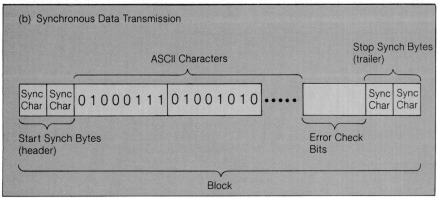

FIGURE 8.3

Asynchronous and synchronous transmission. So that devices receiving data transmission can decode the beginnings and ends of data strings and check for transmission errors, the character strings are transmitted asynchronously or synchronously. Synchronous transmission takes less time because groups of characters are transmitted as blocks with no start and stop bits between characters.

is due to three factors: (1) the time needed for device A (at the receiving end) to change from receive to transmit mode, (2) the time required for device A to transmit to device B a request for confirmation that all is ready for transmission, and (3) the time required for device A to receive the confirmation that device B is ready to receive. The half-duplex transmission mode is frequently used for linking microcomputers via telephone lines.

Full-duplex transmission sends data in both directions simultaneously, similar to two trains passing each other in different directions on side-by-side tracks (Figure 8.4). This transmission mode eliminates the problem of transmission delay, but it is more expensive than the other two modes because it requires special equipment. Full-duplex transmission is used primarily for mainframe communications.

DATA TRANSMISSION MEDIA

To get from here to there, data must move *through* something. A telephone line, a cable, or the atmosphere are all transmission *media*, or *channels*. But before the data can be communicated, it must be converted into a form suitable for com-

FIGURE 8.4

Data traffic moves in simplex, half-duplex, or full-duplex modes.

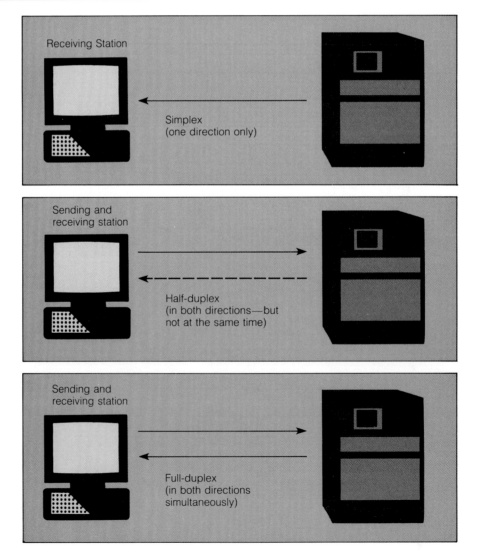

munication. The three basic forms into which data can be converted for communication are as follows:

1. Electronic pulses or charges (used to transmit voice and data over telephone lines)
2. Electromagnetic waves (similar to radio waves)
3. Pulses of light

The form or method of communication affects the maximum rate at which data can be moved through the channel and the level of noise that will exist—for example, light pulses travel faster than electromagnetic waves, and some types of satellite transmission systems are less noisy than transmission over telephone wires. Obviously, some situations require that data be moved as fast as possible; others don't. Channels that move data relatively slowly, like telegraph lines, are *narrowband* channels. Most telephone lines are *voiceband* channels, and they have a wider bandwidth than narrowband channels. *Broadband* channels (like coaxial cable, fiber-optic cable, microwave circuits, and satellite systems) transmit large volumes of data at high speeds.

The transmission media used to support data transmission are telephone lines, coaxial cables, microwave systems, satellite systems, and fiber-optic cables. Understanding how these media function will help you sort out the various rates and charges for them and determine which is the most appropriate in a given situation.

TELEPHONE LINES

The earliest type of telephone line was referred to as *open wire*—unsheathed copper wires strung on telephone poles and secured by glass insulators. Because it was uninsulated, this type of telephone line was highly susceptible to electromagnetic interference; the wires had to be spaced about 12 inches apart to minimize the problem. Although open wire can still be found in a few places, it has almost entirely been replaced with cable and other types of communications media.

Cable is insulated wire. Insulated pairs of wires twisted around each other—called *twisted-pair cable*—can be packed into bundles of a thousand or more pairs (Figure 8.5). These wide-diameter cables are commonly used as telephone lines today and are often found in large buildings and under city streets. Even though this type of line is a major improvement over open wire, it still has many limitations. Twisted-pair cable is susceptible to a variety of types of electrical interference (noise), which limits the practical distance that data can be transmitted without being garbled. (To be received intact, digital signals must be "refreshed," or strengthened, every 1 to 2 miles through the use of an amplifier and related circuits, which together are called *repeaters*. Although repeaters do increase the signal strength, which tends to weaken over long distances, they can be very expensive.) Twisted-pair cable has been used for years for voice and data transmission; however, newer, more advanced media are replacing it.

COAXIAL CABLE

More expensive than twisted-pair wire, **coaxial cable** (also called *shielded cable*) is a type of thickly insulated copper wire (Figure 8.5) that can carry a larger volume of data—about 100 million bits per second, or about 1,800 to 3,600 voice calls at once. The insulation is composed of a nonconductive material covered by a layer of woven wire mesh and heavy-duty rubber or plastic. Coaxial cable is similar to the cable used to connect your TV set to a cable TV service. Coaxial cables can also be bundled together into a much larger cable. This type of communications line has become very popular because of its capacity and reduced need for signals to be refreshed (every 2 to 4 miles). Coaxial cables are most often used as the primary communications medium for locally connected networks in which all computer communication is within a limited geographic area, such as in the same building. Computers connected by coaxial cable do not need to use modems. Coaxial cable is also used for undersea telephone lines.

MICROWAVE SYSTEMS

Instead of using wire or cable, **microwave** systems use the atmosphere as the medium through which to transmit signals. These systems are extensively used for high-volume as well as long-distance communication of both data and voice in the form of electromagnetic waves similar to radio waves but in a higher frequency range.

Microwave signals are often referred to as "line of sight" signals because they cannot bend around the curvature of the earth; instead, they must be relayed from point to point by microwave towers, or relay stations, placed 20 to 30 miles apart (Figure 8.6). The distance between the towers depends on the curvature of the surface terrain in the vicinity. The surface of the earth typically curves about 8

FIGURE 8.5

Twisted wire (d) is being phased out as a communications medium by coaxial cable (b, c) and even more sophisticated media such as microwave and fiber optics.

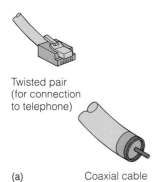

Twisted pair
(for connection
to telephone)

(a)   Coaxial cable   (b)

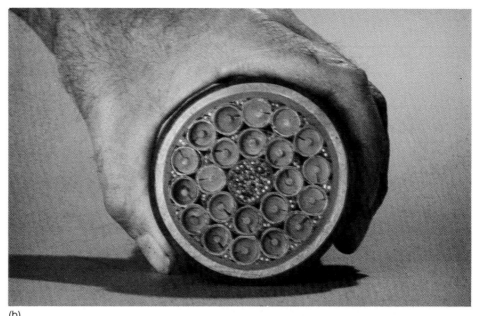

(c)

(d)

inches every mile. The towers have either a dish- or a horn-shaped antenna. The size of the antenna varies according to the distance the signals must cover. A long-distance antenna could easily be 10 feet or larger in size; a disk of 2 to 4 feet in diameter, which you often see on city buildings, is large enough for small distances. Each tower facility receives incoming traffic, boosts the signal strength, and sends the signal to the next station.

The primary advantage of using microwave systems for voice and data communications is that direct physical cabling is not required. (Obviously, telephone lines and other types of cable must physically connect all points in a communications system.) More than one half of the telephone system now uses microwave transmission. However, the saturation of the airwaves with microwave transmissions has reached the point where future needs will have to be satisfied by other communications methods, such as fiber-optic cables or satellite systems.

SATELLITE SYSTEMS

Satellite communications systems transmit signals in the gigahertz range—billions of cycles per second. The satellite must be placed in a geosynchronous orbit, 22,300 miles above the earth's surface, so it revolves once a day with the earth (Figure 8.7). To an observer, it appears to be fixed over one region at all times. A **satellite** is a solar-powered electronic device that has up to 100 transponders (a *transponder* is a small, specialized radio) that receive, amplify, and retransmit signals; the satellite acts as a relay station between satellite transmission stations on the ground (called *earth stations*).

Although establishing satellite systems is costly (owing to the cost of a satellite and the problems associated with getting it into orbit above the earth's surface and compensating for failures), satellite communications systems have become the most popular and cost-effective method for moving large quantities of data over long distances. The primary advantage of satellite communications is the amount

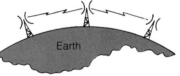

Microwave line-of-sight links

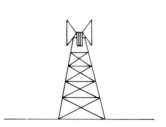

Microwave tower

FIGURE 8.6

Microwave relay station. Microwaves must be relayed from point to point along the earth's surface because they cannot bend.

of area that can be covered by a single satellite. Three satellites placed in particular orbits can cover the entire surface of the earth, with some overlap.

However, satellite transmission does have some problems:

1. The signals can weaken over the long distances, and weather conditions and solar activity can cause noise interference.

2. A satellite is useful for only 7 to 10 years, after which it loses its orbit.

3. Anyone can listen in on satellite signals, so sensitive data must be sent in a secret, or encrypted, form.

FIGURE 8.7

Satellite communications. (a) The satellite orbiting the earth has solar-powered transponders that receive microwave signals from the earth's surface, amplify the signals, and retransmit them to the earth's surface (b). Part (c) illustrates how the various communications media can work together as communications links. (d) AT&T long-distance communications center.

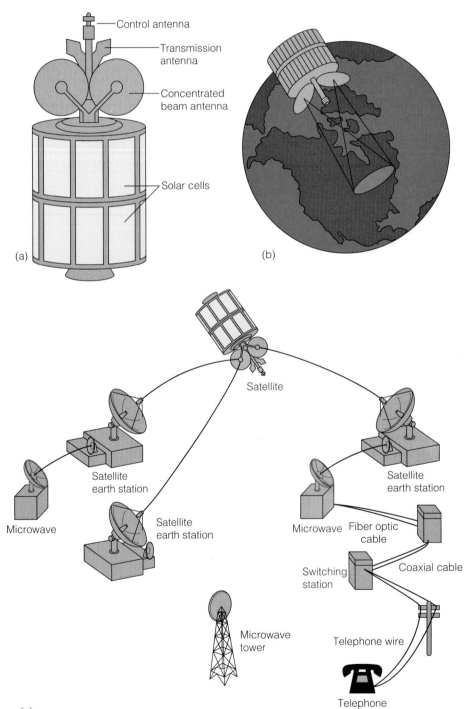

4. Depending on the satellite's transmission frequency, microwave stations on earth can jam, or prevent, transmission by operating at the same frequency.

5. Signal transmission may be slow if the signals must travel over very long distances.

Companies must lease satellite communications time from suppliers such as Westar (Western Union), Telstar (AT&T), Satellite Business Systems (partially owned by IBM), Galaxy (Hughes Aircraft), RCA, Comstar, and the American Satellite Company. Large companies that have offices around the world benefit the most from satellite communications.

FIBER OPTICS

Although satellite systems are expected to be the dominant communications medium for long distances during the 90s, fiber-optics technology is expected to revolutionize the communications industry because of its low cost, high transmission volume, low error rate, and message security. Fiber-optic cables are replacing copper wire as the major communications medium in buildings and cities; major communications companies are currently investing huge sums of money in fiber-optics communications networks that can carry *digital* signals, thus increasing communications and capacity. (Computers connected by fiber-optic cables do not need to use modems.)

In **fiber-optics** communications, signals are converted to light form and fired by laser in bursts through insulated, very thin (2,000ths of an inch) glass or plastic fibers (Figure 8.8). The pulses of light represent the "on" state in electronic data representation and can occur nearly 1 billion times per second—nearly 1 billion bits per second can be sent through a fiber-optic cable. Equally important, fiber-optic cables aren't cumbersome in size: A fiber-optic cable (insulated fibers bound together) that is only 12 inches thick is capable of supporting nearly 250,000 voice conversations at the same time (soon to be doubled to 500,000). However, since

FIGURE 8.7

(*continued*)

(d)

the data is communicated in the form of pulses of light, specialized communications equipment must be used.

Fiber-optic cables are not susceptible to electronic noise and so have much lower error rates than normal telephone wire and cable. In addition, their potential speed for data communications is up to 10,000 times faster than that of microwave and satellite systems. Fiber-optic communications is also very resistant to illegal data theft, because it is almost impossible to tap into it in order to listen to the data being transmitted or to change the data without being detected; in fact, it is currently being used by the Central Intelligence Agency. Another advantage to fiber-optic transmission is that electrical signals don't escape from the cables—in other words, the cables don't interfere with sensitive electrical equipment that may be nearby. Given its significant advantages, it is not surprising that fiber-optic cable is much more expensive than telephone wire and cable.

AT&T has developed undersea optical fiber cables for transatlantic use in the belief that fiber optics will eventually replace satellite communications in terms of cost-effectiveness and efficiency. The Japanese have already laid an underwater fiber-optic cable. Sprint uses a fiber-optic communications network laid along railroad rights-of-way in the United States that carries digital signals (analog voice signals are converted to digital signals at company switching stations).

DATA COMMUNICATIONS HARDWARE

Much of the hardware used in data communications is operated by technical professionals and is rarely of immediate consequence to the user unless it stops working—when you're calling from New York and can't reach your division office in London, for example. However, you should become familiar with certain types of common business communications hardware: modems, which were mentioned briefly in the section on analog and digital signals, multiplexers, concentrators, controllers, front-end processors, and protocol converters.

FIGURE 8.8

Fiber optics. Laser-fired light pulses (representing the "on" state in the binary system of data representation) are fired through very thin glass or plastic fibers.

MODEMS

Modems are probably the most widely used data communications hardware in business. They are certainly the most familiar to microcomputer users who communicate with one another or with a larger computer. As you learned earlier in this chapter, the word **modem** is actually a contraction of *mo*dulate and *dem*odulate. A modem's basic purpose is to convert digital computer signals to analog signals for transmission over phone lines, then to receive these signals and convert them back to digital signals.

A modem allows the user to directly connect the computer to the telephone line (Figure 8.9). Modems transmit and receive data at speeds from 300 to 9,600 or more bits per second (bps). Transmitting a 10-page single-spaced report would take about 20 minutes at 300 bps, about 5 minutes at 1,200 bps, and about 2½ minutes at 2,400 bps.

Modems are either internal or external. An **internal modem** (Figure 8.9) is located on a circuit board that is placed inside a microcomputer (actually plugged

---

FIGURE 8.9

Modems. An internal modem (a) is placed inside the computer; an external modem (b) remains outside the computer. In both cases, the phone remains connected for voice communication when the computer is not transmitting.

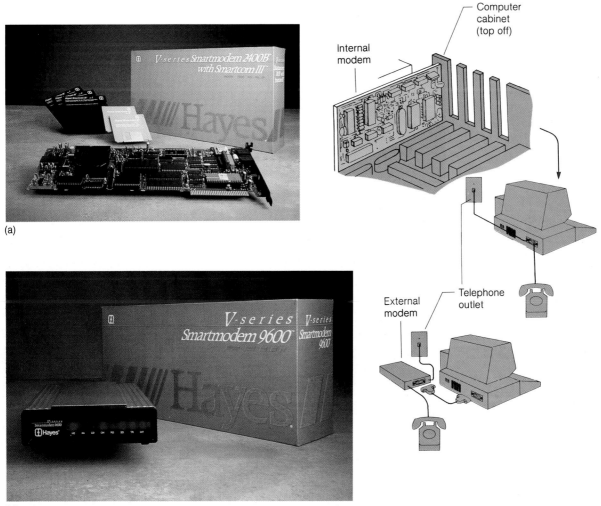

(a)

(b)

into an expansion slot). The internal modem draws its power directly from the computer's power supply. No special cable is required to connect the modem to the computer. An **external** direct-connect **modem** is an independent hardware component—that is, it is outside the computer—and uses its own power supply (Figure 8.9). The modem is connected to the computer via a cable designed for the purpose.

Business users who deal with modems and data communications must be sure they are communicating with compatible equipment. Like other types of computer hardware and software, not all modems work with other modems, and not all modems work with the same type of software. In addition, microcomputer communications software packages—such as ProComm, Smartcom II and III, Crosstalk XVI—require users to set their systems at specific "parameters" so that their microcomputer can "talk" to another computer using the same parameters. Parameters include speed of data transmission, parity scheme, direction of traffic, and so forth. The software package manual tells users how to set software parameters and how to use a small screwdriver to set certain switches, called DIP (dual inline package) switches, in the external modem cabinet. These software packages allow "smart" modems (with certain types of chips) to do more than simply transmit and receive; for example, you can arrange for automatic dialing and transmission, printing of incoming text, and storage of incoming data on disk.

MULTIPLEXERS, CONCENTRATORS, AND CONTROLLERS

When an organization's data communications needs grow, the number of lines available for that purpose often become overtaxed, even if the company has leased one or more private telephone lines—called *dedicated lines*—used only for data communications. *Multiplexing* optimizes the use of communications lines by allowing multiple users or devices to share one high-speed line (Figure 8.10), thereby reducing communications costs. Multiplexing can be done by multiplexers, concentrators, or controllers.

Briefly, a **multiplexer** is a data communications hardware device that allows 8, 16, 32, or more devices (depending on the model) to share a single communications line. Messages sent by a multiplexer must be received by a multiplexer of the same type. The devices differentiate individual messages and direct them to their recipients.

A **concentrator,** which also allows many devices to share a single communications line, is more "intelligent" than a multiplexer because it can be programmed to temporarily store some transmissions and forward them later. It is also used to multiplex low-speed communications lines onto one high-speed line.

A **controller** also supports a group of devices (terminals and printers) connected to a computer. It is used in place of a multiplexer and acts to control functions for the group of terminals.

FRONT-END PROCESSORS

In some computer systems, the main computer is connected directly into the multiplexer, controller, or concentrator. In other systems, it is first hooked to a **front-end processor,** a smaller computer that relieves the larger one of many data traffic management and communications functions (Figure 8.11). In effect, the front-end processor acts as a "mediator" between the network and the main computer, allowing the main computer to concentrate on processing and improving the responsiveness of the system to the user.

PROTOCOLS AND PROTOCOL CONVERTERS

One of the most frustrating aspects of data communications between different types of computers, especially between a microcomputer and a larger computer system, is that they often use different communications protocols. A **protocol** is the formal set of rules for communicating, including rules for timing of message exchanges, the type of electrical connections used by the communications devices, error detection techniques, means of gaining access to communications channels, and so on. To overcome this problem, a specialized type of intelligent multiplexer called a **protocol converter** can be used. Protocol converters are available that even allow a microcomputer operating in asynchronous mode to talk with a large IBM

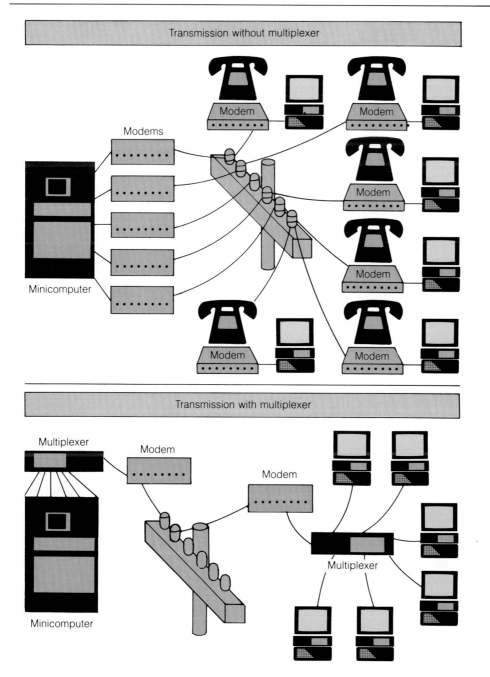

FIGURE 8.10

This figure shows the basic difference between computer communications with and without the use of a multiplexer.

mainframe computer operating in synchronous mode. This type of device is being used by more and more companies that want to establish effective communications between personal computers and the main computer system and with printing devices.

Some groups are working on the establishment of a standard protocol for data transmission. For example, IBM has released the Systems Network Architecture (SNA) for its own machines, and the International Standards Organization (ISO)

FIGURE 8.11

A smaller computer, called a *front-end processor*, is often used to relieve the main computer of many communications functions.

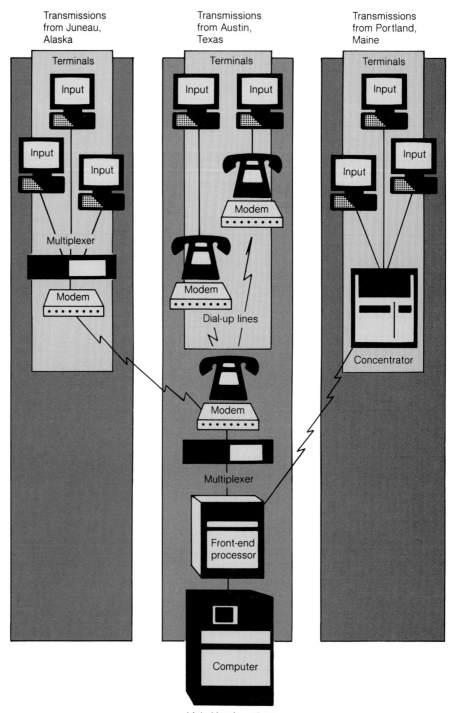

has released its set of protocol standards, called the Open Systems Interconnection (OSI). However, just because standards exist does not mean that they will be used by everyone or that they can be enforced.

ISDN (Integrated Services Digital Network) is a set of standards put out by the Consultative Committee for International Telegraphy and Telephony (CCITT). The ISDN standards are designed to set rules for a worldwide digital communications network that could simultaneously support voice, data, and video traffic over telephone wires (traditionally an analog communications medium). For ISDN to work, users will have to replace their existing telephones with ISDN telephones and insert an ISDN board in their PCs.

DATA COMMUNICATIONS SOFTWARE

Even with the best communications hardware, you won't be able to communicate with another computer without communications software. Most **communications software** packages enable you to perform the basic functions of sending files between computers and communicating with a communications service (communications services, systems, and utilities are described shortly). However, most users have business requirements that extend beyond these basic communications tasks. For example, if you want to transmit data only at night to take advantage of low phone rates, your communications software must provide a strong **script language,** like a programming language, that will enable you to automate this process. The most popular communications packages include Crosstalk, DynaComm, HyperAccess 5, Mirror III, Procomm Plus, Relay Gold, and Smartcom III.

A useful communications package provides a number of capabilities beyond basic communications functions. The package should provide a wide range of communications protocols (described earlier), or sets of rules, that govern the meaningful transfer of data between two or more computers or services. Most communications programs include protocols for communicating with popular communications services such as CompuServe. (Both the sending and receiving party must be using the same protocol in order for data transmission to be successful.) In addition, some communications programs offer protocols that automatically compress a file, or reduce the space it takes up on a storage device, before it is sent, so that the speed of data transmission is lessened. If you often need to send and retrieve complex data such as spreadsheets and programs, make sure your software includes an efficient error-checking protocol.

If you're concerned with speed, make sure your communications software can support sending data at a rate of more than 9,600 bps. In addition, if you want to perform operations on a remote computer, such as downloading a file to another computer, make sure the communications software supports remote control of communications. If most of your communications tasks involve remote communications, purchase a special program that provides more flexibility for communicating remotely.

Of all the communications software features to be familiar with before purchasing a package, the capabilities and ease of use of the script language can be the most critical to users. The script language enables you to save time when performing tasks particular to your needs. For example, before a vacation, you can use the script language to instruct your computer to send and retrieve data a specified number of times when you're gone. In addition, you can program a script language to simplify the task of establishing communication with complex information systems.

Fortunately, much attention has been given in recent years to improving the user interface of most communications packages so that they are easier to use. Now, most include easy menu systems. In addition, the documentation that accompanies communications software has improved. Helpful illustrations and improved writing make it much easier for the first-time user to communicate.

COMMUNICATIONS NETWORKS: CONNECTIVITY

As we have talked about communications media and hardware, we have occasionally referred to communications *networks*. Networks are often used by business workers, and chances are good that you will become acquainted with one or more types of communications networks in your job.

Information and resources gain in value if they can be shared. A **network** is simply a collection of data communications hardware, computers, communications software, and communications media connected in a meaningful way to allow users to share information and equipment. The three most common types of networks are private, public, and international.

A **private network** is specifically designed to support the communications needs of a particular business organization. Many organizations with geographically separated facilities and a need for a large volume of data and voice communications implement or install their own private communications networks. The Southern Pacific Railroad was one of the first organizations to develop its own comprehensive microwave communications network to facilitate communication along all its rail lines. Its microwave towers can be seen along any of the major rail lines.

A **public network,** in contrast, is a comprehensive communications facility designed to provide subscribers (users who pay a fee) with voice and/or data communications over a large geographical area (in some cases coast to coast). Public networks such as Bell Telephone and AT&T Communications are sometimes referred to as *common carriers*. Some public communications networks offer **teleconferencing** services—electronically linking several people by phone, computer, and video (Figure 8.12). Still other communications networks enable users to participate in **multimedia conferences,** during which users can not only see and hear one another but also work on text and graphics projects *at the same time*.

FIGURE 8.12

Teleconferencing. These people are participating in a teleconferencing session. They are connected by voice, video, and computer through public network communications facilities.

The term **international network** is used to describe a communications network specifically designed to provide users with intercontinental voice and data communications facilities. The majority of these networks use undersea cable or satellite communications. Western Union and RCA provide international networks.

NETWORK CONFIGURATIONS

A number of different network configurations, or shapes, are used to satisfy the needs of users in different situations. The basic types of configurations are star (and hierarchical) network, bus network, and ring (and token ring) network. Although each network configuration is actively used today by private, public, and international communications networks, you will most likely come into contact with one in the context of a local area network.

A **local area network (LAN)** is a private communications network, connected by a length of wire, cable, or optical fiber, and run by special networking software that serves a company or part of a company that is often located on one floor or in a single building (Figure 8.13). A LAN is similar to a telephone system: in the latter, any telephone connected to the system can send and receive information; the same principle is true in the former. Any computer hooked up to the network can send and receive information. The LAN is generally owned by the company that is using it.

Chances are that the microcomputer you will use in your office will be part of a local area network. LANs allow office workers to share hardware (such as a laser printer or storage hardware), to share software and data, and to essentially make incompatible units compatible. The LAN also provides a communications link to outside communications systems, and it can be connected to other local area networks in different locations, either by public communications lines or by **dedicated lines**—lines leased by the company for its transmission purposes only. Note that modems are not always needed *within* a local area network; special hardware and software are used instead.

A **metropolitan area network (MAN)** links computer resources that are more widely scattered—such as among office buildings in a city. A **wide area network (WAN)** links resources scattered around the country or the world (Figure 8.14). The communications hardware discussed earlier—modems, multiplexers, and so on—would be used to link various LANs together and to link parts of a MAN or a WAN.

FIGURE 8.13

LAN. One of the world's busiest local area networks is at the Hong Kong Stock Exchange. Of course, such a local network can use communications lines to hook up to networks in other parts of the world.

STAR NETWORK

The **star network**, a popular network configuration, involves a central unit that has a number of terminals tied into it. These terminals are often referred to as *nodes*. This type of network configuration is well suited to companies with one large data processing facility shared by a number of smaller departments. The central unit in the star network acts as the traffic controller between all the nodes in the system. The central unit is usually a host computer or a **file server**. The host computer is a large computer, usually a mainframe. A file server is usually a microcomputer with a large-capacity hard disk storage device that stores shared data and programs. The file server acts as the network's "traffic cop."

The primary advantage of the star network is that several users can use the central unit at the same time—the star is sometimes used to link microcomputers to a central database. However, its main limitation is that the whole network is affected if the main unit "goes down" (fails to function). In this case, since the

FIGURE 8.14   WAN. This wide area communications network was used by CBS to transmit the 1992 Winter Olympics from France to the United States. (Adapted from Don Foley, *The Arizona Republic*, February 16, 1992, p. 33.)

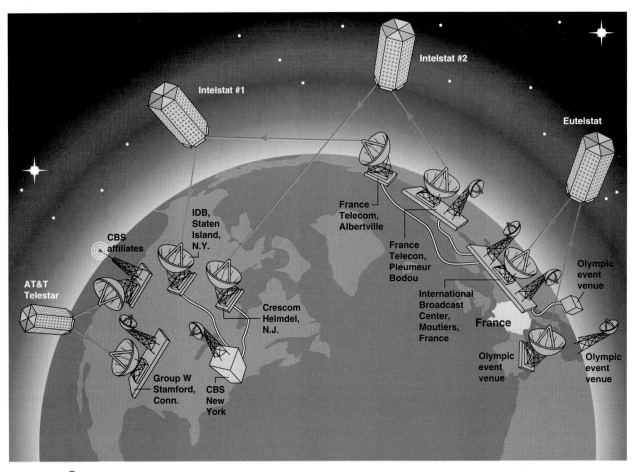

Satellite transmission

Microwave transmission

Satellite

Television transmission

Fiber-optic communication

Drawings show how parts of the transmission system relate to each other; their locations are not exact.

nodes in the system are not designed to communicate directly with one another, all communication stops. Also, the cost of cabling the central system and the points of the star together can be very high.

When a number of star networks are configured into a single multilevel system, the resulting network is often referred to as a **hierarchical, or tree, network** (Figure 8.15). In this type of network a single host computer still controls all network activity. However, each (or some) of the computers connected into the main computer in the first level of the star has a star network of devices connected to it in turn.

Hierarchical network configuration is often used by large companies with a main communications center linked to regional processing centers. Each regional processing facility acts as a host computer to smaller offices or branch computer facilities within the region. The lowest-level computer facilities allow the users to conduct some stand-alone applications processing. The regional computer facilities are used to manage large business information resources (usually in the form of regional databases) and to provide processing support that the smaller computers cannot handle efficiently.

FIGURE 8.15   Hierarchical network. This type of network configuration is basically a star network with smaller star networks attached to some of the nodes.

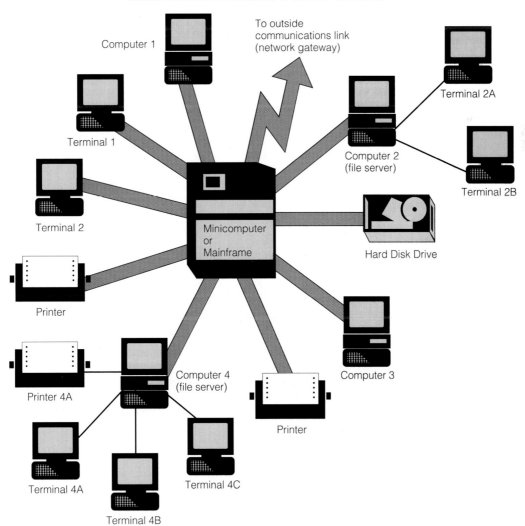

Use of computers in manufacturing is not just for the mammoth Fortune 500 companies. For his daughter who wanted to open a clothing store, a University of Dayton electrical engineering professor devised a computer-based dressmaking program for tailors. An optical scanner "reads" a person's body, producing figures that can be translated into a personalized dress or suit pattern.

Still, the most dramatic uses of computers have been those employed by large organizations. Once, taking inventory at computer-maker Hewlett-Packard's New Jersey division required the equivalent of 120 hours of a person's time, plus an additional two to three weeks to get the information key-punched and tabulated. Today, two people using electronic wands to scan bar codes on each product finish in less than six hours, and the data is ready immediately.

Moving bar codes from supermarkets to warehouses and factories has produced dramatic productivity gains. Indeed, companies now need entirely too much information in their computer systems for it to be keyed in manually. On an assembly line, laser scanners can read bar codes of up to 360 objects per second. The codes enable a company to keep track of individual lots or products, to track production rates, and do quality control and inventory, all without the need for paper.

Another form of computer technology becoming more frequently used in factories and warehouses is the industrial robot. A Reynolds Metals plastics plant in Virginia uses a robot that stacks a pallet with boxes, then moves it to an automatic pallet wrapper, where it is shrinkwrapped in plastic film. Employees are happier because they are less fatigued at the end of a shift compared to earlier times, when this work had to be done by hand.

Nowadays the factory is being reinvented from the top down. Computer simulations are used to recreate the factory floor on a computer screen, including machine tools, robots, and materials-handling vehicles. Manufacturing processes can then be tried out before a single machine is put in place. With computer-integrated manufacturing (CIM), a product that is ordered may be available the next day. Using computer-aided design (CAD), the part is designed on a video screen. Then, with computer-aided engineering (CAE), it is analyzed for performance. Finally, with computer-aided manufacturing (CAM), the part is produced by an automated system on the shop floor.

Some of the lessons or ideas developed for the factory floor are now being used in other areas. Unlike factory robots, so-called *field*, or *service*, *robots* are mobile and are able to work in nonmanufacturing environments that are hazardous or inaccessible to humans. Field robots equipped with wheels, tracks, legs, and fins are being used to clean up hazardous-waste sites, inspect nuclear power plants, do bomb disposal, and perform maintenance on offshore oil rigs. ∎

BUS NETWORK

In a **bus network,** a number of computers are connected by a single length of wire, cable, or optical fiber (Figure 8.16). All communications travel along this cable, which is called a *bus* (not the same type of bus as the CPU buses we discussed in Chapter 3). There is no host computer or file server. The bus network is often used to hook up a small group of microcomputers that share data. The microcomputers are programmed to "check" the communications that travel along the bus to see if they are the intended recipients. The bus network is not as expensive as the star network, and, if one computer fails, the failure does not affect the entire network. However, the bus network is not as efficient as the star network.

RING NETWORK

A **ring network** is much like a bus network, except the length of wire, cable, or optical fiber connects to form a loop (Figure 8.17). This type of configuration does not require a central computer to control activity. Each computer connected to the network can communicate directly with the other computers in the network by using the common communications channel, and each computer does its own independent applications processing. When one computer needs data from another computer, the data is passed along the ring. The ring network is not as susceptible to breakdown as the star network, because when one computer in the ring fails, it does not necessarily affect the processing or communications capabilities of the other computers in the ring.

TOKEN RING NETWORK

In early 1986, IBM announced a new local area network for personal computers using the ring network configuration. The new network was called the **token ring network** (Figure 8.18). Before the token system was established, existing ring networks used the following approach:

- A computer with a message to transmit monitored network activity, waited for a lull, and then transmitted the message.

- This computer then checked to determine if other computers in the network were trying to transmit a message at the same time. (Overlapping transmission might have garbled its message.)

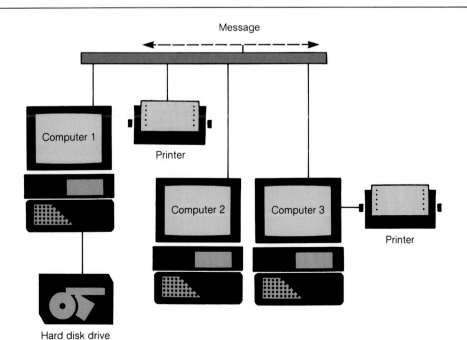

Message

Computer 1

Printer

Computer 2   Computer 3

Printer

Hard disk drive

FIGURE 8.16

Bus network. All messages are transmitted to the entire network, traveling from the sender in both directions along the cable. Each microcomputer or device is programmed to sense uniquely directed messages (one signal out of many). The bus network does not necessarily have to be in a straight line; for example, it can be U-shaped.

- If two or more computers did try to send messages at the same time, then both waited a different random period of time and tried to retransmit their messages.

Obviously, this procedure led to some message garbling and loss of time and productivity. In the token ring network, designed to eliminate these problems, a predefined pattern of bits, or *token*, is passed from computer to computer in the network. When a computer receives the token, it is allowed to transmit its message. Then the token is passed on. This method for transmitting messages (which can also be used in the bus network) prevents two computers from transmitting at the same time. The IBM token ring network is expensive but efficient. It can link up to 250 stations per ring over distances of about 770 yards, and separate rings can be linked to form larger networks.

FIGURE 8.17

Ring network. In this type of network configuration, messages flow in one direction from a source on the loop to a destination on the loop. Computers in between act as relay stations. If one computer fails, it can be bypassed, and the network can keep operating.

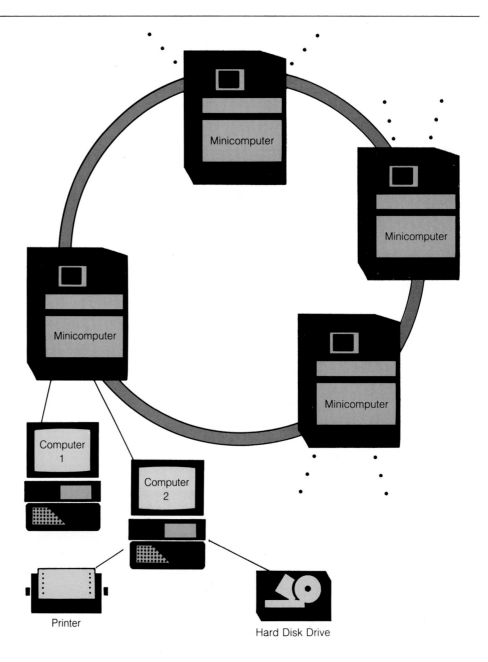

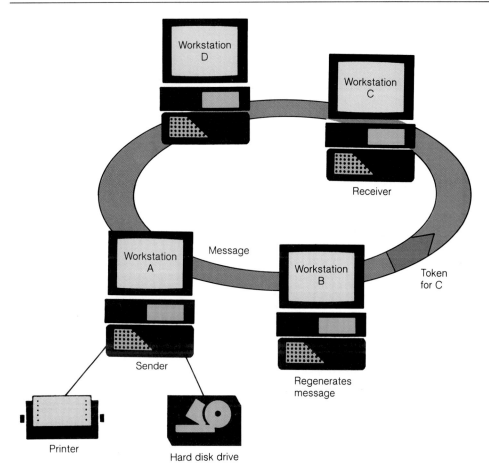

FIGURE 8.18

Token ring network. In this type of ring network, each computer can get exclusive access to the communications channel by "grabbing" a "token" and altering it before attaching a message. The altered token acts as a message indicator for the receiving computer, which in turn generates a new token, freeing up the channel for another computer. Computers in between the sender and the receiver examine the token and regenerate the message if the token isn't theirs. Thus, only one computer can transmit a message at a time.

COMMUNICATIONS SERVICES, SYSTEMS, AND UTILITIES

If you have a microcomputer, a modem, a telephone, and data communications software, you can hook up to public networks and sell a printer, buy new software, play a game with one or more people, solve a complex problem by researching information in a database or having a conference with several experts, buy stock, book a plane reservation, send flowers, receive mail—all from your desk. Public and academic networks provide users with the vast resources of (among other things) databases, teleconferencing services, information services, electronic stock trading, shopping, and banking.

PUBLIC DATABANKS/INFORMATION SERVICES

Many industries and professions require access to large volumes of specialized information to conduct business. For example, a law firm must have access to a law library and other specialized legal information. Medical professionals must have access to a tremendous volume of pharmaceutical and research-related information. To serve such needs, **public databanks,** or **information services,** were created by a number of organizations to provide users with access, for a fee, to large databanks, or databases. (In addition to the fee, the user pays regular phone rates for hook-up time.) The user accesses the databank with a terminal or a personal computer through one of the major common carrier networks, like AT&T (telephone lines). The databases contain information that covers a wide range of topics, such as health, education, law, humanities, science, government, and many others.

Some of the largest organizations providing public databases are Mead Data Central, Lockheed Information Systems, Systems Development Corporation, Data Resources, Inc., Interactive Data Corporation, Dow Jones Information Service, and CompuServe (Table 8.1). Some specialized 24-hour services do information searches for users to enable them to stay current in their field.

Mead Data Central provides two very extensive public database services: LEXIS and NEXIS. The LEXIS database provides users with access to a tremendous pool of legal information for use in research. It incorporates data from a variety of sources, including federal, state, and municipal court opinions, federal regulations, and a broad collection of recent publications in legal periodicals. The NEXIS database provides users with access to a huge amount of bibliographic data that has been collected from hundreds of magazines, newspapers, specialized newsletters, and other sources. In addition, NEXIS offers access to the complete text of the *Encyclopaedia Britannica*. Students working on term papers and theses can make extensive bibliographic resource searches by using an information service like NEXIS.

Lockheed Information Systems provides a public database service through its Dialog Information Service subsidiary. The Dialog system provides users with access to close to 100 separate databanks covering a variety of areas, including science, business, agriculture, economics, energy, and engineering. Dialog is regarded as the largest supplier of bibliographic data to computer users. To promote the use of the system after normal business hours, a special microcomputer-oriented service (called Knowledge Index) is made available at reduced rates.

Systems Development Corporation offers an information service called Orbit Search Service. This service allows users access to over 70 specialized databases. Many of the databases available can also be accessed through the Dialog system.

Data Resources, Inc., and Interactive Data Corporation both offer users access to a variety of statistical databanks covering such industries as banking, economics,

TABLE 8.1

Public Information Services*

Title	Number	Cost
CompuServe CompuServe Inc.	800-848-8199	$6–12 per hour
Dialog Dialog Information Services, Inc.	800-334-2564	$30–300 per hour
Dow Jones Dow Jones & Co.	800-225-3170	$60–174 per hour
GEnie G.E. Information Service	800-638-9636	$6–18 per hour
LEXIS Mead Data Central	800-543-6862	$39 per hour
NEXIS Mead Data Central	800-229-9597	$39 per hour
Prodigy	800-PRO-DIGY	$12.95 per month

*This table provides a partial list of available information services. Each information service provides access to many different databases. With most information services, hourly rates vary depending on when you use the service (hour and day), the speed of your modem, and the database you use. In addition to hourly fees, many information services require you to pay an initial membership fee.

insurance, transportation, and agriculture. The sources for their data include Chase Econometric Associates, Value Line, Standard & Poor's, and their own staff of economists.

The Dow Jones Information Service provides users with access to one of the largest statistical databanks and a news retrieval service. The statistical databanks cover stock-market activity from the New York and American stock exchanges. In addition, a substantial amount of financial data covering all of the corporations listed on both exchanges, as well as nearly a thousand others, is maintained. The Dow Jones News/Retrieval system allows users to search bibliographic data on individual businesses and broad financial news compiled from a variety of sources, including *Barron's* and the *Wall Street Journal.*

Since the early 1980s, several new information services have been created to provide microcomputer users at home with easy access to the statistical and bibliographic databanks and other services. The most popular of these are Prodigy and CompuServe. To access Prodigy, you need a microcomputer and a keyboard, a modem, a telephone line, and Prodigy software (which includes written documentation for using the service). The Prodigy software includes communications functions that enable you to communicate with the Prodigy service. If you want to store or print out the information you download from the information service, you also need a secondary storage device (disk drive) and a printer. Prodigy provides access to a wide variety of services, including electronic banking and shopping. In addition, you can obtain the latest news, weather forecasts, and stock quotes, or choose from the many educational and entertaining games that are offered by the Prodigy service (Figure 8.19). Up to six family members can obtain a password—their own sequence of keystrokes to type in—to the system and can customize it to suit their needs.

Many people would say that Prodigy's greatest attraction is its low cost. Most other on-line services assess hourly fees, whereas Prodigy assesses one monthly fee (which is usually lower than one hour on another on-line service). The major disadvantage of Prodigy is its inability to download financial data into another program, such as a spreadsheet program. Prodigy treats financial data graphically. You can print a graph, but you can't download the data that Prodigy used to generate the graph. In addition, Prodigy keeps track of only current data. Prodigy's market reports contain information from the last two trading days on NASDAQ and the New York and American stock exchanges and the past 10 business days on the Dow Jones Industrial.

CompuServe provides more in-depth and extensive capabilities than does Prodigy. Among its services, CompuServe keeps track of company and market performance for the past 16 years and enables you to download financial data to another software program. It is also more expensive. Like Prodigy, to use CompuServe you need a microcomputer and a keyboard, a modem, and a telephone line. In addition, you need a communications software package such as Smartcom or Crosstalk XVI. Then you have to contact the service through its 800 number and arrange to become a subscriber. As a subscriber, you are assigned two codes, or passwords, to type in when you want to log on to the information service. Like most services, CompuServe provides you with written instructions for using its system's commands.

ELECTRONIC SHOPPING

Another type of public network service that is popular with users is **electronic shopping** (Figure 8.20). To use this service, you dial into a network such as Prodigy or CompuServe (by using your computer keyboard) and select the electronic shopping category: A menu of major categories of items available is presented and you select one. You can then browse through the catalog—shown on the screen—looking for the desired item. When you find the item, you use your keyboard to place an order and enter a previously assigned identification number and perhaps a credit card number (sometimes the credit card number is included in the user I.D. information). You can even get cost-comparison information for several similar items before you order one.

The variety of goods available through electronic shopping has grown rapidly over the past few years and now includes a wide range of name-brand goods at discount prices from nationally known stores and businesses. In fact, users now not only buy products but also make travel reservations through electronic shopping.

FIGURE 8.19

Prodigy log-in screen

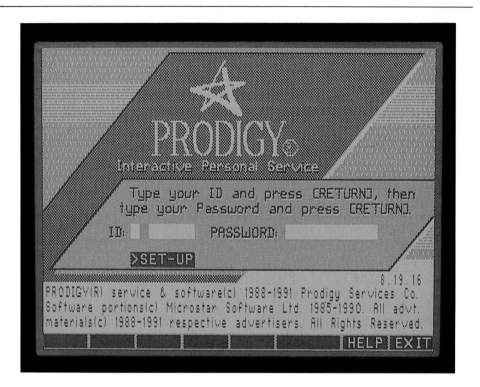

FIGURE 8.20

Modems and communications software allow the microcomputer user who subscribes to certain public network services to shop at home. This CompuServe shopping screen displays a partial list of SOFTEX applications software packages for sale to the CompuServe subscriber.

```
≡
File    Edit    Services    Special                              6:23
CompuServe+

SOFTEX Selections

 1 AMBIZ-PAK/IBM            IBM PC  $50.00
 2 Mail List Manager        IBM PC  $35.00
 3 TagCommand! for Ventura P IBM PC $79.95
 4 Tally Ho! Financial Calc IBM PC  $49.95
 5 Teledoll                 IBM PC  $49.95
 6 Teledoll-Plus            IBM PC  $89.95
 7 UPMover for Ventura Publi IBM PC $49.95
 8 Byte Size Calendar       IBM PC  $21.95
 9 Byte Size Calculator     IBM PC  $21.95
10 Byte Size Mail/Phone List IBM PC $29.95
11 Byte Size Stock Portfolio IBM PC $29.95
12 Byte Size DOS Shell      IBM PC  $29.95
13 PRNTLABL Label System    IBM PC  $15.00
14 Byte Size General Ledger IBM PC  $49.95
15 Byte Size Labeler        IBM PC  $39.95


Enter choice or <CR> for more !
F1=Help  F10=Menu bar  F5=Logging [OFF]  F6=Printer [OFF]
```

ELECTRONIC BULLETIN BOARDS

The **electronic bulletin board service (BBS)** (Figure 8.21) is a popular information service that allows subscribing users to place messages and advertisements into the system and also scan existing messages in the system. For example, suppose you have an item you would like to sell or trade—an automobile, bicycle, motorcycle, sports equipment, or even a microcomputer or some software. After setting up your computer and modem with your communications software, you would dial the information service and select the electronic bulletin board mode. Next you would compose an electronic 3-by-5-inch card describing the item(s) for sale and include an electronic mailbox number to which inquiries can be directed. You can check back for responses over a period of days, or whenever appropriate.

Electronic bulletin boards are also used simply to exchange information between computers in remote locations, such as offices in different parts of the country, or even within a company at one location. As long as the sending and receiving computers have modems attached and have established an account with the same BBS, one user can upload data to the BBS for the other to download. Since data on a BBS is stored in a basic text format, any microcomputer can read it. This is one method for getting around the problem of moving data between machines that store data in incompatible formats. For example, to convert an IBM file into an Apple Macintosh format (IBMs and Macintoshes use different machine languages), the IBM file could be sent to the BBS, at which point the Macintosh user could retrieve it.

The procedure for scanning the bulletin board is very straightforward. Once you have entered the electronic bulletin board mode, you simply identify the type of item you would like to search for and let the computer do the work for you. You can also scan *all* the messages.

ELECTRONIC MAIL

Electronic messages can also be sent via **electronic mail,** or **E-mail,** which uses a special communications line rather than a telephone line. Electronic mail is often used within companies to exchange memos, make announcements, schedule meetings, and so forth. Each user has a "mailbox"—an electronic file—with a number and a password to limit access to approved users. To send a message, the

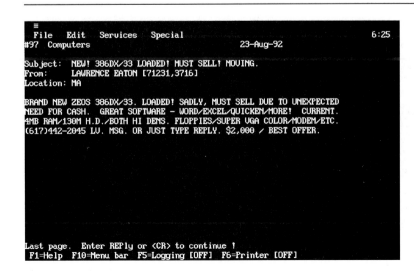

FIGURE 8.21

Electronic bulletin boards allow users to "post" messages on particular topics, read messages from other people, and reply to messages. This CompuServe bulletin board screen shows a for-sale notice posted by a user from Massachusetts.

user types in the recipient's mailbox number, the password, and then the message. Approximately 12.4 million people are sending 1.2 billion messages via E-mail each year—about a 3,000% increase in 10 years. Until recently, there were almost no links between different E-mail systems. However, new developments such as AT&T Mail, cc: Mail, MCI Mail, and ALL-In-1 are making links possible.

ELECTRONIC BANKING AND INVESTING

In the past few years, many major financial institutions have begun to offer customers a new service referred to as **electronic banking.** This service allows customers to access banking and investment services via a terminal or personal computer from the comfort of their offices or homes. The customer just uses the keyboard to dial the local-access telephone number into the electronic service. When the communications link has been established, the user is prompted to enter an identification code. If the code is accepted, the user can request a number of electronic financial services, including:

- Viewing the balances in checking and savings accounts
- Transferring funds between checking and savings accounts
- Directing that certain utility bills be paid directly by the bank
- Verifying the latest rates available on certificates of deposit, passbook savings accounts, and other investment options
- Following the stock market and entering buy and sell orders for stocks

COMPUTER VIRUSES

The proliferation of relatively low-cost, high-tech communications devices and powerful microcomputers has created a breeding ground for a new kind of computer bug—the computer virus.

Normal bugs are accidental programmer's errors that are weeded out of a system's software during testing. **Viruses** are *intentional* bugs that are usually created by sophisticated, obsessive computer programmers and users (often called *hackers* or *crackers*)—sophisticated programming skills are usually required to create a virus. These viruses consist of pieces of computer code (either hidden or posing as legitimate program code) that, when downloaded or run, attach themselves to other programs and files and cause them to malfunction. Sometimes the viruses are programmed to lie dormant for a while before they become active; thus, they can be spread from disk to disk and system to system before they are detected (Figure 8.22). The viruses are transmitted by downloading through modems from electronic bulletin boards and networks, and through shared disks. They reproduce themselves over and over again. In recent years, some major companies, universities, and government agencies have had their systems disabled by computer viruses. More than 110 different viruses have been detected to date; because so many critical aspects of modern life depend on computer programs, the destructive potential of viruses has become a threat to all of us.

What exactly do viruses do? Among other things, they can rename programs, alter numeric data, erase files, scramble memory, turn off the power, reverse the effect of a command—or simply display a message without damaging the system. For example, in 1988 the so-called Meta-Virus was unleashed on users of a particular software system. This virus did not actually damage the system; rather, it was intended to create anxiety on the part of the users. The message that popped up on the user's screen said:

WARNING! A serious virus is on the loose. It was hidden in the
program called 1987 TAXFORM that was on this bulletin board last
year. By now, it is possible that your system is infected even if
you didn't download this program, since you could easily have
been infected indirectly. The only safe way to protect yourself
against this virus is to print all files onto paper, erase all
the disks on your system, buy fresh software disks from the
manufacturer, and type in all your data again. FIRST! Send this
message to everyone you know, so they will also protect
themselves.

In early 1992, many computer users were worried about the Michelangelo virus,
which was programmed to wipe out hard disk files on the anniversary of the Italian

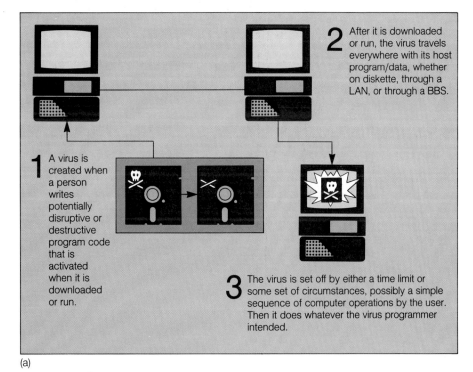
(a)

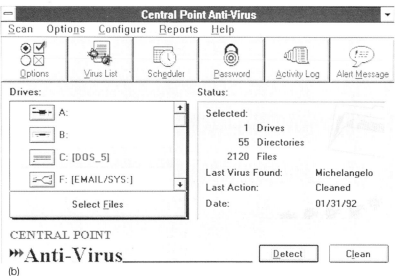
(b)

FIGURE 8.22

(a) How a computer virus can spread. Just as a biological virus disrupts living cells to cause disease, a computer virus—introduced maliciously—invades the inner workings of computers and disrupts normal operations of the machines. (Adapted from Knight-Ridder Tribune News/Stephen Cvengros, *Chicago Tribune*, October 6, 1989, Section 1, p. 2.) (b) A screen from Central Point's Anti-Virus software. Note the disk drive designations on the left: A and B represent floppy disk drives, and C is the hard disk drive. F represents an electronic mail connection. At the top of the screen is the title bar, under which you see a menu bar with several options. Under that is a row of "buttons"; the user points to the buttons with the mouse pointer and clicks the mouse button to quickly open up frequently used option files.

Renaissance artist Michelangelo's birthday, March 6. Many of these users scanned their files with virus-detection software and eliminated this virus before the date arrived (Figure 8.22).

Other programs are like viruses in that they are created to cause problems for users. *Trojan horses* act like viruses, but they don't reproduce themselves. *Worms* use up available space by rewriting themselves repeatedly throughout the computer's memory. What can users do to protect themselves? First, they can obtain free or low-cost software programs (called *freeware* or *shareware*) that detect and cure common viruses—for example, Virus RX, Virus Detective, VirusCheck, Interferon, and Symantec Antivirus. These programs come with instructions for use. Also, personal computer users should:

- Make backup copies of their data on a regular basis.
- Increase the use of the write/protect tabs on their diskettes. With 5¼-inch diskettes, this involves putting a plastic sticker (write/protect tabs are included in every box of diskettes) over the write/protect notch. With 3½-inch diskettes, this involves sliding down a plastic notch on the back of the diskette.
- Don't use master disks. Make working copies and store the masters in a safe place.
- Avoid use of computer games from bulletin board services.
- Avoid downloading from bulletin board services.
- Be cautious with whom they network, share data, or share applications software programs, or avoid sharing at all.

Table 8.2 provides a list of common virus-related terms.

TABLE 8.2

Virus-Related Terms

Antidotes	Programs that help remove viruses
Bug	Programmer error
Counterhacker	One who is in the business of identifying hackers
Crashing	A term used to describe a computer system that is being halted by a virus
Finger hacker	One who obtains access codes from a service like U.S. Sprint Telephone, using a programmable memory telephone
Hacker	A sophisticated, obsessive computer programmer who creates computer code that can cause a computer system to malfunction
Password	A code used to gain entrance into a computer system so that data can be accessed
Replicate	To copy or repeat
Scan programs	Used to detect viruses
Vaccines	Programs that prevent machines from being infected with viruses
Virus	An intentional bug created by a computer user (usually a programmer) that can cause harm to data stored in a computer system and cause a computer system to malfunction
Virus strain	A particular virus with its own unique characteristics
Worm	A type of virus that repeats (replicates) itself on a disk, thus destroying critical data and computer code

FACSIMILE (FAX)

Today, the question "what is your fax number?" is almost as common as asking for someone's telephone number. In fact, most business cards today include both a telephone number and a fax number. In what seems like a very short time, many businesses and individuals have adopted the fax (*fax* is short for *facsimile*, meaning *reproduction*) as the standard communications medium. A **fax** is a copy of a document that is sent using fax hardware (described in the following paragraphs) through the phone lines to another location that has fax hardware. The process of sending or receiving a fax is called **faxing**—faxing a document is faster than sending it through the mail or using an overnight courier service. If you are in charge of bringing the fax capability to your home or office, you have two choices. You can either purchase a stand-alone fax machine or you can purchase a fax board, which fits into an expansion slot in your system unit. Both methods have their advantages.

A stand-alone **fax machine** (Figure 8.23) is composed of a scanner for input, a thermal printer for output, and a modem so that text and graphics can be sent across the phone lines. Because the phone line is the transmission medium, each machine is usually given its own fax number, which is used the same way as a telephone number. To send a fax, put the document you want to fax into the fax

FIGURE 8.23 (a) Stand-alone fax machine; (b) Intel fax board

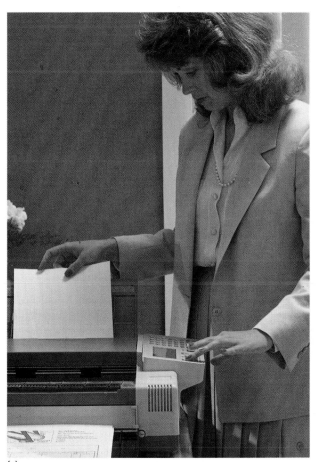

(a)

(b)

machine, punch in the number of the fax machine you want to send to, and then press a button to transmit the document. The scanner moves the document through the machine and transmits that data to a receiving fax machine. Some fax machines can also transmit photos, and some have many options for such functions as number storage and automatic dialing, security checks, transaction record, printouts, and voice communication. The more options, the more expensive the fax machine.

A **fax card** (Figure 8.23) is essentially an internal fax modem that differs from conventional modems in that it can send and receive both text and graphics and can typically send and receive at a faster rate (9,600 bits per second versus 2,400 bps). Since fax cards don't provide users with all the capabilities of the stand-alone fax machines, they typically cost hundreds of dollars less. However, they require special software to function. A microcomputer with a fax board can receive faxed images and display them on the screen. It can also print them out on a printer. It can fax documents to another computer with a fax board or a fax machine.

When using a fax card, if you want to match the capabilities of the stand-alone fax machines, you would have to purchase a scanner so that you can fax documents that don't originate in your PC, such as newspaper clippings. The scanner converts paper images into computer-usable files that can then be faxed, using the fax board, to a fax machine in another location or to a PC that is configured with a fax board. The fax board you use must be compatible with the type of

---

Digital Convergence: "The Mother of All Industries"

A remarkable transformation is coming about that may change everything. It's called the *Digital Revolution*, or *Digital Convergence*—the merger of four huge industries: computers, communications, consumer electronics, and entertainment. According to Apple Computer Inc. chairman John Scully, this convergence—what he calls "the mother of all industries"—could be worth more than $3 trillion by the year 2000.

The blurring of industries will come about, it is predicted, as information, sound, video, text, and images become converted to digital bits—0s and 1s—that can be decoded by similar hardware. Everything is expected to go digital—from the images of photos, graphics, and films to the analog waves of telephone, radio, and television. In time, the electronic world could be a huge melting pot of a new digital order.

In many ways, the Digital Revolution is well along. We have seen digital compact disks supplant vinyl LP records. Recently, digital audio tape (DAT) has proven to be much superior to conventional audiocassettes. Europe and Canada are leading the way toward digital audio broadcasting, bringing the quality and reliability of CDs to radio. Electronic imaging has taken a step forward with the digital camera, which requires no film developing and which allows images to be transmitted as digital files via computer modem to, for example, electronic pictures desks at newspapers. Family photos can now be stored on "photo CDs," which in turn can be manipulated on microcomputers as digitized images. This brings to the home market the digital techniques of "morphing," as professional film makers call it, whereby an image can be digitally changed to another by a computer—for example, putting one person's head on another person's body.

Many companies currently send digital information over telephone lines, communicating with digital beepers, for example. As present cellular telephone channels fill up, producing more garbled calls, the cellular telephone industry has geared up to convert to digital transmission in large cities. Around the corner is HDTV—high-definition television—for which the Federal Communications Commission is supposed to approve a U.S. digital standard in late 1993. Although Japan already has HDTV, it is stuck with the old analog wave signal. U.S. broadcasters could be broadcasting digital high-definition signals to home HDTV sets in 1996. HDTV and digital video is expected to make advances in teleconferencing, video telephones, electronic cameras, and interactive education systems.

What's holding up the Digital Revolution? As so often happens in technological matters, the main sticking point is lack of agreement about standards. There is no standard format for digitizing, integrating, and manipulating all the information around us. Yet another problem is how to go about converting older materials, such as newspapers, photographs, and music, into digital form, presently an expensive, time-consuming task. Clearly, if the new digital world is to take place, it will take a lot of cooperation between hardware, software, and communications companies and perhaps many years.

Still, the prospect of such convergences promises opportunities. For example, ultimately they could lead to a wireless, pocket-size "personal communicator" or "personal digital assistant." This gadget would combine a personal computer, pager, appointment book, address book, and even "electronic book" and pocket CD player—all in a hand-held box operated by a pen or voice commands.

scanner you want to use, because not all fax boards drive every scanner. In addition, if you want to print a faxed document, make sure the fax board in your computer is compatible with your printer. When using a fax board, the added expense of purchasing a scanner and possibly a printer increases the total cost of your fax system.

Deciding whether to purchase a stand-alone fax machine or a fax board may depend on the amount of space you have on your desktop (for a fax machine) or whether you have an expansion slot in your PC (for the fax board).

Some computers use fax to improve customer services. For example, Borland (a software company) offers callers who have fax capabilities a menu of choices via telephone. The caller punches in responses on the telephone buttons and then receives chosen information faxed automatically within minutes by a computer.

SUMMARY

- When people speak, the sound travels as *analog signals*—continuous signals that repeat a certain number of times over a certain period (*frequency*) at certain *amplitudes* (degrees of loudness). Telephone lines carry analog signals. Computers, in contrast, use digital signals—discontinuous (discrete) pulses of electricity (on) separated by pauses (off).

- When they communicate, the sending and receiving computers must use *modems* (*mo*dulate/*dem*odulate) to convert the digital signals into analog signals for transmission and then back again into digital signals for reception. Modems can be *internal* (built into the computer or inserted on an add-on card or board) or *external* (connected to the computer and the telephone by cable).

- When signals are transmitted from computer to computer, patterns of bits coded to represent data are sent one bit at a time. For the receiving computer to be able to determine where one character of data ends and another starts, data is sent either *asynchronously* or *synchronously*.

- In asynchronous transmission, each string of bits that make up a character is bracketed by control bits—a start bit, one or two stop bits, and an error check bit, or parity bit. Most microcomputers use asynchronous transmission.

- In synchronous transmission, characters are sent as blocks with flags inserted as identifiers at the beginning and end of the blocks. This type of transmission is used by large computers to transmit huge volumes of data at high speeds.

- Data communications technology must also consider the direction of data traffic: *simplex* (one way only), *half-duplex* (two-way traffic but only one direction at a time), or *full-duplex* (two-way traffic passing at the same time).

- The media most commonly used for communication are *telephone wires* (*open* and *twisted-wire*), *coaxial cables*, atmosphere (*microwave* and *satellite systems*), and *fiber-optic cables*. Each of these media differs in terms of the form of the transmitted data (electrical pulses, electromagnetic waves, or light pulses), the rate at which data moves through it, and its susceptibility to noise and "eavesdropping."

- The hardware typically used to communicate between computers includes *modems, multiplexers, concentrators, controllers, front-end processors*, and microcomputer *protocol converters*.

- Multiplexers, concentrators, controllers, and front-end processors all allow multiplexing—the sharing of one high-speed communications line by multiple users or devices. A concentrator, which is like a multiplexer, is more "intelligent" because it can store and forward transmissions. A controller performs more functions than a multiplexer or a concentrator. A front-end processor, a smaller computer connected to the main computer, not only allows multiplexing but also relieves the main computer of many routine data traffic management and communications functions.

- To communicate, the sending and receiving computers must follow the same rules, or *protocols*. In the case of microcomputer communications, the software parameters can be set on both ends to agree. In other cases, *protocol converters* must be used. For example, a protocol converter could be used to allow a microcomputer in asynchronous mode to communicate with a mainframe operating in synchronous mode.

- Companies often set up communications *networks*, which are collections of data communications hardware, computers, communications software, and communications media connected in a meaningful way to allow users to share data and information.

- Three basic types of networks are private, public, and international. *Private networks* support the communications needs of particular business organizations. *Public networks* provide paying subscribers with voice or data communications over a large geographical area. *International networks* provide users with intercontinental voice and data communications facilities.

- Networks can be set up in different shapes: star (and hierarchical) network, bus network, and ring (and token ring) network. The normal business user may encounter one of these network shapes in the context of a *local area network (LAN)*, which is a private network that serves a company or part of a company that is located on one floor, in a single building, or in offices within approximately 2 miles of each other.

- The *star network* uses a host computer or a *file server* connected to a number of smaller computers and/or terminals, called *nodes*. The nodes are not designed to communicate directly with one another, so if the main computer fails, the whole network "goes down."

- In a more complicated star network called a *hierarchical*, or *tree, network*, some nodes have devices connected to them in smaller star networks.

- In a *bus network*, a number of computers are connected to a single communications line. In this network, if one computer fails, the others can continue to operate.

- A *ring network* is much like a bus network, except that the communications line forms a loop. This network has no central computer, and each computer connected to the network can communicate directly with the others.

- In the *token ring network*, predefined patterns of bits, or tokens, are passed from computer to computer. The computer with the token can transmit; the others cannot. This setup prevents the garbling of messages that occurs when more than one computer tries to transmit at the same time.

- The business user can benefit from computer-to-computer communications using a number of public services and utilities to access data and information. *Public databanks* provide information about such topics as health, education, law, the humanities, science, and government. To use these databanks, the user pays a fee plus the regular phone charges. *Public information services* also provide the user with such conveniences as *electronic shopping, banking and investing, electronic bulletin boards*, and *electronic mail*.

- More and more offices today have the ability to send and receive faxes by using either a fax machine or a fax board. A *fax machine* is composed of a scanner (for input), a thermal printer (for output), and a modem so that text and graphics can be sent across the phone lines. A *fax card* is essentially an internal fax modem on a board that can be inserted into an expansion slot in your PC. Fax cards can also send and retrieve both text and graphics. If you want to fax images that don't originate in your PC, you must purchase a scanner.

KEY TERMS

amplitude, p. 183
analog signal, p. 183
asynchronous trans-
    mission, p. 184
bus network, p. 203
coaxial cable, p. 187
communications
    software, p. 197
concentrator, p. 194
controller, p. 194
dedicated line, p. 199
demodulation, p. 183
digital convergence,
    p. 182
digital signal, p. 183
electronic banking,
    p. 210
electronic bulletin
    board service (BBS),
    p. 209
electronic mail,
    p. 209
electronic shopping,
    p. 207
external modem, p. 194
fax, p. 213

fax card, p. 214
fax machine, p. 213
faxing, p. 213
fiber optics, p. 191
file server, p. 200
frequency, p. 183
front-end processor,
    p. 194
full-duplex, p. 186
half-duplex, p. 185
hierarchical network,
    p. 201
information service,
    p. 205
internal modem, p. 193
international network,
    p. 199
local area network
    (LAN), p. 199
metropolitan area
    network (MAN),
    p. 199
microwave, p. 188
modem, p. 184, 193
modulation, p. 183

multimedia conference,
    p. 198
multiplexer, p. 194
network, p. 198
networking, p. 182
private network, p. 198
protocol, p. 195
protocol converter,
    p. 195
public databank, p. 205
public network, p. 198
ring network, p. 203
satellite, p. 189
script language, p. 197
simplex, p. 185
star network, p. 200
synchronous trans-
    mission, p. 185
teleconferencing, p. 198
token ring network,
    p. 203
tree network, p. 201
virus, p. 210
wide area network
    (WAN), p. 199

EXERCISES

SELF-TEST

1. List four transmission media that are used for data communications.
    a. _____   b. _____   c. _____   d. _____

2. To communicate between computers across wire phone lines, you need a _____ at both the sending and receiving locations.

3. Whereas computers "understand" _____ signals, the telephone line can usually transmit only _____ signals.

4. For a microcomputer to communicate with a mainframe, it must be configured with the necessary hardware and software to allow it to support _____ transmission.

5. A _____ communications link can support two-way traffic, but data can travel in only one direction at a time.

6. Asynchronous transmission, commonly used in microcomputers, is faster than synchronous transmission. (true/false)

7. Pulses of light are sometimes used to represent data so that it can be communicated over a distance. (true/false)

8. List three popular network configurations.
   a. _____   b. _____   c. _____

9. _____ optimizes the use of communications lines by allowing multiple users or devices to share one high-speed line, thereby reducing communications costs.

10. _____ transmission sends data in both directions simultaneously, similar to two trains passing each other in different directions on side-by-side tracks.

11. Satellite communications systems transmit signals in the gigahertz range—billions of cycles per second. (true/false)

12. A _____ is a standard set of rules for communicating.

13. A _____ is a collection of data communications hardware, computers, communications software, and communications media connected in a meaningful way to allow users to share information and equipment.

14. The term _____ refers to electronically linking several people by phone, computer, and video so that they can hold a meeting.

15. The _____ _____ _____ _____ is a popular information service that allows subscribing users to place messages and advertisements into the system and also scan existing messages in the system.

16. A _____ consists of pieces of computer code intentionally created by programmers or users that, when downloaded or run, attaches itself to other programs and files and causes them to malfunction.

17. List two hardware devices that you could choose from to bring a fax capability to your home or office.
   a. _____   b. _____

18. _____ _____ technology is expected to revolutionize the communications industry because of its low cost, high transmission volume, low error rate, and message security.

19. In contrast to a private network, a _____ _____ is a comprehensive communications facility designed to provide subscribers with voice and/or data communications over a large geographical area.

20. _____ _____ is a system often used within companies to electronically transmit memos and announcements and to schedule meetings.

SOLUTIONS   (1) telephone lines, microwave, satellite, fiber optics; (2) modem; (3) digital, analog; (4) synchronous; (5) half-duplex; (6) false; (7) true; (8) ring, token ring, bus, star, tree; (9) multiplexing; (10) full-duplex; (11) true; (12) protocol; (13) network; (14) teleconferencing; (15) electronic bulletin board service; (16) virus; (17) fax machine, fax card; (18) fiber-optic; (19) public network; (20) electronic mail

SHORT ANSWER

1. When might you encounter electronic communications in the business environment?

2. What are modems used for?

3. What is the function of a multiplexer?

4. Explain the difference between analog and digital signals.

5. What does a microcomputer user need to do in order to communicate synchronously?

6. What is the main function of a front-end processor?

7. What is meant by the term *protocol* as it relates to communicating between two computers?

8. What does the term *digital convergence* mean?

9. Describe the difference between synchronous and asynchronous transmission modes and how they affect the speed with which data can be communicated.

10. What is a communications network? What are the three main types of network?

PROJECTS

1. You need to purchase a computer to use at home to perform business-related tasks. You want to be able to communicate with the network at work so that you can use its software and access its data. To do this you need to know what hardware and software exists at work. Include the following in a report:
   a. A description of the hardware and software used at work
   b. A description of the types of tasks you will want to perform at home
   c. The name of the computer you would buy (include a detailed description of the computer, such as the RAM capacity and disk storage capacity)
   d. The communications hardware/software you would need to purchase
   e. A cost estimate

2. Are the computers at your school or work connected to a network? If so, what are the characteristics of the network? What advantages does the network provide in terms of hardware and software support? What types of computers are connected to the network (microcomputers, minicomputers, and/or mainframes)? Specifically, what software/hardware is allowing the network to function?

3. Using current articles and publications, research the history of ISDN, how it is being used today, and what you think the future holds for it. Present your findings in a paper or a 15-minute discussion.

4. "Distance learning," or "distance education," uses electronic links to extend college campuses to people who otherwise would not be able to take college courses. College instructors using such systems are able to lecture "live" to students in distant locations. Is your school involved in distance learning? If so, research the system's components and uses. What hardware does it use? Software? Protocols? Communications media?

5. With 17 million to 20 million fax machines in the world and with sales growing about 15% annually, this communications technology is becoming a convenient source of information dissemination. For example, 10 daily U.S. newspapers are offering or experimenting with weekday fax editions. If you were to start a fax-information business, what group of information buyers would you target? How would you prepare your faxes? How often would you fax? How would you contact and establish your clientele? How much would you charge for your service? How would you get your data, and what type of computer-based system would you set up?

CHAPTER 9

DATABASE MANAGEMENT SYSTEMS

Where does the power come from in a computer-based information system? Although your first answer may be "hardware and the speed with which it can process data," if you think about it a bit longer you will probably realize that the *real* power comes from the data. From data comes information, and access to information offers power. But the amounts of data being handled by companies in computer-based systems have grown so large in recent years that managing data properly has become a sophisticated operation.

PREVIEW

When you have completed this chapter, you will be able to:

Explain what a database is

Describe the difference between file management systems and database management systems

Describe how database management systems software relates to hardware and the user

Identify the advantages and disadvantages of the three database models and of database management systems in general

Explain the importance of database administration within an organization

CHAPTER OUTLINE

Why Is This Chapter Important?

What Is a Database Management System?

Data Management Concepts
    File Management Systems

Database Management Systems
    Hardware: Storage Counts
    Software: In Control
    Data Dictionaries and Transaction Logs

Database Models
    Hierarchical Database Model
    Network Database Model
    Relational Database Model

Designing a Database
    Matching the Design to the Organization
    Logical Design
    Physical Design

Database Administration
    Why Administer?
    The Job of the Database Administrator

Advantages and Disadvantages of the DBMS

Who Owns the Database?

Summary

Key Terms

Exercises

Managers need information to make effective decisions. The more accurate, relevant, and timely the information, the better informed management will be when making decisions. Now we turn our attention to the *organization* of the data that makes up the information. In many companies data was (and certainly still is) collected on a grand scale, even redundantly; that is, the same element of data was entered more than once and appeared in more than one file—computerized or not. Nevertheless, data needed for a report was often unavailable or at least not available in a form appropriate to the situation. And to extract data from uncoordinated files was difficult.

By the early 1970s it was apparent that traditional file-handling concepts were often no longer adequate to handle the large amounts of data and the sophisticated and complex informational needs of a business's computer-based information system. To improve the quality of management information—and information for users in general—as well as the ease with which it could be produced, a new tool was developed: the database management system.

In general, database management concepts are the same for large computer systems and for microcomputers. As a general business user, you will most likely be using a microcomputer or a terminal to access data stored in a **database**—a large group of stored, integrated (cross-referenced) data elements that can be retrieved (usually from a minicomputer or a mainframe) and manipulated with great flexibility to produce information. It is therefore important for you to understand not only what a database is but also what a database management system is, so that you can put them to effective use in your job.

WHAT IS A DATABASE MANAGEMENT SYSTEM?

A database is a large group of stored, integrated (cross-referenced) data—usually organized in files—that can be retrieved and manipulated to produce information. A **database management system (DBMS)** is a comprehensive software tool that allows users to create, maintain, and manipulate the database to produce relevant management information. By *integrated* we mean that the file records are logically related to one another so that *all* data on a topic can be retrieved by simple requests. The database management systems software represents the interface between the user and the computer's operating system and database (Figure 9.1).

Picture a typical corporate office with a desk, chairs, telephones, and a row of file cabinets along the wall. A wide variety of business data is stored in these cabinets. If the files have been carefully organized and maintained, then any piece of data that needs to be retrieved can quickly be located and removed. However, if the data has not been properly filed, some time and effort will be expended to find it. And, regardless of how carefully the files have been organized and maintained, you will always need to retrieve related pieces of data. For example, suppose you need to review the customer files for all invoices for payments due in

FIGURE 9.1

DBMS software as interface. The database management system is the facilitator that allows the user to access and manipulate integrated data elements in a database.

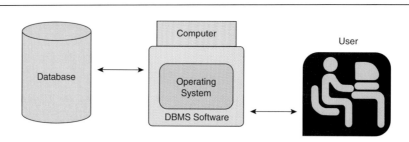

excess of $2,500 and prepare a simple report. How would you accomplish this task? First, you would probably go through the customer files in alphabetical order, folder by folder. You would examine each invoice in the folders to determine if the amount is in excess of $2,500 and remove and copy each invoice that meets the criterion. You would then have to refile the copies you removed (and risk misfiling them). When you had examined all the customer folders and copied all the appropriate invoices, you would then review the copies and put together your report. Imagine how much time this could take. If there are a lot of customers, you would need to spend hours, if not days.

Now let's look at the situation in a different way. The environment is the same, except that, instead of file cabinets, you have a microcomputer or a terminal and DBMS software that has access to a customer database file (Figure 9.2). In this file a row of customer data is referred to as a *record*, and an individual piece of data within a record, such as a name, is referred to as a *field*. (See Table 9.1 and Figure 9.3 for a review of the filing and database terminology introduced in Chapter 4.) To get the invoice data you need, you would do something like this:

- Turn on the computer and the printer.
- Start up the DBMS software.
- Give the command to "open up" the customer database file stored on your disk, which is similar in concept to manually opening up the customer drawer in a file cabinet.
- Give the command to search all the records in the database file and display copies of the records that meet your criterion (that is, the names of people with unpaid invoices greater than $2,500). If you were using dBASE IV, a popular microcomputer DBMS, the command would look something like:

```
LIST FOR INV_AMOUNT > 2500
```

If you were using SQL (Structured Query Language), the command would look like this:

```
SELECT NAME FROM CUSTOMER
    WHERE INV_AMOUNT > 2500
    ORDER BY NAME
```

In response to this command, all the records in the file that have an invoice amount greater than $2,500 will be listed on the screen. (The SQL command would also sort the listing into order by name.) This whole procedure would take perhaps only five minutes or less.

Customer Name	Date	Item Ordered	Quantity Ordered	Invoice Amount
Arthene Ng	02/12/92	4065	6	2510.67
Pamela Robert	02/13/92	4128	7	1510.62
Jeff Arguello	02/13/92	4111	1	1905.00
Sylvia Arnold	02/14/92	4007	6	2950.93
Richard Mall	02/14/92	4019	1	63.55
Alan Steinberg	02/14/92	4021	3	1393.00
Harry Filbert	02/14/92	4106	2	940.56
Frances Chung	02/15/92	4008	5	2717.00
Bruce Chaney	02/15/92	4007	8	1720.00

Field   Record

File

FIGURE 9.2

Customer database file. This figure illustrates only a small section of our hypothetical customer file. Data stored electronically in a DBMS can be much more easily retrieved than data stored in file cabinets.

TABLE 9.1

Short Glossary of Database
Terminology

Alphanumeric (character) data: data composed of a combination of letters, numbers, and other symbols (like punctuation marks) that are not used for mathematical calculations

Bit: contraction of *binary digit*; either 1 ("on") or 0 ("off") in computerized data representation

Character: the lowest level in the data hierarchy; usually one letter or numerical digit; also called **byte** (8 bits)

Data: the raw facts that make up information

Database: a large collection of stored, integrated (cross-referenced) records that can be maintained and manipulated with great flexibility; the top level in the data hierarchy

Entity: any tangible or intangible object or concept about which an organization wishes to store data; entities have attributes, such as name, color, and price

Field, or attribute, or data element: a group of related characters (*attribute* is also a column of a relation in a relational database, discussed later); the second-lowest level in the data hierarchy

File: a group of related records; the fourth level from the bottom in the data hierarchy

Information: data that has value to, or that has been interpreted by, the user

Key: a unique field within a record that uniquely identifies the record

Numeric data: data composed of numeric digits (numbers); used for mathematical calculations

Record: a group of related fields; the third level from the bottom in the data hierarchy (analogous to a *tuple*, or *row*, in a relational database, as described later)

FIGURE 9.3

Data hierarchy. These figures show how most of the data terms in Table 9.1 fit into the data hierarchy (first introduced in Chapter 4).

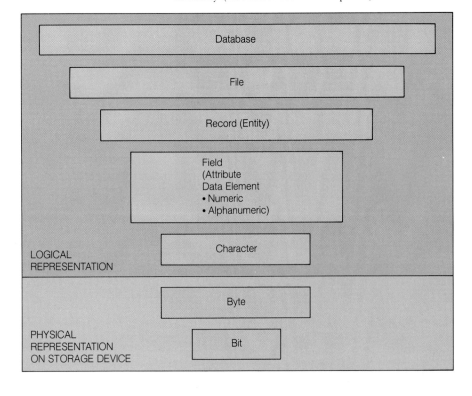

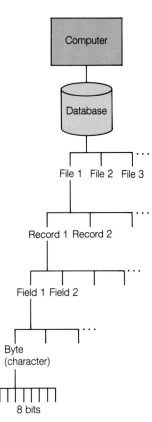

The DBMS is a software tool designed to manage a large number of integrated, shared electronic "file cabinets." You describe the type of data you wish to store, and the DBMS is responsible for creating the database file(s) and providing an easy-to-use mechanism for storing, retrieving, and manipulating the data.

In small businesses, databases may be both created and operated by the user. In moderate- to large-size businesses with extensive computer systems, the corporate database is usually created by technical information specialists such as the database administrator, but the database management system is acquired by the information systems department. Users generate and extract data stored by the database management system.

DATA MANAGEMENT CONCEPTS

The DBMS approach for storing and retrieving data in computer-usable form has evolved to allow users to easily retrieve and update data that is in *more than one file*. But before we describe why the DBMS approach is significant, and to facilitate your understanding of it, we will first describe in more detail the traditional system it evolved from—the file management system.

FILE MANAGEMENT SYSTEMS

Computers were placed in commercial use in 1954, when General Electric Company purchased a UNIVAC (Universal Automatic Computer) for its research division. At first, the processing performed was straightforward. Applications software programs tended to be sequentially organized and stored in a single file on magnetic tape that contained all the elements of data required for processing. The term **file management system** was coined to describe this traditional approach to managing business data and information (Figure 9.4). However, file management systems did not provide the user with an easy way to group records within a file or to establish relationships among the records in different files. As disk storage became more cost-effective and its capacity grew, new software applications were developed to access disk-based files. The need to access data stored in more than one file was quickly recognized and posed increasingly complex programming requirements.

The most serious problems of file management systems involve:

- Data redundancy
- Difficulty of updating files and maintaining data integrity
- Lack of program and data independence

In the case of **data redundancy,** the same data elements appear in many different files and often in different formats, which makes updating files difficult, time consuming, and prone to errors. For example, a course grades file and a tuition billing file may both contain a student's ID number, name, address, and telephone number. Obviously, having many copies of the same data elements takes up unnecessary storage space.

In addition to wasted space, data redundancy creates a problem when it comes to **file updating.** When an element of data needs to be changed—for example, student address—it must be updated in *all* the files, a tedious procedure. If some files are missed, data will be inconsistent—that is, **data integrity** is not maintained—and reports will be produced with erroneous information. (*Data integrity* generally refers to the quality of the data—that is, to its accuracy, reliability, and timeliness. If data integrity is not maintained, data is no longer accurate, reliable, and/or timely.)

Another limitation of file management systems has to do with the lack of **program independence** and **data independence.** This lack of independence means that different files established in different arrangements, such as some with the date first and expense items second and others vice versa, cannot be used by the same program. Programs must be written by programmers to use a specific file format. This process takes the programmer a large amount of time and costs the company a great deal of money.

To deal with these problems and the ever-growing demands for a flexible, easy-to-use mechanism for managing data, the concept of a database was developed.

DATABASE MANAGEMENT SYSTEMS

As mentioned earlier, the term *database* describes a collection of related records that forms an integral base of data that can be accessed by a wide variety of applications programs and user requests. In a database management system, data needs

FIGURE 9.4

(a) Traditional file management approach. In old file management systems, some of the same data elements were repeated in different files. (b) In database management systems, data elements are integrated, thus eliminating data redundancy.

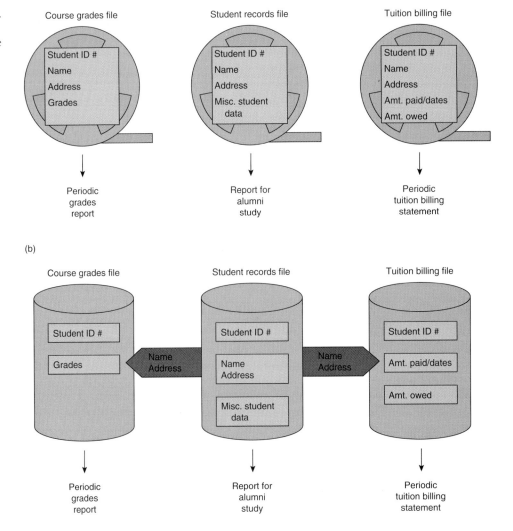

to be entered into the system only once. When the user instructs the program to sort data or compile a list, the program searches quickly through the data in memory (or in storage), copying needed data into a new file for the purpose at hand. However, the user's instructions do not change the original set of data in any way. (Database administrators may change the data later, when they update the database.)

How is this done? Through software—the database management system (DBMS). However, the software must be considered together with the hardware and the database because the type and capacity of certain hardware components and the size of the database will affect both the sophistication and the efficiency of the DBMS software.

HARDWARE: STORAGE COUNTS

Storage capacity is crucial to the operation of a database management system. Even the many megabytes of hard disk storage in an efficient, modern microcomputer can't handle the many gigabytes of data that move through some large corporations. However, not all organizations need minicomputer-based database management systems. Recent advances in the speed and the capacity of hard disk drives for microcomputers have made microcomputer-based database management systems possible for some organizations. (In general, one must have a minimum of 100 MB of hard disk space to run a microcomputer-based DBMS.)

Because database files represent a significant (in many organizations the most important) business resource, they must be protected from damage, loss, and unauthorized use. The most common way to protect the corporate database from loss or damage is to periodically make backup copies of it. In large database systems, backup copies are usually made on one or more reels of standard ½-inch magnetic tape. The backup process for large corporate databases requires the involvement of computer operations specialists. The most popular form of backup for microcomputer hard disks is the tape streamer, or streaming tape unit (Chapter 4). These devices are small, fast, and so easy to use that the user can perform the backup operation unassisted.

SOFTWARE: IN CONTROL

A database management system is an integrated set of software programs that provides all the necessary capabilities for building and maintaining database files, extracting the information required for making decisions, and formatting the information into structured reports. It is intended to:

- *Make data independent of the applications programs being used, so that it is easy to access and change.* Say, for example, you have created a student database with many student records. After some time, you decide to change the structure of the student database to include phone numbers. With a DBMS you can do this and still use the applications program you were using before you changed the database structure, because the data's organization is independent of the program being used.

- *Establish relationships among records in different files.* The user can obtain *all* data related to important data elements. For example, the user can obtain student course and address information from the student database while at the same time viewing the student's payment status from the billing database.

- *Eliminate data redundancy.* Because data is independent of the applications program being used, it can be stored a single time in any file that can be accessed, for example, by the student billing applications program or the grade-averaging program.

- *Define the characteristics of the data.* The user can create a database to store data based on particular informational needs.
- *Manage file access.* For example, the DBMS can "examine" user requests and clear them for access to retrieve data, thus keeping data safe from unauthorized access.
- *Maintain data integrity.* Because data is not stored redundantly, it needs to be updated only in one place.

Using DBMS software, personnel can request that a program be run to produce information in a predefined format or extract information in a specific way. For example, if you are the manager of a school's registration department, you may want to review a report of the classes that currently have space available; however, the manager of the school's finance division may want to use the same data to generate a report on courses that had low enrollment over the past two years to determine whether to continue offering these courses.

The easiest way to view a DBMS is to think of it as a layer of software that surrounds the database files (Figure 9.5). The DBMS software usually includes a query language, report writers, utilities, and an applications program language interface (usually called the *data manipulation language,* or *DML*). Each of these will be described in the following sections.

QUERY LANGUAGE

Most managers and other users find a **query language** for data retrieval (see also Chapter 7) to be the most valuable aspect of DBMS software. Traditionally, many

---

FIGURE 9.5

DBMS software. The software that comprises the functions of a database management system can be thought of as a layer that surrounds the database files. Among other things, this software provides the user interface, which allows the user to interact easily with the system.

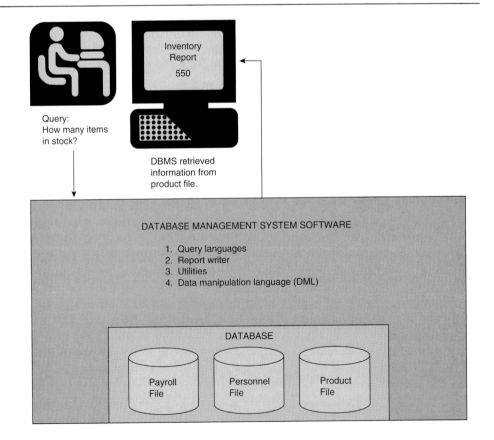

Query: How many items in stock?

DBMS retrieved information from product file.

DATABASE MANAGEMENT SYSTEM SOFTWARE

1. Query languages
2. Report writer
3. Utilities
4. Data manipulation language (DML)

DATABASE

Payroll File   Personnel File   Product File

Inventory Report 550

managers rely on the information provided by periodic reports. However, this creates a problem when a decision must be made *now* and the information required to make it will not be produced until the end of the week. The objective of a query language is to allow people to use simple English (or the language of the company they're working with) to produce information on demand that is also in simple English. To be effective, a query language must allow the user to phrase requests for information in a very flexible fashion. For example, take a request for inventory information. Here are some examples of questions that the user could ask using a query language when a single file is involved:

- List all items in the inventory database for which the quantity on hand equals zero. (Immediate orders would have to be placed to restock these items.)
- List all items in the database for which the quantity on hand is less than or equal to the reorder point. (This information would be used to process regular orders for restocking inventory.)

Here are examples of questions that the user could ask using a query language when more than one file is involved:

- List the names and addresses of all customers who ordered items that were out of stock and that are now in stock. (This would involve using both the customer file and the inventory file and would show a listing of all customers who should be notified by mail that the items they ordered were now available for pickup.)
- List the phone numbers of customers who ordered items that were out of stock and that aren't going to be restocked. (This would also involve using both the customer file and the inventory file and would show a listing of all customers who should be notified by phone that the item they ordered would no longer be carried in inventory.)

You, the user, can learn to use a typical query language effectively with about eight hours of instruction and practice. Once you have this skill, you can prepare a special report in a few minutes instead of several days or weeks. Several powerful query languages, including Structured Query Language (SQL), dBASE III Plus, dBASE IV, Oracle, and R:base System V, exist for use with microcomputers.

REPORT WRITER

The **report writer** aspect of DBMS software simplifies the process of generating reports after querying the DBMS system for information. The procedure is usually fairly easy and involves specifying column headings for the items to be included in the report, as well as any totals, subtotals, or other calculations (Figure 9.6).

Some DBMS software also includes **screen generators** to simplify the process of making data readily accessible to users. Screen generators display preformatted "forms" on the screen that users fill in to retrieve, modify, and/or add data.

UTILITIES

The utilities part of the DBMS software is used to maintain the database on an ongoing basis. This includes such tasks as:

- Creating and maintaining the data dictionary (described in more detail later in the chapter)
- Removing records flagged for deletion (most DBMSs have built-in protection schemes to prevent users from accidentally deleting records. To delete unwanted records from the database, the user must first mark, or "flag," them for deletion and then give the command to actually remove the flagged records)

- Establishing control of access to portions of the database (protecting the database against unauthorized use)
- Providing an easy way to back up the database and recover data if the database is damaged
- Monitoring performance
- Preventing data corruption when multiple users attempt to access the same database simultaneously

DATA MANIPULATION LANGUAGE (DML)

The user needs the **data manipulation language (DML)** software in the DBMS to effect input to and output from the database files; in other words, all programs, including the query language, must go through the DML, which comprises the technical instructions that make up the input/output routines in the DBMS. Each applications program that is written needs certain data elements to process to produce particular types of information. A list of required elements of data is contained within each applications program. The DML uses these lists, identifies the elements of data required, and provides the link necessary to the database to supply the data to the program. (In some cases, the data manipulation language is embedded in the query language.)

DATA DICTIONARIES AND TRANSACTION LOGS

Once a DBMS has been implemented, two types of files are constantly in use besides the database files—the **data dictionary** and a transaction log.

The information in the data dictionary varies from one DBMS to another. In general, the data dictionary maintains standard definitions of all data items within the scope of the database, including:

- What data is available
- Where the data is located
- Data attributes (descriptions)
- Who owns or is responsible for the data
- How the data is used
- Who is allowed to access the data for retrieval

FIGURE 9.6

DBMS-generated report

```
Page No.        1
01/01/92

              INVENTORY ITEMS
        QUANTITY-ON-HAND < REORDER POINT

PRODUCT NUMBER DESCRIPTION          SUPPLIER

           202 HAMMERS              A
           207 NAILS                B
           213 WRENCHES             C
           202 SCREW DRIVERS        B
           309 BROOM                C
           310 MOPS                 A
           315 POWER CABLES         C
           300 EXTENSION CORDS      A
```

- Who is allowed to update or change the data
- Relationships to other data items
- Security and privacy limitations

The dictionary is used constantly by the DBMS as a reference tool (Figure 9.7). When an applications program requests elements of data as part of a query, the DBMS refers to the data dictionary for guidance in retrieving them. The database administrator, whose job we'll discuss in more detail later, determines what the data dictionary contains.

The **transaction log** (Figure 9.7) contains a complete record of all activity that affected the contents of a database during the course of a transaction period. This log aids in backup and in rebuilding database files (recovery) if they are accidentally destroyed or damaged. If a backup copy is made each time a database file is updated and a transaction log is created to document the current transaction period's activity, then recovery from the loss of the current copy of the database file(s) is simple. In this case, the previous day's copy of the database is considered to be the current copy, which is then updated by using the most current transaction log.

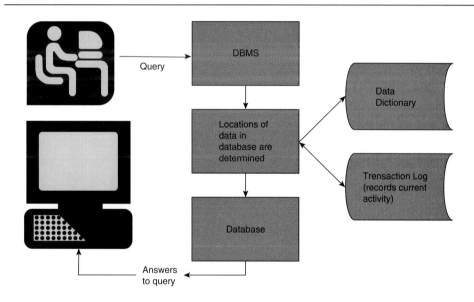

FIGURE 9.7

Data dictionary and transaction log. The bottom of the figure shows dBASE IV's data dictionary for an EMPLOYEE database located on drive A (A:).

Database management systems for microcomputers do not automatically create a transaction log file. Special provisions must be made in the program design to accommodate this requirement. Database management systems for minicomputers and mainframes usually build the transaction log automatically.

DATABASE MODELS

Three popular models are used to organize a database:

1. Hierarchical
2. Network
3. Relational

These three models have evolved gradually as users and computer specialists gained experience in using database management systems. They differ in terms of the cost of implementation, speed, degree of data redundancy, ease with which they can satisfy information requirements, and ease with which they can be updated.

In use since the late 1960s, the hierarchical and network database models were first developed and used principally on mainframe computers. The concepts behind the relational database model were pioneered in the early 1970s. This database model, which takes advantage of large-capacity direct access storage devices, has been used extensively on microcomputers and is also being used more and more on larger computers for large-scale applications.

HIERARCHICAL DATABASE MODEL

In the **hierarchical database model,** data is organized into related groups much like a family tree (Figure 9.8). The model comprises two types of records—parent records and child records. **Parent records** are higher in the structure of the model than **child records.** Each "child" can have only one "parent"; that is, each record may have many records below it but only one record above it. The record at the highest level, or top of the "tree," is called the root record. The **root record,** which is the key to the model, connects the various branches.

To store or retrieve a record in a hierarchical model, the DBMS begins at the root occurrence and moves downward through each of the occurrences until the correct record is located. There is no connection between separate branches in this type of model. See, for example, the route that is followed in Figure 9.8 to locate the record of travel expenses for the second week in April.

The primary advantage of the hierarchical database model is the ease with which data can be stored and retrieved, as well as the ease with which data can be extracted for reporting purposes.

The main disadvantage of this type of database model is that records in separate groups—in Figure 9.8, for example, medical, travel, and life insurance are separate groups—cannot be directly related without a great deal of effort. For example, the Moser Corporation might want to compare by month and by year the different expense amounts of each category to answer such questions as "What percentage is each yearly expense amount of the total of all expenses for the year?" and "What is the average expense amount for each month and for the year?" But the user is confined to retrieving data that can be obtained from the established hierarchical links among records. Also, if you delete a parent from the model, you automatically delete all the child records. In addition, modifying a hierarchical database structure is complex and requires a trained and experienced programmer who knows all the physical connections that exist between records. Another restriction is the inability to implement hierarchical models without a great deal of redundancy.

NETWORK DATABASE MODEL

The **network database model** (Figure 9.9) is somewhat similar to the hierarchical model, but each record can have more than one parent. This model overcomes the principal limitation of the hierarchical model because it establishes relationships between records in different groups. Any record can be related to any other data element.

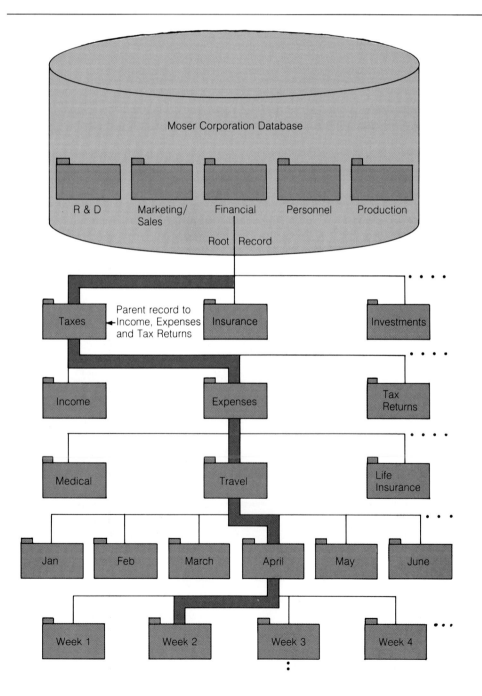

FIGURE 9.8

Hierarchical database model for the Moser Corporation. In this database model, which looks somewhat like a family tree, a parent record can have many child records, but each child record can have only one parent record. The root record is the topmost record.

2

Figure 9.9 shows the expense types and expense periods for the first quarter of a year for the Moser Corporation as part of a network database model. With this type of model, it would be easy to compare weekly or monthly expense amounts or to determine what percentage travel expenses are of all expenses for the first quarter.

The primary advantage of the network database model is its ability to provide sophisticated logical relationships among the records. However, as in the hierarchical model, the user is limited to retrieving data that can be accessed using the established links between records.

RELATIONAL DATABASE MODEL

The **relational database model** (Figure 9.10) is made up of many tables, called *relations*, in which related data elements are stored. The relations—similar in concept to files—are made up of rows and columns, and they provide data to the user about an *entity* class. A row (similar to a record) is called a *tuple*, and a column (similar to a field) is called an *attribute*. All related tables must have a common data item, or key field. Thus, any data stored in one table can be linked with any data stored in any related table. The main objective of the relational database model is to allow complex logical relationships between records to be expressed in a simple fashion.

Relational databases are useful because they can cross-reference data and retrieve data automatically. Users do not have to be aware of any "structure" to use a relational database, and they can use it with little effort or training.

The main disadvantage of the relational model is that searching the database can be time consuming, so it has primarily been used with smaller databases on microcomputers. Indeed, the relational model has become the most popular database model for microcomputer-based database management systems such as dBASE III, dBASE IV, and Paradox. However, the relational model is finding more and more applications on mainframes and minicomputers.

FIGURE 9.9

Network database model for the Moser Corporation

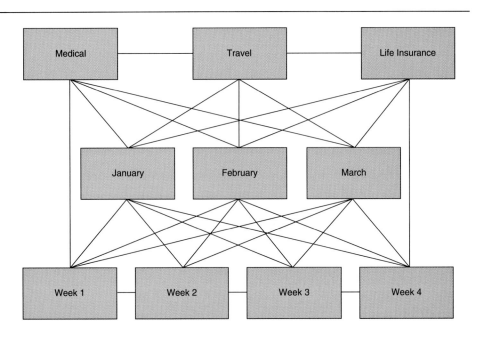

DESIGNING A DATABASE

Many users in the microcomputer environment will design a database and will actually build and implement it using a microcomputer DBMS; however, users are less involved in database design and development when the database management system is intended to be used in minicomputer and mainframe computer environments. (Users are highly involved in defining what data needs to be stored in the database, though.) In these situations, design and development are carried out by trained and experienced information system specialists.

MATCHING THE DESIGN TO THE ORGANIZATION

Most users working with microcomputer-based DBMS software focus on a very specific set of objectives and information processing needs—that is, their own. For many small applications this is a satisfactory approach. However, the objectives must be broader when working with a large corporation, a large computer system, and more complex and sophisticated DBMS software. And the plans for the use of the database management system must be integrated with the long-range plans for the company's total information system. The information processing needs of the entire corporation must be considered and viewed in terms of a corporate database that facilitates the collection, maintenance, and sharing of data among all the company's organizational units. Once the general information needs have been established, the design process can proceed. This process usually comprises two distinct phases of activity—the logical design phase and the physical design phase.

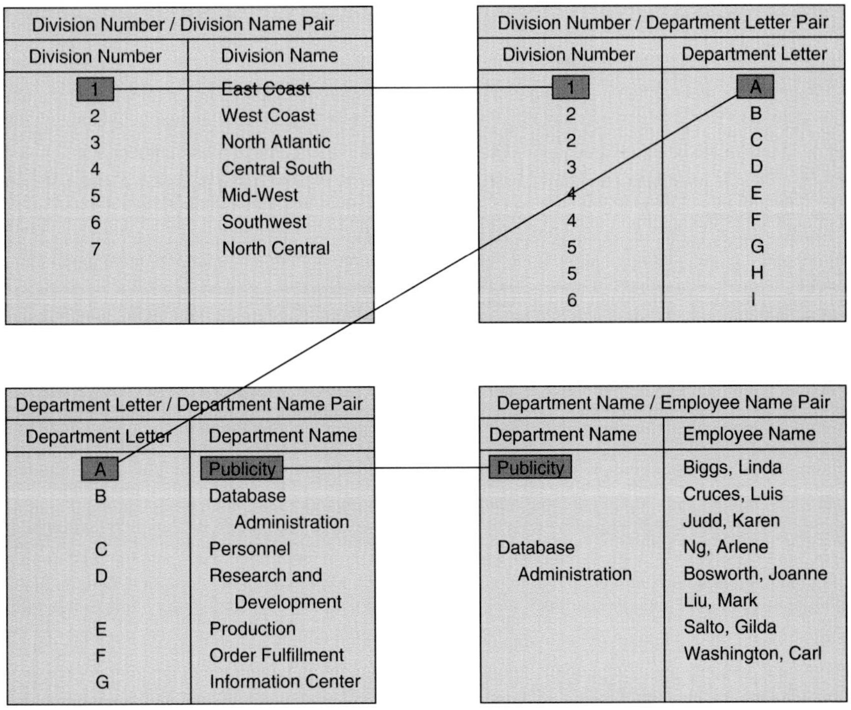

FIGURE 9.10

Relational database model

COMPUTERS AND CAREERS

INFORMATION

There is a new business breed: "infopreneurs," specialized entrepreneurs moving to exploit opportunities for products and services provided by advances in computers and communications. The real value of information, it has been pointed out, is when it becomes knowledge. This is where the infopreneurs come in.

Infopreneurs transform existing information into new uses. They identify and create new markets by developing new information services and products. Examples are those who have bought the electronic rights to printed lists of names. The telephone Yellow Pages, for instance, appear not only in book form but also in computer form, giving rise to databases that can create different kinds of lists or be sent over communications lines.

Two examples of how the information business works are as follows: Dow Jones News/Retrieval takes information collected by the company's news organizations, such as *The Wall Street Journal*, splits it into news, financial data, and stock prices, and sells them separately. An organization that tracks commercial ocean-going ships, Lloyd's Maritime Data Network, sells the information to shippers, who can use it to negotiate better deals with carriers.

Half the electronic information sold in the United States is financial, used for stock trading and the like. However, there are other uses for databases and communications. For instance, instead of using advertisements and personnel agencies, some companies searching for the right person for the right job use computerized files of resumes offered by industry associations, alumni groups, and entrepreneurs such as Computer Assisted Recruitment International of Schaumberg, Ill. Comp-U-Card is a merchandise broker that takes orders from home shoppers—either by telephone or modem-linked computer—for thousands of products. CheckFree, of Columbus, Ohio, offers home-computer users an automatic bill-paying service, working with any bank you choose.

Nearly all occupations now have their own specialized information services. Most major law firms, for example, use Mead Data Central's LEXIS service, a computer-based research system for lawyers. Mead also owns Micromedex, which sells information on poisons, drugs, and emergency care to several hospitals and poison centers. Many catalog mailers pay Claritas Corp., a marketing consulting firm, to tell them how to reach certain kinds of prospective buyers, whose lifestyles can be identified according to the ZIP codes they live in.

As computer-based information has become more a part of every industry and occupation, investigative journalists have found that being able to sift through electronic databases is as important as a notepad and good shoes. Indeed, some journalists feel that the only way that reporters can monitor enormous organizations such as government agencies is to get access to computer-based files.

Where will all this deluge of information end? Reportedly the Library of Congress alone doubles its volume every 10 years. As the Information Society continues to grow, more and more people will specialize in the creating and selling of information. ∎

Logical Design

Logical database design refers to *what* the database is as opposed to *how* it operates; in other words, the logical design is a detailed description of the database model from the business perspective rather than the technical perspective. The logical design of a database involves defining user information needs, analyzing data element requirements and logical groupings, finalizing the design, and creating the data dictionary. The major focus is on identifying every element of data necessary to produce the required management information systems reports and on the relationship among the records. This process involves defining two distinct views of the database—the schema and the subschema.

Schema refers to the organization of the database in its entirety, including the names of all the data elements and how the records are linked in useful ways. A **subschema** is part of the schema; it refers to the manner in which certain records are linked in ways useful to a *particular* user—perhaps to produce a report or satisfy certain queries (often called *user-views*). In other words, because the data in a database should *not* be accessible to all the employees of a company, subschemas are designed into a DBMS that limit users in certain functional areas within the company—such as accounting and marketing—to certain files and records in the database.

Defining Database-User Information Needs

The objective of the first step in logical design is *information requirements analysis*—to identify specific information needs and to group them logically. For example, let's assume that in your small business you have indicated that the following elements of data must be collected about each employee:

PERSONNEL DEPARTMENT	PAYROLL DEPARTMENT
Employee name	Employee name
Home address	Home address
Phone	Pay rate
Hire date	Number of dependents
Department	Deductions
Job title	Year-to-date (YTD) pay
Salary level	
Date of last review	
Date of next review	
Performance rating	
Number of dependents	
Office location	
Extension	

Analyzing Data Elements and Logical Groups

This step in logical design involves composing subschemas. First, the list of data elements that users have identified as necessary is analyzed to:

- Identify redundant data elements
- Identify the natural groups into which data elements can be organized
- Identify groups of data elements needed for specific applications programs

You'll note that there are three redundant elements of data in the items listed above for the personnel and payroll departments: employee name, home address, and number of dependents. And the items can be organized into at least four natural groups: employee data, position data, performance data, and salary data. The elements of data could be grouped as follows:

EMPLOYEE DATA	PERFORMANCE DATA
Employee number	Employee number
Name	Hire date
Home address	Date of last review
Home phone	Performance rating
POSITION DATA	Date of next review
Employee number (needed as identifier)	SALARY DATA
Department	Employee number
Job title	Pay rate
Office location	YTD pay
Extension	Deductions
	Number of dependents

Second, the major output reports to be produced from the database are identified along with the elements of data that will be required for each report. For example, if we know that we will need reports on the dates when employees are due for their next performance evaluations, we would include the following data elements: employee number, name, hire date, date of last review, performance rating, date of next review, and pay rate. This grouping of data elements would be considered a subschema.

FINALIZING THE DESIGN

The final step in the logical design of a database is to combine and refine the logical subsets of data—the *subschemas*—into an overall logical view of the relationships among all elements to be stored in the database—the *schema*. The schema includes a description of all the data elements to be stored, the logical records into which the data elements will be grouped, and the number of individual database files or relations to be maintained within the framework of the DBMS.

PHYSICAL DESIGN

Once the logical design of the database has been defined, the next step is to proceed with the physical design. The **physical database design,** also called the *internal view* of the database, involves the specification of exactly *how* the data will be arranged and stored on the direct access storage devices allocated for use by the DBMS. The objective of the physical design is to store data so that it can be updated and retrieved in the quickest and most efficient way possible.

One of the main considerations in the development of the physical design is the users' data access patterns. In other words, how often will certain data elements need to be retrieved by the users? Knowing the patterns can improve speed and efficiency. Information about them is gathered during the logical design stage, often by counting the number of times users will access data elements by manual methods (such as opening a file drawer for a specific folder). Users' access patterns often change, so whatever physical design is developed must be continually reviewed and updated when necessary to conform to actual access patterns.

Note that microcomputer DBMS users are not involved in the physical design of the DBMS, since that is determined by the type of DBMS package they have purchased.

DATABASE ADMINISTRATION

The effective use of a database within an organization requires a great deal of cooperation and coordination. User requirements and needs throughout an organization need to be frequently reviewed, and the overall security and integrity of the database must be ensured. Organizations working with DBMSs quickly recognized the need for an individual or a group of individuals to coordinate all related activities and needs and to control the database. A **database administrator (DBA)** undertakes this function.

WHY ADMINISTER?

As we mentioned earlier, the development and implementation of a corporatewide database is a major task that requires the complete support of management, a substantial amount of human resources and user involvement, and often the expenditure of large sums of money. This task needs to be coordinated. In addition, the data in the database often represents the company's most precious asset: It must be managed well, so that it is not misused or damaged.

THE JOB OF THE DATABASE ADMINISTRATOR

The responsibilities for administering the database activities within an organization are usually assigned to an individual or a small group of individuals, depending on the size of the organization and the scope and complexity of the database. The database administrator has six major responsibilities.

1. *Database design.* The DBA plays a key role in both the logical and the physical design phases. He or she guides the definition of the database content and the creation of the database dictionary, as well as set data classification and coding procedures and backup and restart/recovery procedures.

2. *Database implementation and operation.* The DBA guides the use of the DBMS on a daily basis. Among other things, this includes adding and deleting data, controlling access to data, detecting and repairing losses, instituting restart/recovery procedures when necessary, and assigning space used on secondary storage devices.

3. *Coordination with user.* The DBA receives and reviews all user requests for additional DBMS support. The administrator establishes feasibility, resolves redundant or conflicting requests, and assists in the process of establishing priorities for the requests. In addition, the DBA is responsible for establishing and enforcing organizationwide DBMS standards for such things as techniques for accessing data, formats in which data elements will be stored, and data element names.

4. *Backup and recovery.* The DBA is responsible for preparing a plan for periodically backing up the database(s) and for establishing procedures for recovering from the failure of the DBMS software or related hardware components.

5. *Performance monitoring.* The DBA constantly monitors the performance of the DBMS, using specialized software to calculate and record operating statistics. If a problem occurs, such as a decrease in responsiveness, the DBA must identify the problem and take steps to improve performance.

6. *System security.* The DBA is responsible for designing and implementing a system of DBMS security that controls who has access to the database

files, which DBMS operations can be performed, and which applications programs can be accessed. This system often involves the assignment of user identification codes and passwords.

Experience has shown that organizations that have a well-organized and well-staffed database administration department achieve much greater success in the use of the database management system to manage business information resources than do organizations without such a department.

ADVANTAGES AND DISADVANTAGES OF THE DBMS

The principal advantages of the DBMS approach include:

- *Elimination of data redundancy.* More storage becomes available when maintenance of redundant data elements among traditionally separate application files is rendered unnecessary.

- *Easy file updating.* Because there is only one copy of each data element, all applications have access to the most current data. In traditional systems in which the same element of data was kept on several different files, ensuring that all copies of the data element were updated when changes were made was a problem.

- *Data independence and simplification of program maintenance.* In a DBMS the programs are much more independent of the data than in traditional file processing systems. Previously, programs had to include a substantial amount of information about the format and structure of the fields and records in each file accessed. In a DBMS, this information is contained in the data dictionary; the programs do not need to contain these details. In traditional systems, when a change in format of one or more data elements was necessary, each program that used the data element had to be modified. In a DBMS only the data dictionary needs to be updated.

- *Increased user productivity.* The ability of a DBMS to respond quickly to user requests for additional information without involving the user in technical language manipulation encourages faster and more efficient work. The report generators and query languages associated with database management systems make them easy to use.

- *Increased security.* Centralized control of access to and use of the database is easily established. With traditional file-processing systems, the data was too fragmented for effective security to be exercised.

- *Standardization of data definitions.* Before database management systems, each applications program could define similar elements of data with different names. However, the use of data dictionaries standardizes the names and descriptions of data elements.

Some disadvantages to using a database management system include:

- Database management systems are complex; extensive planning and a substantial amount of technical expertise are needed to implement and maintain a system.

- The costs associated with the development and operation of a corporatewide DBMS can be substantial in terms of software and hardware acquisition, technical support personnel, and operations personnel.

- The consolidation of an entire business's information resources into a DBMS can create a high level of vulnerability. A natural disaster, a fire, or even a hardware- or software-related problem can cause the loss of the current version of the database files. This could be fatal for a business unless proper precautions were taken. A very thorough framework of policies and procedures must be established to ensure that backup copies of the database files are made on a regular basis, that a transaction log is maintained, and that documentation exists for recovery procedures.

WHO OWNS THE DATABASE?

Before ending this chapter we need to say a few words about who owns a given type of database. Small and large databases can all be classified as individual, company, distributed, or proprietary.

The *individual database* is basically a microcomputer database used by one person. The data is usually stored on a large-capacity hard disk. For example, an independent certified public accountant (CPA) may build and maintain an individual database of customer and account information. In this case, the individual user owns the database.

The *company database*, or *shared database*, is shared by the users of one company, which owns the database. The data is usually stored on a minicomputer or a mainframe and managed by a DBA. Users are linked via a LAN (local area network, discussed in Chapter 8) to the database through terminals or microcomputer workstations.

The *distributed database* is shared by the users of one company, which owns the database, but the data is not stored where the users are, as it is with a company database. Instead, the data is made accessible to users through a variety of communications networks. For example, users with microcomputers and hard disks could be linked by a WAN (wide area network, discussed in Chapter 8) that is linked to a mainframe.

The *proprietary database* is a huge database that functions as an information service, such as CompuServe, Prodigy, and Dow Jones News/Retrieval (which were discussed in Chapter 8). The proprietor owns the database in this case.

FIGURE 9.11

Several popular DBMS software packages for microcomputers

SUMMARY

- *Database management systems* (DBMSs) are comprehensive software tools that allow users to create, maintain, and manipulate an integrated base of data.

- *File management systems* used to be the only way of managing data and files. In these systems, data was stored in a series of unrelated files on tape or disk. The major problems associated with file management systems are
    1. Data redundancy—the same data appears in more than one file.
    2. Tedious updating procedures—because the same data appeared in many places, updating files was time consuming.
    3. Poor data integrity—if some redundant data elements were missed during file updating, they were no longer current and could cause inaccurate information to be produced.
    4. Lack of data and program independence—programmers could not use the data file to develop new programs because the data and the programs were restricted by existing formats. To update either the applications program or the data file became a major task.

- Database management systems were developed to:
    1. Make data independent of the programs, so that it is easy to access and change
    2. Eliminate data redundancy
    3. Establish relationships among records in different files
    4. Define data characteristics
    5. Manage file directories
    6. Maintain data integrity
    7. Provide a means of securing access to the database

- DBMS software often uses a *query language* as an interface between the user and the system. This interface allows users to easily ask questions of the DBMS and obtain information to answer the questions and produce reports.

- DBMS software also includes capabilities to simplify *report writing* and maintain the database (utilities) as well as to allow different applications programs to use the database by means of a *data manipulation language*, or DML.

- During the design of the database, a *data dictionary* is constructed that contains all the data descriptions used by the DBMS to locate and retrieve data.

- The DBMS also can include a *transaction log* of current activity. This log can be used to update necessary backup copies of the database in case of failure of or damage to the operating database system.

- A DBMS structure usually falls into one of three categories:
    1. Hierarchical
    2. Network
    3. Relational

    These models differ in terms of the cost of implementation, speed, degree of data redundancy, ease with which they can satisfy information requirements, and ease with which they can be updated.

- The *hierarchical database model* resembles a family tree; the records are organized in a one-to-many relationship, meaning that one parent record can have many child records. Records are retrieved from a hierarchical model by starting at the root record at the top and moving down through the structure. There is no connection between separate branches.

- The *network database model* is similar to the hierarchical model, but each child record can have more than one parent record, and it also allows relationships between records in different groups. Also, access to the database can be made from a number of points—not just from the top.

- The *relational database model* is made up of many tables, called *relations*, in which related data elements are stored. The data elements are in rows, called *tuples*, and columns, called *attributes*. The main objective of the relational database model is to allow complex logical relationships between records to be expressed in a simple fashion.

- In general, the hierarchical and network models are less expensive to implement and allow faster access to data. However, they are more difficult to update and aren't as effective at satisfying information requirements as the relational model can be. Because the hierarchical and network models are older than the relational model, they are used most often on large computers. The newer relational model is used extensively on microcomputers; however, because relational models are so flexible in satisfying information requests and because they aren't difficult to update, relational models are being used more and more on large computers.

- The process of database design is usually carried out exclusively by specialists; however, users may have occasion to set up small databases for microcomputers.

- The main responsibilities of a database administrator include:
  1. Guiding database design
  2. Overseeing database implementation and operation
  3. User coordination
  4. Backup and recovery
  5. Performance monitoring
  6. System security

- In general, the main advantages of database management systems are
  1. Elimination of data redundancy
  2. Increased ease of file updating
  3. Increased data independence and simplification of program and maintenance
  4. Increased user productivity and efficiency
  5. Increased security
  6. Standardization of data definitions

- The main disadvantages are
  1. Complexity
  2. High cost of implementation
  3. Vulnerability of consolidated business data in a central database

KEY TERMS

child record, p. 232
database, p. 222
database administrator (DBA), p. 239
database management system (DBMS), p. 222
data dictionary, p. 230
data independence, p. 226
data integrity, p. 225
data manipulation language (DML), p. 230

data redundancy, p. 225
file management system, p. 225
file updating, p. 225
hierarchical database model, p. 232
logical database design, p. 237
network database model, p. 233
parent record, p. 232
physical database design, p. 238

program independence, p. 226
query language, p. 228
relational database model, p. 234
report writer, p. 229
root record, p. 232
schema, p. 237
screen generator, p. 229
subschema, p. 237
transaction log, p. 231

EXERCISES

SELF-TEST

1. An individual piece of data within a record is called a _____.
2. If an element of data in a database needs to be changed, it must be changed in *all* the files in order for data _____ to be maintained.
3. A group of related records is called a _____.
4. *Data redundancy* means that an element of data (field) is repeated in many different files in a database. (true/false)
5. Microcomputers always had the storage capacity to handle database management systems. (true/false)
6. If you have a collection of related records that forms an integral base of data that can be accessed by a wide variety of applications programs and user requests, then you have a _____.
7. DBMS software can manage file access by "clearing" users through the use of passwords. (true/false)
8. The aspect of DBMS software that simplifies the process of generalizing reports is called a _____ _____.
9. The most sophisticated database model that allows complex logical relationships among records in many different files is the _____ database model.
10. A microcomputer-based database owned by one person is called an _____ database.
11. One key field must be the same in all related tables in a relational database. (true/false)
12. To use a microcomputer-based DBMS, you should probably have a minimum of _____ of hard disk storage space.
13. Old file-handling methods did not provide the user with an easy way to establish relationships among records in different files. (true/false)
14. A _____ _____ allows the user to phrase requests for information from a database in a very flexible fashion.
15. A special file in the DBMS called the _____ _____ maintains standard definitions of all data items within the scope of the database.
16. dBASE III, dBASE IV, and Paradox are popular microcomputer DBMS packages. (true/false)
17. Ensuring backup and recovery of a database is not one of the functions of a database administrator. (true/false)
18. The _____ _____ contains a complete record of all activity that affected the contents of a database during the course of a transaction period—such as one day.
19. _____ refers to the logical organization of a database in its entirety.
20. _____ refers to the manner in which certain records are linked in ways useful to a particular user.

SOLUTIONS (1) field; (2) integrity; (3) file; (4) true; (5) false; (6) database; (7) true; (8) report writer; (9) relational; (10) individual; (11) true; (12) 100 MB; (13) true; (14) query language; (15) data dictionary; (16) true; (17) false; (18) transaction log; (19) schema; (20) subschema

SHORT ANSWER

1. Why is a database management system important to many organizations?
2. What are the three main problems with old file management systems?
3. What is a query language in a DBMS?
4. What does the data dictionary in a DBMS provide?
5. What used to be the main limitation to microcomputer-based DBMSs?
6. What is the difference between a distributed database and a proprietary database?
7. Give three main advantages of a DBMS over old file-handling approaches; give three main disadvantages.
8. Name four functions of a database administrator.
9. What is the main difference between the logical design and the physical design of a database?
10. Why are microcomputer DBMS users usually involved in the logical design of the database but not in the physical design?

PROJECTS

1. Interview someone who works with or manages the database at your school or university. What types of records make up the database, and which departments use it? What types of transactions do these departments enact? Which database structure is used? What are the types and sizes of the storage devices? Was the software custom written?

2. What types of databases do you think would include information about yourself? Prepare a brief summary.

3. Contact TRW Credit, P.O. Box 14008, Orange, CA 92613, and ask for a credit report in your name (the report comes from their huge database). If you are in their database, are there any mistakes in the report? If so, how do you think the incorrect data came to be in your file? (Be sure to inquire about any costs involved before you tell TRW to send the report.)

4. People's resistance to change, sometimes called *social inertia,* may come about simply because change is stressful to many people. Employees in organizations undergoing change from familiar, old procedures to new, computer-based procedures often resist the efforts of trainers and administrators to institute the new programs. If you were a new database administrator in a large company converting to a new computer-based DBMS, what are some things you would tell people to lessen their resistance?

5. Look through magazines such as *PC Computing, PC Magazine, PC World, MacWorld,* and *MacUser* for microcomputer DBMS ads. Make a list of the functions advertised to help the user and also list the hardware requirements mentioned for each one. How do you think you could use a microcomputer DBMS in your profession, job, or other activities?

CHAPTER 10

MANAGEMENT INFORMATION SYSTEMS AND SYSTEM DEVELOPMENT

To be functional, systems and databases need to be tied clearly to business or professional goals, objectives, and plans. Indeed, data and systems have no meaning until they are put into the context of what a business does. To be useful as a resource—just as people and money are resources for a company—data and data processing systems must be *managed* according to a company's needs. *Management information systems*, also called *information resource management*, provide the means and the methods to manage the components of the computer-based information cycle—hardware, software, data/information, procedures, and people—as well as its four phases—input, processing, storage, and output.

PREVIEW

When you have completed this chapter, you will be able to:

Describe a basic management information system and explain its role in an organization

Describe the levels of management, the five basic functions of managers, and the types of decisions typically made at each level

Distinguish among transaction processing systems, management information systems for middle management, and decision support systems

Briefly explain the functions of an information center

Identify the six phases of an information system's development life cycle

Describe the role of the user in information systems development

CHAPTER OUTLINE

Why Is This Chapter Important?

Information Systems: What They Are, How They Work

What Is Management?

What Is a Management Information System?
    Levels of Management: What Kinds of Decisions Are Made?
    The Role of the MIS in a Business

How Does Management Make Decisions?
    Step 1—Problem Recognition and Identification
    Step 2—Identification and Evaluation of Alternatives
    Step 3—Alternative Selection
    Step 4—Action
    Step 5—Follow-up

What Kind of Information Does Management Use to Make Decisions?

Types of Management Information Systems
    Transaction Processing System (TPS)
    Management Information System (MIS)
    Decision Support System (DSS)

Developing and Implementing a Management Information System

Information Centers

Systems Analysis and Design
    The Systems Development Life Cycle (SDLC)
    Phase 1—Analyze the Current System
    Phase 2—Define the New System Requirements
    Phase 3—Design the New System
    Phase 4—Develop the New System
    Phase 5—Implement the New System
    Phase 6—Postimplementation Evaluation and Maintenance
    What Skills Does the User Need?

Summary

Key Terms

Exercises

WHY IS THIS CHAPTER IMPORTANT?

Information technology can ruin our lives unless we think of ways to get it under control. Without an organized approach to managing information, we may drown in an ocean of available information, unable to make decisions. Although knowledge may well be power, we must remember that information does not equal knowledge.

What should managers do to change an information technology into an intelligence technology to assist with decision making and efficient, productive, and high-quality business operation? In other words, how can users of an information system do their jobs better and not just shuffle overwhelming amounts of data and information from input to storage, from storage to processing and back to storage, and from processing to output? The answer: through management information systems. By understanding the principles of information management, users can help exploit technology to accomplish business and professional goals. As more and more hardware, software, and data are shared by multiple users, users are becoming more and more involved in the on-line functioning and management of the entire information system.

INFORMATION SYSTEMS: WHAT THEY ARE, HOW THEY WORK

Chapter 2 described the computer-based information system as comprising five parts—hardware, software, data/information, procedures, and people. The fourth component (procedures) includes manual and computerized procedures and standards for processing data into usable information. A *procedure* is a specific sequence of steps performed to complete one or more information-processing activities. In some organizations, these processing procedures are carried out only by the staff; in others they are carried out by a combination of the staff and the computer specialists.

If you walk into a busy discount consumer-products showroom, stand in a corner, and observe the activities taking place, you will probably see the following kinds of activities: Customers come in and browse around, looking at the display cases. Some customers decide to buy items and begin to fill out order forms. If they are completed properly, the order forms are taken at the counter by a clerk and placed into a *queue*—that is, in line to be processed. If an order form is not complete, the clerk asks the customer questions and completes it. Then a stock person takes the completed order forms into the stockroom or warehouse and returns with the goods. A clerk takes each order form, marks it "Filled," and rings up the sale on the cash register. All these activities form a procedure that is part of the *sales order entry system* (Figure 10.1).

A business is made up of many procedures, grouped logically into systems. The types of information systems found in companies vary according to the nature and the structure of the business; however, the systems commonly found in many businesses include payroll, personnel, accounting, and inventory.

Businesses receive data from a variety of sources, including customers who purchase products or services, vendors from whom supplies are ordered, banks, government agencies, and insurance companies—just to name a few. Information systems help organizations process all this data into *useful* information. One of the most important purposes of a business's information system, then, is to satisfy the knowledge requirements of management.

WHAT IS MANAGEMENT?

You know what an information system is. After we consider what *management* consists of, we will see how the two concepts can be put together as a management information system.

Management often refers to those individuals in an organization who are responsible for providing leadership and direction in the areas of planning, organizing, staffing, supervising, and controlling business activities. These five functions, which are the primary tasks of management, may be defined as follows:

1. *Planning* activities require the manager to formulate goals and objectives and develop short- and long-term plans to achieve these goals.

2. Management's responsibility for *organizing* includes the development of an organizational structure and a framework of standards, procedures, and policies designed to carry out ongoing business activities.

3. *Staffing* refers to management's responsibility for identifying the personnel needs of the organization and selecting the personnel, as well as training staff. Many companies have personnel managers to take charge of these activities.

4. *Supervising* refers to management's responsibility to provide employees with the supervision, guidance, and counseling necessary to keep them highly motivated and working productively toward the achievement of company objectives. This includes the recognition of good work, perhaps through certificates or bonuses, and concrete suggestions about how to improve performance. Companywide educational seminars may also be held to upgrade employees' knowledge of the company in general or perhaps to help them deal with stress and improve their health.

5. *Controlling* refers to management's responsibility to monitor organizational performance and the business environment so that steps can be taken to improve performance and modify plans as necessary in response to the mar-

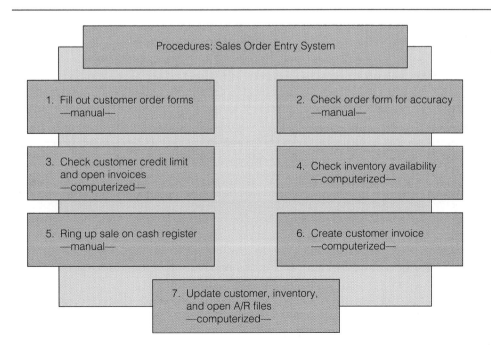

FIGURE 10.1

This group of related procedures makes up a simple sales order entry system.

ketplace. This includes keeping alert to new opportunities in the market-place and recognizing new business opportunities.

Each primary management function involves making decisions, and information is required to make good decisions. Thus, to fulfill its responsibilities, management must set up information systems and subsystems.

What Is a Management Information System?

A **management information system (MIS)** comprises computer-based processing and/or manual procedures to provide useful and timely information to support management decision making in a rapidly changing business environment. MIS systems enable *information resource management (IRM)*. The MIS system must supply managers with information quickly, accurately, and completely.

The approaches that companies take to develop information systems for management differ depending on the structure and management style of the organization. However, the scope of an MIS is generally companywide, and it services management personnel at all three traditional organizational levels:

1. Low-level, or operating, management
2. Middle management
3. Upper, or top, management

The primary objective of the MIS is to satisfy the need that managers have for information that is *more summarized and relevant to the specific decisions that need to be made* than the information normally produced in an organization and that is *available soon enough to be of value in the decision-making process*. The information flows up and down through the three levels of management and is made available in various types of reports.

Levels of Management: What Kinds of Decisions Are Made?

Each level of management (Figure 10.2) can be distinguished by the types of decisions made, the time frame considered in the decisions, and the types of report information needed to make decisions.

Operating Management
The lowest—and the largest—level of management, **operating management,** deals mostly with decisions that cover a relatively narrow time frame. Operating management, also called *supervisory management*, actualizes the plans of middle management and controls daily operations—the day-to-day activities that keep the organization humming. Examples of operating managers are the warehouse manager in charge of inventory restocking and the materials manager responsible for seeing that all necessary materials are on hand in a manufacturing firm to produce the product being manufactured.

Most decisions at this level require easily defined information that relates to the current status and activities within the basic business functions—for example, the information needed to decide whether to restock inventory. This information is generally given to low-level managers in **detail reports** that contain specific information about routine activities. Because these reports are structured—that is, their form is predetermined—and daily business operations data is readily available, their processing can easily be computerized.

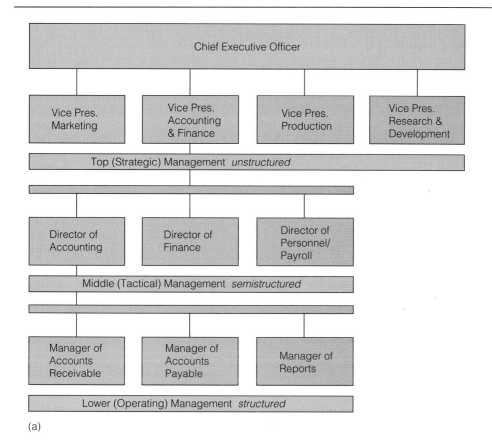

(a)

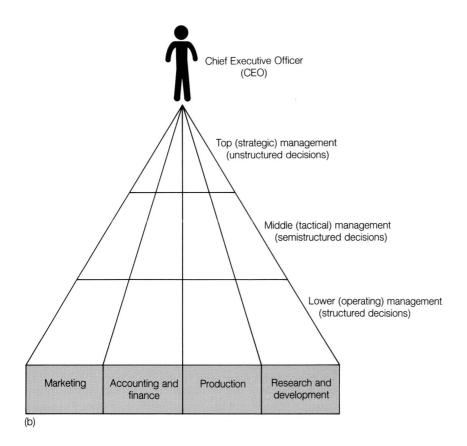

(b)

FIGURE 10.2

Three levels of management, three kinds of decisions. Different types of decisions are made depending on the level of management. The higher a manager is in an organization's hierarchy, the more decisions he or she must make based on information that is increasingly less structured. The four basic business functions or departments that top managers control are marketing, accounting and finance, production, and research and development. (a) This part of the figure shows the organizational hierarchy from a vertical perspective, focusing on the department of accounting and finance; (b) this part of the figure shows the hierarchy as a pyramid to indicate that there are fewer managers at higher levels of management.

Managers at this level, often referred to as **operational decision makers,** typically make structured decisions (Figure 10.3a). A **structured decision** is a predictable decision that can be made by following a well-defined set of routine procedures. For instance, a manager may not know exactly when inventory will need to be restocked, but he or she knows that a decision to restock must be made soon. This type of decision can easily be programmed as a part of computer-based data processing—for example, identifying the reorder point for a particular part or when to apply a discount to a customer's invoice.

MIDDLE MANAGEMENT

The **middle** level of **management** deals with decisions that cover a somewhat broader range of time and involve more experience. Some common titles of middle managers are plant manager, division manager, sales manager, branch manager, and director of personnel. The information that middle managers need involves review, summarization, and analysis of historical data to help plan and control operations and implement policy that has been formulated by upper management. This information is usually given to middle managers in the form of **summary reports,** which show totals and trends—for example, total sales by office, by product, by salesperson, or total overall sales—and **exception reports,** which show out-of-the-ordinary data—for example, inventory reports that list only those items that number fewer than 10 in stock. These reports may be regularly scheduled (periodic reports), requested on a case-by-case basis (on-demand reports), or generated only when certain conditions exist (event-initiated reports).

Periodic reports are produced at predetermined times—daily, weekly, monthly, quarterly, or annually—and commonly include payroll reports, inventory status reports, sales reports, income statements, and balance sheets. **On-demand reports** are usually requested by a manager when information is needed that focuses on a particular problem. For example, if a customer wants to establish a large charge account, a manager might request a special report on the customer's payment and order history. **Event-initiated reports** usually deal with a change in conditions that requires immediate attention, such as an out-of-stock report or a report on an equipment breakdown.

Managers at the middle level of management are often referred to as **tactical decision makers** who generally deal with semistructured decisions. A **semistructured decision** is a decision that, unlike a structured decision, must be made without a base of clearly defined informational procedures. In most cases, a semistructured decision (Figure 10.3b) is complex, requiring detailed analysis and extensive computations. Examples of semistructured decisions include deciding how many units of a specific product should be kept in inventory, whether or not to purchase a larger computer system, from what source to purchase personal computers, and whether to purchase a multiuser minicomputer system. At least some of the information requirements at this level can be met through computer-based data processing.

UPPER MANAGEMENT

The **upper** level of **management** deals with decisions that are the broadest in scope and cover the widest time frame. Typical titles of managers at this level are chief executive officer (CEO), president, treasurer, controller, executive vice president, and senior partner. Top managers include only a few powerful people who are in charge of the four basic functions of a business—marketing, accounting and finance, production, and research and development. Decisions made at this level are unpredictable, long-range, and related to the future—not just past and/or current activities; therefore, they demand the most experience and judgment.

A company's MIS must be able to supply information to upper management as needed in periodic reports, event-initiated reports, and on-demand reports. The information must show how all the company's operations and departments are related to and affected by one another. The major decisions made at this level tend to be directed toward (1) strategic planning—for example, how growth should be financed and which new markets should be tackled first; (2) allocation of resources, such as deciding whether to build or lease office space and whether to spend more money on advertising or the hiring of new staff members; and (3) policy formulation, such as determining the company's policy on hiring minorities and providing employee incentives. Managers at this level are often referred to as **strategic decision makers.**

Upper management typically makes unstructured decisions (Figure 10.3c). An **unstructured decision** is the most complex type of decision that managers are faced with. Because these decisions are rarely based on predetermined routine procedures, they involve the subjective judgment of the decision maker. As a result, this type of decision is the hardest to support from a computer-based data processing standpoint. Examples of unstructured decisions include deciding five-year goals for the company, evaluating future financial resources, and deciding how to react to the actions of competitors.

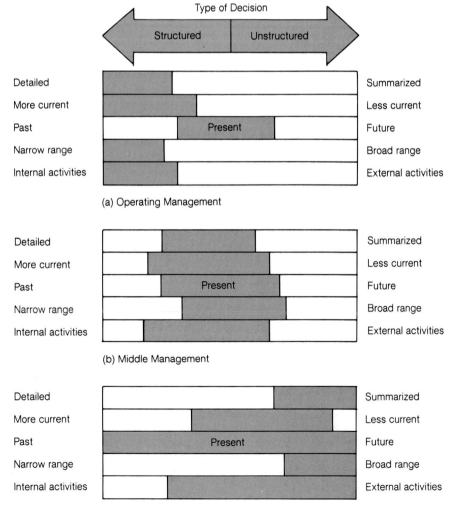

(a) Operating Management

(b) Middle Management

(c) Top Management

FIGURE 10.3

(a) Structured decisions are typically made at the operating level of management by following clearly defined routine procedures. Operating managers need information that is detailed, focused on the present, and concerned with daily business activities.

(b) Semistructured decisions, typically made at the middle-management level, involve information that does not necessarily result from clearly defined, routine procedures. Middle managers need information that is detailed and more summarized than information for operating managers and that compares the present with the recent past.

(c) Unstructured decisions, typically made at the upper level of management, are supported by the management information system in the form of highly summarized reports. The information should cover large time periods and survey activities outside (as well as inside) the company.

THE ROLE OF THE MIS IN A BUSINESS

Now that you know what we mean by *managers* and understand their need for the right kinds of information, we can go on to describe in more detail the role of the management information system. First, as we have already pointed out, an MIS must provide managers with information (reports) to help them perform activities that directly relate to their specific areas of responsibility. Second, a management information system must provide managers with information about other functional areas of the business—accounting and finance, marketing and sales, production, and research and development—so that they can coordinate their departmental activities with activities in these areas.

But *how* do managers use information to make decisions? To understand how an MIS works, you must know something about the decision-making process.

HOW DOES MANAGEMENT MAKE DECISIONS?

Management styles vary. Some managers follow their instincts and deal with situations on a case-by-case basis. Other managers use a more systematic and structured approach to making decisions. If we approach decision making systematically, we can view it as a process involving five basic steps, as shown in Figure 10.4. Bear in mind that feedback, or review of the gathered information, is analyzed at each step, which may necessitate revisions or a return to a previous step. For example, suppose a company decides in Step 2 to purchase one of two software packages to help with in-house publishing; at Step 3 the company discovers that one of the two software manufacturers has gone out of business. The process must return to Step 2 to evaluate other software alternatives.

STEP 1—PROBLEM RECOGNITION AND IDENTIFICATION

In the first step of the decision-making process, the manager acknowledges a problem that affects the business. Take, for example, a small business like Bowman, Henderson, and Associates (BH&A), which provides training in the use of microcomputer hardware and software. The demand for training has grown so fast that the staff cannot handle it, and the facilities cannot support an increase in the number of students that can be taught per session. The fact that a problem exists becomes obvious when management notices that the staff is too busy to take a day off and everyone is always running around trying to take care of last-minute details. The seriousness of the problem becomes evident when staff morale begins to drop and potential customers are turned away.

STEP 2—IDENTIFICATION AND EVALUATION OF ALTERNATIVES

In the second step of the decision-making process, management considers various alternatives for solving the problem. In the case of BH&A, alternatives include (1) adding more staff and offering training in the existing facilities during expanded training hours (perhaps evenings and weekends) and (2) adding more staff, purchasing additional equipment, and leasing additional training facilities. Once the alternative courses of action have been identified, they must be examined and compared in terms of anticipated costs and benefits.

Step 3—Alternative Selection

When each alternative has been carefully explored, the next step is to select the one that appears to best meet the manager's objectives. The logical choice would be the alternative that offers the most benefits for the least cost. However, the manager must ensure that the chosen action is not in conflict with other activities or organizational objectives.

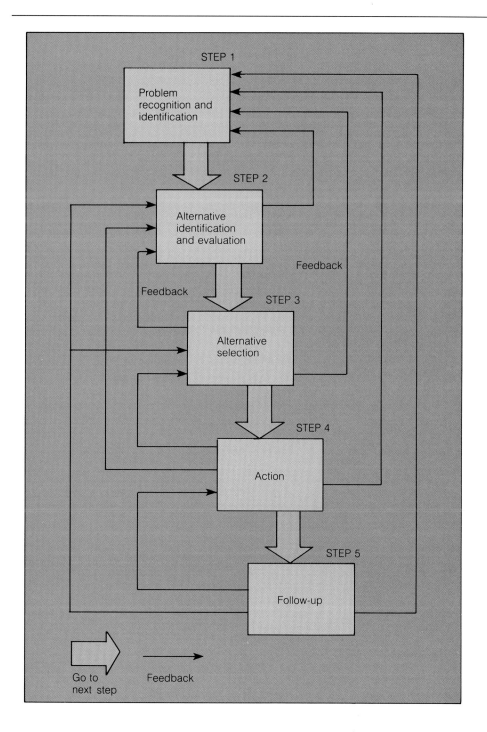

FIGURE 10.4

Five steps of the decision-making process. At any step, feedback—a review of gathered information—may require the return to any of the previous steps.

STEP 4—ACTION

Once management has decided how to solve the problem, it must act on the decision. Suppose BH&A management selected the alternative that involved adding more staff and scheduling the use of existing facilities for additional hours. Implementing this decision would probably involve (1) defining specific staff requirements and skills, (2) advertising for additional staff, (3) interviewing prospective staff members, (4) selecting the best candidates, (5) notifying existing customers of the additional staff and expanded hours, and (6) scheduling the use of the facility during the new hours of operation.

STEP 5—FOLLOW-UP

In the final step of the decision-making process, management follows up on its choice of action to determine if it has been successful. Management assesses the degree to which original objectives and anticipated benefits are being achieved and takes corrective action when necessary. If the solution to the original problem has created a new problem, a new decision-making process begins to solve it.

WHAT KIND OF INFORMATION DOES MANAGEMENT USE TO MAKE DECISIONS?

Because decisions are made on the basis of information, the decision-making process is greatly affected by the scope and quality of the information provided by the MIS. This information is produced by processing data from three sources:

1. Internally generated data (produced by normal data processing systems of the business)
2. Data provided by higher or lower levels of management
3. Externally generated data (produced by sources outside the company)

Information, as required by management, has three distinct properties that vary in significance, depending on the organizational level and type of decision being made:

1. Level of summarization
2. Degree of accuracy
3. Timeliness

As we mentioned in the discussion of the three management levels, the degree to which information needs to be *summarized* increases as the level of management goes up. Conversely, the lower the level of management, the more detailed the information needs to be. Top managers do not want to wade through mountains of details to make a decision. They want to be able to identify problems and trends at a glance in summary reports and exception reports; that is, they need only essential information, not nonessential details. Operational managers, however, need details on daily operations to make decisions regarding scheduling, inventory, payroll, and so on.

Of course, information must be *accurate* for wise decisions to be made. (Remember: garbage in, garbage out.) The higher the accuracy of the information, the higher the cost of the processing system, because more controls—both manual and computer-based—must be installed to increase the accuracy of output information. Some areas such as inventory may be able to live with an accuracy rate of 90–95%, but this rate is probably too low for the accounting department.

The *timeliness* of management information involves how soon the information is needed and whether it needs to relate to the past, the present, or the future. When decisions are time-sensitive (must be made quickly), the information system must accommodate this need.

In general, to support the making of intelligent and knowledgeable decisions, information generated at all levels of management must be:

- Correct (be accurate)
- Complete (include all relevant data)
- Current (be timely)
- Concise (include only the relevant data)
- Clear (be understandable)
- Cost-effective (be efficiently obtained)
- Time-sensitive (be based on historical, current, and/or future information and needs as required)

TYPES OF MANAGEMENT INFORMATION SYSTEMS

The more structured the problem, the easier it is to develop computer-based processing support to produce the information needed to solve it. As an organization matures in its use of the computer, the extent to which it uses computers to produce information for decision making grows.

TRANSACTION PROCESSING SYSTEM (TPS)

The support of day-to-day business operating activities, or *transactions*, is usually the first and most important objective of an information system. These activities involve the processing of data received from external sources, as well as data generated internally. A computer-based **transaction processing system (TPS),** also called an *operations information system (OIS)* or an *electronic data processing (EDP) system*, is focused at the operating level of a business (Figure 10.5). The management information produced by transaction processing systems usually consists of detail reports of daily transactions (such as a list of items sold or all the accounting transactions that have been recorded in various ledgers and registers) or future transactions (such as lists of items that need to be ordered).

A TPS usually operates only within one functional area of a business—in other words, marketing, accounting and finance, production, and research and development each has its own transaction processing system. Database management systems (covered in Chapter 9) were designed to solve the problems involved with sharing computer-based files among the four functional areas. Although the reports generated by a TPS are useful to lower-level managers, they are not helpful to middle managers, who need more summarized information with a wider perspective. Thus, management information systems were developed to take care of middle management's information needs.

MANAGEMENT INFORMATION SYSTEM (MIS)

A **management information system (MIS),** also called *an information reporting system*, provides middle management with reports that summarize and categorize information derived from all the company databases. The purpose of the reports is to allow management to spot trends and to get an overview of current business activities, as well as to monitor and control operational-level activities. (Although the term *management information system* is used to refer to *any* type of information system for managers, it is also used to refer specifically to *middle* management information systems.)

The scope of the reports and the characteristics of their information vary according to their purpose. In general, there is less need at the middle-management level for instant information than there is at the operational level. As you have seen, the reports can be periodic (such as income statements and balance sheets), on demand, or event-initiated, and they can summarize information or report on exceptional events or conditions. Examples of reports generated by an MIS are sales region analyses, cost analyses, annual budgeting reports, capital investment analyses, and production schedules.

DECISION SUPPORT SYSTEM (DSS)

The **decision support system (DSS),** a set of special computer programs and particular hardware, establishes a sophisticated system to produce information not regularly supplied by transaction processing or middle management information systems. This information is analyzed by the DSS and used for unstructured decision making. (TPSs and MISs do not analyze the information they produce.) DSSs are generally used by top management (although they support all levels of management), combine sophisticated analysis programs with traditional data access and retrieval functions, can be used by people who are not computer specialists, and emphasize flexibility in decision making. They are used to analyze unexpected

FIGURE 10.5

Three information systems for three levels of management

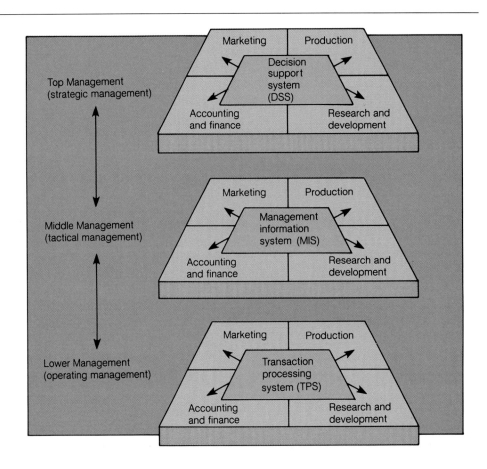

problems and integrate information flow and decision-making activities. A DSS may use database management systems (Chapter 9), query languages (Chapter 9), financial modeling or spreadsheet programs, statistical analysis programs, report generators, and graphics programs to provide information.

To reach the DSS level of sophistication in information technology, an organization must have established a transaction processing system and a management information system. But these two types of systems are not designed to handle unpredictable information and decisions well. Decision support systems are designed to handle the unstructured types of decisions—the "what if" types of decisions—that traditional management information systems were not designed to support (Figure 10.6). Moreover, decision support systems provide managers with tools to help them better model, analyze, and make decisions about the information they have. Indeed, some people regard decision support systems as a separate type of information system altogether, not just a management information system for top management.

Although most DSSs are designed for large computer systems, electronic spreadsheet packages and database management packages are used by many businesspeople as tools for building a DSS for microcomputers. As microcomputers become more and more powerful, more and more microcomputer-based MISs will include a DSS using a database management system. The popularity of spreadsheet software among managers is due to the fact that it allows managers to examine a variety of business situations—that is, to "see what would happen" if business conditions changed—and to make projections, or guesses, about future developments based on sophisticated computer-based data analysis. Decision support systems designed for large computer systems collect large amounts of data and analyze it in more ways and with greater efficiency than a microcomputer spreadsheet does.

Decision support systems generally fall into two distinct categories: general and institutional. A general DSS produces information that can be used in making a wide variety of management decisions. The electronic spreadsheet is an ideal tool for the development of general decision support systems for microcomputers. An institutional DSS is much more industry- and function-specific. Examples include a DSS for the medical profession (including hospitals), which supports decision making in the areas of administration, patient diagnosis, determination and monitoring of drug dosages, medical records, and so on, and a DSS for the advertising profession, which supports strategy in presenting products.

DSS HARDWARE
In most cases, the computer hardware in a DSS is used mainly by management personnel. It is not uncommon to find a high-level manager sitting in front of a

---

1. If we discontinue selling baseball bats, will fewer people come into our stores?

2. If we add a new clothing line, will more people come into our stores?

3. How will offering the customer a 10% discount for all purchases totaling over $35 affect next year's net income?

4. What effect will hiring 50 additional sales employees have on the company's overall performance (i.e., profit)?

5. What effect will modernizing our stores have on sales?

FIGURE 10.6

Decision support system. These processing questions represent the types of questions a top manager might ask a DSS. (These questions would not be keyed into the computer word by word exactly as you see here; the manager would use a query language, such as SQL.)

computer terminal or a personal computer to take advantage of the company's DSS. The terminal would be connected to a large multiuser computer system; the personal computer would have some processing capabilities of its own, but it would also need to be able to connect with the larger computer system for data exchange. In addition, personal printers and hardcopy graphics output devices (such as a plotter or a color ink-jet printer) are often available to the manager. The manager's collection of computer hardware is often called an *executive workstation.*

PEOPLE

The users of a DSS must be reasonably comfortable working with the hardware and DSS software to be effective. Many managers develop substantial skills in using some of the microcomputer-based packages, such as electronic spreadsheets, that provide decision-support processing capabilities. The software used for DSSs on large computer systems is generally too complex for people who are not computer specialists to handle; the manager would use it only on a simple level—to ask questions and obtain reports.

Because a DSS is tailored to meet specific management information requirements, the nonmanagement user would not likely be directly involved with it. However, this type of user might be involved in gathering data to be processed by the DSS and then used as information for management.

DSS SOFTWARE

DSS applications software is usually very complex in terms of the instructions of which it is composed. As mentioned earlier, many different types of programs can make up a DSS. In most cases, it can be divided into three levels: database management systems software, query language, and specialized software or languages.

Database management software provides managers with the ability to collect, maintain, manipulate, and retrieve huge amounts of data.

A query language, allows people to use software easily, without having to learn countless lists of codes and procedures.

Specialized software or languages are used to develop decision-making models. Some organizations purchase industry-specific modeling software for such common activities as financial risk analysis and forecasting (predicting future performance and conditions). However, the most sophisticated DSS users develop their own custom-made business activity and decision-making models.

The following list identifies some of the major differences between a management information system (MIS) and a decision support system (DSS):

- MIS users *receive* reports or information from the system, whereas DSS users interact with the system.
- MIS users can't direct the system to support a specific decision in a specific way, whereas DSS users can.
- MISs generate information based on the past, whereas DSSs use information from the past to create scenarios for the future.
- MIS activity is initiated by middle management, whereas DSS activity is usually initiated by top management.

DEVELOPING AND IMPLEMENTING A MANAGEMENT INFORMATION SYSTEM

The task of developing and implementing any type of management information system is a formidable one, requiring a great deal of planning. Business environments change rapidly, so unless management has great foresight (and the support of good specialists and user input), an information system may be obsolete by the time it is implemented.

The successful development of a management information system requires:

- A long- and a short-range plan for the company; a company must have plans for the future to be able to decide what to do tomorrow, next week, and next month
- A commitment from management to allocate the personnel and resources necessary to get the job done
- A staff of technical specialists with the skills necessary to develop the computer-based parts of the system based on user input

The most important step in undertaking the development of an MIS is the formation of a project development team (which would follow the steps of systems analysis, design, and development discussed in the following section on systems analysis and design). The team should be made up of managers, information system users, and technical computer specialists. All the team members should be familiar with the company's business objectives, current activities, and problems. And all must come to a general understanding of how the business operates. This task is not easy because many managers understand only how their own departments work but know little, if anything, about other departments; many managers have difficulty explaining how their own departments work; and many users, managers, and computer specialists use jargon—special vocabulary and expressions—to explain what they do. Jargon is not generally understood by everyone.

INFORMATION CENTERS

In an effort to further support management decision making, many large organizations have established **information centers** as part of their management information system. The person in charge of the information center is called the chief information officer (CIO). The people who staff an information center are technical experts on the hardware, software, and procedures that the company is using. The staff acts as "troubleshooters"—consultants and problem solvers. However, they focus not only on technology, as they did in the earlier years of computer-based information systems, but also on the goals, productivity, and quality of the business.

The user is the person the information center was created for; the user is the only customer. If the user wants to request a computer, the information center staff will assist in identifying what kind of computer is appropriate. A user with an operating problem with hardware or software would call the information center for help, or for service requests and replacement parts. Information center staff also show users how to use available software to create their own customized applications and provide general training sessions for hardware and software use. In large systems with a mainframe computer, the information center will also assist users in accessing and storing data.

The information center may be a separate department that services the entire company, or each functional area—such as marketing or production—may have its own information center. (The current trend is toward integrating information resource management into all the functional departments of a company.) Here are some of the typical activities of an information center:

- Education in high-level languages and development tools
- Assistance in accessing data

- Assistance in debugging programs
- Assistance with applications, queries, and reports employing high-level languages
- Consultation on appropriate tools and methodologies for developing an application
- Provision of reference materials on information center resources
- Liaison with other information-processing groups (such as database specialists) that support information center resources
- Maintenance of a catalog of available applications and databases

SYSTEMS ANALYSIS AND DESIGN

Systems analysis and design, as performed by systems analysts, seeks to analyze systematically the data input, data flow, and information output within the context of a particular business. No matter what your position in an organization, you will undoubtedly come in contact with a systems development life cycle (SDLC). Although it takes a lot of training to become a systems analyst, the user is always involved in defining the needs of a system.

How might you have to deal with systems development? You may be a manager whose staff is unable to handle the current workload and who has requested a study to see if a computer will improve the situation. Or you may be a staff member faced with the task of learning how to use and evaluate a new sales order entry system. Perhaps the division vice president has decided that some departments need computers, and you are asked to submit a report on your department's need for one.

The extent to which your job brings you in contact with your company's **systems development life cycle (SDLC)**—the formal process by which companies build computer-based information systems—will vary depending on a number of factors, including the size of the organization, your job description, your relevant experience, and your educational background in information-processing concepts, tools, and techniques. In large companies, the SDLC is usually a formal process with clearly defined standards and procedures. Although the technical aspects of each phase of the cycle will undoubtedly be handled by computer specialists, you will likely interface with these specialists.

For example:

- It may be necessary for you to explain how the current system works in your department—the manual procedures you use or what you do to support an existing computer-based system.
- You could easily find yourself in a meeting discussing the nature of problems with the current system and how it can be improved.
- You may be required to provide to systems analysts and designers the departmental objectives and requirements that the system must meet. For instance, if you expect to have the new system produce useful reports, then you should plan to assist the computer specialists in designing them.
- As the development of a new system nears completion, you may help in testing it to ensure that it works as expected.
- You may attend briefings and training sessions to learn how the new system will affect your job and what its new operating procedures will be.
- And last, but certainly not least, you will end up using the new system. This may involve preparing data for input or using information produced by the system.

In a sizable company, the SDLC may seem like a large and complex process to which you are only peripherally related; however, your role in it is still important. Although in a small organization you are likely to be involved in more phases of the SDLC, and your role in each phase will tend to be more detailed, you shouldn't assume that the principles of an SDLC apply only to large computer systems and applications. Users often believe that they can purchase a microcomputer and a payroll software package on Monday and have a staff member produce paychecks on Friday. Unfortunately, it just isn't that simple. The basic principles of an SDLC should be followed even at the microcomputer level.

Remember, in the past, many systems (and often the businesses that set up the systems) have failed because the components and the functions of the system were never clearly defined in terms of specific objectives and were not controlled tightly enough, allowing costs to greatly exceed estimates. These problems can be avoided through user participation—*your* participation—in and control of the systems development process. In short, some kind of user involvement throughout the development of a system is critical to the success of a computer-based system in business.

THE SYSTEMS DEVELOPMENT LIFE CYCLE (SDLC)

Businesses are made up of many systems and subsystems, including many manual and mechanized procedures. Some systems are very simple; an order entry system could be just a set of procedures for taking down a telephone order from a customer and seeing that the appropriate catalog item is delivered. Other systems are very complicated; a large company's payroll system involves a number of subsystems for tracking employee turnover, pay rate changes, tax exemption status, types of insurance deductions, overtime rates and bonuses, and so on.

You learned earlier that a system for which a computer is used to perform some of the procedures is called a *computer-based information system*. No computer-based system can stand on its own; people must interact with the system and perform the manual procedures required to feed it raw data, review the information produced, and take appropriate actions.

The scope of an SDLC can vary. In some cases, the effort will be so large that dozens of people will be involved for a year or more. In other cases, the scope will be much smaller—for example, the owner of a two-person graphic design business would not take long to set up an invoice and payment system. In both extremes, however, it is equally important to follow a clearly defined process. The degree of complexity of an SDLC and the amount of effort that goes into each of its phases will vary according to the scope of the project.

WHY DO SYSTEMS DEVELOPMENT PROJECTS FAIL?
The chances are great that a systems development project will fail if a clearly defined SDLC isn't followed. Sometimes, however, even when companies go to the trouble of establishing a formal and comprehensive SDLC, projects still fail to achieve their objectives. Why? Most failures can be traced to a breakdown in communication between the users and the data processing group or among the computer specialists. The reasons for failure often include:

- *Inadequate user involvement.* Users must assume responsibility for educating the analyst about business applications, requirements, and policies. (For example, a system may fail because major functions weren't anticipated in the design—because users didn't make their needs known.)

- *Continuation of a project that should have been canceled.* Often it's tempting to not cancel a project because of the investment already made. Analysts should reevaluate the project at various phases to determine if it remains feasible.

- *The failure of two or more portions of the new system to fit together properly* (called *systems integration*). This often results when major portions of the systems are worked on by different groups of technical specialists who do not communicate well.

Responses to systems failure vary. Project leaders may be fired; usually the systems requirements are reassessed, and the highest-priority requirements are identified so they can be satisfied by a smaller, more controllable system.

WANTED: ORDERLY DEVELOPMENT PROCESS

In most sizable companies, a great deal of money is allocated for information processing functions (hardware, software, and staff support). In such companies, a systems development project that costs more than $1 million is not uncommon. Hundreds, even thousands, of individual tasks may need to be performed as part of the development effort. These tasks may involve many people within an organization, often in several different organizational units. This multiplicity of effort can lead to conflicting objectives and result in a project that is difficult to coordinate. If the process of developing a system bogs down, the final product can be delayed, and the final cost can be more than double the original estimate. To avoid such difficulties, the SDLC is used as a guideline to direct and administer the activities and to control the financial resources expended—in other words, to impose order on the development process. In a small company, the amount of money spent on project development may not be much; however, following the steps of the SDLC is no less significant. Some, but by no means all, risks of ignoring these steps include the following:

- *The new system does not meet the user's needs.* Inaccurate or incomplete information given by users to systems analysts and designers may result in the development of software that does not do what the user needs.
- *The acquisition of unnecessary hardware or too much hardware.* If personal computers and printers are sitting idle most of the time, then probably far too much money has been invested without a clear definition of how much processing power is needed.
- *The acquisition of insufficient hardware.* The system may be inefficient.
- *Software may be inadequately tested and thus may not perform as expected.* Users tend to rely heavily on the accuracy and the completeness of the information provided by the computer. However, if software is not adequately tested before it is given to users, undetected programming logic errors may produce inaccurate or incomplete information.

Different organizations may refer to the systems development life cycle by different names—such as Systems Development Cycle (SDC) or Systems Life Cycle (SLC); however, the general objectives will always be the same. The number of steps necessary to complete the cycle may also vary from one company to another, depending on the level of detail necessary to effectively administer and control the development of the systems. One way to look at systems development is to divide it into six phases:

- *Phase 1*—Analyze current system: identify problems, opportunities, and objectives
- *Phase 2*—Define new system requirements
- *Phase 3*—Design new system
- *Phase 4*—Develop new system
- *Phase 5*—Implement new system
- *Phase 6*—Evaluate performance of new system and maintain system

Figure 10.7 diagrams the six phases of the SDLC. Keep in mind that, although we speak of six separate SDLC phases, one phase does not necessarily have to be completed before the next one is started. In other words, the phases often overlap. The degree of overlap usually depends on the project's size and the amount of resources committed to the project. However, work done on a subsequent phase is subject to change until the work of the preceding phase is completed.

WANTED: PARTICIPANTS

Three groups of personnel are usually involved in an SDLC project: the user group staff members (users), representatives of user management and information-processing management (management), and a technical staff consisting of systems analysts and programmers (computer specialists). The users could come from a number of different departments, particularly in large systems. In smaller systems, the user may be a single individual or department. The systems analysts function as a bridge between the business users and the computer programmers and technicians.

Management participation in systems development is important because it lends support to the efforts underway. The cooperation of all staff members is much easier to obtain when all levels of management have indicated their support for the project. Users must know that management will work with them to minimize any disruption caused by the project. In addition, management needs to review and approve progress as a project proceeds through each phase of the cycle. User management focuses on getting what is required; that is, it makes sure that the system fills all the stated requirements, and it evaluates the system's effect on staff and budget. Certain users, management representatives, and computer specialists form a systems development project management team, which is led by a project leader, a systems analysis specialist.

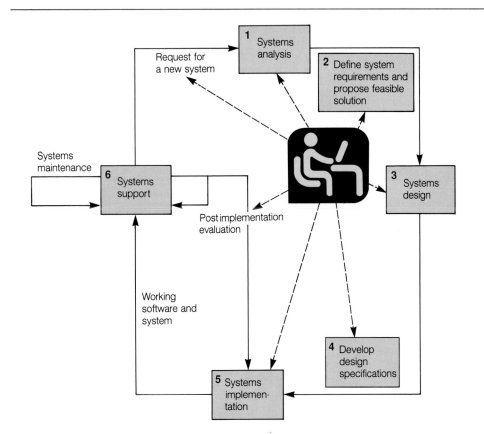

FIGURE 10.7

Typical systems development life cycle. An SDLC commonly includes six phases. After each of the first three phases, management must decide whether or not to proceed to the next phase. User input and review is a critical part of each phase. (Adapted from J. Whitten, L. Bentley, and V. Barlow, *Systems Analysis and Design Methods*, 2nd ed. [Homewood, Ill.: Richard D. Irwin, 1989], p. 82.)

COMPUTERS AND CAREERS

TRANSPORTATION

Dashboards that talk to you? Instrument panels that look like video games? These are the superficial uses of computers in automobiles. By now there are electronic systems for engine controls, smart windshield wipers, suspension control, antilock braking, and fuel regulation. And that is only the beginning.

A computer-based navigation system recently available in Japan uses satellites to plot a vehicle's location. The car's location is indicated on color maps, which are supplied on compact disks; the maps are displayed on a flat 4-inch color screen. A driver can choose from five levels of detail—some maps include the names of thousands of restaurants, hotels, and entertainment facilities and the services they provide. The navigation system can also be used by the drivers of trucks and helicopters; the vehicles can be moving or standing still.

The reverse is also true; managers of fleets of vehicles—trucks, taxis, ambulances, police cars, armored cars, utility repair trucks, and so on—can keep track of vehicles (and even boats and off-road vehicles) through the use of satellite or ground-based navigation transmitters—locally or anywhere in the country. With such position-finding technologies, dispatchers can monitor drivers and give directions whenever they are needed.

Computer sensor systems are also used to control the roadways. For instance, wire sensors are buried every ½ mile along the Long Island Expressway and convey, to a central computer, information on traffic flow. Engineers monitoring this information are able to tap out messages on their keyboards that are displayed on electric signs at various points over the expressway, warning motorists about possible delays.

Fiber-optic sensors are also being applied in "smart skin" technology, in which networks of fiber-optic sensors embedded in the fuselages of airplanes can alert pilots to small stresses and microscopic cracks.

Air transportation has long been a major user of computer technology. If you fly United Airlines into Chicago's O'Hare airport, for instance, your luggage will be moved through an underground baggage area that is the size of three football fields and that processes up to 480 bags a minute. Whereas once baggage handlers had to read each luggage tag individually, now laser scanning sorters read bar codes and route bags down the appropriate conveyor belts. The airport receiving a planeload of luggage knows exactly which flights each bag is being transferred to even before the jet lands.

United also uses a computer-based Gate Assignment Display System (GADS) to reduce flight delays. This software, which runs on Texas Instruments workstations, uses an artificial intelligence program that captured the experience and knowledge of United Airlines operations experts. GADS replaces a system whereby gate assignments were handled by airline experts relying on memory and wall-size scheduling boards to chart arrivals and departures.

Airlines also use computers to make fare adjustments. TWA, for instance, has software that can monitor the fares of competitors and can create pricing scenarios flight by flight and determine the profitability of various fares. Continental Airlines can measure bookings against expectations on nearly a half million future flights and can then revise fares and advertising accordingly.

Even ordinary computer users can take advantage of computers to save on fares. With a microcomputer, modem, communications software, and access to CompuServe or similar "gateway" network, you can link with different airline-reservations services and scan lists of available seats for the best deal. ■

266

Occasionally *steering committees* are formed to help decide how to get started—that is, which systems development projects to work on first. A steering committee is a group of individuals from each department in an organization. It may hear reports from experts about the advantages, disadvantages, and costs of a particular project, after which it must decide whether it is in the organization's interest to implement the project. If it decides to go ahead, the systems development life cycle begins.

GETTING STARTED

The development of a system can be initiated in a number of ways. As we have indicated, a project request can come from a steering committee, which has already evaluated the project's potential benefits. In a large organization, a user department (for example, payroll department, personnel department, or marketing department) may fill out a project request and submit it to management. Or top management may decide on its own to replace an archaic system—for instance, the manual accounting system—with a more modern and efficient one. Project requests may also originate from computer professionals or government. The requests are forwarded to the information-processing department for review. Then the systems development life cycle begins. The following sections will describe some of the basic functions involved in each phase of the SDLC.

PHASE 1—ANALYZE THE CURRENT SYSTEM

The objective of Phase 1 is to gain a clear understanding of the existing system and its shortcomings and to determine opportunities for improvements. (An analysis of the current system takes place regardless of whether it is computer-based or manual.) Figure 10.8 shows some problems identified in a sporting goods store's manual accounting system, as well as areas in which a computer-based system could make improvements.

The participants in this phase are usually the systems analyst, who must gain an understanding of the current system, and the users, who must educate the systems analyst about the current system.

Note: Users should keep in mind that, although systems analysts may be experts about computers and their applications, they are not necessarily knowledgeable about the business functions performed by the user. It is the user's responsibility to make sure the analyst is well informed about the current system.

Some aspects of the current system that are studied include:

- Inputs (transactions)
- Outputs
- Files
- Users' interaction
- Methods and procedures
- Data storage
- Controls
- Existing hardware and software

Improvements to systems can be defined as changes that will result in worth-while benefits. Here are some possibilities for improvement:*

---

*Adapted from K. Kendall and J. Kendall, *Systems Analysis and Design*, Englewood Cliffs, NJ: Prentice Hall, 1992, p. 39.

1. Speeding up a process
2. Streamlining a process through elimination of unnecessary or duplicated steps
3. Combining processes
4. Reducing errors in input through changes of forms and VDT screens
5. Reducing redundant output
6. Improving integration of systems and subsystems
7. Improving user satisfaction with the system
8. Improving ease of customer/supplier/vendor interaction with the system
9. Cutting costs
10. Improving security

FIGURE 10.8

Phase 1 analysis of Sporting Life's current accounting system. These are only a few of the general problems and objectives that may be identified.

```
Sporting Life Problem Definition--Current
Accounting System
The following problems have been detected in
the current accounting system:

1. Because files are spread among many
   filing cabinets in different locations,
   it takes too long to locate the required
   accounting files in order to update them.
   Often a file has been misplaced, or the
   file contains information that belongs
   somewhere else.

2. The procedures for updating all
   accounting files are not clearly defined.
   Mistakes are often made when entering
   accounting data.

3. The files that need to be updated daily
   include the General Ledger, Accounts
   Receivable, Accounts Payable, and the
   payroll files. Because it takes so much
   time to access the files, there is never
   enough time to get the job done;
   consequently, the job is often done
   haphazardly and updated only weekly.

4. Because data is filed in several places
   but under different labels, it is
   difficult to obtain information from the
   accounting files to generate the
   following types of reports:
     Summary reports about the financial
     status of the company (daily, weekly,
     monthly, yearly)
     Reports about the projected growth of
     the company.

Objectives

The new computer-based accounting system
should:

1. Reduce by 50% the amount of time required
   to locate the files that have to be
   updated.
2. Include built-in procedures for the user
   to follow when updating the accounting
   files.
3. Establish built-in controls to reduce
   data input errors.
4. Make it easy to update the accounting
   files daily.
5. Make it easy to obtain information from
   the accounting files to generate reports.
```

The systems analyst studies existing system components not only individually but also how they interact with one another and how people use them. Users can assist the analyst by expanding their own thinking about the components being studied. For example, if you were helping a systems analyst study the existing filing system, you would have to describe *everything* used as a file, including not only files in file cabinets or on disk but also index card boxes, in/out boxes on your desk, the telephone book, notebook, log sheets, materials on your shelf—in other words, anything that is used as reference for obtaining data to help you make decisions. The analyst will also need to know *how* and *when* you use these references/files.

The principal activities in this phase involve gathering data about the current system and then analyzing the data. The analyst can use a number of techniques, including:

- Conducting interviews
- Reviewing policies and procedures
- Collecting sample forms, documents, memos, reports, and so on
- Observing operations
- Using questionnaires to conduct surveys

Needless to say, the systems analyst does not necessarily do these alone. Users themselves can collect data on a current system by using these techniques, perhaps in an organized fashion along with the analyst.

After the analyst has gathered data on the current system, he or she must analyze the facts to identify problems—including their causes and effects—and opportunities for improvement. Some things that the analyst determines are:

- *Minimum, average, and maximum levels of activity*—for example, when do most sales orders come in?
- *Relative importance of the various activities*—this means prioritizing the activities.
- *Redundancy of procedures*—for example, are two users entering the same sales order data at different times?
- *Unusually labor-intensive and/or tedious activities*—manual activities that could be computerized, such as filling out forms to record sales data.
- *Activities that require extensive (complex and/or repetitive) mathematical computation*—such as updating customer charge account balances and interest charges.
- *Procedures that have become obsolete*—perhaps your company's licensing requirements have changed, rendering the old procedures useless.

The analyst can use several tools to assist in the analysis, including:

- Data flow diagrams (DFDs)
- Special software packages, such as Excelerator, a computer-aided software engineering (CASE) tool that, among other things, automates the production of data flow diagrams

A **data flow diagram** uses graphics to show the flow of data through a system—where it originates and where it goes—as well as the boundaries of the system and the information used within the system. Data flowcharts can be used for clarification in any phase of the systems development life cycle. Figure 10.9 shows the standard symbols used in many data flow diagrams.

- The *process* symbol shows what is done to data in the current system—whether it is filed, printed out and forwarded, checked and discarded, and so on.

- The *source* symbol indicates where data has come from—that is, from which departments or individuals.
- The *sink* symbol, indicates where data is going to—that is, it indicates the recipient. For example, a customer order record may be sent by Customer Services (*source*) to Inventory (*sink*).
- The *file* symbol indicates that data is deposited or stored, whether in an index card file or on magnetic tape, in a file cabinet or on a desk notepad.
- *Vectors* (arrows or flowlines) show the direction of the data flow.

To give you an example of how data flow symbols are used, Figure 10.10 diagrams how Sporting Life processes customer orders.

The first phase of the SDLC usually concludes with a report to management. The objectives of the Phase 1 report are to provide management personnel in affected departments and in the information-processing department with a clear picture of what the system does, how it does it, and what the analysis identified as problems, causes and effects of problems, and areas where improvements can be made. After reading the report, management must be given an opportunity to ask for specific clarification of the points raised in the report and to request a final recommendation from the analyst about whether or not to proceed.

PHASE 2—DEFINE NEW SYSTEM REQUIREMENTS

In Phase 2 the analyst focuses attention on what he or she—and the users—want the new system to do. But before the analyst can design it, he or she has to define the requirements that the new system must satisfy. And the requirements must be defined very carefully; otherwise, the new system might not end up doing what the users hope it will do. Needless to say, these requirements should solve the problems identified in the first phase.

FIGURE 10.9

Data flow diagram symbols. Systems analysts use these symbols to make data flow diagrams throughout the systems development life cycle.

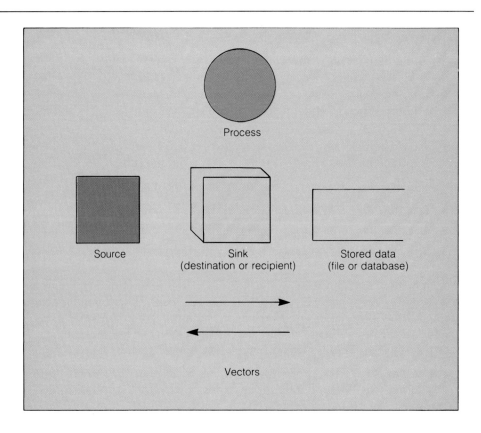

The first requirements to be defined should be the *business* requirements—input, storage, processing, and output—that the system is able to accommodate. For example, do the personnel who fill customer orders find that certain inventory items are often out of stock and therefore want inventory reports to be issued more frequently? Has the number of files required by the current system grown so much that users spend too much time searching for customer account information? The requirement of the new system in this instance is to make the finding of file information quick and easy.

Figure 10.11 shows some of the requirements identified for Sporting Life's payroll processing system.

Once the requirements of a system are known, then both manual and computer-based alternatives are evaluated for new and improved systems. Among the factors affecting what alternatives should be implemented are the availability of computer hardware that is technologically suited to the business's requirements and whose cost fits within the budget of the proposed system. Cost becomes a major factor if software must be created from scratch by a professional programmer, instead of being bought off the shelf (the "make or buy" decision).

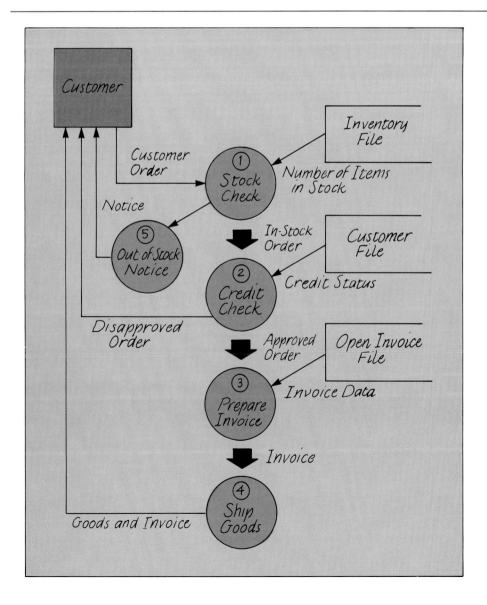

FIGURE 10.10

General data flow diagram of Sporting Life's system of processing orders. When an order is received, the inventory file is checked to make sure enough items are in stock to satisfy the order (1). If there aren't, an out-of-stock notice (5) is given to the customer; otherwise, a credit check is performed (2). If the credit status is poor, the customer's order is not approved; otherwise, an invoice is prepared (3) and the goods and the invoice are given to the customer (4). (Some details are omitted from this diagram for the purpose of simplification.)

The systems analyst can use several common tools to define the new system's requirements and suggest ways of fulfilling these requirements. These tools generally fall into one of two categories: modeling tools and prototyping tools.

Modeling tools are used to document the computer program modules, or components, necessary to the system, using a structured approach. One example of a systems development modeling tool is the **systems flowchart,** which uses its own special set of American National Standards Institute (ANSI) symbols (Figure 10.12). They document the design of a new system, including the flow of data (points of input, output, and storage) and processing activities. The systems flowchart for the accounts receivable portion of Sporting Life's accounting system is shown in Figure 10.13. The activity flows from top to bottom.

FIGURE 10.11

Phase 2 requirements of a sporting goods store's payroll portion of the new accounting system. These are only a few of the requirements that may be identified by the analyst.

```
Sporting Life: Requirements

The requirements for the Sporting Life payroll
processing system are as follows:

1. Increase the number of time cards that can be
   processed once a week by 20% and decrease the
   time it takes to generate paychecks by 15%.

2. Automatically update the personnel file with
   gross pay information when time cards are
   processed.

3. Automatically calculate regular and overtime
   hourly amounts when time cards are processed.

4. Automatically generate weekly-to-date and
   year-to-date personnel income figures when
   time cards are processed.
```

FIGURE 10.12

ANSI systems flowchart symbols. Systems flowcharts use symbols standardized by the American National Standards Institute, just as program flowcharts do (however, not all the symbols are the same).

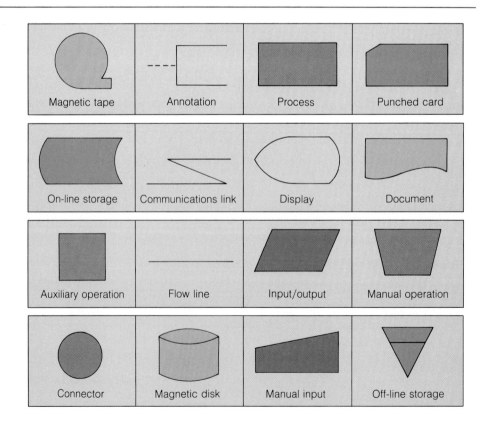

Prototyping tools document the system modules. A prototype is a small-scale working model of a new system module (or of a small system). Analysts use fourth-generation languages and applications generators to quickly generate working models of files, databases, screens, reports, and so on. The objective of prototyping is to get feedback from users as soon as possible. Prototyping also encourages more active participation of users in systems development.

Although we mention modeling and prototyping tools in Phase 2 of the SDLC, these tools will be used throughout the life cycle to continually document design and development progress and to try out program and system modules.

Once the business requirements have been defined, most systems analysts and designers focus on the *output* the system must produce. The output requirements fall into three general categories: hardcopy output (reports, special forms, and so on), softcopy output (displayed on video screen), and computer-usable output (a computer file created during processing for output in one system that is also used as input to another system—for example, a file produced by the payroll system that is later used in the general ledger system).

To define the requirements for hardcopy and softcopy outputs, the analyst usually meets with each user who will be using each type of output and carefully identifies:

- The purpose of the output
- The elements of information it will contain
- How each element will be used
- How often and how fast the output will need to be produced

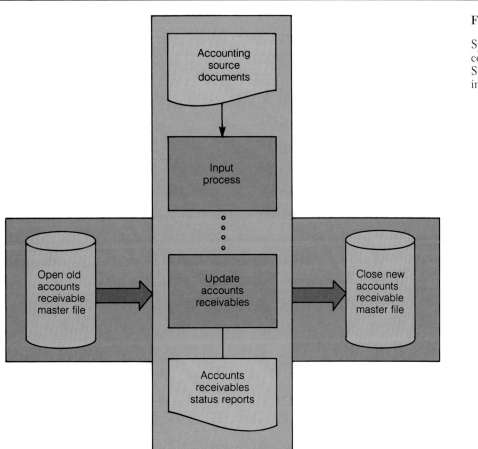

FIGURE 10.13

Systems flowchart for the accounts receivable portion of Sporting Life's new accounting system

In some cases, the analyst will model forms for the user to approve (Figures 10.14 and 10.15).

The storage, processing, and input requirements are closely related to the output requirements. They are determined largely on the basis of where the information in an output is going to come from. The input requirements are formulated in terms of:

- Who will be performing the input procedure
- The elements of data that will be entered

FIGURE 10.14

Specifying the requirements of one type of hardcopy output. This example shows the model of a report form designed with DESIGNAID (Nastec Corp.), a CASE tool. After the form and the system are finalized, the user can call the form up on the screen, insert the appropriate data where the 9s and the Xs appear, and then output the finished report. (X—alphanumeric data; 9—numeric data.)

REPORT LAYOUT CHART

1-10	11-20	21-30	31-40	41-50	51-60	61-70	71-80

12345678901234567890123456789012345678901234567890123456789012345678901234567890

ABC

CORPORATION

PARTS MOVE REPORT

- -

	PART-ID	MGR	APPR	LOCATION	QTY-STOCK	QTY-REQUEST	STATUS
1)	999999	XXX	XX	9,999.99	9,999.99	99/99/99	XXX
2)	999999	XXX	XX	9,999.99	9,999.99	99/99/99	XXX
3)	999999	XXX	XX	9,999.99	9,999.99	99/99/99	XXX
4)	999999	XXX	XX	9,999.99	9,999.99	99/99/99	XXX

FIGURE 10.15

Specifying the contents of one type of softcopy output. This screen example was produced using the "screen painter" in TELON DOM Pansophic, a CASE tool. This prototype provides the user with a model of how a particular screen will look when the system is operative.

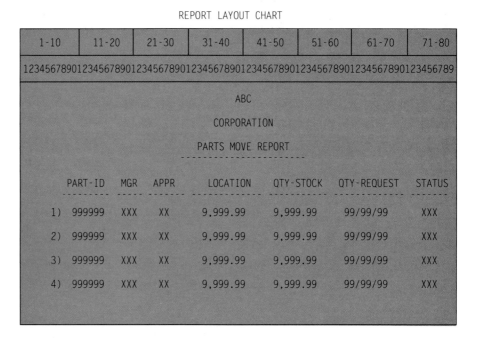

```
PANEL DEFINITION MENU ********** ********** END PROCESSING PERFORMED
COMMAND ==>

FUNCTION: UP   CR-CREATE    UP-UPDATE    PU-PURGE    SH-SHOW    LI-LIST

ITEM     PI  PI-IMAGE    PD-DEFIN
                              FD-FIELD     CE-CONSIS     SL-SEGLOOP
                               (UP)        (CR,UP)       (CR,UP,PU)

MEMBER NAME:
     HEADER TR____
     ID     XXAD_ PRE-CLASS ASSIGN, STUDENT NAME
     DESC   _____

ENTER VALUE FOR SPECIFIC ITEM TO BE PROCESSED:
     1. IMAGE    < > + | \ (INPUT OUTPUT OUTIN SELECT LIT-BREAK CHARACTERS)
                 24 080    (LINE-COLUMN IMAGE SIZE)
                 U         (UPPER/LOWER CASE LITERALS)
     2. DEFIN    Y Y Y Y N (INPUT OUTPUT OUTIN SELECT LITERAL FIELDS LISTED)
     3. FIELD    _____  (NAME OR LINE, COLUMN OR "*PANEL")
     4. CONSIS   _____  (TYPE - "XFEDIT", "SEGEDIT", OR BLANK FOR LIST)
                 _____  (NAME - IF TYPE SPECIFIED)
     5. SEGLOOP  _____  (TYPE - "FILE" OR "TABLE")
                 _____    (FROM NAME OR LINE,COLUMN)
                 _____    (TO NAME OR LINE,COLUMN)
```

- The input screens (the information displayed on the screen that tells the user what data elements to enter)
- The control procedures to be exercised over the data entry process

Storage requirements are defined in terms of the different files that will need to be created to satisfy the processing and output requirements.

Processing requirements deal with processing schedules—that is, when data is to be input, when output is to be produced, and when files are to be updated—and the identification of logical and computational processing activities.

The new system's software requirements must be defined first to determine what type of computer hardware is needed. This may involve modifying equipment already owned or buying new equipment.

EVALUATING ALTERNATIVES

Once the new system's requirements have been defined and ways to satisfy them have been suggested, the analyst should examine *alternative* approaches to satisfying the requirements. This step keeps people from jumping to conclusions. For example, perhaps an expensive conversion to a computer-based system from a manual one is not really necessary. The analyst carefully weighs the advantages and disadvantages of each alternative, including how each might affect the time required to get the new system in place and its estimated cost. The company can modify existing software, hire computer specialists to develop it from scratch, or buy software packages off the shelf and perhaps modify them, if necessary. Hardware and software to support the new systems should be selected, but they do not have to be purchased and in use before design begins.

SYSTEMS REQUIREMENTS REPORT

When all the requirements have been defined, they are usually summarized as a part of the *New Systems Requirements Report*. The detailed specifications are used as a basis for proceeding (or not) with the next phase of activity: design of the new system. If the company is going outside its organization to develop a new system, its systems requirements report may also contain a document called a *request for proposal* (RFP). This document is used when a company wants to get bids from vendors for prices of software, hardware, programs, supplies, or service. It lists the systems requirements and any limitations.

PHASE 3—DESIGN THE NEW SYSTEM

The third phase of the SDLC focuses on the design of the new system. To determine how the new system will be constructed, the analyst analyzes the requirements defined in Phase 2. The activities in this phase are carried out primarily by computer specialists—that is, programmers. Users may have little direct involvement in the design phase; however, their responses are critical when a programmer needs clarification of logical or computational processing requirements. Users should also continue to be involved in the final approval of procedures that provide for user interface with the system—such as what type of dialog will show up on the terminal—and of proposed report forms, both hardcopy and softcopy. After all, the analysts can leave when their job is done; the users must live with the system!

Phase 3 involves two main objectives: to design the new system and to establish a sound framework of controls within which the new system should operate. The tools and methods used to document the development of the design and the controls vary according to the preferences of the computer specialists and, if there is one, the standards and procedures of the information-processing department. Systems flowcharts, program flowcharts, hierarchy-input-processing-output

(HIPO) packages, structured design and programming, and prototyping are commonly used tools.

CASE (computer-assigned software engineering) tools are also used in Phase 3. CASE tools provide computer-automated support for structured design techniques; they speed up the design process and improve the quality of systems development and documentation. CASE tools are built around the concept of a *project dictionary*, which stores all the requirements and specifications for all elements of data to be used in the new system. (The term *project dictionary* is replacing the term *data dictionary*, which is now being used in a database management context; see Chapter 9.)

Among other outputs, CASE tools can generate:

- Graphics tools such as data flow diagrams, flowcharts, structure charts, and data models
- Reports on file contents, properties of data elements, and rules of logic
- Prototypes
- Quality analysis reports
- Programming code for writing software programs
- Project management tools
- Cost/benefit analyses

Figure 10.16 gives you an idea of how these capabilities relate to one another. In addition to Excelerator, CASE tools include Design Aid, Information Engineering Workbench, and Analyst/Designer Toolkit.

FIGURE 10.16

Some computer-assisted software engineering (CASE) capabilities. This figure shows how the capabilities relate to one another and to the people involved in the systems development process. (Adapted from J. Whitten, L. Bentley, and V. Barlow, *Systems Analysis and Design Methods*, 2nd ed. [Homewood, Ill.: Richard D. Irwin, 1989], p. 127.)

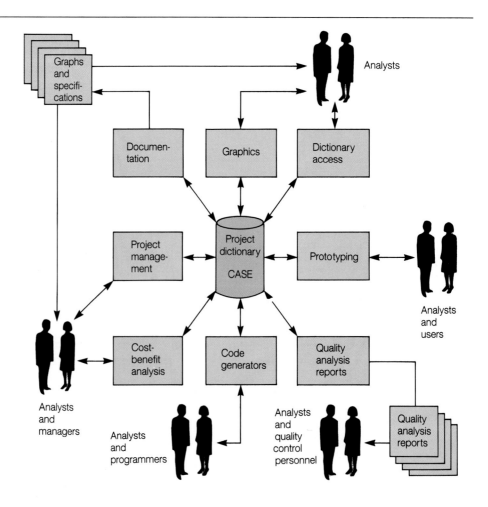

CONTROLS AND SECURITY

New systems must be designed to operate within a framework of controls, a system of safeguards that protect a computer system and data from accidental or intentional damage, from input and output inaccuracies, and from access by unauthorized persons. As computer systems become increasingly easier to use, and as software becomes more user friendly, the importance of designing adequate security controls into an information system grows. Controls involve the physical environment of the system (the buildings, rooms, doors, and computer hardware), the manual procedures performed by users and computer specialists, and the computerized processing procedures.

Physical security controls include the use of:

- *Passes and passwords.* Employees and authorized visitors may be required to wear badges or carry passes or cards in order to gain access to the computer building or room.

- *Encryption devices.* Data sent over telecommunications lines is put into secret code by equipment known as "encryption devices." This code can be decoded only by an authorized person using similar equipment at the other end of the line.

- *Safeguards against environmental disasters.* As far as possible, the system should be protected against disasters such as fire, flood, earthquake, electrical surges, power failures, and so on. Backup procedures must also be designed to protect the system's files.

- *Documentation library and file library.* Documentation and storage media should be kept in special rooms and checked out only to personnel who have a current assignment.

- *Locks.* Machines not in use should be locked up.

Manual procedure controls include:

- *Keeping a log.* All users of the company's system should sign in and sign out in a log book.

- *Separate employee functions.* If possible, employees' jobs should not overlap; for example, a computer operator should not also be a programmer, and users and computer operators should have access only to those parts of the system and documentation that directly involve their particular routine activities.

- *Creating a disaster plan.* Procedures should be established for all users (and other employees) to follow in case of a disaster.

- *Documented procedures for distributing output.* For example, reports may be kept in a secured area until distribution; users may be asked to sign a delivery sheet when they receive a report; reports may be shredded after use instead of being thrown away.

Computerized processing security controls include the use of:

- *Passwords.* Users must type in passwords to gain access to the computer system. These passwords should be changed frequently by the computer information department and should not be logically obvious.

- *Software restrictions.* The software program can be written to include user profiles to be activated when a person logs in to authorize that person as a user.

- *Dial-back routines.* When a person dials up a computer (with a Touch-Tone phone), the computer asks him or her for a password. After the person gives the password, the computer disconnects the line and checks to see if the caller's phone number matches an authorized phone number in its files. If a match is found, the computer calls the person back; if no match is found, the computer alerts an authorized user that an attempt at unauthorized entry to the system was made.

- *Standards for input data and data verification.* The system should include a program for verifying accuracy of input.

This list of controls is not complete; you may be able to think of additional ways systems analysts, designers, and users can write security measures into their systems design. However, you can see that systems controls are an important consideration during the design phase.

The completion of the design phase of the SDLC is marked by three events. First, the analyst/designer completes, organizes, and assembles the new systems design documentation, including records of the general and applications controls, by using a combination of the tools and techniques discussed earlier in the chapter. Second, the systems analyst(s) and information processing management meet to review the technical soundness of the design. Third, systems designer(s), user management, and information processing management meet to present and review the design. The outcome of the last meeting is a decision either to approve the design and proceed to the next phase of the SDLC (systems development) or to revise the design before continuing. Although the decision to discard a project entirely would most likely happen at an earlier phase, it is still possible to terminate the project at this time.

PHASE 4—DEVELOP THE NEW SYSTEM

A company that is changing from a manual to a computer-based system (or modifying an existing computer-based system) cannot run out and buy hardware in Phase 1 because it doesn't yet know what the new system is supposed to do. The company shouldn't make purchases during Phase 2 either because, although its requirements have been established, the new system has not yet been designed. During Phase 3, the system has been designed but not yet accepted. It's not until Phase 4 that the system is accepted and development begins. Now the company can acquire software and hardware.

During Phase 4, four major activities occur:

1. Acquire software
2. Acquire hardware
3. Train the users
4. Test the new system

ACQUIRE SOFTWARE
If the software is not purchased off the shelf, it must be written by programmers.

ACQUIRE HARDWARE

- If some computers have already been acquired, additional units need to be compatible.
- The minimum amount of main memory to satisfy the processing requirements must be established.
- If processing will involve extensive mathematical calculations, special math coprocessor chips may need to be installed in some computers.
- The video display units will need to be high resolution for certain applications like graphics. If graphics are required, graphics adapter cards and RGB monitors may be required for certain computers.

- The storage requirements should be carefully analyzed to help determine what size system to purchase.
- The quality, volume, and type of printed output to be produced must be considered in determining the types of printers required.
- Delivery schedules for all equipment must be established.
- Hardware locations must be determined.
- The number of users the system will need to support now—and in a year or two—must be set.
- The amount of multiusing and multitasking required must be established.
- The type of operating system that will ensure program compatibility and efficiency must be determined.
- Computer communications needs must be evaluated.

Once hardware needs have been identified, the company must determine which vendor to choose.

- The financial stability of the vendor should be strong. You want the vendor to be in business when you call for assistance.
- The vendor should have a qualified technical support staff for ongoing maintenance and repair (toll-free lines are invaluable).
- The vendor should have staff available to assist in setting up the equipment and making sure it is ready to operate.
- The vendor should have staff available to provide training in the use of the equipment.

TRAIN THE USERS

The users (and the computer operators) must be trained to use the new hardware and software. Training can often start before the equipment is delivered; for example, the vendor may give training seminars on its own premises or provide temporary training equipment.

TEST THE NEW SYSTEM

Several methods may be used to test the new system. Sample data will be fed into the system to see that it performs correctly. Testing may take several months. Of course, any bugs must be eliminated.

PHASE 5—IMPLEMENT THE NEW SYSTEM

The process of developing a new system costs a great deal of time, energy, and money. However, even a beautifully designed and developed system can fail to meet its objectives if it is not carefully implemented. In this phase, the company converts from the old system to the new system.

The implementation phase, which gets the new system up and running, involves creating the final operating documentation and procedures, converting files, and using the new system.

The computer operators and system users must have detailed documentation in order to use the new system properly and efficiently. Figure 10.17 shows a sample documentation package.

In addition, a new computer-based system cannot be used until all the data files are converted into computer-usable form. When a manual system is computerized, file conversion can become a monumental task. The time and effort required to sort through and key in the data—and the corresponding cost of doing it—are great. Outside assistance may be required for large file conversion tasks.

If an existing computer-based system is being changed to a new system, the files can be converted by a computer program.

There are four basic approaches to implementing a new system: direct implementation, parallel implementation, phased implementation, and pilot implementation. The concepts behind the four approaches are diagramed in Figure 10.18.

In *direct implementation*, the change is made all at once. The old system is halted on a planned date and the new system is activated. This approach is most often used for small systems or larger systems for which a model was previously developed and thoroughly tested.

Parallel implementation involves running the old system and the new system at the same time for a specified period. The results of using the new system are compared to those of the old system. If the performance of the new system is satisfactory, use of the old system is discontinued.

Some systems are just too broad in scope or are so large that they must be implemented in phases to avoid the traumatic effect of trying to implement all the components at once. Implementation is more easily handled one phase at a time—*phased implementation*.

FIGURE 10.17

Sample documentation package

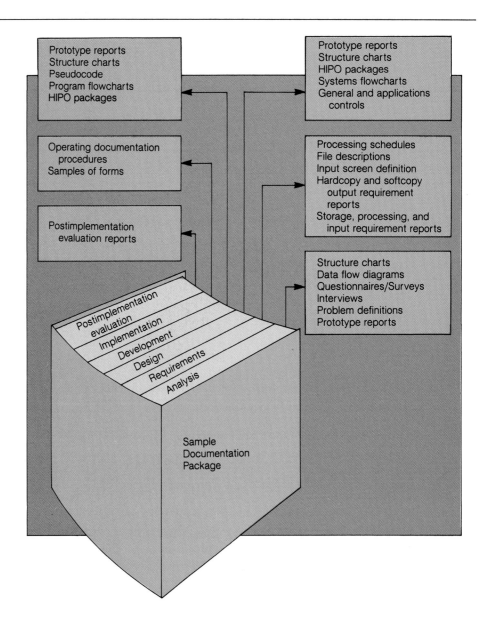

If a system is to be implemented at many locations in a widely dispersed company, the task can be very difficult to manage all at once. To implement the system at one location at a time—and ensure that it is working correctly before moving on to other locations—is safer. This is called *pilot implementation.*

PHASE 6—POSTIMPLEMENTATION EVALUATION AND MAINTENANCE

Two very important activities take place after the new system has been implemented: postimplementation evaluation and maintenance. Systems maintenance is not actually part of the systems *development* life cycle; it refers to adjustments and enhancements, or additions, that need to be made to the system after it has been implemented. Adjustments may be needed because, as users gain experience in using the new system, they may discover minor processing errors. Or government reporting regulations may change, creating new requirements for a system to satisfy. Companies must remember to budget funds to pay for the maintenance of their systems.

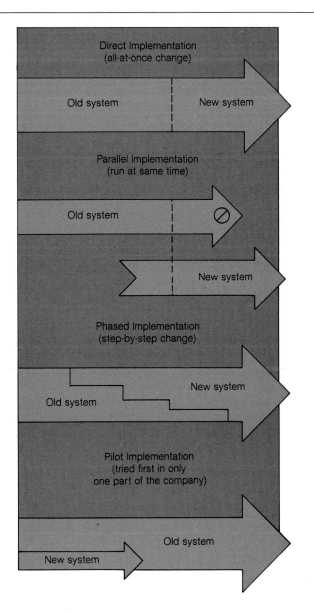

FIGURE 10.18

Four approaches to systems implementation

After a new system has been in operation for several months and any necessary maintenance has been done, a formal evaluation—called a *postimplementation evaluation*—of the new system takes place. This evaluation determines either that the new system is meeting its objectives or that certain things need to be done so that it will.

The end of the final step in the SDLC is marked by the preparation of a system evaluation report. The report summarizes the extent to which the system meets the original objectives and includes a list of enhancements to be considered for future development and implementation.

WHAT SKILLS DOES THE USER NEED?

Now that you have learned a bit about systems analysis and design, you're probably wondering what you will have to know in a typical business situation. Figure 10.19 reviews the points at which you, the user, may interact with the systems development life cycle. Whether or not you will need to use any of the tools and techniques for analyzing and documenting systems and their development depends on the type of organization you're with and the level of expertise you have gained. But, in most cases, you will need only a basic understanding of the life cycle used at your place of business and the objectives of each phase. You will need to develop your ability to communicate effectively with computer specialists to help your company operate efficiently and profitably. If you can't communicate your business needs clearly, your requirements may not be met by the new system.

SUMMARY

- *Management information systems* are organized standards and procedures, both computer-based and manual, for processing data into useful information.
- Management information systems are used by three levels of management:
  1. *Operating management*
  2. *Middle management*, or *tactical management*
  3. *Upper management*, or *strategic management*
- The types of decisions made differ according to the level of management. Operating management typically makes *structured, short-term decisions*. Middle management generally makes *semistructured decisions* based on information that is less detailed (summarized to some degree). Upper management typically makes *unstructured decisions*, which are the most difficult to computerize because they are made with the most subjective judgment. Unstructured decisions are broad in scope, long range, and often unpredictable and future-oriented.
- Information must be made available to management in the form of reports. Operating management generally uses *detail reports* that are issued on a regular, or periodic, basis. Middle and top management use *summary reports* and *exception reports* that are issued periodically or on demand or that are initiated by an event.
- Managers generally follow five steps when making decisions:
  1. Problem recognition and identification
  2. Identification and evaluation of alternatives
  3. Selection of alternative
  4. Action
  5. Follow-up
- The data managers use is generated internally (by normal data processing systems), externally (by sources outside the company), or by other levels of management.

- The information generated by processing the data into reports differs in level of summarization, degree of accuracy, and degree of time sensitivity, according to the management level.
- Three general types of management information systems exist to satisfy management's need for information:
  1. *Transaction processing system (TPS)*, which supports day-to-day operating activities and is used mostly by operating management.
  2. *Management information system (MIS)*, which supports the decision making of middle management by providing reports that summarize and categorize information derived from data generated on the transaction level.
  3. *Decision support system (DSS)*, which supports the decision making of top management through a sophisticated software setup designed to answer "what if" questions and aid in making projections. Most DSSs are designed

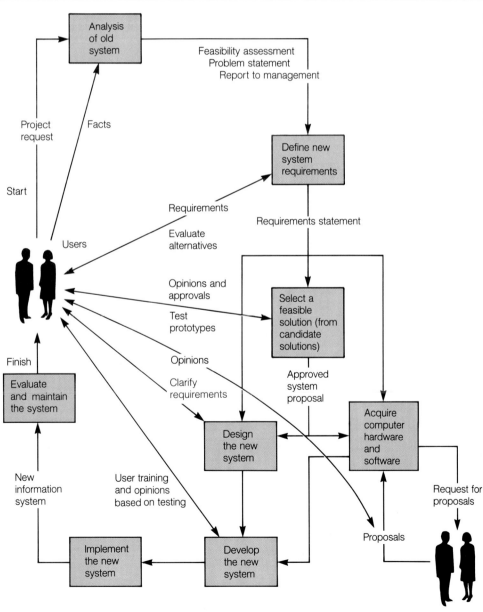

FIGURE 10.19

User interaction with the systems analysis and design life cycle. This diagram reviews the points at which you, the user, may interact with systems analysts and designers.

for large computer systems, although electronic spreadsheets and database management systems software can be used to build a type of DSS for microcomputers.

- *General decision-support systems* produce information that can be used to make a wide variety of management decisions.

- *Institutional decision-support systems* are much more industry- and function-specific.

- *Information centers*, staffed by experts on a company's hardware, software, and business procedures, are also being used to help managers and users in general to satisfy their ever-growing need for training and information.

- The *systems development life cycle (SDLC)* is the formal process by which organizations build computer-based information systems. Systems development life cycles may be known by different names and comprise varying numbers of phases, but their principles are basically the same. The participants in the SDLC are users, information processing staff, management of all departments, and computer specialists (programmers and analysts).

- Users participate in the systems analysis and design process by explaining to analysts and designers how they use the current system and what they think is wrong with it.

- An SDLC can be divided into six phases:

  Phase 1—Analyze current system: gather data; analyze data; summarize to management and recommend whether to proceed with the next phases of the SDLC.

  Phase 2—Define new systems requirements: categorize requirements according to input, output, processing, and storage; prepare systems requirements report; evaluate alternatives; prepare request for proposal.

  Phase 3—Design new system: define the technical design of the new system; establish controls; continue to assemble documentation; build project dictionary.

  Phase 4—Develop new system: create or select software; choose vendors; acquire hardware; train users and operators; test new system.

  Phase 5—Implement new system: create final documentation and procedures; convert files; get the new system running.

  Phase 6—Evaluate performance of new system and maintain new system: determine whether new system is meeting objectives; make necssary adjustments.

KEY TERMS

computer-assisted
  software engineering
  (CASE) tools, p. 276
data flow diagram
  (DFD), p. 269
decision support system
  (DSS), p. 258
detail report, p. 250
event-initiated report,
  p. 252
exception report, p. 252
information center,
  p. 261

management, p. 249
management infor-
  mation system
  (MIS), p. 250, 257
middle management,
  p. 252
modeling tools, p. 272
on-demand report,
  p. 252
operating management,
  p. 250
operational decision
  maker, p. 252

periodic report, p. 252
prototyping tools,
  p. 273
semistructured decision,
  p. 252
strategic decision
  maker, p. 253
structured decision,
  p. 252
summary report, p. 252
systems analysis and
  design, p. 262

systems development
  life cycle (SDLC),
  p. 262
systems flowchart,
  p. 272

tactical decision
  makers, p. 252
transaction processing
  system (TPS), p. 257

unstructured decision,
  p. 253
upper management,
  p. 252

EXERCISES

SELF-TEST

1. A _____ is a specific sequence of steps performed to complete one or more information-processing activities.

2. What are the five functions of management?
   a. _____   b. _____   c. _____
   d. _____   e. _____

3. A _____ _____ _____ comprises computer-based processing and/or manual procedures to provide useful and timely information to support management decision making.

4. The lowest level of management is strategic management. (true/false)

5. Operating management deals with structured decisions and needs detailed information. (true/false)

6. Middle management makes _____ decisions.

7. Decision support systems are used mainly by upper management. (true/false)

8. The five steps involved in making a decision are:
   a. _____   b. _____   c. _____
   d. _____   e. _____

9. What are the three distinct properties of information?
   a. _____   b. _____   c. _____

10. A transaction processing system supports day-to-day business activities. (true/false)

11. A decision support system supplies information not regularly supplied by transaction processing systems and (middle) management information systems. (true/false)

12. A manager's collection of computer hardware is often called an _____ _____.

13. The people who staff an _____ _____ are technical experts on the hardware, software, and procedures that a company is using in its information system.

14. Name four of the functions of an information center:
    a. _____   b. _____   c. _____   d. _____

15. The process of building a small, simple model of a new information system is called _____.

16. Name three ways of gathering data in Phase 1 of the SDLC.
    a. _____   b. _____   c. _____

17. What are the four methods of implementing a new system?
    a. _____   b. _____   c. _____   d. _____

18. A _____ _____ stores all the requirements and specifications for all elements of data to be used in a new system.

19. _____ _____ is when the old system is halted on a given date and the new system is activated.

20. Users are never involved in systems development. (true/false)

SOLUTIONS   (1) procedure; (2) planning, organizing, staffing, supervising, controlling; (3) management information system; (4) false; (5) true; (6) semistructured; (7) true; (8) problem recognition and identification, identification and evaluation of alternatives, alternative selection, action, follow-up; (9) level of summarization, degree of accuracy, timeliness; (10) true; (11) true; (12) executive workstation; (13) information center; (14) [any four from pages 261–262]; (15) prototyping; (16) conduct interviews, observe operations, conduct surveys, review policies and procedures; (17) direct, phased, parallel, pilot; (18) project dictionary; (19) direct implementation; (20) false

SHORT ANSWER

1. What steps should management follow to make decisions?

2. What is a decision support system?

3. What is the primary function of an information center?

4. Briefly describe the six phases of the SDLC.

5. What is a management information system, and what is its role in an organization?

6. What are transaction processing systems typically used for?

7. Describe some differences between a management information system and a decision support system.

8. What is the difference between a structured decision and a semistructured decision, and which type of decision is easier to support from a computer-based data processing standpoint?

9. Why is it important for users to understand the principles of the SDLC?

10. Describe a few different types of security controls that can be used by an organization to protect a computer system and data from accidental or intentional damage.

PROJECTS

1. Decision support systems often take years to develop. Given this long development period, some experts argue that the system will be obsolete by the time it is complete and that information needs will have changed. Other experts argue that no alternatives exist. By reviewing current computer publications that describe management information systems, formulate an opinion about this issue.

2. Does your school or place of employment have an information center? If so, interview the chief information officer and report on the services and functions of the center. Can the CIO identify the various levels of management within the departments that use the center? To whom does the CIO report? What kinds of user input were requested when the center was being set up? Does the center use any sophisticated decision support software? Whom

does the center serve, and what kind of reports does it provide? What kinds of services does the center offer to students?

   If your school or place of employment does not have an information center, interview the CIO of a local company that does have one.

3. Using recent computer publications, research the state of the art of computer-assisted software engineering (CASE) tools. What capabilities do these tools have? What do you think the future holds for CASE tools?

CHAPTER 11

ADVANCED TOPICS

Is it really possible for computers to think like human beings? Not yet, but perhaps that time is coming. Developments in areas such as artificial intelligence, robotics, expert systems, and virtual reality show that computers are indeed becoming increasingly "intelligent." Professionals who are at the forefront of their disciplines make sure they are aware of new developments in computer technology. As an intelligent user, you should, too.

PREVIEW

When you have completed this chapter, you will be able to:

Describe artificial intelligence and explain its influence on robotics, natural language processing, and virtual reality

Explain what expert systems are and how they affect business

Describe the object-oriented approach to programming, including how it is different from other programming approaches and how it influences business

CHAPTER OUTLINE

Why Is This Chapter Important?

Artificial Intelligence

    What Is AI Supposed to Do?

    Robotics

    Natural Language Processing and Fuzzy Logic

Expert Systems: Human Expertise in a Computer

    Implications for Business

Virtual Reality

Object-Oriented Programming

    Advantages and Disadvantages

    Why Should Users Be Familiar with Object-Oriented Programming?

Summary

Key Terms

Exercises

The topics of artificial intelligence, expert systems, and object-oriented programming are receiving widespread attention from researchers, businesses, and the media. In this chapter, we describe why so much interest is focused on these areas and how you can expect to be impacted by the research done in these areas now and in the future.

ARTIFICIAL INTELLIGENCE

For years, researchers have been exploring the way people think, in hopes of creating a computer that thinks like a person. And little doubt exists that **artificial intelligence (AI)** has the complete attention of computer scientists; indeed, it is their main focus for the present and the future. However, no agreement exists about what artificial intelligence is. Existing definitions are contradictory. Some experts say that AI is the science of making machines do things that would require intelligence if done by a person. Others state that, if we can imagine a computer that can collect, assemble, choose among, understand, perceive, and know, then we have artificial intelligence. Still others believe that there is no such thing as intelligence that is "artificial" and that, therefore, the term *knowledge-based system* should be used.

Why do the definitions differ? First of all, there is not—and never has been—a single agreed-on definition of human intelligence. Second, agreement on the point at which a machine exhibits intelligence is difficult to achieve. For example, years ago, when a computer could play tic-tac-toe, some researchers considered it to be intelligent because it could choose the next best possible move and could beat its human opponents. Today, most researchers no longer think that a machine's ability to play tic-tac-toe is enough to reflect intelligence. Other characteristics have been added to our definition of *intelligent behavior*—for example, the ability to reason logically and respond creatively to problems.

WHAT IS AI SUPPOSED TO DO?

The aim of AI is to produce a generation of systems that will be able to communicate with us by speech and hearing, use "vision" (scanning) that approximates the way people see, and be capable of intelligent problem solving. In other words, AI refers to computer-based systems that can mimic or simulate human thought processes and actions. Some of the primary areas of research within AI that are of particular interest to business users are robotics, natural language processing, virtual reality, and expert systems.

ROBOTICS

According to *Webster's Ninth New Collegiate Dictionary*, a **robot** is an automatic device that performs functions ordinarily ascribed to human beings or that operates with what appears to be almost human intelligence. In the field of artificial intelligence, there are *intelligent robots* (also called *perception robots*) and *unintelligent robots*. Most robots are unintelligent; that is, they are programmed to do specific tasks, and they are incapable of showing initiative (Figure 11.1). An unintelligent robot cannot respond to a situation for which it has not been specifically programmed. Intelligence is provided either by a direct link to a computer or by on-board computers that reside in the robot. Robotic intelligence is primarily a question of extending the sensory (for example, vision) and mobility competence of robots in a working environment (Figure 11.2). One future application of intelligent robotics is a machine that is small enough to swallow. It will be able to scan intestinal walls with a miniature camera, searching for possible tumors, and send the images to a doctor watching a monitor. Then, under instructions from the doctor, it will take a tissue sample.

In the future, reasoning ability will be incorporated into robots, thus improving their ability to behave "intelligently." For example, robot vision has already been successfully implemented in many manufacturing systems (Figure 11.3). To "see," a computer measures varying intensities of light of a shape; each intensity has a numbered value that is compared to a template of intensity patterns stored in memory. One of the main reasons for the importance of vision is that production-line robots must be able to discriminate among parts. General Electric, for example, has Bin Vision Systems, which allow a robot to identify and pick up specific parts in an assembly-line format (Figure 11.4).

Another area of interest is the "personal" robot, familiar to us from science fiction. Existing personal robots exhibit relatively limited abilities, and whether a sophisticated home robot can be made cost-effective is debatable. B.O.B. (Brains On Board) is a device sold by Visual Machines that can speak (using prerecorded

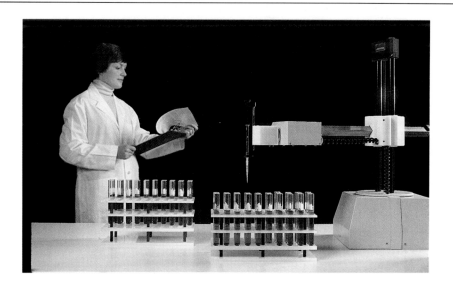

FIGURE 11.1

Unintelligent laboratory robot

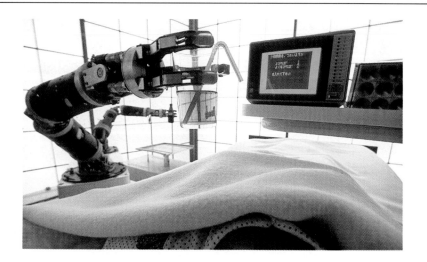

FIGURE 11.2

Intelligent robot feeding a patient in a Japanese hospital

phrases), follow people around using infrared sensors, and avoid obstacles by using ultrasonic sound. Software will allow the robot to bring its owner something to drink from the refrigerator. Another type of personal robot is the Spimaster, built by Cybermotion. This security robot patrols up to 15 miles per shift, collecting

FIGURE 11.3

Robot vision

FIGURE 11.4

Some industrial robots use claws to pick up objects and insert them into various parts of machinery.

video images and recording data. If it senses a problem, it heads for the trouble zone and sounds alarms on-site and at security headquarters.

The performance limitations of personal robots reflect the difficulties in designing and programming intelligent robots. In fact, we have just begun to appreciate how complicated such mundane tasks as recognizing a can of Pepsi in the refrigerator can be. Another concern is that, if a robot does in fact become intelligent, what would stop it from deciding that work is something to avoid?

NATURAL LANGUAGE PROCESSING AND FUZZY LOGIC

The goal of **natural language processing** is to enable the computer to communicate with the user in the user's native language, for example, English. The primary difficulty in implementing this kind of communication is the sheer complexity of everyday conversation. For example, we readily understand the sentence "The spirit is willing, but the flesh is weak." One natural language processing system, however, understood this sentence to mean "The wine is agreeable, but the meat has spoiled." It turns out that the system must have access to a much larger body of knowledge than just a dictionary of terms. People use their world knowledge to help them understand what another person is saying. For example, we know the question "Coffee?" means "Do you want a cup of coffee?" But a computer would have difficulty understanding this one-word question.

Alan Turing, a famous British mathematician, proposed several years ago a method by which the intelligence—or natural language processing capacity—of a computer can be tested. In this test, a person is seated in front of two computer terminals; one terminal is directed by a computer and the other is directed by a human (through a keyboard). The subject is supposed to hold conversations (using a keyboard) with each terminal and then guess which one is run by a human. Hugh Loebner, a New York businessman, with support from the National Science Foundation and the Alfred P. Sloane Foundation, has offered a $100,000 prize for the first computer system that can pass the Turing test by fooling the subject into thinking he or she is communicating with a person. In November of 1991 a competition based on the Turing test was held in Boston's Computer Museum. Five out of ten judges were fooled by a computer program called PC Therapist III, from Thinking Software Inc., which won a $1,500 prize. The $100,000 prize is still up for grabs!

The post office is currently using a language-processing system that was developed by Verbex to speed up the sorting and delivery of mail that doesn't include a ZIP code. After the human mail sorter reads the address into a microphone, the computer responds in an electronic voice with the correct ZIP code.

Most existing natural language systems run on large computers; however, scaled-down versions are now available for microcomputers. Intellect, for example, is the name of a commercial product that uses a limited English vocabulary to help users orally query databases on both mainframes and microcomputers. One of the most successful natural language systems is LUNAR, developed to help users analyze the rocks brought back from the moon. It has access to extensive detailed knowledge about geology in its knowledge database and answers users' questions.

One relatively new concept being used in the development of natural languages is fuzzy logic. Classical logic has been based on either/or propositions. For example, to evaluate the phrase "The cat is fat," classical logic requires a single cut off point to determine when the cat is fat, such as a specific weight for a certain length. It is either in the set of fat cats or it is not. However, "fat" is a vague, or "gray," notion; it's more likely that the cat is "a little fat." **Fuzzy logic** works by allowing partial membership in a set. If the cat weighs 25 pounds, then it probably has 1.00 membership in the set. If it weights 15 pounds, it may have a partial, 0.70 membership. By allowing for partial membership in sets, fuzzy logic has made it simpler and more efficient to control electronic products.

Artificial intelligence has the potential to solve many problems; however, it may create some as well. For example, some people think that AI is dangerous because it does not address the ethics of using machines to make decisions nor does it require machines to use ethics as part of the decision-making process. However, in spite of these concerns, AI has been used to develop yet another system—the expert system—to support decision making in many areas, including the business environment.

Expert Systems: Human Expertise in a Computer

Beginning in the mid-1960s, a new type of system, called an **expert system,** began to be developed to support management in the decision-making process. This new type of system, which represents one of the first practical applications of artificial intelligence, is an exciting addition to the kinds of computer systems available to businesses. However, expert systems are designed to be users' *assistants*, not *replacements*.

An expert system solves problems that require substantial expertise to understand. The system's performance depends on the body of facts (knowledge) and the heuristics (rules of thumb) that are fed into the computer. Knowledge engineers gather, largely through interviews, the expert knowledge and the heuristics from human experts in the field for which the computer-based system is being designed to support decisions—fields such as medicine, engineering, or geology. (For example, in the field of medicine, one question that might be asked of an expert system is whether one treatment is better for a patient than another one.) The responses recorded during the interviews are codified and entered into a knowledge base that can be used by a computer. An expert system has the capacity to store the collection of knowledge and manipulate it in response to user inquiries; in some cases, it can even explain its responses to the user.

An expert system has four major program components:

1. Natural (software) language interface for the user
2. Knowledge base (like a database, where the facts are stored)
3. Inference machine (software that solves problems and makes logical inferences)
4. Explanation module (which explains its conclusions to the user)

One of the most famous expert systems—an older system now being replaced by updated ones—is MYCIN, a system that diagnoses infectious diseases and recommends appropriate drugs. For example, bacteremia (bacteria in the blood) can be fatal if it is not treated quickly. Unfortunately, traditional tests for it require 24 to 48 hours to verify a diagnosis. However, MYCIN provides physicians with a diagnosis and recommended therapy within minutes. To use MYCIN, the physician enters data on a patient; as the data is being entered, MYCIN asks questions (for example, "Is patient a burn patient?"). As the questions are answered, MYCIN's inference machine "reasons" out a diagnosis: "IF the infection is primary bacteria, AND the site of the culture is a gastrointestinal tract, THEN there is evidence (0.7) that the identity of the organism causing the disease is Bacteroides." The "0.7" means that MYCIN "thinks" there is a 7 out of 10 chance that this diagnosis is correct. This pattern closely follows that of human thought; much of our knowledge is inexact and incomplete, and we often reason using odds (such as "There's a 40% chance it's going to rain") when we don't have access to complete and accurate information.

I f medicine isn't quite like this in every locality, it probably won't be long until it is!

Every physician and hospital in town is hooked up by telephone to a medical information system, a specialized database. Doctors can admit or discharge a patient to and from the hospital, without leaving their offices. They can check on how much and what kind of medication a patient has received, what kind of laboratory tests have been run, and whether the patient has been moved from one bed to another. Besides having access to patient records, physicians and other professionals concerned with the patient's health have insurance and Medicare information. When the patient leaves the hospital, the schedule of medication given on discharge will also be available to the on-line physician.

In a significant step toward the future, computers are now being used to help doctors make diagnoses, do surgical procedures, and keep up with rapid changes in medicine. A system called DXplain contains data on thousands of case histories and more than 2,000 diseases, including the latest on AIDS. A physician can build a clinical case description by entering patient signs, symptoms, and lab data; DXplain then presents the physician with a ranked list of diseases that should be considered possibilities. The physician can also ask the system questions, such as why a particular disease does not appear on the list.

Many medical schools are now using computer programs to teach surgical procedures via screen animation. Some schools are using virtual reality techniques to allow medical students to practice these procedures *before* they do them on people.

As costs skyrocket and insurance companies switch to fixed-scale reimbursement for treatment, computerization also helps hospitals to manage their costs. Sacred Heart Hospital in Eau Claire, Wisc., installed a 90-terminal electronic information system and found it could save on hiring the equivalent of 50 full-time employees. It was also able to increase the speed of processing doctors' orders from 20 minutes to 5. At Latter Day Saints Hospital in Salt Lake City, the computer-based system known as the Help Evaluation through Logical Processing (HELP) system can assist physicians in selecting the right medicine mix. At Moses Cone Memorial Hospital in Greensboro, North Carolina, all medical, radiology, laboratory, and pharmacy records are integrated on the same system.

Computers are beginning to find specialized uses in medicine and health not even thought of a decade ago. For instance, plastic surgeons now use computers and videos to show patients what they might look like after a facelift, breast reduction, or other cosmetic surgery. Robots have been devised to perform tasks for those with physical disabilities. Other devices help the 13 million Americans who have some trouble speaking, reading, or writing. Computers also help children with cerebral palsy, Down's syndrome, and other problems to mitigate their disabilities by helping them to display and improve their skills.

It is possible that some day you will carry a plastic "smart card" that contains your entire medical history. Such a card could be put into a computer at hospitals, physicians' offices, and pharmacies around the country and provide details as to your chronic illnesses, allergies, and adverse reactions. ■

Gensym Corporations's G2 Real-Time Expert system is used in Mrs. Baird's Bakery (a large independent bakery in Fort Worth) for scheduling and monitoring the production of baked goods. The system takes care of scheduling such tasks as ingredient mixing and oven operations—don't plan on finding a burned cookie at Mrs. Baird's! The Residential Burglary Expert System (REBES) is an expert system that uses certain rules of thumb to help a detective investigate a crime scene. REBES, which acts like a partner to the detective, might ask "Did the intruder search the entire house? If so, an accomplice might be involved" or "Was valuable jewelry taken but cheaper jewelry left behind? If so, thieves may be professionals/repeaters." Examples of other expert systems are XCON, a system that puts together the best arrangement of Digital Equipment Corporation (DEC) computer system components for a given company; DENDRAL, a system that identifies chemical compounds; PROSPECTOR, a system that evaluates potential geological sites of oil, natural gas, and so on; and DRILLING ADVISOR, a system that assists in diagnosing and resolving oil-rig problems.

Capturing human expertise for the computer is a time-consuming and difficult task. Knowledge engineers are trained to elicit knowledge (for example, by interview) from experts and build the expert system. The knowledge engineer may program the system in an artificial intelligence programming language, such as LISP or PROLOG, or may use system-building tools that provide a structure. Tools allow faster design but are less flexible than languages. An example of such a tool is EMYCIN, which is MYCIN without any of MYCIN's knowledge. A knowledge engineer can theoretically enter any knowledge (as long as it is describable in rules) into this empty shell and create a new system. The completed new system will solve problems as MYCIN does, but the subject matter in the knowledge base may be completely different (for example, car repair).

Expert systems are usually run on large computers—often dedicated artificial intelligence computers—because of these systems' gigantic appetites for memory; however, some scaled-down expert systems (such as the OS/2 version of KBMS, Knowledge Base Management System) run on microcomputers (Figure 11.5). Negotiator Pro from Beacon Expert Systems, Inc., for IBM and Apple Macintosh computers, helps executives plan effective negotiations with other people by examining their personality types and recommending negotiating strategies. Scaled-down systems generally do not have all the capabilities of large expert systems, and most have limited reasoning abilities. LISP and PROLOG compilers are available for microcomputers, as are some system-building tools such as EXPERT-EASE, NEXPRET, and VP-Expert, which allow relatively unsophisticated users to

FIGURE 11.5

KBMS screen showing the development of a scheduling program that will work across multiple platforms in any environment—for example PCs, minicomputers, mainframes, networks.

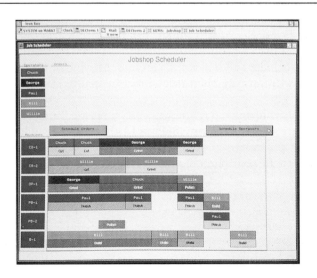

build their own expert system. Such expert-system building software tools are called *shells*.

IMPLICATIONS FOR BUSINESS

Expert systems are becoming increasingly important to business and manufacturing firms. However, it is difficult to define what constitutes "expertise" in business. Defining expertise in business (unlike in some other areas, notably math, medicine, and chemistry) is a formidable task because of its general and "soft" nature; that is, "business" is not made up of a specific set of inflexible facts and rules. Some business activities, however, do lend themselves to expert system development. DEC has developed several in-house expert systems, including ILPRS (which assists in long-range planning) and IPPMS (which assists in project management). Other examples are TAXMAN, which evaluates the tax consequences of various proposed business reorganization schemes; AUDITOR, which helps auditors assess a company's allowance for bad debts; and TAXADVISOR, which makes tax planning recommendations.

Another issue that inhibits the use of expert systems in business is that businesses want systems that can be integrated into their existing computer systems. Many existing expert systems are designed to run in a stand-alone mode. Furthermore, who will use the expert system? Who will be responsible for its maintenance? Who will have authority to add and/or delete knowledge in the expert system? What are the legal ramifications of decisions made by an expert system? These and other questions will have to be answered before expert systems are fully accepted in the business environment.

Cost is also a factor. Associated costs include purchasing hardware and software, hiring personnel, publishing and distribution costs (if the expert system is used at more than one location), and maintenance costs, which are usually more than the total of any costs already incurred. The costs can easily run into the many thousands of dollars. However, over the last few years, the number of implementations of expert systems has exploded from the hundreds to the thousands as businesses realize the benefits of better performance, reduced errors, and increased efficiency. In addition, less expensive micro-based tools are becoming increasingly powerful and available to businesses.

VIRTUAL REALITY

Want to take a trip to the moon? Be a race car driver? See the world through the eyes of an ocean-bottom creature or your cat? Without leaving your chair, you can experience almost anything you want through the form of AI called **virtual reality (VR)** (Figure 11.6), also known as *artificial reality* and *virtual environments*. In virtual reality, the user experiences a computer-generated environment called *cyberspace*; he or she is inside a world instead of just observing an image on the screen. To put yourself into virtual reality, you need special hardware—a headset called *Eyephones*, with 3-D screens and earphones, and gloves called *DataGloves*, which collect data about your hand movements and recognize commands from hand gestures. The headset includes a head-tracking device to enable the viewpoint to change as you move your head. The hardware uses software, such as Body Electric, that translates data into images and sound.

Aside from entertainment, artificial reality can provide instructional simulation situations to help people learn to exercise skills under varying conditions—skills such as driving, flying, outer space operations, police work, and disaster management, to name but a few. Architects are currently using virtual reality systems

---

to allow clients to "test" their houses—walk through them and try out room sizes and designs—before building plans are finalized. Medical schools are starting to use virtual reality to teach surgical procedures to medical students.

OBJECT-ORIENTED PROGRAMMING

Before we describe the fundamentals of the object-oriented approach to programming, we must familiarize you with a few terms and a bit of history. First, a software program, created by a professional programmer, is a group of related instructions that perform specific processing tasks. A group of software programs is referred to as a software package, or software application. The coded instructions contained in most of the software packages in use today were typed by a software programmer one line at a time—usually in one of the programming languages

FIGURE 11.6
(a) Jason Lanier, CEO and founder of VPL Research, wears a black spandex DataGlove with fiber-optic sensors to interact with computer-generated worlds that can be seen in 3-D while wearing the Eyephones seen on top of the monitor. Images from a demonstration world are projected behind him. (b) At VPL, Lou Ellyn Jones wears a data suit she designed; Bea Holster, a VPL electronic technician, makes an adjustment and Asif Ernon, a manufacturing engineer, adjusts the computer connection. Just as the DataGlove enables the user to interact, with hand gestures, in a virtual world, the bodysuit lets the wearer use the entire body to interact with a program. (c) At NASA Ames Research Center, two program developers demonstrate a virtual reality program they developed with a physician. The program enables doctors or students to manipulate the anatomy of a human leg. (d) Gary Reinagle of the Resource Center for the Handicapped takes a virtual reality tour of Seattle. Gary is a quadraplegic.

(a)

(b)

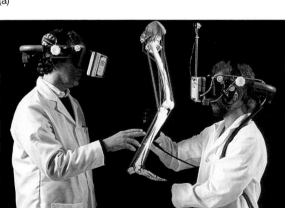
(c)

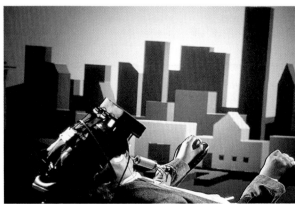
(d)

discussed in Chapter 7 (such as C, Pascal, or Ada). One of the disadvantages of this traditional approach to creating programs is that much time is spent writing program segments that have already been written. This happens for a few reasons. Programmers don't tend to share their work with other programmers and often will take ownership of the code they develop. Therefore, it is possible that a programmer down the hall or at another location is programming something very similar. In addition, a programmer might have to write the same or slightly modified code over and over again in many different applications. For example, for many of the different applications programs developed, the programmer must write the same instructions for the user interface, or what the user sees on the screen. This process is very time consuming and can be quite expensive.

To solve the problems of redundancy and time waste in program development, **object-oriented programming** treats each software program segment as an object—or discrete unit or module—that can be used repeatedly in different applications and by different programmers. Therefore, programmers won't have to spend time reinventing the wheel.

Imagine for an instant that you are viewing an automobile production line. As a component is moved down the production line, other components, such as seats, doors, windows, and engine, are added to it until a completed car emerges at the end of the assembly line. Each car is made up of individual components, or objects, that are designed to be attached to other components. The individual components were probably manufactured in different parts of the world and were purchased for use in this current line of automobiles.

Object-oriented programming brings production-line efficiency to the area of microcomputer programming. Whereas an object in the production line is an individual component of the automobile, an *object* in an object-oriented program is a collection of related procedures (software instructions) and data that constitute one component of the entire applications program. The idea behind object-oriented programming is that programmers can pick and choose already-programmed objects to be included in a larger application, just as car makers pick and choose the components they want to include in their car models. For example, if the programmer wants to include a pull-down menu on the screen, he or she can choose the pull-down menu object instead of writing the code for the pull-down menu from scratch.

Clockenspiel's Common View is an object-oriented language that enables developers to use the same objects in applications written for the Microsoft Windows operating environment (described in Chapter 7). Common View includes more than 350 objects for creating user-interface windows on the screen.

Advantages and Disadvantages

A major advantage of using object-oriented technology to develop software applications is that the resulting application is more likely to be error-free than if a traditional programming language and writing process are used. In addition, most new software applications incorporate graphic user interfaces. It is easier to program a graphic user interface by using an object-oriented language such as Smalltalk (developed by Xerox Palo Alto Research Center) or Digitalk Inc.'s Look and Feel Kit than it is to program using the C language, which has in the recent past been the language of choice among sophisticated programmers.

In short, object-oriented programming techniques provide the software developer with the following benefits:

- Productivity is enhanced
- Number of errors is kept to a minimum

- Source code (actual program instructions) can be reused
- Applications are easier to maintain

What this means to a business is that, once a programmer becomes familiar with object-oriented techniques, it will take less time for the programmer to generate an initial working application, less time in the future for the programmer to generate additional working applications (because objects from the previous application can be used), and less time to update and maintain existing applications. The bottom line: Business can save a lot of money in programming fees.

One drawback to implementing object-oriented technology is that it is initially difficult to learn for the programmer who is accustomed to using traditional programming languages. Traditional programs are code-based; object-oriented languages are object-based (component-based). Furthermore, object technology doesn't keep code and data separate, a fact that requires a programmer to look at a program in an entirely different way. Nonetheless, much excitement has surrounded the topic of object-oriented programming over the past several years, and the momentum behind this new approach to designing software applications is gaining speed.

WHY SHOULD USERS BE FAMILIAR WITH OBJECT-ORIENTED PROGRAMMING?

If your business needs a new applications program, you should consider employing an object-oriented approach, because, as described earlier, your business can save a lot of money in programming fees. Businesses in the computer industry have been focusing on using object-oriented approaches for the past several years and plan to do so in the future. IBM and Apple Computer, Inc. are currently working together on object-oriented programming technologies that would enable networks (described in Chapter 8) using different operating environments to interact, or communicate. Microsoft is currently planning on releasing an object-oriented version of Windows in 1994. In addition, Lotus Development Corporation has been working on modifying and enhancing its Lotus 1-2-3 spreadsheet by using object-oriented programming to update its graphic user interface. The company's main objective is to establish a standard user interface that can be used on different processing platforms.

Experts in the field of object-oriented programming predict that as object-oriented languages become easier to use, users, or nonprogrammers, will be able to develop simple applications by using object-oriented techniques.

SUMMARY

- *Artificial intelligence* (AI) is basically the science of making machines do what humans can do. The following are some of the primary areas of research within AI: robotics, natural language processing, virtual reality, and expert systems.
- A *robot* is an automatic device that performs activities normally performed by human beings. Robots can be categorized according to whether they are intelligent or not. An unintelligent robot can carry out specific tasks, namely those that it was programmed to perform; most robots are unintelligent. An intelligent robot, or perception robot, is capable of showing initiative. Much research in recent years has focused on developing robots that can respond to the spoken word and see.

- The goal of *natural language processing* is to enable a computer or robot to communicate with the user in the user's native language.

- *Virtual reality* enables the user to experience a computer-generated environment; in other words, the user feels like he or she is actually experiencing an environment rather than just looking at it on the screen.

- *Expert systems*, an application of artificial intelligence, are also used in the business world to aid in the support of decision making. An expert system is a collection of knowledge (and rules for using it, or heuristics) gathered by knowledge engineers from human experts and fed into a computer system.

- *Object-oriented programming* uses a programming method that treats individual program segments as *objects* that can be used repeatedly in other applications. Object-oriented programming helps to streamline the programming process by increasing productivity and decreasing the number of programming errors. In addition, applications created with object-oriented programming techniques are easier to maintain over time.

KEY TERMS

artificial intelligence (AI), p. 290
expert system, p. 294
fuzzy logic, p. 293

natural language processing, p. 293
object-oriented programming, p. 299

robot, p. 290
virtual reality, p. 297

EXERCISES

SELF-TEST

1. A _____ is an automatic device that performs functions that are ordinarily performed by a human being.

2. The goal of _____ _____ _____ is to enable the computer to communicate with the user in the user's native language.

3. An _____ robot cannot respond to a situation for which it has not been specifically programmed.

4. _____ _____, which are based on a body of facts, help to solve problems that require substantial expertise to understand.

5. An _____, in an object-oriented program, is a collection of related procedures, or software instructions, and data.

6. A new concept being used in the development of natural language processing is _____ _____, which doesn't base decisions on either/or propositions.

7. A form of AI that lets you experience almost anything, such as viewing the world through the eyes of a monkey, is called _____ _____.

8. An _____ robot is often referred to as a perception robot.

9. The primary areas of research within _____ _____ are robotics, natural language processing, virtual reality, and expert systems.

10. The _____ approach to programming was developed to solve the problems of redundancy and time waste in program development.

SOLUTIONS   (1) robot; (2) natural language processing; (3) unintelligent; (4) expert systems; (5) object; (6) fuzzy logic ; (7) virtual reality [or artificial reality]; (8) intelligent; (9) artificial intelligence; (10) object-oriented

SHORT ANSWER

1. Why is it so difficult to define *artificial intelligence?*
2. What is natural language processing?
3. What is an expert system?
4. Describe the relationship between the Turing test and research into artificial intelligence and natural language processing.
5. What benefits do object-oriented programming techniques provide? To whom?
6. What are the four main components of an expert system?
7. Why is it so expensive to develop an expert system?
8. What inhibits many companies from using expert systems?
9. What is meant by the term *virtual reality?*
10. What is the difference between an intelligent robot and an unintelligent robot?

PROJECTS

1. Research virtual reality in current computer magazines and other popular periodicals such as *Time* and *Newsweek.* What do you think of this new technology? What would you use it for? How could it be applied in educational settings?
2. During the 1990s you can expect expert systems to be used for the monitoring and control of a growing number of complex systems. Research what expert systems are currently being used and then focus on one that is of particular interest to you. Who developed the expert system? How long did it take? What are the hardware requirements for supporting the expert system? How is the expert system updated? Who uses the expert system and how is information retrieved from it?
3. Using computer magazines and other periodicals, research the state-of-the-art of object-oriented programming. Who is using object-oriented techniques? What companies have switched from using traditional programming techniques to using object-oriented techniques? Why? Has the transition been difficult?
4. Explore how natural language processing is being used today. What companies are using it? What are the benefits? What are the limitations? What are the hardware requirements? Is it expensive to design and then implement a natural language system? Is fuzzy logic being incorporated into natural language processing systems?

CHAPTER 12

ETHICS, PRIVACY, AND SECURITY

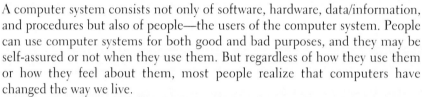

A computer system consists not only of software, hardware, data/information, and procedures but also of people—the users of the computer system. People can use computer systems for both good and bad purposes, and they may be self-assured or not when they use them. But regardless of how they use them or how they feel about them, most people realize that computers have changed the way we live.

The deeper computer technology reaches into our lives, the more questions we should be asking ourselves. For example: What are the consequences of the widespread presence of computer technology? Is computer technology creating more problems than it's solving? In the following sections we examine some critical issues related to the widespread use of computers.

PREVIEW

When you have completed this chapter, you will be able to:

■

Discuss the issue of computers and the unethical invasion of privacy through the use of databases and networks

■

Name some of the things that credit-reporting bureaus are doing to improve report accuracy and protect data

■

Discuss the major laws passed in the United States to protect citizens' privacy and prevent the misuse of computers

■

Define *computer crime* and give some examples of it, along with ways to protect computer security

■

Discuss the major hazards for computer systems

■

Define *software piracy* and describe what freeware, shareware, and public domain software are

CHAPTER OUTLINE

Why Is This Chapter Important?

Computers and Privacy
 Databases
 Electronic Networks
 Major Laws on Privacy

Computer Hazards
 Crime and Criminals
 Other Hazards

Computer Security

Computers and Copyright Violation
 Software Piracy
 Shareware, Freeware, and Public Domain Software
 Electronic Manipulation of Copyrighted Material

A Last Word

Summary

Key Terms

Exercises

"How did they get my name?" "I've just been denied a job on the basis of an error-ridden credit report!" "My employer got hold of my medical records!" "Someone used my social security number to set up some fraudulent accounts!" "Can XYZ Inc. really sell data on my financial history to that marketing organization?" "Someone took a copyrighted photograph of mine, changed it slightly, and had it printed without my permission in a famous magazine!" "Mary wants to copy my applications software programs, since she can't afford to buy her own. Do you think I should let her?"

Such questions and comments are heard frequently these days. Unfortunately, their answers and solutions are heard less often. Indeed, many people are not aware of the extent of the problems relating to the ethical uses of computer technology, let alone the rights and duties they may have in using it. If you are to be a responsible member of the Information Age, you need to know about computers and privacy, hazards, security, and copyright violation.

COMPUTERS AND PRIVACY

One definition of **ethics** is that it is a set of moral values or principles that govern the conduct of an individual or a group. People in most countries agree that they are entitled to the right of privacy—the right to keep personal information, such as credit ratings and medical histories, from getting into the wrong hands. The right of privacy from an electronic "invasion" into the realm of personal data has become a serious ethical issue.

Some of the computer-related privacy issues involve the use of large databases and electronic networks, and the enactment of certain laws.

DATABASES

Large organizations around the world are constantly compiling information about most of us. For instance, in the United States, social security numbers are routinely used as key fields in databases for organizing people's employment, credit, and tax records. As part of the billing process, telephone companies compile lists of the calls made, the numbers called, the time the calls were made, and so on. Using a special telephone directory called a reverse directory that lists telephone numbers followed by the names of the number holders, governmental authorities and others can easily get the addresses and other details about the persons we call. Credit card companies keep similar records.

Professional data gatherers, or "information resellers," collect personal data and sell it to direct marketers, fund-raisers, and others. In the United States, even some motor-vehicle departments sell the car-registration data they collect. From this data database companies have been able to collect names, addresses, and other information about the majority of American households. Some privacy experts estimate that the average person is on 100 mailing lists and in 50 databases at one time. This invasion of privacy raises three issues:

1. How do you feel about personal information being spread without your consent? What if a great deal of information about your shopping habits—collected without your consent—were made available to any small or large business that wanted it? Until they dropped the project, Lotus Development Corporation and Equifax, Inc. were preparing to do just that.

On highways and bridges in some states—Texas, Louisiana, and Oklahoma, for example—toll-collecting systems read tags affixed to cars. When a car passes through a toll plaza, a machine records the tag's ID number and then, at the end of the month, bills the driver for tolls. The states say that the system cuts down on traffic and smog. But privacy advocates say the system could also give state government a powerful new tool to monitor its citizens; it will know when they're gone and which way they've traveled.

What if you discovered that your employer was using your medical records to make decisions about placement, promotion, and firing? A survey done in the United States in 1988 found that half of the *Fortune* 500 companies were using employee medical records to make these decisions.

2. How do you feel about the spread of inaccurate information? Mistakes made in one computer file may find their way into other computer files. For example, many people find that their credit records contain errors. And even if you get the mistake corrected in one file, it may not be corrected in other files.

Robert Ellis Smith, a U.S. lawyer, was worried enough about inaccuracy in the collection and dissemination of personal information to do something about it. In the early 1970s, as the use of computers became widespread, he worried that government and businesses could know too much about an individual's life and lifestyle. And what they knew quickly became a commodity for marketers. Smith said: "What I soon discovered was that there was often not any need for the information that was being collected, or respect for its accuracy." Smith has successfully been party in a suit against TRW, Inc., a major U.S. credit-reporting company. The result of the suit is to make it easier for consumers to correct errors in their credit reports. TRW has agreed to set up toll-free numbers for consumers to call with credit report questions. It will also make its reports easier to read and create a set of strict new rules for handling consumer complaints about credit report errors.

However, credit-reporting companies also do background investigations on individuals for potential employers. Their reports are sometimes incorrect, and the result is that, for no valid reason, the applicant is not hired. To prevent this, consumer groups advocate the following:

- *Improved accuracy*: Credit bureaus should take responsibility for correcting mistakes, no matter where the data came from, and, they should inform other credit reporters of errors.
- *Free reports*: Consumers are entitled to a free copy of their credit reports once a year, not just when they are denied credit.
- *Privacy protection*: Consumers should be given a clear chance to prevent sales of personal data to marketers.
- *Improved service*: Credit-denial notices should include a list of consumers' rights. Investigations of errors should take 30 days, tops.
- *Better enforcement*: The Federal Trade Commission should be given more power to penalize credit reporters for violating the law.*

Fortunately, U.S. law allows its citizens to gain access to records about themselves that are held by credit bureaus and by governmental agencies (we'll discuss this in more detail later).

3. How do you feel about anonymous individuals and large companies profiting from the personal activities that make up your life? "Whose life is it, anyway?"

Business Week, July 29, 1991, p. 70.

ELECTRONIC NETWORKS

Suppose you use your company's electronic mail system—or an electronic bulletin board service—to send people a political message that includes some unflattering remarks against a particular group. Later you find the boss has been spying on your exchange or that the BBS has screened your messages and not sent them.

In the United States, some legislation has been introduced to control unannounced electronic "spying"—**electronic surveillance**—by supervisors. For example, one proposed law would require employers to provide prior written notice of electronic monitoring and supply some sort of audible or visual signal to alert employees that monitoring was occurring. However, most commercial electronic bulletin board services commonly restrict libelous, obscene, and offensive material through the use of electronic surveillance.

Many people believe that, in a nation linked by electronic mail, there has to be fundamental protection against other people reading or censoring messages or taking action because of their contents. Indeed, in October 1991, in a case involving CompuServe, a New York Federal Court ruled that a computer network (information service) company is not legally liable for the contents of the information it disseminates. But some people think that there has to be a limit on the potentially libelous, offensive, or otherwise damaging contents of some messages, in spite of any existing rights to free speech and freedom from censorship. For example, the Prodigy information service network has a policy of prescreening its members' public notes. It warns its members that it won't carry messages that are obscene, profane, or otherwise offensive. But who determines exactly what is "obscene," "profane," or "offensive"?

MAJOR LAWS ON PRIVACY

- U.S. **Fair Credit Reporting Act of 1970:** This law is intended to keep mistakes out of credit bureau files. Credit agencies are barred from sharing credit information with anyone but authorized customers. Consumers also have the right to review and correct their credit records and to be notified of credit investigations for insurance and employment. However, credit agencies may share information with anyone they reasonably believe has a "legitimate business need." The term "legitimate" is not defined.

- U.S. **Freedom of Information Act of 1970:** This law gives citizens the right to look at data concerning themselves that is stored by the U.S. government. However, sometimes a lawsuit is necessary to gain access to the data

- U.S. **Privacy Act of 1974:** This law restricts U.S. governmental agencies in the way they share information about American citizens. It prohibits federal information collected for one purpose from being used for a different purpose. However, some exceptions written into the law permit federal agencies to share information anyway.

- U.S. **Right to Financial Privacy Act of 1979:** This act sets procedures that U.S. governmental agencies must follow when examining customer records in a bank. However, the law does not cover state and local governments.

- U.S. **Computer Fraud and Abuse Act of 1986:** This law was passed to allow the prosecution of people who gain unauthorized access to computers and databases. However, people with legitimate access can get into computer systems and then create mischief without penalty.

- U.S. **Video Privacy Protection Act of 1988:** This act prevents retailers in the United States from selling or disclosing video-rental records without the customer's consent or a court order. (The same restrictions do not apply to more important files, such as medical and insurance records.)

- U.S. **Computer Matching and Privacy Protection Act of 1988:** This law sets procedures for using computer data for verifying a person's eligibility for federal benefits or for recovering delinquent debts. Individuals are given a chance to respond before the government takes any adverse action against them. However, computer data can still be used for law-enforcement or tax reasons.

Since the late 1970s, seven European nations have enacted a patchwork of data protection laws. But Italy, Belgium, Spain, Portugal, and Greece have passed none. The matter of data protection and privacy remains one of the many barriers to a Europe that is a truly unified economic entity. If the European nations were to adopt a single privacy standard, however, current thinking is that it could be stricter than U.S. and Canadian laws (Figure 12.1).

Because many of the records stored by nongovernmental organizations are not covered by existing laws, privacy is still largely an ethical issue, not entirely a legal one. However, many people have indicated that they are concerned about controlling who has the right to personal information and how it is used. The following list summarizes the Code of Fair Information Practice, recommended in 1977. The code has been adopted by many information-collecting businesses in the United States, but many people would like to see it written into law.

1. *No secret databases:* There must be no secret record-keeping systems containing personal data.

2. *Right of individual access:* Individuals must be able to find out what information about them is in a record and how it is used.

3. *Right of consent:* Information about individuals obtained for one purpose cannot, without their consent, be used for other purposes.

4. *Right to correct:* Individuals must be able to correct or amend records of information about them.

5. *Assurance of reliability and proper use:* Organizations creating, maintaining, using, or disseminating records of identifiably personal data must make sure the data is reliable. They must take precautions to prevent such data from being misused.

FIGURE 12.1

THE PRIVACY FUROR

The European Commission's proposal would:

▶ Prevent companies from keeping personal data or ID numbers without the person's O.K.
▶ Let consent be withdrawn at any time and permit damage suits if such privacy rights are infringed
▶ Require file-keepers to set up a security system to bar unauthorized access
▶ Ban electronic profiles of individuals based on what they buy or do through computer networks
▶ Bar transmission of data to countries without similar protections

COMPUTER HAZARDS

Personal data in a computer database may not be protected if the computer itself is not kept safe from criminals, natural disasters, and other hazards.

CRIME AND CRIMINALS

A **computer crime** is committed when a person uses computer technology or knowledge of computers in an illegal activity. To catch computer criminals, computers are programmed to do a lot of double-checking; but if the criminal evades the double-checks, he or she may not get caught. Police have a hard time tracking down computer criminals, because fingerprints and other traditional forms of evidence are irrelevant. Most computers use passwords to try to stop people from fooling around with sensitive data, but some programmers can get around the passwords. Typically, computer criminals who were caught used to be dealt with more leniently in court than other types of criminals—for example, someone who stole $100,000 from an electronic file received a lesser sentence than someone who used a gun and robbed a store of $1,000. But that situation is changing. Computer criminals are being dealt with more harshly than they used to be.

In general, computer criminals are of four types:

1. *Employees:* In this case, the crime can be theft. Of course, it can be theft of physical property, such as equipment and software. But often it is theft of proprietary information, money in electronic accounts, or computer time for private purposes. For example, two Bank of Boston employees were fired in late 1991; one for using the computer system to handicap horse races and the other for using the computer to run his Amway business—which took up 600 MB of memory! In addition, an employee may have a grudge and introduce program bugs into the system.

2. *Outside users:* Suppliers or clients may have access to a company's computer system. These authorized users may obtain confidential passwords or find other ways of committing computer crimes.

3. *"Hackers" and "crackers":* **Hackers** are people who gain unauthorized access to a computer system for fun. **Crackers** gain unauthorized access for malicious purposes—that is, to create trouble. For example, they may steal technical information or introduce a virus into the system.

4. *Organized crime:* People in organized crime use computers for illegal purposes, such as to keep track of stolen goods or illegal gambling debts. In addition, counterfeiters and forgers use microcomputers and printers to produce sophisticated-looking documents, such as checks and driver's licenses.

People are becoming more and more creative in the ways they use computers to commit crimes. Some of the more common types of computer crime are:

1. *Damage:* Disgruntled employees sometimes attempt to destroy computers, programs, or files. They may also attempt to infect the computer system with a virus (viruses were covered in Chapter 9).

2. *Theft:* Theft may be of hardware, software, data, or computer time. People steal equipment, and they steal data or use (steal) their company's computer time to run a sideline business.

3. *Unauthorized copying:* Software piracy is the unauthorized copying of software disks for personal use (covered in more detail later in the chapter).

4. *Manipulation:* Gaining entry into someone's computer network and manipulating, or changing, the data can cause unpredictable damage.

OTHER HAZARDS

Other dangers to computers and computer systems include the following:

- *Natural hazards:* Computer systems can be damaged or destroyed by fires, floods, wind, hurricanes, tornadoes, and earthquakes. Even home computer users must be aware of the importance of storing backup disks of programs and data in safe locations in the event of a natural disaster.

- *Civil strife and terrorism:* Wars, insurrections, terrorism, and sabotage are greater risks in some parts of the world than in others, but these occurrences can definitely destroy a computer system. For example, during a period of civil unrest in November of 1991, looters in Zaire destroyed six years of medical data used in AIDS research. The looters stole all the computers and the data had not been backed up.

- *Technological failures:* Hardware and software failures can be caused by power surges and power outages. To protect themselves against power changes, many microcomputer users purchase surge protectors and uninterruptible power supply units (Chapter 13). Also, users of hard disks should always remember to make backup copies of disk files, on diskettes or tape, in case the hard disk crashes.

- *Human errors*: Remember the phrase "garbage in, garbage out"? "Garbage" can mean mistakes made in data entry. Perhaps the data entry person's finger slipped while typing—imagine what an incorrectly placed decimal point could do—or perhaps he or she had incorrect data to begin with. Or, it can mean programming errors. Mistakes can also happen if the procedures for data entry are not clear. For example, are time measurements to be entered in minutes or seconds? Are distances to be entered in feet or meters? Can the user input "Y" instead of "yes"?

Unfortunately, people tend to regard computer-generated information as gospel, in spite of the sizable potential for input error (Figure 12.2).

COMPUTER SECURITY

Controls must be built into computer systems to ensure **security,** the protection of data, hardware, and software from unauthorized use as well as from damage from intrusions, sabotage, and natural disasters. In general, ensuring computer system security involves:

- *Restricting access*: Security experts are constantly devising ways to protect computer systems from being accessed by unauthorized persons. Sometimes guards are posted in company computer rooms, to check the identification of everyone who enters. Sometimes locks are put on microcomputers and ID numbers are etched on computer equipment. Disks, diskettes, and tapes are kept in locked containers and/or rooms. Passwords may be issued to people to use to gain access to computer files. (Passwords are the secret words or numbers that must be entered into a computer system before it will operate.)

    Some security systems use biometrics, the science of measuring individual body characteristics (Figure 12.3)—using machines that can recognize one's fingerprints, signature, voice, or even photographs.

- *Anticipating disasters*: Ensuring physical security means protecting hardware from possible human and natural disasters. Data security is concerned with

---

Rex Reed, writer and sometime actor, ordered a bed from a Manhattan department store.

Three months passed. Then came the long-anticipated announcement: the bed will be delivered on Friday.

Reed waited all day. No bed.

Having disposed of his other bed, he slept on the floor.

Next day deliverers brought the bed but couldn't put it up. No screws.

On Monday, men appeared with the screws. But they couldn't put in the mattresses. No slats. "That's not our department."

Reed hired a carpenter to build them; the department store's slats finally arrived 15 weeks later.

Undaunted, Reed went to the store to buy sheets. Two men came up and declared "You're under arrest." Why? "You're using a stolen credit card. Rex Reed is dead."

Great confusion. Reed flashed all his identity cards. The detectives apologized— and then tore up his store charge card. Why? "Our computer has been told that you are dead. And we cannot change this."

FIGURE 12.2

One result of input errors. (From *Time* magazine, reprinted in *The Secret Guide to Computers*, 14th edition, p. 542. Russ Walter, 22 Ashland St. #2, Somerville, MA 02144-3202.)

protecting software and data from unauthorized tampering or damage. Most large organizations have a disaster recovery plan that describes ways to continue operations following a disaster until normal computer operations can be restored.

- *Backing up data:* If a disaster occurs, computer equipment may be replaced, but data may not be—unless it was backed up. And, the backup files should be kept in a safe place that is in a location different from the location of the original data files (Figure 12.4).

- *Using encryption:* Data transmitted over communications lines can be secured by encryption to prevent eavesdropping. **Encryption** is the encoding of data by converting the standard data code into a proprietary (secret) code for transmission. After transmission, the data is converted back into standard code.

COMPUTERS AND COPYRIGHT VIOLATION

SOFTWARE PIRACY

Software piracy, or theft, has become a major concern to software writers and manufacturers. However, the act of piracy is not quite as dramatic as it sounds.

FIGURE 12.3   Computer security: New ways to keep hackers and crackers out. (Adapted from *Fortune,* December 16, 1991, p. 14.)

Estimates show that U.S. business and government agencies lose more than $1 billion a year to hackers and other high-tech criminals.

Limiting access to files and databases is the key defense. Most Americans use all-too-obvious passwords to log on to their machines, employing such giveaways as their street address, dog's name, or spouse's well-known nickname.

To make access more secure, an increasing number of companies are issuing their employees "tokens," which the user carries. The tokens look like credit cards and display a row of numbers that, through the wonders of modern technology, changes every 60 seconds. To log on to most systems using tokens, the user first types in his or her password then this number. The computer, which is in sync with the numerals, allows entry.

Another mode of computer security involves biometrics. It goes beyond passwords (what you know) and tokens (what you have) to biological features (what you are). See below for how four such systems work.

Voice I.D.

Computer recognizes user's voice. Strength: Completely mobile and makes access from phone possible. Weakness: Expensive; static can block access.

Retinal I.D.

A ray of light looks at map of blood vessels on back of eyeball. Strength: Similar technology can already open doors. Weakness: Eye safety is still a concern.

Fingerprint I.D.

Identification through a "reader" gadget attached to computer. Strength: Fingerprints are unique. Weakness: Limited mobility—user must carry brick-size reader.

Lip Prints

User kisses screen. Fanciful technology in earliest stages. Strength: Lip patterns are unique. Weakness: Makeup, chapped lips and cold sores can block signal.

In most cases it simply means illegally copying private domain (copyrighted) software onto blank disks. (It *is* legal for buyers of software to make backup copies on blank disks.) Because much software—from games to sophisticated publishing programs—is expensive, it's tempting to avoid buying an off-the-shelf package by accepting a friend's offer to supply free copies. But, according to the Copyright Act of 1976, the Software Copyright Act of 1980, and the Computer Software Piracy and Counterfeiting Amendment of 1983, this practice is illegal. It is also unethical.

Computer programmers and software companies often spend years developing, writing, testing, and marketing software programs—only to lose many royalty dollars to software "pirates." If you spent several years writing a book, only to lose royalties through the distribution of illegally copied volumes, how would you feel? The issue is the same.

What you're really buying when you purchase software is the **license** to use the software (Figure 12.5). However, vendors include different restrictions with the licenses they sell. When you purchase a software package, make sure that you read the license agreement and send in the registration card, if any, so that you will receive information on new versions and other updates.

Some software companies write copy-protect programs into their software to prevent illegal copying; other software authors offer free or inexpensive copies of their programs, called *freeware* and *shareware*.

Shareware, Freeware, and Public Domain Software

Shareware, freeware, and public domain software are all a kind of noncommercial software usually distributed through bulletin board systems (Chapter 8). Shareware costs something—but much less than commercial software packages—and freeware and public domain software usually cost nothing.

Shareware is distributed on request for an evaluation period, after which the user pays a registration fee or returns the software. After the user pays the registration fee—or licensing fee—he or she is usually sent documentation, and, in some cases, additional support and notification of updates.

The following story was related by Russ Walter, who writes and produces a popular guide to computers.

"On my own hard disk, the only file that's critical is TRAN, which contains the details of every transaction that generated income or an order. Since it's too long to copy onto floppies quickly, I copy it instead to a file called TRANBAK on the same hard disk. Copying TRAN to TRANBAK takes just a few seconds, so I do it every day. If I ever lose TRAN, I just tell the computer to rename TRANBAK to TRAN. Simple!

"But what happens if my whole hard disk suddenly goes bad, so that I lose TRAN and TRANBAK simultaneously? To prepare for such a calamity, once a week I copy TRAN onto floppies. I also keep paper records of all transactions that occurred during the week.

"Hard disks are fairly reliable. The only time calamity struck me was when I disobeyed the rules. On a summer afternoon when I was rushing to finish some research, I risked using the computer when the temperature was in the high 90s. I was sorry! The hard disk's outermost tracks—which contain the directory and the fundamental formatting information—burned up. (As we computer junkies say, 'The tracks *fried*.') When I tried using the disk the next day, the computer told me the disk didn't exist. After saying a few prayers and other things, I got a new hard disk and restored the previous week's TRAN from floppies."

FIGURE 12.4

Backup tale. (From Russ Walter, *The Secret Guide to Computers*, 14th ed., © 1990 by Russ Walter, 22 Ashland St. #2, Somerville, MA 02144-3202.)

Freeware authors do not charge for their software, but they may limit its distribution. Sometimes these authors ask for feedback from users regarding any bugs in and incompatibilities with the program.

Public domain software is entirely in the public domain—that is, it carries no copyrights—and carries no restrictions. Users who use public domain software should keep in mind that software reliability may be an issue. It may have been copied many times and have been altered or tampered with in the process. Also, it may have a virus. Users should install a virus-protection program on their computers and scan all shareware, freeware, and public domain disks before using the programs on those disks.

ELECTRONIC MANIPULATION OF COPYRIGHTED MATERIAL

Most people are aware that they need to obtain permission to print text and illustrations that are copyrighted by others. Permission to reprint usually involves paying the copyright holder a fee and inserting a credit line—which gives the copyright holder's name—with the reprinted text or illustration. However, now that illustrations, including photos, can be scanned into a computer system and altered using certain types of software, a new type of copyright violation is occurring: the alteration of photos and other art without the permission of the copyright holder. Computer users in the field of desktop publishing need to be especially aware of the copyright restrictions of the materials they are working with.

FIGURE 12.5   This part of a Microsoft software licensing agreement clearly indicates that the product is for a single user; copying for additional users is illegal.

IMPORTANT—READ CAREFULLY BEFORE OPENING SOFTWARE PACKET(S). Unless a separate multilingual license booklet is included in your product package, the following License Agreement applies to you. By opening the sealed packet(s) containing the software, you indicate your acceptance of the following Microsoft License Agreement.

Microsoft License Agreement

(Single-User Products)

This is a legal agreement between you (either an individual or an entity) and Microsoft Corporation. By opening the sealed software packet(s) you are agreeing to be bound by the terms of this agreement. If you do not agree to the terms of this agreement, promptly return the unopened software packet(s) and the accompanying items (including written materials and binders or other containers) to the place you obtained them for a full refund.

MICROSOFT SOFTWARE LICENSE

1. GRANT OF LICENSE. Microsoft grants to you the right to use one copy of the enclosed Microsoft software program (the "SOFTWARE") on a single computer. The SOFTWARE is in "use" on a computer when it is loaded into temporary memory (i.e., RAM) or installed into your permanent memory (e.g., hard disk, CD-ROM, or other storage device) of that computer. However, installation on a network server for the sole purpose of distribution to one or more other computer(s) shall not constitute "use" for which a separate license is required.

2. COPYRIGHT. The SOFTWARE is owned by Microsoft or its suppliers and is protected by United States copyright laws and international treaty provisions. Therefore, you must treat the SOFTWARE like any other copyrighted material (e.g. a book or musical recording) except that you may either (a) make one copy of the SOFTWARE solely for backup or archival purposes, or (b) transfer the SOFTWARE to a single hard disk provided you keep the original solely for backup or archival purposes. You may not copy the written materials accompanying the SOFTWARE.

3. OTHER RESTRICTIONS. You may not rent or lease the SOFTWARE, but you may transfer the SOFTWARE and accompanying written materials on a permanent basis provided you retain no copies and the recipient agrees to the terms of this Agreement. You may not reverse engineer, decompile, or disassemble the SOFTWARE. If the SOFTWARE is an update or has been updated, any transfer must include the most recent update and all prior versions.

4. DUAL MEDIA SOFTWARE. If the SOFTWARE package contains both 3.5" and 5.25" disks, then you may use only the disks appropriate for your single-user computer. You may not use the other disks on another computer or loan, rent, lease, or transfer them to another user except as part of the permanent transfer (as provided above) of all SOFTWARE and written materials.

A LAST WORD

What are some of the other ethical issues that have arisen as a result of using computers in the workplace and in other aspects of daily life?

Many universities incorporate into their computer science curriculum a course on ethics. For example, in 1990, Polytechnic University in Brooklyn added a course to its curriculum: Information, Society, and Man. This course teaches students that computing professionals have a responsibility to act in an ethical manner. Especially in a networked environment, where many different computers are connected together, professionals maintaining the network have a serious responsibility to hundreds of people they will never see—a responsibility to maintain privacy and accuracy of data, among other things.

Interestingly, although other disciplines have long followed codes of ethics—for example, the goal of a civil engineer is to build public structures that are *safe*—strict codes of ethical standards have not been defined in the world of computing. Computer industry observers predict that users and computer professionals alike will be faced with more and more ethical *dilemmas*, or "gray areas," in the future.

For example, many people focus on the freedom from repetitive and boring work that computers give. This is certainly welcome in many situations, but we must remember that what is boring and routine work to one person may be life-saving employment to another. Traditionally, in the United States, many low-level jobs are held by young people and immigrants with language problems. Therefore, what at first seems like an advantage of computerization may really be a disadvantage. McDonald's restaurants came to this conclusion not too long ago when they decided not to eliminate the jobs of people who take orders at the front counters and replace the human order-takers with machines that customers would use to key in their own orders. And maintaining human contact is still better for business.

More and more, information is replacing energy as society's main resource. Many people are concerned that too much emphasis has been put on what the computer can do to streamline business and too little on how it may be affecting the quality of our lives. For example, is it distorting the meaning of thought? That is, is it absurd and dangerous to attribute the capabilities of thinking and creativity to a computer? People have experience, convictions, and cultural traditions. Are these qualities being devalued? If so, perhaps we are heading into an era in which machine-like qualities of speed and problem solving will be valued more highly than what used to be called *humane* qualities. As a result, many people believe computers have the potential to contribute to worker dissatisfaction.

Consider again the potential for computer-based systems in business to be used to monitor employees. What if computers were (and many already are) programmed to check your speed, the pauses you make, the breaks you take, the rate of keying errors? Would it be fair for the company to do this to make sure it retains only the most efficient workers and thus increase the value of goods and services it has to sell? Or would this detract from your dignity as a human being—your right to do some things better than you do others? And would this type of company get high-quality decisions from its employees—or would the employees be too afraid to work creatively? One major labor union in the United States, the AFL-CIO, has taken the position that electronic surveillance "invades workers' privacy, erodes their sense of dignity, and frustrates their efforts to do high-quality work by a single-minded emphasis on speed."

In addition, a growing percentage of the work force is working at home. Workers can communicate with their offices via a microcomputer and special communications software. In many cases, this arrangement enables workers in metropolitan areas to get work done instead of sitting in traffic. However, how does working at home affect employee morale, efficiency, and motivation? How does the employer maintain control of the employee? With these issues in mind, is the employee who works at home really more productive? Or not?

Another important issue relates to the disabled. For most of us, computers make our lives more convenient. But for some—people with disabilities—computers play a much greater role. Computers have the potential of equalizing the workplace by enabling people with mobility, vision, and hearing impairments to do the same work as someone who isn't handicapped. Some disabled workers have difficulty holding down more than two keys at once or using a mouse. Blind workers need special translator hardware so they can read text and numbers. Fortunately, many add-on products are available to adapt standard microcomputers to the needs of the disabled, including voice translators for the blind and software that modifies the way the keyboard and the mouse are used. However, products like these vary in sophistication and are usually quite expensive. As a result, very few companies make these purchases. Aren't these companies discriminating against the handicapped? Many legislators are actively working to pass a bill that will make this form of discrimination illegal.

This chapter covered only a few of the many computer-related issues that are being discussed today. Keep an important thought in mind, however: Although these problems certainly deserve everyone's attention, they should not obscure the opportunities that will be opened to you if you know how to use computers in your chosen occupation.

SUMMARY

- The development of computers and large electronic databases has facilitated the collection of information about individuals. In the past, this information has been sold to marketing groups without the individual's consent. Many people believe this is an unethical practice.

- The information that is collected about individuals and then transmitted to credit-reporting companies is often error-ridden, causing people to be denied loans and jobs, in addition to causing other problems.

- Seemingly private information about individuals—such as medical records—has been disseminated to others—such as employers—and used to make decisions about which the individuals may know nothing.

- Consumer groups are trying to correct the problems involving data collection and dissemination and make information sellers more responsible by advocating:
  1. *Improved accuracy:* Information sellers must correct mistakes in the data, no matter where it came from.
  2. *Free reports:* At the request of an individual, information sellers must provide a copy of the individual's report for free once a year.
  3. *Protect privacy:* Companies that sell data must give an individual a clear chance to prevent sales of personal data to marketers.
  4. *Improved service:* Credit denial notices should include a list of consumers' rights. Investigations of errors should take no more than 30 days.
  5. *Better enforcement:* Credit reporters should be penalized for violating the law.

- The use of electronic communications and information networks has also raised ethical concerns about the censorship of some messages and the electronic "spying" on message contents by supervisors in companies and directors of information services.

- The United States has passed seven major laws in an attempt to protect individual privacy and regulate the selling of information:
  1. *Fair Credit Reporting Act of 1970:* Intended to keep mistakes out of credit bureau files; credit agencies are barred from sharing credit information with

anyone but authorized customers; consumers also have the right to review and correct their credit records and to be notified of credit investigations for insurance and employment.

2. *Freedom of Information Act of 1970:* Gives citizens the right to look at data concerning themselves that is stored by the U.S. government.

3. *Privacy Act of 1974:* Restricts governmental agencies in the way they share information about American citizens; prohibits federal information collected for one purpose from being used for a different purpose.

4. *Right to Financial Privacy Act of 1979:* Sets strict procedures that U.S. governmental agencies must follow when they want to examine customer records in a bank.

5. *Computer Fraud and Abuse Act of 1986:* Allows the prosecution of people who gain unauthorized access to computers and databases.

6. *Video Privacy Protection Act of 1988:* Prevents retailers in the United States from selling or disclosing video-rental records without the customer's consent or a court order.

7. *Computer Matching and Privacy Protection Act of 1988:* Sets procedures for using computer data for verifying a person's eligibility for federal benefits or for recovering delinquent debts.

- The *Code of Fair Information Practice* was recommended in 1977 and has been adopted by many U.S. businesses. Though not yet law, the code recommends:
  1. *No secret databases*   3. *Right of consent*
  2. *Right of individual access*   4. *Assurance of reliability and proper use*

- A *computer crime* is committed when a person uses computer technology or knowledge of computers in an illegal activity. It can include:
  1. Employee theft of hardware, software, proprietary information, electronic funds, or company time on the computer (for example, by running a private business); a disgruntled employee can also introduce bugs or viruses into a company system.
  2. Outside users with access to a company's computer system may abuse their privileges to steal information or funds or to introduce bugs or viruses.
  3. Hackers or crackers may gain unauthorized access to a system and steal information or introduce viruses.
  4. People in organized crime may use computers for illegal purposes.

- In addition to being subject to theft and sabotage, computer systems may be damaged by natural hazards, civil strife and terrorism, technological failures, and/or human errors. Because of these dangers, computer systems must be made as secure as possible, and all data must be backed up. Ideally, the backup disks or tape should be kept in a different, safe location.

- *Computer security* includes:
  1. Restricting access to the system by the use of guards and passwords
  2. Locking some equipment and rooms and engraving ID numbers on the equipment
  3. Using biometrics to identify and clear users
  4. Anticipating disasters
  5. Backing up data
  6. Using encryption for data transmissions over communications lines

- *Software piracy* is the illegal copying of copyrighted software onto blank disks for unauthorized use.

- When a user buys software, he or she is really buying a *license* to use that software; he or she is not authorized to make and give copies to anyone else.

- *Shareware* is software distributed on request—usually through an electronic bulletin board service—for which the user pays a small fee if he or she wishes to keep it. Shareware carries a copyright.

- *Freeware* is free software usually distributed in a limited fashion through an electronic bulletin board service.
- *Public domain software* is free software without any copyright and usually distributed through a bulletin board service.
- Copyrighted photos and illustrations may not be electronically manipulated without the copyright holder's consent.

KEY WORDS

computer crime, p. 309
Computer Fraud and
    Abuse Act of 1986,
    p. 308
Computer Matching
    and Privacy
    Protection Act of
    1988, p. 309
cracker, p. 310
electronic surveillance,
    p. 308

encryption, p. 312
ethics, p. 306
Fair Credit Reporting
    Act of 1970, p. 308
Freedom of Information
    Act of 1970, p. 308
freeware, p. 314
hacker, p. 310
license, p. 313
Privacy Act of 1974,
    p. 308

public domain software,
    p. 314
Right to Financial
    Privacy Act of 1979,
    p. 308
security, p. 311
shareware, p. 314
software piracy, p. 312
Video Privacy
    Protection Act of
    1988, p. 308

EXERCISES

SELF-TEST

1. _____ is a set of moral values or principles that govern the conduct of an individual or a group.

2. In the United States, it is not possible for someone to use another person's social security number to set up bank accounts and obtain credit cards. (true/false)

3. _____ _____ involves the electronic monitoring by a supervisor of employees' work performance.

4. The U.S. Freedom of Information Act of 1970 gives citizens the right to look at data concerning themselves that is stored by the U.S. government. (true/false)

5. In the United States, video-rental stores can sell customers' video-rental records without the customers' consent. (true/false)

6. A _____ _____ is committed when a person uses computer technology or knowledge of computers in an illegal activity.

7. _____ are people who gain unauthorized access to a computer system for fun; _____ gain unauthorized access for malicious purposes.

8. Computer _____ is the protection of information, hardware, and software from unauthorized use as well as from damage.

9. The encoding of data from a standard code into a secret proprietary code for protection from eavesdropping during data transmission is called

_____.

10. If a user copies copyrighted software onto blank disks and uses the copies as backup, he or she is committing software piracy. (true/false)

SOLUTIONS (1) ethics; (2) false; (3) electronic surveillance; (4) true; (5) false; (6) computer crime; (7) hackers, crackers; (8) security; (9) encryption; (10) false

SHORT ANSWER

1. List five things that consumer groups believe credit-reporting companies should do to better serve customers.
2. List and briefly describe the seven privacy laws enacted in the United States.
3. Define *computer crime* and give a few examples.
4. What does the phrase "garbage in, garbage out" mean?
5. How can users help prevent data damage or loss from natural disasters and technological failures?
6. What is data encryption used for?
7. List at least four ways of ensuring the security of a computer system.
8. Define *software piracy*.
9. What is shareware?
10. What danger might exist in electronically manipulating photos and other illustrations?

PROJECTS

1. What's your opinion about the issue of free speech on an electronic network? Research some recent legal decisions in various countries, as well as some articles on the topic, and then give a short report about what you think. Should the contents of messages be censored? If so, under what conditions?
2. People especially susceptible to electronic surveillance while they are working include those who work for airlines; hotel, rental car, mail-order, insurance, telephone, and credit card companies; or federal, state, and local U.S government departments and agencies. For example, recently an airline reservation employee took a call from a distraught man who had to book a flight to go to his sister's funeral. The employee purposely spent extra time with the man because he was upset. Later, she was reprimanded by a supervisor who said that her work had been monitored and that she had taken too long with the call, thus losing revenue for the airline.

   Give a short report taking a position for or against the electronic surveillance of employees during work time. Be sure to consider what the opposite position's points would be and refute them.
3. *Privacy for Sale*, by Jeffrey Rothfeder (Simon & Schuster, 1992), catalogues major and minor "horror stories" from the recent annals of America's constantly growing computer state. For example, one man, who did not smoke or drink and who was in good health, was shocked when he was told by an insurance company that he would have to pay an exhorbitant premium for disability insurance. Why? Because he was an alcoholic, the insurance company said. The man, who was not an alcoholic, finally discovered that the source of the misinformation was a little-known Massachusetts company that is said to control the largest collection of medical records in the United States.

   Mr. Rothfeder gives some specific suggestions for protecting personal information. Obtain a copy of his book from the library or a bookstore, and prepare a short report on some of the major privacy issues he identifies and his suggestions for protecting privacy.

COMPUTERS AND DISABILITIES*

THE FUTURE

A primary interest of mine is the application of computer technology to the needs of the handicapped. Through the application of computer technology, handicaps associated with the major sensory and physical disabilities can largely be overcome during the next decade or two. I am confident of this development because of the fortunate matching of the strengths of early machine intelligence with the needs of the handicapped. The typical disabled person is missing a specific skill or capability but is otherwise a normally intelligent and capable human being. It is generally possible to apply the sharply focused intelligence of today's machines to ameliorate these handicaps. A reading machine, for example, addresses the inability of a blind or dyslexic person to read, probably the most significant handicap associated with the disability of blindness.

In the early 21st century lives of disabled persons will be far different than they are today. For the blind, reading machines will be pocket-sized devices that can instantly scan not only pages of text but also signs and symbols found in the real world. These machines will be able to read with essentially perfect intonation and with a broad variety of voice styles. They will also be able to describe pictures and graphics, translate from one language to another, and provide access to on-line knowledge bases and libraries through wireless networks. Most blind and dyslexic persons will have them, and they may be ubiquitous among the rest of the population.

Blind persons will carry computerized navigational aids that will perform the functions of seeing-eye dogs, only with greater intelligence than today's canine navigators. Attempts up to now at electronic navigational assistants for the blind have not proved useful. Unless such a device incorporates a level of intelligence at least comparable to a seeing-eye dog, it is not of much value. This is particularly true since modern mobility training can provide a blind person equipped only with an ordinary cane with substantial travel skills. I personally know many blind people who can travel around town and even around the world with ease. With the intelligent navigational aids of the future, travel skills for the blind will become even easier.

Ultimately, compact devices will be built that combine both reading and navigational capabilities with the ability to provide intelligent descriptions of real-world scenes on a real-time basis. At that stage of machine evolution they are probably more accurately called *seeing* machines. Such a machine would be like a friend that could describe what is going on in the visible world. The blind user could ask the device (verbally or in some other way) to elaborate on a description, or he could ask it questions. The visual sensors of such a device could be built into a pair of eyeglasses, although it may be just as well to pin it on the user's lapel. In fact, these artificial eyes need not only look forward; they may as well look in all directions. And they may have better visual acuity than normal eyes. We may all want to use them.

The deaf will have hearing machines that can display what people are saying. The underlying technology required is the Holy Grail of voice recognition: combining large-vocabulary recognition with speaker independence and continuous speech. Early versions of speech-to-text aids for the deaf should appear over the next decade. Artificial hearing should also include the ability to intelligently translate other forms of auditory information, such as music and natural sounds, into other modalities, such as vision and touch.

---

*By Raymond Kurzweil, *The Age of Intelligent Machines*, Cambridge, Mass.: Massachusetts Institute of Technology, 1990, pp. 441–443.

Eventually we may find suitable channels of communication directly into the brain to provide truly artificial sight and hearing. But in any case, there will certainly be progress in restoring lost hearing and sight.

The physically handicapped (paraplegics and quadriplegics) will have their ability to walk and climb stairs restored, abilities that will overcome the severe access limitations wheelchairs impose. Methods to accomplish this will include exoskeletal robotic devices, or powered orthotic devices, as they are called. These devices will be as easy to put on as a pair of tights and will be controlled by finger motion, head motion, speech, and perhaps eventually thoughts. Another option, one that has shown promise in experiments at a number of research institutes, is direct electrical stimulation of limb muscles. This technique effectively reconnects the control link that was broken by spinal cord damage.

Those without use of their hands will control their environment, create written text, and interact with computers using voice recognition. This capability already exists. Artificial hand prostheses controlled by voice, head movement, and perhaps eventually by direct mental connection, will restore manual functionality.

Substantial progress will be made in courseware to treat dyslexia (difficulty in reading for neurophysical reasons other than visual impairment) and learning disabilities. Such systems will also provide richer learning experiences for the retarded.

Perhaps the greatest handicap associated with sensory and physical disabilities is a subtle and insidious one: the prejudice and lack of understanding often exhibited by the general public. Most handicapped persons do not want pity or charity; instead, they want to be respected for their own individuality and intelligence. We all have handicaps and limitations; those of a blind or deaf person may be more obvious, but they are not necessarily more pervasive or limiting. I have worked with many disabled persons, and I know from personal experience that they are as capable as other workers and students at most tasks. I cannot ask a blind person to drive a package across town, but I can ask him to give a speech or conduct a research project. A sighted worker may be able to drive a car, but he will undoubtedly have other limitations. The lack of understanding many people have of handicapped persons is evident in many ways, some obvious, some subtle. By way of example, I have had the following experience on many occasions while eating a meal with a blind person in a restaurant. The waiter or waitress will ask me if my blind friend wants dessert or if he wants cream in his coffee. While the waiter or waitress obviously intends no harm or disrespect, the message is clear. Since there is no indication that the blind person is also deaf, the implication is that he must not be intelligent enough to deal with human language.

A not unimportant side benefit of intelligent technology for the handicapped should be a substantial alteration of these negative perceptions. If the handicaps resulting from disabilities are significantly reduced, if blind people can read and navigate with ease, if deaf persons can hold normal conversations on the phone, then we can expect public perceptions to change as well. When blind, deaf, and other disabled persons take their place beside us in schools and the workplace and perform with the same effectiveness as their nondisabled peers, we shall begin to see these disabilities as mere inconveniences, as problems no more difficult to overcome than poor handwriting or fear of public speaking or any of the other minor challenges that we all face. ∎

CHAPTER 13

PURCHASING AND MAINTAINING A MICROCOMPUTER SYSTEM

In Chapters 2 through 5 we described the different input, processing, storage, and output components common to microcomputer systems, including their approximate cost. Chapters 6, 7, and 8 covered applications software, systems software, and communications. As you can see, it's easy to spend a few thousand dollars on a microcomputer system! Given this substantial investment, *carefully* consider your processing needs before pulling out your checkbook. And remember to maintain your microcomputer on a daily basis so that it will have a long and problem-free life.

PREVIEW

When you have completed this chapter, you will be able to:

Explain what should be considered before purchasing a
microcomputer system

Maintain a microcomputer system on a daily basis so that it can
be relied on over time

Explain some of the health concerns associated with frequent computer use,
and describe some of the ergonomic options open to users

CHAPTER OUTLINE

13

Why Is This Chapter Important?

Purchasing a System: What to Consider
    What Software and Hardware Will You Need?
    PC Clones: A Good Bet?
    Macintoshes
    Where to Go
    Other Practical Considerations

Maintaining a System
    Temperature
    Turning the Computer On/Off
    Plugging in the System
    Dust and Pollutants
    Other Practical Considerations
    Backing Up Your Microcomputer System

Ergonomics: Health Issues
    Physical Health
    Mental Health

Summary

Key Terms

Portable Checklist for Buying a Microcomputer System

Many different microcomputers—with different features and processing capabilities—exist on the market today. If you, or your company, are in the market to purchase a microcomputer you should consider carefully your processing needs. Not only should you define your software and hardware requirements clearly before you purchase a microcomputer system, but you should also investigate the company from which you are buying the computer to make sure it will offer support in the long run.

Despite the substantial investment they have made, many users treat their microcomputers with no more respect than a desktop calculator or a telephone. Would you leave a record album in the direct sunlight for long? If so, you would have an unusable record album on your hands because the surface would become wrinkled or warped. Similarly, you shouldn't leave your microcomputer in the direct sunlight because microcomputers are very sensitive to temperature changes. Temperature is only one factor that will affect the life of your computer. We'll cover others.

In this chapter we provide you with a few simple rules that will help you purchase a microcomputer system and maintain it over time.

PURCHASING A SYSTEM: WHAT TO CONSIDER

"You need an 80 MB hard disk." "You must purchase a laser printer." "By all means, purchase *this* word processing package." Purchasing a microcomputer system involves doing some research, listening to a lot of advice, and ultimately making a number of different purchasing decisions. Many people will buy hardware and software solely at the recommendation of a friend. Although recommendations are helpful, if you don't do additional research, you may find yourself spending more for a system that offers features you will never use. In this section we provide advice on choosing software and hardware to support your processing needs and explain what to consider before you purchase a microcomputer **clone**—that is, a microcomputer that is virtually identical to and compatible with the brand of computer it is copying. In addition, we describe some factors that should affect where you purchase a microcomputer system.

WHAT SOFTWARE AND HARDWARE WILL YOU NEED?

If you are a first-time buyer of a microcomputer, you should choose your applications software *first* (Figure 13.1), after you identify your processing needs. For example, do you want to generate documents? Budgets? Graphics? In color? Will others use the computer? If so, what are their processing needs? Depending on your needs, you will need to purchase one or more applications software packages.

Once your applications software needs have been determined, choose the compatible hardware models and systems software that will allow you to use your applications software efficiently and expand your system if necessary. (Sometimes the systems software is automatically included with the computer.)

The documentation (user's manual) that accompanies the applications software you purchase will list the minimum hardware requirements necessary to run the software. For example, your microcomputer must have a *minimum* of 640 K RAM to run many software programs on the market today. And if your objective is to output graphics, you must make sure that your printer is compatible with your software and will support graphics. By choosing your applications software first, you will ensure that all your processing requirements will be satisfied: You

FIGURE 13.1

Choose your software first, after you have determined processing needs. Then choose hardware that will run your chosen software.

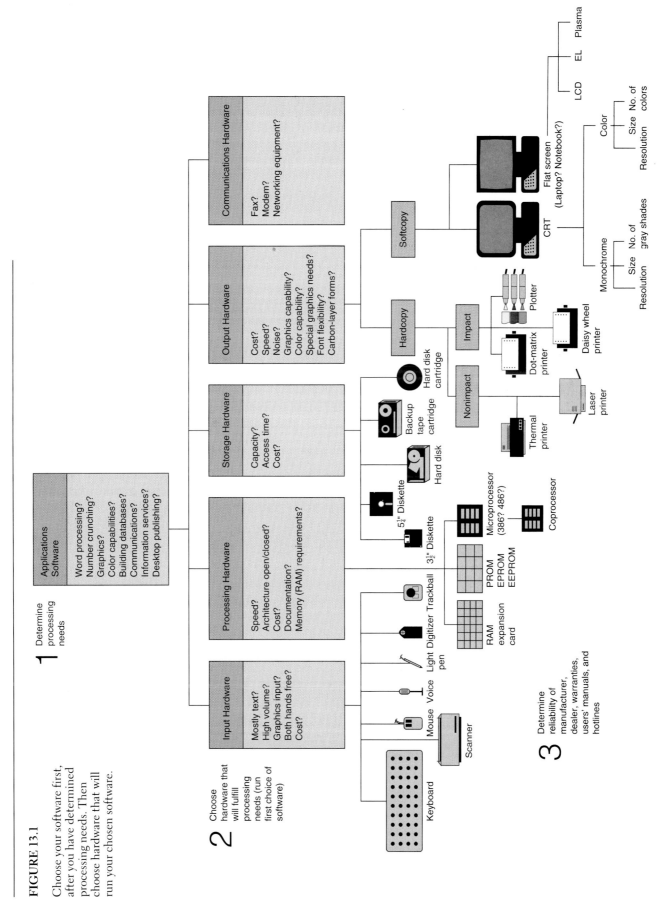

won't be forced to buy a software package that is your second choice simply because your first software choice wasn't compatible with the hardware or systems software already purchased.

When you go to work in an office, chances are that the computer hardware and systems software will already be in operation, so if you have to choose anything, it will most likely be applications software to help you do your job. If you do find yourself in a position to choose applications software, make sure not only that it will satisfy the processing requirements of your job, but also that it is compatible with your company's hardware and existing software.

PC CLONES: A GOOD BET?

It depends. There are good clones and bad clones. But if you ask some important questions before making a purchase, you will end up with a compatible system for a good price.

- Is the microcomputer accompanied by proper and adequate documentation? This is extremely important. If your microcomputer needs to be repaired or upgraded, the computer technician will want to look at the technical documentation that accompanies your system. No matter what the price, if the system comes without documentation, you should not buy it.
- Is the ROM chip a known PC compatible? If the answer is "yes," then you will be able to run all the software (generally) that is written for the microcomputer your machine is a clone of.
- Are the characteristics of the motherboard—the main circuit board—similar to those of the PC's motherboard? If they are, then PC adapter boards (such as expanded memory or video adapter boards) will work in the clone.
- Is the system covered by a warranty? The system should be covered by a 6- to 12-month warranty. If something fails during that time, the manufacturer should repair it at no cost.
- If the system fails after the warranty period, will parts be available? The manufacturer should service your computer after the warranty period expires. In other words, watch out for fly-by-night manufacturers.

Companies like NCR have conducted studies that prove their computers are 100% compatible with the microcomputer they are cloning. This type of information is useful to the microcomputer clone buyer; ask your dealer about such studies.

Because IBM microcomputers are very popular in the business environment, computer makers often manufacture IBM clones and sell them with their own manufacturing label (Figure 13.2). Don't think that a microcomputer with an IBM label is better than an IBM clone—clones are sometimes more powerful and typically less expensive than the machines they copy. As a result, IBM clones have become extremely popular and have achieved a niche of their own in the marketplace. When IBM makes a change in its microcomputer line, you can be sure that other compatibles, or clones, will appear that incorporate those changes. The microcomputers that have been cloned the most are the IBM PC and IBM XT microcomputers (based on the 8088 microprocessor chip) and the IBM AT microcomputer (based on the Intel 80286 microprocessor chip).

MACINTOSHES

Since Apple Computer, Inc., introduced the first Macintosh microcomputer in 1982, it has remained popular with many people who were impressed with its "user-friendly" graphic interface. In contrast to pre-Windows IBM PCs, the Macintosh was not command-oriented; in other words, users worked with icons, menus, and the mouse to issue commands instead of having to memorize many DOS commands and type them in on the computer. However, the Macintosh was not—and still is not—used in business as much as the IBM and IBM clones.

Then, with the introduction in 1985 of Adobe's PostScript page description language for the Mac, desktop publishing was essentially invented. Thus the Macintosh line of microcomputers became essential to many types of people in publishing, design, illustration, and typesetting. Although PostScript desktop publishing programs—such as Ventura and PageMaker—are now available for the IBM, the Macintosh—especially the high-end Quadra 950 (Figure 13.3)—is still preferred by many people in desktop publishing and related areas.

Basically, the Mac can do anything the IBM can do, and many people still insist it's easier to use than IBM microcomputers (even with Windows). Although Macs are generally more expensive than IBMs and IBM clones, most of them come with built-in hardware features that are costly extras on IBM clones, including networking capability, sound, and 256-color video. And you can expand Macs without opening the cover or adding circuit boards: just plug add-on devices into special sockets on the back of the system unit. Also, it's getting easier to swap files between the two systems—with extra software that costs around $69, all Macs

The Compaq computer on the right is a clone of the IBM computer on the left.   **FIGURE 13.2**

(a)

(b)

FIGURE 13.3

The Apple Quadra 950

can accept floppy disks formatted on an IBM PC. (Macs with System 7 operating system software include this special software.) Newer Macs have a floppy disk drive called a *Superdrive*, which can handle floppies formatted on an MS-DOS machine.

One possible drawback to using a Mac is that although there's plenty of Mac-compatible software equal to or better than DOS or Windows programs in word processing, spreadsheets, desktop publishing, and graphics, there's relatively little in some other areas. These include sophisticated databases, business accounting, and programs for creating custom applications.

WHERE TO GO

The following three factors should greatly influence where you purchase a microcomputer:

1. The company's reputation
2. The warranty agreement
3. The price

Since each of these factors influences the others, they can't be described independently.

If a local computer store has been in business for a few years, you can be reasonably confident that it has tested the waters and won't go out of business. Purchasing a computer from a local computer store offers a number of advantages, including:

- Manufacturers generally support warranties on computers sold through dealers. Should anything happen to the computer in 6–12 months, parts and labor are covered by the manufacturer's **warranty**, or agreement between the manufacturer (and sometimes the seller) and purchaser. If a computer has a problem, you will likely experience it in the first 6–12 months anyway, so a 6–12 month warranty is a fair deal. If a computer is sold through someone other than an authorized dealer—computers sold in this way are referred to as *gray-market computers*—many manufacturers ignore the manufacturer's warranty.

- Since the computer store is local, you have a convenient place to take the computer if it needs to be serviced.

- You can establish personal contacts at the computer store should you have questions about your system.

If you are *very* careful, you can purchase a microcomputer and peripheral equipment from a mail-order company for a substantial discount. Unfortunately, some computer manufacturers like IBM, Compaq, NEC, and Apple don't sell directly to mail-order companies because the mail-order companies don't usually offer support to their customers. Some manufacturers, however, do support their warranties no matter who sells the computer, including AT&T, Everex, Toshiba, and Zenith. *Make sure your microcomputer is supported by a warranty before purchasing it.*

Computer magazines such as *Byte, PC World, PC Computing, Personal Computing, InfoWorld, MacWorld,* and *MacUser* all contain advertisements for mail-order companies. Although many mail-order companies have solid reputations, some don't. If you don't do the following homework before making a purchase through a mail-order company, you may be abandoned with little or no hardware, a computer that doesn't work, or one that has no warranty.

- Check back issues of the magazine to see if the advertisement has been running regularly. If it has, the company has been paying its bills.

- Check the ad for a street address. If no street address exists—only a P.O. box—it is possible that the company may be a temporary operation.
- Compare the prices offered by different mail-order companies. If the price you are eyeing is more than 25% lower than the competition, you might be looking at something that is too good to be true.
- Make sure the system's price includes all the features and peripherals that you want. For example, make sure the price includes a monitor and a keyboard.
- Make sure the system you purchase is covered by a manufacturer's warranty. Many major computer manufacturers don't honor warranties on computers sold through mail-order companies.
- In addition, you may want to check with the Better Business Bureau or local consumer protection department in the company's area to find out more details about the company.

If everything adds up, you have found yourself a good deal. Of course, you still won't have the personalized support that you get when purchasing a computer from a local store.

OTHER PRACTICAL CONSIDERATIONS

Following are a few more guidelines that will help you in choosing a microcomputer system:

1. Determine the maximum amount of money you can spend. Don't spend money on fancy functions you don't need or may never use!
2. After you decide what you want the system to do for you and have chosen your software, determine what the minimum hardware requirements are to run the software. These requirements are listed in the documentation that accompanies each software program. Pay special attention to RAM requirements.
3. Determine if any of your hardware needs to be portable.
4. To ensure the possibility of upgrading the computer in the future, choose one designed with open architecture.
5. Determine if your system must be compatible with another system—either in your office or in another context—or with software you or your office is already using. If so, be sure to choose compatible hardware, and make sure that any systems software that comes with the computer is compatible also.
6. If possible, buy everything (computer, keyboard, monitor, printer, and so on) at one place, so you have to make only one phone call to ask questions and solve problems.
7. Consider having someone from the computer store or outlet come to your office to set up the system, install the software, and make sure everything is running properly. (Independent professionals can also do this for you.) It's also a plus if the seller offers training classes.
8. Buy a monitor and a keyboard that are comfortable to use; try them out first. Check the RAM requirements of your monitor (Table 13.1).
9. Determine how much storage you will need and buy accordingly.
10. Determine if you need color in either hardcopy or softcopy output.
11. Determine your most common output needs. For example, will you need to print out forms with many carbon layers? Will you be outputting

mostly business letters or internal memos? Will you also need to output graphics?

12. Determine your communications needs.

See the end of the chapter for a portable checklist that you can take with you when you decide to purchase a microcomputer. To help you further, Figure 13.4 interprets a few hardware and software ads to start you on the way to understanding them.

Maintaining a System

A microcomputer system presents a sizable investment—from a few hundred to a few thousand dollars. Even so, many users don't take care of this investment, which leads to system abuse and failures. Most microcomputer problems could have been prevented by regular maintenance. Maintaining a system properly—on an ongoing basis—is easy, and will pay for itself many times over by reducing hardware malfunctions and data loss and increasing the life of your computer.

In this section you will learn how to maintain your microcomputer system by following some simple procedures and words of advice.

Temperature

Computer systems should be kept in an environment with as constant a temperature as possible. In cold climates, where office temperatures are controlled by an automatic thermostat causing warmer temperatures during the day and much cooler temperatures at night, microcomputers tend to have the most system failures. The ideal room temperature for microcomputers ranges from 60 to 90 degrees Fahrenheit when the system is on and from 50 to 110 degrees when the system is off. But maintaining a constant temperature in an environment is more important than the number of degrees.

The following problems can eventually occur if a microcomputer system is subjected to substantial changes in temperature in short amounts of time:

- The chips inside the system unit can work their way out of their sockets in the system boards. In addition, the chip connectors can corrode more quickly so that they become brittle and crack.

TABLE 13.1

How Much Memory Do You Need to Support Different Color Combinations at Varying Resolutions?

	Resolution		
	640 × 480	800 × 600	1,024 × 768
4 bits per pixel (16 colors)	150 K	234 K	384 K
8 bits per pixel (256 colors)	300 K	469 K	768 K
16 bits per pixel (65,536 colors)	600 K	938 K	1,536 K
24 bits per pixel (16,777,216 colors)	900 K	1,407 K	2,304 K

AST Premium Exec
386 /25 60MB
- VGA w/32 gray shades
- 4MB RAM
- 60/80MB HD

$1799 80MB $1999

This notebook computer has a 386 microprocessor and a clock speed of 25MHz; it comes with a 60MB or 80MB hard disk, 4MB of RAM and a VGA monitor.

PS™ 486DX-33MHz 64K Cache
- 4MB RAM
  Expandable to 32MB
- 120MB Maxtor
- 1.2MB 5.25" and 1.44MB 3.5" Floppy Drives
- 2 Serial, 1 Parallel, and 1 Game Ports
- 101 Enhanced Keyboard
- High Quality 3 Button Mouse
- 1MB Trident SVGA Card
- WEN 14" 1024x768 SVGA monitor

$1595

This microcomputer system has a 486 microprocessor and a clock speed of 33 MHz. It has 4MB of RAM with 64K of cache memory, a $5\frac{1}{2}$-inch floppy disk drive, several ports for hooking up peripheral devices, a keyboard with a separate keypad, a mouse, a graphics adapter board, and a 14-inch Super VGA monitor with a resolution of 1,024 x 768.

TI PostScript Laser Printer

- PostScript Laser Printer
- 9PPM, AppleTalk Optional
- Small Footprint

This laser printer can print text and graphics on the same page, using the PostScript page description language.

It prints 9 pages per minute, can be used with both Macintosh and IBM computers, and takes up only a small amount of space on the desktop.

Macintosh IIcx 2/40
- 1.4 MB High Density Floppy Drive
- MC8030 Microprocessor
- 16MHz Clock Speed
- 2MB of RAM
- 40MB Hard Drive
- 3 NuBus expansion slots for custom configuration

This Macintosh can be upgraded with expansion cards.

Multimedia System
CD-ROM, High Tech Sound, & 16 Million Colors
24-Bit SVGA! 486-33 w/256K Cache, DOS 5.0 & Windows 3.1 w/Mulitmedia Ext. v1.0

- Intel 486DX CPU, Made in USA Motherboard
- 4 MB (expandable to 64 MB) 8 MB add $180
- 120 MB Maxtor or Conner Hard Drive – 200 MB add $200
- 24-Bit SVGA Card w/1 MB up to 16 Million Colors
- Viewsonic 6 Non-interlaced Super VGA Monitor (1024x768)
- Teac 1.44 MB 3.5" Floppy Drive
- Teac 1.3 MB 5.25" Floppy Drive
- 2 Serial, 1 Parallel, 1 Game Port, I/O Card
- Naxiswitch 101-Key Enhanced Keyboard
- Microsoft Compat. Mouse w/Pad
- DOS 5.0 with Manual
- Window 3.1 w/Manual & Muitimedia Ext. 1.0
- Sound Blaster Pro Mulitmedia Kit Including:
  CD ROM
  Sound Blaster Pro
  & 4 CD Software Package

$2745

- 24-bit Super VGA
- 486 microprocessor
- 33MHz clock speed
- 256K cache memory
- DOS 5.0 operating system software
- Windows 3.1 graphic user interface
- Multimedia software
- 4–64MB of RAM
- 120–200MB hard disk
- Monitor resolution of 1,024 x 768
- $3\frac{1}{2}$-inch floppy disk drive
- $5\frac{1}{4}$-inch floppy disk drive
- Various ports for connecting peripherals
- Keyboard with separate numeric keypad
- CD-ROM drive with software and optical disks

EPSON
ACTION LASER II

$695

- 512KB-4MB
- 6ppm laser engine
- HPLJ II Compatible
- 14 fonts
- Accepts HP font cartridge

This printer is available with 512K–4MB of RAM; it prints 6 pages per minute, is also compatible with microcomputers that use a Hewlett-Packard LaserJet Series II printer, comes with 14 different type styles and sizes, and can use Hewlett-Packard cartridges of additional type styles and sizes.

- Hard disks suffer from dramatic changes in temperature, which can cause read/write problems. If a new hard disk drive has been shipped in a cold environment, manufacturers usually recommend that users wait for a few hours to a day before operating the hard disk.

These problems are caused by the expansion and contraction that naturally occurs when materials are heated and then cooled. The bottom line is that changes in temperature are stressful for microcomputer systems. Therefore, don't place your system near heating vents, in direct sunlight, or directly in front of cold-air blasts.

TURNING THE COMPUTER ON/OFF

Sudden changes in temperature can cause lasting damage to a computer system. When a computer system is turned on, it is subjected to the *most* extreme change in temperature—computers are relatively cool when they are off and become quite warm when they are turned on. For this reason, the fewer times a system has to be turned on, the longer it will remain in good working order. Ideally, a microcomputer system should be kept on continuously—24 hours a day, 7 days a week; however, because of the issue of security during nonbusiness hours and continuous power consumption, it is unlikely that the typical office worker can keep his or her machine running all the time. A better solution is to keep the system on all day so that it is turned on and off only once each day.

One myth that we would like to dispel is that leaving a microcomputer system on will wear down a hard disk. By running a hard disk continuously, you are greatly reducing any stress on the drive due to temperature variations. This will reduce the potential of any read/write failures that are caused by such variations and improve the life of the drive. If you can't leave your microcomputer system on continuously, at least let the system warm up for 15 minutes or so before reading from or writing to the drive. By remembering this simple rule, you will improve the reliability of the data stored on your disk.

If you do leave your system on all the time, make sure that the screen automatically goes blank after a few minutes if the keyboard or other input device isn't used. Many manufacturers include this feature with their computer systems—if not, special software is available that will do this for you. If your screen doesn't go blank, the phosphors on the screen can burn, leaving a permanent image on the screen (Macintosh computers typically don't show these phosphor burn effects). The monitors in airports that display flight information show these phosphor-burn effects.

PLUGGING IN THE SYSTEM

Many users plug a number of different system components into one power strip that contains a number of different plug outlets (Figure 13.5). However, certain types of equipment, including coffee makers, laser printers, and copy machines, can cause voltage *spikes* (surges of electricity), which can do damage to a computer that is connected to the same line. Therefore, it's best to keep your computer on a line separate from other equipment. If you must connect peripheral equipment on the same power line, turn on that equipment *before* turning on the computer.

If your computer is in an environment that is susceptible to power surges or power outages, you should plug your system into a surge suppressor or uninterruptible power supply (Figure 13.6). **Surge suppressors** are devices into which you can plug your microcomputer system, and which in turn are connected to the power line. Costing between $20 and $200, surge suppressors help protect the power supply and other sensitive circuitry in your computer system from voltage spikes. An **uninterruptible power supply (UPS)** is also used to protect your hardware from the damaging effects that a power surge can have on your computer system. In addition, should you lose power, they will keep your system running for around 8-30 minutes, providing you with plenty of time to save your work and shut the system down. The cost of a UPS system is determined by the amount of time it can continue to provide power to your computer system after the power has been cut off. Prices range from around $300 to many thousands of dollars.

DUST AND POLLUTANTS

As an experiment, when your computer is on, light a match in front of a diskette drive and notice where the smoke goes. The smoke is inhaled by the system unit!

Most microcomputers are configured with a fan inside the system unit. The fan is mounted near the power supply and causes air to be drawn into the system unit through any possible opening and then blown out. Systems are designed this way to allow for the even cooling of the microcomputer system. Unfortunately, in this process, dust, smoke, and any other pollutants in the air are drawn into the system unit. Over time these particles will insulate the system unit and prevent it from cooling properly. In addition, some of these particles can conduct electricity, causing minor electrical shorts in the system. (However, be sure not to block the vents; otherwise, the system will overheat.)

Diskette drives are especially susceptible to dust and other pollutants because they provide a large hole through which air flows. The read/write heads in the disk drive won't work accurately if they are contaminated with foreign particles. (Hard disks aren't at risk because they are stored in airtight containers.) For this reason, many companies enforce "No Smoking" policies in rooms where computers are present.

If you want to clean the diskette drives in your computer system (the read/write heads can become dusty over time, and dust can reduce the reliability with

FIGURE 13.5

Multiplug extender

(a) Uninterruptible power supply (UPS); (b) surge suppressor   **FIGURE 13.6**

(a)

(b)

which they can store and retrieve data), an easy method does exist. You must first purchase a head-cleaning disk from a local computer store. Head-cleaning disks come in two basic styles—that is, wet or dry. The wet-cleaning disk uses a liquid cleaning agent that has been squirted onto the disk, and the dry-cleaning disk uses an abrasive material that has been put onto the cleaning disk. Most computer professionals recommend using the wet system, because the dry system can actually damage the read/write heads of the disk if it is used too often. To use a cleaning disk, simply put it into the disk drive and run a program (that is stored on the disk) to make the disk spin. When the disk spins in the disk drive, the read/write heads touch the surface of the cleaning disk and are wiped clean. In a clean (smoke-free) office environment, diskette drives should be cleaned once a year. In a smoking environment, diskette drives should be cleaned every 3–6 months.

The diskette drives aren't the only system components that should be cleaned periodically. If a microcomputer system is operated in a dirty environment, such as on the floor of a lumber shop, it should also be cleaned every 3–6 months. But in most office environments, the cleaning should be done every one to two years. You can either clean the appropriate components yourself or hire a professional to clean them for you. If you aren't familiar with the process of cleaning a microcomputer, hire a professional.

OTHER PRACTICAL CONSIDERATIONS

Shocks and vibrations are bad for computer disk drives. Therefore, you should also keep the following considerations in mind:

- Never place an impact printer (dot-matrix or daisy wheel printer) on the same surface as the computer.
- Don't drop or throw objects onto the surface on which the computer is located.
- If you place your system unit on the floor to free up desk space, make sure it's not in a place where you will accidentally kick it or people will bump into it.

BACKING UP YOUR MICROCOMPUTER SYSTEM

The scenario: You've stored a year's worth of client information on your hard disk. You are able to retrieve client information easily onto the screen. You have confidence in your computer system until the hard disk crashes; the read/write heads fall onto the surface of the disk, making the disk unusable and causing the loss of all the data stored on the disk! Well, at least you have a backup copy of your client files. What? You don't?

One of the most important tasks involved in maintaining a microcomputer system is to make copies of—or a backup of—your data files. A popular rule of thumb is to never let the time between backups go longer than the amount of data it represents that you are willing to lose in a disk disaster. Depending on the amount of activity on a system, hard disks should be backed up at the end of each day or each week. All managers should make sure that office policies include backup procedures.

PROCEDURES
When making backup copies, you must decide how often you want to back up your data. Do you want to back up the entire hard disk or simply the files that have been changed since the last backup? Perhaps you want to make daily copies

of the files that have been changed and, at the end of the week, make a backup copy of the entire disk, including software and data files. Whatever the procedures, they should be defined clearly and followed routinely.

Also, remember that backup must be done on **removable media**—storage media that can easily be removed from the system and stored remotely. Some businesses configure microcomputers with two hard disks. The first hard disk is the work disk onto which all the current processing activities and updated files are stored. The second hard disk is used as a backup disk—the contents of the first disk are copied onto the second. This is not advisable. Suppose the microcomputer system is subjected to a massive power surge? The contents of *both* disks will be destroyed. Or suppose the entire microcomputer system is stolen? Once more, you won't have any backup files.

Once data has been backed up, it is important to clearly label and date the backup media.

HARDWARE AND SOFTWARE
Diskettes are still used in some cases as backup media. All microcomputer systems come with at least one diskette drive, so without a substantial hardware investment in a **dedicated backup system**—hardware and software used only for backup purposes—the user can back up the contents of a hard disk onto removable media (diskettes). Backup software for diskette systems is available that assists in the backup process, prompting the user to "insert a new diskette, please" when one diskette becomes full. One such program is called FASTBACK, by 5th Generation Systems. However, using diskettes to back up a hard disk is slow.

Magnetic tape is the more commonly used storage medium for backing up hard disks. With a hard disk of 20 MB or higher, a reliable tape storage unit is a good investment (Figure 13.7). Tape backup units can easily support 60 MB or more and are fast and accurate. Once you decide to purchase a tape backup unit, you must decide on what software to purchase to run the tape system. Many tape

FIGURE 13.7

Magnetic tape is often used for backing up hard disks. This photo shows exterior and interior views of various backup units. The tape cartridge is inserted in the slot on the front.

backup manufacturers write their own software. In addition to your specific needs, you should be sure that the software offers the following capabilities:

- Files can be backed up individually or all at once.
- Several backups can be copied onto a single tape.
- A backup can span more than one tape.
- The backup data can be verified to ensure that it was recorded reliably on the tape.

By paying special attention to the temperature of your system, the number of times you turn it on/off, how it is plugged in, the quality of the air surrounding the system, and routine backup procedures, you will increase the life of your computer system.

ERGONOMICS: HEALTH ISSUES

Even though the cost of computers has decreased significantly, they are still expensive. Why have them, then, unless they can make workers more effective? Ironically, in certain ways computers may actually make people less productive. Many of the problems that affect productivity are commonly experienced by people working in data-entry-intensive positions, such as clerks and word processors. However, such problems may also be experienced by anyone whose job involves intensive use of the computer. As a result, interest in ergonomics has been increasing, and greater effort is being made to avoid health risks. Basically, **ergonomics** is the science of human-comfort engineering—especially comfort in the area of computer use.

PHYSICAL HEALTH

Sitting in front of a screen and using a keyboard for long periods may lead to eyestrain, headaches, back pain, and repetitive strain injury. Of course, adopting such commonsense measures as taking frequent rest breaks and using well-designed computer furniture can alleviate some of the discomfort. However, other suggestions have also proven useful (Figure 13.8).

1. AVOID EYESTRAIN AND HEADACHE
The use of computer screens requires focusing the eyes on items at a closer range than our eyes are designed for. Focusing on the screen at this close range for long periods of time can cause eyestrain, headaches, and double vision. To avoid these problems, take a 15-minute break every hour or two. Minimize reflected glare on the screen by keeping the screen away from windows and other sources of bright light. (If necessary, purchase an antiglare screen or a glare shield for your existing screen.) The screen should be three to four times brighter than room light. In addition, the computer screen, the keyboard, and anything you are reading while typing should all be positioned at the same distance from your eyes—about 20–24 inches away. Clean the screen of dust from time to time.

2. AVOID BACK AND NECK PAIN
Make sure equipment is adjustable. You should be able to adjust your chair for height and angle, and the chair should have good back support. The monitor should be able to tilt and swivel, and the keyboard should be detachable (so you can place it on your lap, for example).

3. AVOID EFFECTS OF ELECTROMAGNETIC FIELDS

VDTs generate electromagnetic field (EMF) emissions, which can pass through the human body. Even though the fact has not been proved, some observers believe that EMF emissions could be involved in miscarriages and possibly some cancers. (In the United States, the Environmental Protection Agency (EPA) and the Federal Drug Agency (FDA) are studying this issue.) For this reason, older monitors should be replaced with new, low-emission monitors (Table 13.2).

Also, try to sit 2 feet away from your monitor and at least 3 feet away from any neighboring monitors.

The ergonomic work office. (From *PCToday*, April 1992, p. 19.)   **FIGURE 13.8**

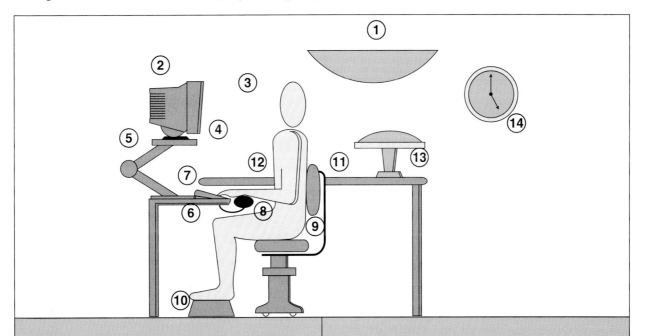

1. Indirect Lighting — Fixtures that bounce light off ceilings or walls provide a soft light that is less likely than harsh light to reflect off monitor screens and create glare.

2. Monitor Height — The top of the monitor should be no higher than eye level.

3. Monitor Distance — 16 to 22 inches is recommended for visual acuity; 24 inches or more is recommended if there are emission concerns.

4. Monitor Display — High-resolution, noninterlaced screen with dark letters on a light background, with an antiglare screen coating or antiglare filter.

5. Adjustable Monitor Support — The monitor should move up and down, forward and back, and tilt on its axis.

6. Keyboard Support — Adjustable from 23 to 28 inches in height. Operator's arm should hang straight down from the shoulder and bend 90 degrees at the elbow and enable the operator to type without flexing or hyperextending the wrist.

7. Keyboard — Adjustable tilt to enable the typist to keep hands in a straight line with the wrists and forearms.

8. Wrist Rest — Rounded, padded adjustable support for the heel of the hand or forearm, without constricting the wrist.

9. Seat Height — Adjustable from 16 to 19 inches. Users should be able to bend their hips and knees at 90 degrees and sit with their feet flat on the floor.

10. Foot Rest — Keeps user from having to support legs and feet while working.

11. Back Support — Backrest should adjust up, down, forward, and backward to support the lumbar portion of the spine in the small of the back.

12. Work Surface Height — A comfortable height for reading, writing, drawing, and other nonkeyboard work.

13. Reading Light — An independent light source for reading letters, reports, books, etc.

14. Clock — Schedule regular breaks, preferably 5 minutes per hour.

4. AVOID REPETITIVE STRAIN INJURY (RSI)

Repetitive strain injury—also known as *repetitive motion injury* and *cumulative trauma disorder*—is the name given to a number of injuries resulting from fast, repetitive work. RSI causes neck, wrist, hand, and arm pain. The recent publicized increase in RSI problems is mainly the result of increasing computer keyboard use and bar code scanner use (for example, grasping items in the grocery cart and moving them past the bar code scanner mounted in the counter at the supermarket).

An RSI called *carpal tunnel syndrome* is particularly common among people who use computers and certain types of scanners intensively. This syndrome involves damage to nerves and tendons in the hands. RSI is basically caused by four factors:

- *Repetition and duration*—Prolonged, constant, and repetitious movements such as typing irritate tendons and nerve casings, causing them to swell.

- *Force*—The harder a person strikes the keys, the more likely he or she is to suffer injury.

- *Joint angle*—Flexing, raising, or twisting hands to reach the keys constricts the carpal tunnel (pinches the medial nerve running through the wrist).

TABLE 13.2   Your Low-Emissions Choices*

Manufacturer	Product	Monitor Type	Price
American Mitac	L1420	14-inch VGA	$ 795
Cornerstone Technology	DualPage Display	19-inch monochrome	$2,495
	DualPage Display	19-inch gray-scale	$2,845
CTX Int'l	5468	14-inch VGA	$ 599
	5468-NI	14-inch VGA noninterlaced	$ 699
IBM	8515 Color Display	14-inch VGA	$ 950
NEC Technologies	MultiSync 3DS	14-inch multiscan	$1,049
Qume	QM835VLF	14-inch VGA	$ 699
Sigma Designs	L-View	19-inch monochrome	$2,195
	L-View	19-inch gray-scale	$2,495
	PageView	15-inch monochrome	$1,299
	SilverView	21-inch monochrome	$2,195
	SilverView	21-inch gray-scale	$2,995

WHERE TO BUY

American Mitac
410 E. Plumeria Dr.
San Jose, CA 95134
800/648-2287

Cornerstone Technology
1990 Concourse Dr.
San Jose, CA 95131
408/435-8900,
408/435-8998 (fax)

CTX Int'l, Inc.
20530 Earlgate St.
Walnut, CA 91789
714/595-6146

IBM
1133 Westchester Ave.
White Plains, NY 10604
800/426-2468

NEC Technologies Inc.
1255 Michael Dr.
Wood Dale, IL 60191
800/632-4636

Qume Corp.
500 Yosemite Dr.
Milpitas, CA 95035
800/457-4447

Sigma Designs, Inc.
46501 Landing Pkwy.
Fremont, CA 94538
415/770-0100

*From "Consumer Watch," *PC World*, May 1991, p. 46.

- *Prolonged constrained posture*—Holding any position without moving places excessive strain on muscles and tendons.

For some victims, the pain of carpal tunnel syndrome is so intense that they cannot open doors or shake hands. Left untreated, this syndrome can cause atrophied muscles and permanent nerve damage. To avoid RSI, take frequent short rest breaks instead of infrequent long ones. Experts also advise getting plenty of sleep and exercise, maintaining appropriate weight, sitting up straight, and learning stress-management techniques.

MENTAL HEALTH

Computers often create mental/psychological irritants that can turn out to be counterproductive.

1. *Avoid noise:* Computer users sometimes develop headaches and experience tension from being exposed to noisy impact printers and to the high-pitched, barely audible squeal produced by some computer monitors. Indeed, some people, particularly women, who hear high-frequency sounds better than men do, may be affected by the noise even when they are not conscious of hearing it. Sound-muffling covers are available for some printers. However, to avoid ending up in a high-tension state because of monitor squealing, the advice again is to take frequent short rest breaks.

2. *Avoid stress from electronic supervision:* Research shows that workers whose performance is supervised electronically suffer more health problems than do those watched by human supervisors. For instance, a computer may monitor the number of keystrokes a data-entry clerk completes in a day or the time a customer-service person takes to handle a call. Such monitoring may force a pace that may lead to RSI problems and mental stress. One study found that electronically supervised employees reported great boredom, high tension, extreme anxiety, depression, anger, and severe fatigue.

SUMMARY

- Before purchasing a microcomputer you should always determine what your specific processing needs are and then what applications software will satisfy those needs. Once you've identified the applications software, you should choose hardware and systems software that will be compatible with your applications software. In the business environment, you will most likely be involved with choosing only applications software because systems software and hardware will already be in place. If you are in a position to purchase a microcomputer and want to save some money, you may want to explore purchasing a microcomputer *clone*. Before purchasing a clone, however, make sure it is accompanied by thorough technical documentation and a warranty for parts and labor.

- When deciding where to purchase a microcomputer, make sure the company has a good reputation and sells its computers at competitive prices. Local computer companies offer purchasers more personalized service than do mail-order companies. But the computers purchased through mail-order companies are often sold at a substantial discount. Before purchasing from a mail-order company, check on the company to make sure you're getting an honest deal.

- When you purchase a microcomputer system, pay attention to such ergonomic issues as screen emission and keyboards with wrist support.
- Once you've purchased a microcomputer, take care of it by maintaining it on a daily basis. Don't subject your computer to sudden changes in temperature or vibrations. Try to keep the computer on continuously—or turn it on and off only once during the day.
- Don't plug your microcomputer system in on the same line as other hardware peripherals (such as a printer). If you must do this, however, then turn the peripherals on before you turn on the microcomputer. It is also important to incorporate backup procedures into your daily or weekly routine.
- Use a surge suppressor to protect your computer against power surges, or "spikes." Use an uninterruptible power supply to provide you with enough time to save your work and shut down your system if the power goes out.
- Be sure to use proper lighting and furniture and to take frequent breaks while using your microcomputer.

KEY TERMS

clone, p. 324
dedicated backup
   system, p. 335
ergonomics, p. 336

removable media,
   p. 335
surge suppressor, p. 332

uninterruptible power
   supply (UPS), p. 333
warranty, p. 328

PORTABLE CHECKLIST FOR BUYING A MICROCOMPUTER SYSTEM

PRICE RANGE (INCLUDING PERIPHERALS)

_____ up to $1,000   _____ up to $3,000   _____ up to $5,000

_____ up to $2,000   _____ up to $4,000   _____ more than $5,000

USES (SOFTWARE NEEDED)

(*Note: All applications software chosen must run with compatible systems software.*)

_____ Writing letters and reports; preparing professional papers (word processing software)

_____ Personal finance; budgeting and planning; taxes (spreadsheet software)

_____ Programming (programming language, such as BASIC, COBOL, Pascal, FORTRAN)

_____ Business applications; finance management, accounting, planning, scheduling, inventory and sales management (spreadsheet, DBMS and/or graphics software)

_____ Entertainment (software games)

_____ Education (tutorial software)

_____ Mailing lists (word processing software; DBMS software)

_____ Publishing newsletters and brochures (word processing, graphics, desktop publishing software)

_____ Multimedia programs

_____ Information retrieval from public information services (communications software)

_____ Personal record-keeping (desktop management software)

_____ Creating art and graphics for use in published materials (graphics and desktop publishing software)

_____ Communications software

_____ CAD/CAM software

_____ Conversion software for cross-platform use (IBM–Macintosh)

TOTAL projected cost for software $_____

HARDWARE

(*Check your chosen software's documentation for minimum hardware requirements and compatibility restrictions; when no requirements are given in the documentation, check your own preferences.*)

1. _____ System must be compatible with other systems? (Y/N) If yes,

what kind: _____

2. _____ How much main memory do I need? _____ 640 K RAM; _____ 1 MB RAM; _____ 2 MB RAM; _____ 4 MB RAM; _____ 8 MB RAM

3. _____ 16-bit processor; _____ 32-bit processor (number of bits that the microprocessor needs to handle at once)

4. _____ 16 MHz (clock speed); _____ 25 MHz; _____ 33 MHz; _____ other

5. _____ Microcomputer must be portable? (Y/N) (_____ laptop; _____ notebook)

6. _____ Monochrome screen; _____ color screen (_____ RAM requirements; _____ low emission?)

7. _____ CGA; _____ EGA; _____ VGA; _____ other (_____ screen resolution, or clarity of image)

8. _____ Number of colors or gray shades

9. _____ Screen can tilt and swivel? (Y/N)

10. _____ Size of screen (_____ appropriate to resolution?)

11. _____ System cabinet can be put on floor to save desk space? (Y/N)

12. _____ Detachable keyboard?

13. _____ QWERTY keyboard; _____ other keyboard

14. _____ Numeric keypad?

15. _____ Number of required function keys

16. _____ Voice input?

17. _____ Single floppy disk drive; _____ dual floppy disk drive

18. _____ 20 MB hard disk; _____ 40 MB; _____ 60 MB; _____ 80 MB; _____ 120 MB

19. _____ Tape backup?

20. _____ Surge protector; _____ uninterrupted power supply?

21. _____ Mouse; _____ trackball

22. _____ Dot-matrix printer; _____ laser printer
_____ color capability; _____ graphics capability
_____ multiple-form capability; _____ font availability
_____ speed; _____ noise level; _____ quality of text output

23. _____ Modem (_____ internal; _____ external)

24. _____ Fax (_____ internal; _____ external; _____ handle photos?)

25. _____ Scanner (_____ color? _____ gray-scale? _____ slides? _____ photos?)

26. _____ Is system upgradeable?

27. _____ Any multimedia hardware needs? Identify: _____

28. _____ Uses what kind of systems software?

TOTAL projected cost for hardware $_____

SUPPORT

Investigate the following:

1. Manufacturer's reputation and length of time in business
2. Dealer's reputation and length of time in business
3. Warranties
4. Quality of documentation (user's manuals): easy to follow? detailed?
5. Hotline availability to solve problems in emergencies
6. Location and availability of repair services
7. Availability of training
8. Will dealer install?

Key Dates
in the History and Future
of Information Processing*

YEAR	EVENT
Less than 100,000 years ago	*Homo sapiens* begin using intelligence to further goals.
More than 5,000 years ago	The abacus, which resembles the arithmetic unit of a modern computer, is developed in the Orient.
3000–700 B.C.	Water clocks are built in China in 3000 B.C., in Egypt approx. 1500 B.C., and in Assyria 700 B.C.
2500 B.C.	Egyptians invent the idea of thinking machines: citizens turn for advice to oracles, which are statues with priests hidden inside.
427 B.C.	In the *Phaedo* and later works Plato expresses ideas, several millennia before the advent of the computer, that are relevant to modern dilemmas regarding human thought and its relation to the mechanics of the machine.
approx. 420 B.C.	Archytas of Tarentum, a friend of Plato, constructs a wooden pigeon whose movements are controlled by a jet of steam or compressed air.
approx. 415 B.C.	Theaetetus, a member of Plato's Academy, creates solid geometry.
387 B.C.	Plato founds the Academy for the pursuit of science and philosophy in a grove on the outskirts of Athens. It results in the fertile development of mathematical theory.
293 B.C.	Euclid, also a member of Plato's Academy, is the expositor of plane geometry. He writes the *Elements*, a basic mathematics textbook for the next 2,000 years.
c. 200 B.C.	In China artisans develop elaborate automata, including an entire mechanical orchestra.
725	A Chinese engineer and a Buddhist monk build the first true mechanical clock, a water-driven device with an escapement that causes the clock to tick.
1540, 1772	The technology of clock and watch making results in the production of more elaborate automata during the European Renaissance. Gianello Toriano's mandolin-playing lady (1540) and P. Jacquet-Droz's child (1772) are famous examples.
1617	John Napier invents Napier's Bones, of significance to the future development of calculating engines.
1642	Blaise Pascal perfects the Pascaline, a machine that can add and subtract. It is the world's first *automatic* calculating machine.
1694	Gottfried Wilhelm Liebniz, an inventor of calculus, perfects the Liebniz Computer, a machine that multiplies by performing repetitive additions, an algorithm still used in modern computers.
1726	Jonathan Swift, in *Gulliver's Travels*, describes a machine that will automatically write books.
1805	Joseph-Marie Jacquard devises a method for automating weaving with a series of punched cards. This invention will be used many years later in the development of early computers.

*Adapted from Raymond Kurzweil, *The Age of Intelligent Machines*, Cambridge, Mass.: Massachusetts Institute of Technology, 1990, pp. 465–483.

1821	Charles Babbage is awarded the first gold medal by the British Astronomical Society for his paper "Observations on the Application of Machinery to the Computation of Mathematical Tables."
1821	Michael Farraday, widely recognized as the father of electricity, reports his discovery of electromagnetic rotation and builds the first two motors powered by electricity.
1822	Charles Babbage develops the Difference Engine, but its technical complexities exhaust his financial resources and organizational skills. He eventually abandons it to concentrate his efforts on a general-purpose computer.
1829	The first electromagnetically driven clock is constructed.
1832	Charles Babbage develops the principle of the Analytical Engine, which is the world's first computer and can be programmed to solve a wide variety of logical and computational problems.
1835	Joseph Henry invents the electrical relay, a means of transmitting electrical impulses over long distances. The relay serves as the basis for the telegraph.
1837	Samuel Finley Breese Morse patents his more practical version of the telegraph, which sends letters in codes consisting of dots and dashes.
1843	Ada Lovelace, Lord Byron's only legitimate child and the world's first computer programmer, publishes her own notes with her translation of L. P. Menabrea's paper on Babbage's Analytical Engine.
1846	Alexander Bain uses punched paper tape to send telegraph messages, greatly improving the speed of transmission.
1847	George Boole publishes his first ideas on symbolic logic. He will develop these ideas into his theory of binary logic and arithmetic—a theory that is still the basis of modern computation.
1854	An electric telegraph is installed between Paris and London.
1855	William Thomson develops a successful theory concerning the transmission of electrical signals through submarine cables.
1861	San Francisco and New York are connected by a telegraph line.
1864	Ducos de Harron develops a primitive motion-picture device in France.
1866	Cyrus West Field lays a telegraph cable across the Atlantic Ocean.
1876	Alexander Graham Bell's telephone receives U.S. Patent 174,465, the most lucrative patent ever granted.
1879	G. Frege, one of the founders of modern symbolic language, proposes a notational system for mechanical reasoning. This work is a forerunner to the predicate calculus, which will be used for knowledge representation in artificial intelligence.
1885	Boston is connected to New York by telephone.
1886	Alexander Graham Bell, with a modified version of Thomas Alva Edison's phonograph, uses wax discs for recording sound.
1888	William S. Burroughs patents an adding machine. This machine is modified four years later to include subtraction and printing. It is the world's first dependable key-driven calculator and will soon win widespread acceptance.
1888	Heinrich Hertz experiments with the transmission of what are now known as radio waves.
1888	The first commercial roll-film camera is introduced.
1890	Herman Hollerith, incorporating ideas from Jacquard's loom and Babbage's Analytical Engine, patents an electromechanical information machine that uses punched cards. It wins the 1890 U.S. Census competition, with the result that electricity is used for the first time in a major data processing project.

1894	Guglielmo Marconi builds his first radio equipment, which rings a bell from 30 feet away.
1896	A sound film is first shown before a paying audience in Berlin.
1896	Herman Hollerith forms the Tabulating Machine Company, which will become IBM.
1897	Alexander Popov, a Russian, uses an antenna to transmit radio waves, and Guglielmo Marconi, an Italian, receives the first patent ever granted for radio. Marconi helps organize a company to market his system.
1899	The first recording of sound occurs magnetically on wire and on a thin metal strip.
1900	Herman Hollerith introduces an automatic card feed into his information machine to process the 1900 census data.
1900	The entire civilized world is connected by telegraph, and in the United States there are more than 1.4 million telephones, 8,000 registered automobiles, and 24 million electric light bulbs. Edison's promise of "electric bulbs so cheap that only the rich will be able to afford candles" is thus realized. In addition, the Gramophone Company is advertising a choice of five thousand recordings.
1901	Marconi, in Newfoundland, receives the first transatlantic telegraphic radio transmission.
1904	John Ambrose Fleming files a patent for the first vacuum tube, a diode.
1906	Reginald Aubrey Fessenden invents AM radio and transmits by radio waves to wireless operators on U.S. ships off the Atlantic Coast. The transmission includes a Christmas carol, a violin trill, and for the first time the sound of a human voice.
1907	Lee De Forest and R. von Lieben invent the amplifier vacuum tube, known as a triode, which greatly improves radio.
1911	Herman Hollerith's Tabulating Machine Company acquires several other companies and changes its name to Computing-Tabulating-Recording Company (CTR). In 1914 Thomas J. Watson is appointed president.
1913	Henry Ford introduces the first true assembly-line method of automated production.
1913	A. Meissner invents a radio transmitter with vacuum tubes. Radio-transmitter triode modulation is introduced the following year, and in 1915 the radio-tube oscillator is introduced.
1921	Czech dramatist Karel Capek popularizes the term *robot*, a word he coined in 1917 to describe the mechanical people in his science-fiction drama *R.U.R.* (Rossum's Universal Robots). His intelligent machines, intended as servants for their human creators, end up taking over the world and destroying all mankind.
1923	Vladimir Kosma Zworkin, the father of television, gives the first demonstration of an electronic television-camera tube, using a mechanical transmitting device. He develops the iconoscope, an early type of television system, the following year.
1924	Thomas J. Watson becomes the chief executive officer of CTR and renames the company International Business Machines (IBM). IBM will become the leader of the modern industry and one of the largest industrial corporations in the world.
1925	Vannevar Bush and his co-workers develop the first analog computer, a machine designed to solve differential equations.
1926	The era of talking motion pictures is introduced by *The Jazz Singer*, starring Al Jolson.
1928	John von Neumann presents the minimax theorem, which will be widely used in game-playing programs.
1928	Philo T. Farnsworth demonstrates the world's first all-electronic television, and Vladimir Zworkin receives a patent for a color television system.
1929	FM radio is introduced.
1930	Vannevar Bush's analog computer, the Differential Analyzer, is built at MIT. It will be used to calculate artillery trajectories during World War II.

1932	RCA demonstrates a television receiver with a cathode-ray picture tube. In 1933 Zworkin produces a cathode-ray tube, called the iconoscope, that makes high-quality television almost a reality.
1937	Building on the work of Bertrand Russell and Charles Babbage, Alan Turing publishes "On Computable Numbers," his now-celebrated paper introducing the Turing machine, a theoretical model of a computer.
1937	The Church-Turing thesis, independently developed by Alonzo Church and Alan Turing, states that all problems solvable by a human being are reducible to a set of algorithms, or more simply, that machine intelligence and human intelligence are essentially equivalent.
1940	John V. Atanasoff and Clifford Berry build an electronic computer known as ABC. This is the first *electronic* computer, but it is not programmable.
1940	The 10,000-person British computer war effort known as Ultra creates Robinson, the world's first operational computer. It is based on electromechanical relays and is powerful enough to decode messages from Enigma, the Nazis' first-generation enciphering machine.
1941	Konrad Zuse, a German, completes the world's first fully *programmable* digital computer, the Z-3, and hires Arnold Fast, a blind mathematician, to program it. Fast becomes the world's first programmer of an *operational* programmable computer.
1943	The Ultra team builds Colossus, a computer that uses electronic tubes 100 to 1,000 times faster than the relays used by Robinson. It cracks increasingly complex German codes and contributes to the Allies' winning of World War II.
1944	Howard Aiken completes the first American programmable computer, the Mark I. It uses punched paper tape for programming and vacuum tubes to calculate problems.
1945	Konrad Zuse develops Plankalkul, the first high-level language.
1946	John Tukey first uses the term *bit* for *binary digit*, the basic unit of data for computers.
1946	John von Neumann publishes the first modern paper on the stored-program concept and starts computer research at the Institute for Advanced Study in Princeton.
1946	John Presper Eckert and John W. Mauchley develop ENIAC, the world's first fully electronic, general-purpose (programmable) digital computer. It is almost 1,000 times faster than the Mark I and is used for calculating ballistic-firing tables for the Army.
1946	Television enters American life even more rapidly than radio did in the 1920s. The percentage of American homes having sets jumps from 0.02% in 1946 to 72% in 1956 and more than 90% by 1983.
1947	William Bradford Schockley, Walter Hauser Brittain, and John Ardeen invent the transistor, a minute device that functions like a vacuum tube but switches current on and off at much faster speeds. It launches a revolution in microelectronics, bringing down the cost of computers and leading to the development of minicomputers and powerful new mainframe computers.
1949	Maurice Wilkes, influenced by Eckert and Mauchley, builds EDSAC, the world's first stored-program computer. Eckert and Mauchley's new U.S. company brings out BINAC, the first American stored-program computer, soon after.
1950	The U.S. census is first handled by a programmable computer, UNIVAC, developed by Eckert and Mauchley. It is the first commercially marketed computer.
1950	Alan Turing's "Computing Machinery and Intelligence" describes the Turing test, a means for determining whether a machine is intelligent.
1950	Commercial color television begins in the U.S.; transcontinental black-and-white television is inaugurated the following year.
1950	Claude Elwood Shannon writes a proposal for a chess program.
1951	EDVAC, Eckert and Mauchley's first computer that implements the stored-program concept, is completed at the Moore School at the University of Pennsylvania.

1952	The CBS television network uses UNIVAC to correctly predict the election of Dwight D. Eisenhower as president of the United States.
1952	The pocket-size transistor radio is introduced.
1952	The 701, IBM's first production-line electronic digital computer, is designed by Nathaniel Rochester and marketed for scientific use.
1955	IBM introduces its first transistor calculator, with 2,200 transistors instead of the 1,200 vacuum tubes that would otherwise be required.
1955	The first design is created for a robot-like machine for industrial use in the U.S.
1955	Allen Newell, J. C. Shaw, and Herbert Simon develop IPL-II, the first AI language.
1955	The beginning space program and the military in the U.S., recognizing the need for computers powerful enough to steer rockets to the moon and missiles through the stratosphere, fund major research projects.
1956	The first transatlantic telephone cable begins to operate.
1956	FORTRAN, the first scientific computer programming language, is invented by John Backus and a team at IBM.
1956	MANIAC I, the first computer program to beat a human being in a chess game, is developed by Stanislaw Ulam.
1956	Artificial intelligence is named at a computer conference at Dartmouth College.
1958	Jack St. Clair Kilby invents the first integrated circuit.
1958	John McCarthy introduces LISP, an early (and still widely used) AI language.
1958–1959	Jack Kilby and Robert Noyce independently develop the chip, which leads to much cheaper and smaller computers.
1959	Dartmouth's Thomas Kurtz and John Kemeny find an alternative to batch processing: timesharing.
1959	Grace Murray Hopper, one of the first programmers of the Mark I, develops COBOL, a computer language designed for business use.
1960	About 6,000 computers are in operation in the United States.
1962	A U.S. company markets the world's first industrial robots.
1962	The first department of computer science offering a Ph.D. is established at Purdue University.
1962	D. Murphy and Richard Greenblatt develop the TECO text editor, one of the first word processing systems, for use on the PDP1 computer at MIT.
1963	AI researchers of the 1960s, noting the similarity between human and computer languages, adopt the goal of parsing natural-language sentences. Susumo Kuno's parsing system reveals the great extent of syntactic and semantic ambiguity in the English language. Kuno's system is tested on the sentence "Time flies like an arrow."
1963	John McCarthy founds the Artifical Intelligence Laboratory at Stanford University.
1964	IBM solidifies its leadership of the computer industry with the introduction of its 360 series.
1964	Daniel Bobrow completes his doctoral work on Student, a natural-language program that can solve high-school-level word problems in algebra.
1964	Gordon Moore, one of the founders of Fairchild Semiconductor Corporation, predicts that integrated circuits will double in complexity each year. His statement will become known as Moore's law and will prove true for decades to come.
1964	Marshall McLuhan's *Understanding Media* foresees electronic media, especially television, as creating a "global village" in which "the medium is the message."
1965	Raj Reddy founds the Robotics Institute at Carnegie-Mellon University. The institute becomes a leading research center for AI.

1965	The DENDRAL project begins at Stanford University, headed by Bruce Buchanan, Edward Feigenbaum, and Nobel laureate Joshua Lederberg. Its purpose is to experiment on knowledge as the primary means of producing problem-solving behavior. The first expert system, DENDRAL, embodies extensive knowledge of molecular-structure analysis. Follow-up work, carried out through the early 1970s, produces Meta-DENDRAL, a learning program that automatically devises new rules for DENDRAL.
Mid-1960s	Computers are beginning to be widely used in the criminal justice system.
Mid-1960s	Scientific and professional knowledge is beginning to be codified in a machine-readable form.
1967	Seymour Papert and his associates at MIT begin working on LOGO, an education-oriented programming language that will be widely used by children.
1967	The software business is born when IBM announces it will no longer sell software and hardware in a single unit.
1968	The film *2001: A Space Odyssey*, by Arthur C. Clarke and Stanley Kubrick, presents HAL, a computer that can see, speak, hear, and think like its human colleagues aboard a spaceship.
1968	The Intel Corp. is founded. Intel will grow to become the dominant manufacturer of microprocessors in the U.S. computer industry.
1970	The floppy disk is introduced for storing data in computers.
1970	Harry Pople and Jack Myers of the University of Pittsburgh begin work on Internist, a system that aids physicians in the diagnosis of a wide range of human diseases.
1971	Kenneth Colby, Sylvia Weber, and F. D. Hilf present a report on PARRY, a program simulating a paranoid person, in a paper entitled "Artificial Paranoia." The program is so convincing that clinical psychiatrists cannot distinguish its behavior from that of a human paranoid person.
1971	The first microprocessor is introduced in the U.S.
1971	The first pocket calculator is introduced. It can add, subtract, multiply, and divide.
1971	Direct telephone dialing on a regular basis begins between parts of the U.S. and Europe.
1971	Daniel Bricklin and Software Arts, Inc. release the first electronic spreadsheet for PCs, *VisiCalc*. The program helps launch the personal computing era by showing the convenience with which information can be handled on a desktop.
1973	Alain Colmerauer presents an outline of PROLOG, a logic-programming language. The language will become enormously popular and will be adopted for use in the Japanese Fifth-Generation Program.
1974	The first computer-controlled industrial robot is developed.
1974	Edward Shortliffe completes his doctoral dissertation on MYCIN, an expert system designed to help medical practitioners prescribe an appropriate antibiotic by determining the precise identity of a blood infection. Work to augment this program with other important systems, notably TEIRESIAS and EMYCIN, will continue through the early 1980s. TEIRESIAS will be developed in 1976 by Randall Davis to serve as a powerful information-structuring tool for knowledge engineers. EMYCIN, by William van Melle, will represent the skeletal structure of inferences.
1974	The SUMEX-AIM computer communications network is established to promote the development of applications of artificial intelligence to medicine.
1975	Benoit Mandelbrot writes "*Les objet fractals: Forme, hasard, et dimension*," his first long essay on fractal geometry, a branch of mathematics that he developed. Fractal forms will be widely used to model chaotic phenomena in nature and to generate realistic computer images of naturally occurring objects.
1975	Medicine is becoming an important area of applications for AI research. Four major medical expert systems have been developed by now: PIP, CASNET, MYCIN, and Internist.

1975	The Defense Advanced Research Programs Agency launches its Image Understanding Program to stimulate research in the area of machine vision.
1975	More than 5,000 microcomputers are sold in the U.S., and the first personal computer, with 256 bytes of memory, is introduced.
1970s	The role of knowledge in intelligent behavior is now a major focus of AI research. Bruce Buchanan and Edward Feigenbaum of Stanford University pioneer knowledge engineering.
1976	Kurzweil Computer Products introduces the Kurzweil Reading Machine, which reads aloud any printed text that is presented to it. Based on omnifont character-recognition technology, it is intended to be a sensory aid for the blind.
1976–1977	Lynn Conway and Carver Mead collaborate on a collection of principles for VLSI design. Their classic textbook *Introduction to VLSI Design* is published in 1980. VLSI circuits will form the basis of the fourth generation of computers.
1977	Steven Jobs and Stephen Wozniak design and build the Apple computer.
1977	Voyagers 1 and 2 are launched and radio back billions of bytes of computerized data about new discoveries as they explore the outer planets of our solar system.
1977	The Apple II, the first personal computer to be sold in assembled form, is successfully marketed.
1978	Total computer units in the United States exceed a half million.
1979	In a landmark study published in the *Journal of the American Medical Association* by nine researchers, the performance of MYCIN is compared with that of doctors on 10 test cases of meningitis. MYCIN does at least as well as the medical experts. The potential of expert systems in medicine becomes widely recognized.
1979	Ada, a computer language developed for use by the armed forces, is named for Ada Lovelace.
1979	Pac Man and other early computerized video games appear.
1979	Hayes markets its first modem, which sets the industry standard for modems in years to come.
Early 1980s	Second-generation robots arrive with the ability to precisely effect movements with five or six degrees of freedom. They are used for industrial welding and spray painting.
Early 1980s	The MYCIN project produces NeoMYCIN and ONCOCIN, expert systems that incorporate hierarchical knowledge bases. They are more flexible than MYCIN.
1981	Desktop publishing takes root when Xerox brings out its Star Computer. However, it will not become popular until Apple's Laserwriter comes on the market in 1985. Desktop publishing provides writers and artists an inexpensive and efficient way to compose and print large documents.
1981	IBM introduces its Personal Computer (PC).
1982	Compact-disk players are marketed for the first time.
1982	A million-dollar advertising campaign introduces Mitch Kapor's Lotus 1-2-3, an enormously popular spreadsheet program.
1982	With over 100,000 associations between symptoms and diseases covering 70% of all the knowledge in the field, CADUCEUS, an improvement on the Internist expert system, is developed for internal medicine by Harry Pople and Jack Myers at the University of Pittsburgh. Tested against cases from the *New England Journal of Medicine*, it proves more accurate than humans in a wide range of categories.
1983	Six million personal computers are sold in the U.S.
1984	Apple Computer, Inc. introduces the Macintosh.
1984	RACTER, created by William Chamberlain, is the first computer program to author a book.

1984	Waseda University in Tokyo completes Wabot-2, a 200-pound robot that reads sheet music through its camera eye and plays the organ with its ten fingers and two feet.
1984	Optical disks for the storage of computer data are introduced, and IBM brings out a mega-RAM memory chip with four times the memory of earlier chips.
1984	Hewlett-Packard brings high-quality printing to PCs with its LaserJet laser printer.
1985	The MIT Media Laboratory creates the first three-dimensional holographic image to be generated entirely by computer.
1985	Aldus Corp. introduces PageMaker for the Macintosh, the first desktop publishing software.
Mid 1980s	Third-generation robots arrive with limited intelligence and some vision and tactile senses.
1986	Dallas police use a robot to break into an apartment. The fugitive runs out in fright and surrenders.
1986	Electronic keyboards account for 55.2% of the American musical keyboard market, up from 9.5% in 1980. This trend is expected to continue until the market is almost *all* electronic.
1986	Technology for optical character recognition represents a $100-million–dollar industry that is expected to grow to several hundred million by 1990.
1986	New medical imaging systems are creating a mini-revolution. Doctors can now make accurate judgments based on views of areas inside our bodies and brains.
1986	Using image processing and pattern recognition, Lillian Schwartz comes up with an answer to a 500-year-old question: Who was the Mona Lisa? Her conclusion: Leonardo da Vinci himself.
1986	Russell Anderson's doctoral work at the University of Pennsylvania is a robotic ping-pong player that wins against human beings.
1986	The best computer chess players are now competing successfully at the senior master level, with HiTech, the leading chess machine, analyzing 200,000 board positions per second.
1987	Computerized trading helps push NYSE stocks to their greatest single-day loss.
1987	Current speech systems can provide any *one* of the following: a large vocabulary, continuous speech recognition, or speaker independence.
1987	Japan develops the Automated Fingerprint Identification System (AFIS), which enables U.S. law enforcement agencies to rapidly track and identify suspects.
1987	There are now 1,900 working expert systems, 1,200 more than last year. The most popular area of application is finance, followed by manufacturing control and fault diagnosis.
1988	Computer memory today costs only 10^{-8} of what it did in 1950.
1988	The population of industrial robots has increased from a few hundred in 1970 to several hundred thousand, most of them in Japan.
1988	In the U.S. 4,700,000 microcomputers, 120,000 minicomputers, and 11,500 mainframes are sold in this year.
1988	W. Daniel Hillis's Connection Machine is capable of 65,536 computations at the same time.
1988	Warsaw Pact forces are at least a decade behind NATO forces in artificial intelligence and other computer technologies.
1989	Computational power per unit of cost has roughly doubled every 18 to 24 months for the past 40 years.
1989	The trend from analog to digital will continue to revolutionize a growing number of industries.

Late 1980s	The core avionics of a typical fighter aircraft uses 200,000 lines of software. The figure is expected to grow to about 1 million in the 1990s. The U.S. military as a whole uses about 100 million lines of software (and is expected to use 200 million by 1993). Software quality becomes an urgent issue that planners are beginning to address.
Late 1980s	The computer is being recognized as a powerful tool for artistic expression.
Early 1990s	A profound change in military strategy arrives. The more developed nations increasingly rely on "smart weapons," which incorporate electronic copilots; pattern recognition techniques; and advanced technologies for tracking, identification, and destruction.
Early 1990s	Continuous speech systems can handle large vocabularies for specific tasks.
Early 1990s	Computer processors operate at speeds of 100 mips.
1990s	Significant progress is made toward an intelligent assistant, a decision-support system capable of a wide variety of administrative and information-gathering tasks. The system can, for example, prepare a feasibility report on a project proposal after accessing several databases and "talking" to human experts.
1990s	Reliable person identification, using pattern-recognition techniques applied to visual and speech patterns, replaces locks and keys in many instances.
Late 1990s	An increasing number of documents never exist on paper because they incorporate information in the form of audio and video pieces.
Late 1990s	Media technology is capable of producing computer-generated personalities, intelligent image systems with some human characteristics.
1999	The several-hundred-billion–dollar computer and information-processing market is largely intelligent by 1990 standards.
2000	Three-dimensional chips and smaller component geometries contribute to a multi-thousandfold improvement in computer power (compared to that of a decade earlier).
2000	Chips with over a billion components appear.
2000	The world chess champion is a computer.
Early 2000s	Translating telephones allow two people across the globe to speak to each other even if they do not speak the same language.
Early 2000s	Speech-to-text machines translate speech into a visual display for the deaf.
Early 2000s	Exoskeletal robotic prosthetic aids enable paraplegic persons to walk and climb stairs.
Early 2000s	Telephones are answered by an intelligent telephone-answering machine that converses with the calling party to determine the nature and priority of the call.
Early 2000s	The cybernetic chauffeur, installed in one's car, communicates with other cars and sensors on roads. In this way it successfully drives and navigates from one point to another.
Early 21st century	Computers dominate the educational environment. Courseware is intelligent enough to understand and correct the inaccuracies in the conceptual model of a student. Media technology allows students to interact with simulations of the very systems and personalities they are studying.
Early 21st century	The entire production sector of society is operated by a small number of technicians and professionals. Individual customization of products is common.
Early 21st century	Drugs are designed and tested on human biochemical simulators.
Early 21st century	Seeing machines for the blind provide both reading and navigation functions.
2010	A personal computer has the ability to answer a large variety of queries, because it will know where to find knowledge. Communications technologies allow it to access many sources of knowledge by wireless communication.
2020–2050	A phone call, which includes highly realistic three-dimensional holographic moving images, is like visiting with the person called.
2020–2070	A computer passes the Turing test, which indicates human-level intelligence.

GLOSSARY

accessory programs Microsoft Windows software tools for organizing the user's desktop, including clock, notepad, calendar, calculator, and cardfile.

access time Average time to locate instructions or data from **secondary** (auxiliary) **storage** device and to transfer this to computer's **main memory** (RAM).

add-ins *See* **add-on utility.**

add-on memory board Circuit board with memory chips plugged into expansion slot on **motherboard** to increase capacity of microcomputer's **main memory.**

add-on (add-in) utility **RAM-resident** software purchased to enhance the features of other applications software products (to provide additional capabilities)—for example, to print output lengthwise instead of across the width of the paper or to improve appearance of the output. Add-on software is loaded *after* the applications software has been loaded.

addressing scheme Computer design feature that determines amount of **main memory** the **CPU** can control at any one time.

algorithm A set of standard operations that guarantees a solution to a problem in a finite number of steps.

Alt key Modifier key on the computer **keyboard;** when a modifier key is pressed along with another key, the function of that other key is modified. The applications software program determines how modifier keys are used.

American National Standards Institute (ANSI) Organization that develops standards for all **high-level programming languages** and related subjects.

American Standard Code for Information Interchange (ASCII) Pronounced "*as*-key." Standard bit code used in data communications, microcomputers, and many minicomputers.

amplitude Size of voltage or magnitude of wave form in data or voice transmission.

analog signal Signal that is continuously varying and that represents a range of frequencies; the telephone system is based on analog signals. *See* **digital signal.**

analytical graphics Graphic forms used to make numeric data easier to understand; the most common analytical graphics forms are bar chart, line chart, pie chart, and XY chart. Analytical graphics are usually *spreadsheet-based;* that is, they are created using a **spreadsheet** software package. *Compare* **presentation graphics.**

ANSI *See* **American National Standards Institute.**

antivirus software Software that identifies the existence of **viruses** in a computer system and may also eliminate viruses the software recognizes.

applications software Program or programs designed to carry out a specific task to satisfy a user's specific needs—for example, to calculate payroll and print out checks. *Compare* **systems software.**

applications software utility Inexpensive program—**RAM-resident** or retrieved from disk—that performs basic "office management" functions for the user. *See* **add-on utility; disk utility; keyboard utility; screen utility.**

arithmetic/logic unit (ALU) Part of the computer's **central processing unit (CPU)** that performs all arithmetic and logical (comparison) functions.

arithmetic operations The operations of addition, subtraction, multiplication, division, and exponentiation.

artificial intelligence The study of intelligence as a collection of information-processing tasks; it is concerned with using computer hardware and software to simulate human thought processes such as imagination and intuition.

ASCII *See* **American Standard Code for Information Interchange.**

asynchronous transmission In data communications, sending one character, or **byte** (8 bits), at a time, each byte preceded by a "start" bit and followed by one or two "stop" bits and an error check bit (or parity bit). An inexpensive and widely used but relatively slow form of data communication. Also called *start-stop transmission.*

auxiliary storage *See* **secondary storage.**

Backspace key Used to move the **cursor** to the left and to simultaneously delete the character to the left.

batch commands Commands used to create batch command files, which automate frequently used command sequences and make procedures easier for users unfamiliar with the computer's operating system. Batch command files are considered **external command files** because their instructions are not loaded into main memory (RAM) at the time the computer is booted.

batch file File created by the user that is a collection of **DOS** commands automatically executed when the user types the name of the batch file after the **system prompt.** This type of file is useful for executing a frequently used series of commands.

binary code Scheme for encoding data using **binary digits.**

binary digit (bit) In binary notation, either 1 or 0. The digit 1 represents an "on" electrical (or magnetic) state; the digit 0 represents an "off" state. A group of adjacent bits (usually 8 bits) constitutes a **byte,** or single character.

bit *See* **binary digit.**

bit-mapped display **Cathode-ray tube** screen display system in which each possible dot is controlled by a single character in memory. Also known as *dot-addressable* or *all-points addressable* display.

block operations By using block operations, a feature of **word processing,** it is possible to move, delete, and copy entire sentences, paragraphs, and pages by issuing commands to the software.

boot To start up the computer and load the necessary software instructions into **RAM.**

bus An "electronic highway" or communications path linking several devices and parts of the **central processing unit (CPU).**

bus network Electronic communications **network** with a number of computers connected by a single length of wire, cable, or optical fiber.

byte Group of contiguous bits, usually 8 bits, that form a character.

cache memory   Special high-speed memory area that the CPU can quickly access; it comprises a small area of RAM created in addition to the computer's main RAM; a copy of the most frequently used data and instructions is kept in the cache so the CPU can look in the cache first—which makes the computer run faster. Cache memory is usually located right on the 386 or 486 microprocessor chip.

Caps Lock key   Keyboard key used to place all the alphabetic keys into uppercase position—that is, capital letters only.

cartridge-tape unit   Device that reads **magnetic tape** in cassette form; often used as alternative type of **secondary storage** to **hard disk** and as backup storage for hard disks.

cathode-ray tube (CRT)   Electronic screen used with computer terminals to display data entered into a computer and information available from it (**softcopy** output); also called *video display screen*.

CD-ROM   *See* **compact disk/read-only memory**.

cell   In a spreadsheet program, this marks the intersection of a column and a row.

central processing unit (CPU)   The "brain" of the computer; the part of the computer composed of electrical circuitry directing most of the computer system's activities. The CPU consists of the **control unit** and the **arithmetic/logic unit (ALU)**, connected by a **bus**.

CGA   *See* **color graphics adapter**.

character   *See* **byte**.

character box   Fixed location on a video display screen where a standard character can be placed. Most screens can display 80 characters of data horizontally and 25 lines vertically, or 2,000 character boxes (called character-mapped display)—the number the electron gun can target. The more **pixels** that fit into a character box, the higher the **resolution** of the resulting image. Each character box is "drawn" according to a prerecorded template stored in read-only memory (ROM).

character-mapped display   *See* **character box**.

character printer   *See* **impact printer**.

characters per second (cps)   Measure of speed of printers and other output devices.

check bit   *See* **parity bit**.

child record   In **hierarchical database**, record subordinate to **parent record**.

chip   Collection of related (integrated) circuits—usually on a wafer made of **semiconductor** material (usually silicon)—designed to work together on a set of tasks; can be as little as 1/4-inch square.

CISC   *See* **Complex Instruction Set Computing**.

clock   Device in **CPU** that synchronizes all operations in a **machine cycle**.

clock speed   The speed at which the **CPU** completes its internal processing tasks; measured in **megahertz (MHz)**.

clone   A copy of a brand-name hardware component. This term typically refers to an IBM-compatible computer.

closed architecture   Attribute of computers that cannot be upgraded by the use of expansion cards; the user cannot open the **system unit**. *Compare* **open architecture**.

coaxial cable   Type of thickly insulated copper wire for carrying large volumes of data—about 1,800–3,600 voice calls at once. Often used in local networks connecting computers in a limited geographic area.

code-oriented   Refers to **desktop publishing**; page description

tion software that displays all the formatting codes on the screen, thus preventing the user from seeing what the page will actually look like until it is printed out. *Compare* **WYSIWYG**.

color dot-matrix printer   Printer that uses the same technology as a monochrome **dot-matrix printer;** however, it uses a color ribbon instead of a black ribbon. Color ribbons usually contain equal bands of black, yellow, red, and blue.

color graphics adapter (CGA)   Expansion card plugged into **expansion slot** in **system cabinet** that allows compatible **monitor** to display **bit-mapped graphics;** must be used with appropriate software; monitor displays four colors as well as monochrome images; used in IBM-type PCs.

color monitor   *See* **RGB monitor**.

command syntax   *See* **syntax**.

communications software   Programs that allow users to access software and data from a computer in a remote location and to transmit data to a computer in a remote location.

compact disk/read-only memory (CD-ROM)   Optical storage disk whose data is imprinted by the disk manufacturer; the user cannot change it or write on the disk—the user can only "read" the data. *Compare* **erasable optical disk; write once, read many (WORM)**.

compatibility   Capability of operating together; can refer to different models of computers, different types of hardware peripherals, and various systems and applications software—not all software is compatible with all computers and other types of hardware, and not all types of hardware are compatible with one another. Incompatibility can often be overcome with the use of **modems** and/or special hardware and software.

compiler   Computer program that translates a **high-level programming language** program (**source code**) into **machine-language** instructions (**object code**) all at once. *Compare* **interpreter**.

Complex Instruction Set Computing (CISC)   A microprocessor chip design used in most of today's **microprocessor chips**. *Compare* **Reduced Instruction Set Computing (RISC)**.

computer   Data processing device made up of electronic and electromechanical components that can perform computations, including arithmetic and logical operations. Also known as **hardware**. By itself, a computer has no intelligence.

computer-aided design (CAD)   The use of a computer and special graphics software to design products.

computer-aided engineering (CAE)   The use of a computer and special software to simulate situations that test product designs.

computer-aided manufacturing (CAM)   The use of computers and special software to control manufacturing equipment; includes **robots**.

computer-assisted software engineering (CASE) tools   Software tools used in systems design, development, and documentation.

computer-based information system   Computer system for collecting data, processing it into information, and storing the information for future reference and output. The system consists of five components: **hardware, software, data/information, procedures,** and **people**. (**Connectivity** is sometimes a sixth component.) It has four major phases of activity: **input, processing, output,** and **storage.**

computer crime Crime committed when a person uses computer technology or knowledge of computers in an illegal activity.

Computer Fraud and Abuse Act of 1986 U.S. law that allows the prosecution of people who gain unauthorized access to computers and databases.

computer graphics *See* **analytical graphics; presentation graphics.**

computer literacy (competency) Basic understanding of what a computer is and how it can be used as a resource; includes some experience with commonly used software packages, such as **word processing, spreadsheet,** and/or **database** software.

Computer Matching and Privacy Protection Act of 1988 U.S. law that sets procedures for using computer data for verifying a person's eligibility for federal benefits or for recovering delinquent debts.

computer professional Person with formal education in technical aspects of computers—for example, a programmer, a systems analyst, or a computer operator.

computer system *See* **computer-based information system.**

concentrator Communications device that multiplexes (combines) low-speed communications lines onto one high-speed line; it is more "intelligent" than a **multiplexer** because it can store communications for later transmission.

connectivity When one computer system is set up to communicate with another computer system, connectivity becomes the sixth system element, after **hardware, software, data/information, procedures,** and **people;** it describes the manner in which the systems are connected.

controller Communications hardware device that supports a group of devices (terminals and/or printers) connected to a computer.

control program *See* **supervisor.**

control unit Part of the **CPU** that reads, interprets, and sees to the execution of software instructions.

CPU *See* **central processing unit.**

cracker Person who gains unauthorized access to a computer system for malicious purposes.

CRT *See* **cathode-ray tube.**

Ctrl key Modifier key on the computer keyboard; when a modifier key is pressed along with another key, the function of that other key is modified. The specific use of modifier keys is determined by the software program.

current disk drive *See* **default disk drive.**

cursor Indicator on video display screen that shows where next data—character, space, command—will be input.

cursor-movement keys Computer keyboard keys, usually marked with arrows, that are used to move the **cursor** around the video screen.

custom software Software that is written by a programmer to a particular organization's specifications.

daisy wheel printer **Impact printer** with plastic or metal disk with typeface impressions of characters on outside tips of spokes; the print character is forced against ribbon and paper.

data Raw, unevaluated facts, concepts, or instructions; after processing, data becomes **information.**

data access area Exposed part of a **disk,** through which the

read/write head inside the disk drive "reads" and "writes" data from and to a disk.

database Large group of electronically stored, integrated (cross-referenced) data that can be retrieved and manipulated to produce information.

database administrator Person who cordinates all related activities and needs for a company's database, including: (1) database implementation; (2) coordination with the user; (3) backup; (4) recovery; (5) performance monitoring; and (6) system security.

database management system (DBMS) Comprehensive software tool that allows users to create, maintain, and manipulate an integrated base of business data to produce relevant management information. A DBMS represents the interface between the user and the computer's **operating system** and **database.**

database management system (DBMS) software Program that allows storage of large amounts of data in different files; the data can be easily cross-indexed, retrieved, and manipulated to produce information for management reports.

database structure The characteristics of every **field** stored in a database; the method according to which a **database management system** organizes records.

data bus Electronic communication link that carries data between components of the computer system.

data dictionary Reference file in a **database management system** that stores information about data that is essential to the management of that data as a resource; it contans the data element names and definitions for all the data to be mantained in data files, to be generated as output, and to be created as input.

data file *See* **file.**

data flow diagram Graphic representation of flow of data through a system; standard **ANSI** symbols are used to represent various activities such as input and processing.

data independence Attribute of data that is stored independently of applications programs being used, so that it is easy to access and change.

data integrity Attribute of data that describes its accuracy, reliability, and timeliness; that is, if data has integrity, then it is accurate, reliable, and timely.

data manipulation language Program that is part of **database management system** software and that effects input to and output from the **database** files; the technical instructions that make up the input/output routines in the DBMS.

data (information) processing Operations for refining, summarizing, categorizing, and otherwise manipulating data into a useful form for decision making.

data redundancy A situation that occurs when the same element of data appears and is maintained in more than one file; a high degree of data redundancy makes updating files difficult.

data storage hierarchy The levels of data stored in a computer file: (1) **files** (broadest level), (2) **records,** (3) **fields,** (4) **bytes,** and (5) **bits** (narrowest level).

DBMS *See* **database management system.**

decision support system (DSS) A sophisticated computer-based information system for assisting high-level managers in planning and decision making on an on-demand basis.

dedicated backup system Hardware and software used only for backup purposes.

dedicated graphics package A software application that functions solely to provide the user with the capability to produce graphics.

dedicated line Communication line created or leased by a company for its own transmission purposes.

default disk drive The disk drive that is automatically affected by commands unless the user specifies another drive.

default values The values, or determinations, that the software assumes are true, unless the user instructs the software otherwise.

Del key Used to delete the character the **cursor** is positioned on.

demodulation Process of using communications hardware to convert **analog** signals sent over a telephone line into **digital** signals so that they can be processed by a receiving computer.

desktop computer *See* **microcomputer.**

desktop management utility Software designed to be available at any time to the user by residing in main memory at all times (**RAM-resident**); it provides many routine office support functions such as calendar organization, dictionary, and calculator.

desktop publishing software Programs that enable user to use a microcomputer, graphics scanners, and a desktop-sized laser printer to combine files created by different software applications packages to produce high-quality publications.

detail report Computer-generated report for **operating** (low-level) **management** that contains specific information about routine activities; such reports are highly structured, and their form is predetermined.

digital Pertaining to the use of combinations of **bits** to represent all quantities that occur in a computation.

digital convergence The merger of the computer, communications, and the consumer electronics and entertainment industries so that all manner of devices exchange data and information in the digital format understood by computers. *See also* **digital**; *compare* **analog.**

digital signal Signal that is discontinuous and discrete; it consists of bursts that form a transmission pattern. Computers communicate with each other in streams of **bits** transmitted as digital signals—a series of on and off electrical pulses. *See* **analog signal.**

digitizer Input device that can be moved over a drawing or a photograph thereby converting the picture to computerized data that can be stored, printed out, or shown on a video display screen. The device can also be moved over an electronic digitizing tablet in order to communicate data to the computer.

digitizing tablet *See* **digitizer.**

direct access storage and retrieval Situation in which records are stored and retrieved in any order. Also called *random access.*

direct entry Nonkeyboard input.

directory commands **Internal command instructions** used in microcomputers to create **directory structures** on a storage device.

directory structure The way a disk is organized into subdirectories.

disk Revolving platter (**secondary storage** medium) on which data and programs are recorded electronically or optically (laser) in the form of spots representing electrical "on" and "off" states.

disk cartridge Form of **secondary storage** consisting of a 5¼- or 3½-inch cartridge containing one or two platters and enclosed in a hard plastic case; the cartridge is inserted into the disk drive much like a music cassette tape.

disk drive Device into which a **diskette (floppy disk), hard disk,** or **disk pack** is placed for storing and retrieving data.

disk drive gate Door of disk drive, which must be closed for the read/write operation to be performed. (Not all computers have disk-drive gates.)

diskette Thin plastic (Mylar) disk enclosed in paper or plastic that can be magnetically encoded with data; standard diskettes are 5¼ or 3½ inches; also known as *floppy disks.*

disk operating system (DOS) **Internal command instructions** for microcomputers; **MS-DOS** and **PC-DOS** have become the industry standard for IBM PC microcomputers; **OS/2** is used on IBM's PS/2 Series microcomputers; **Apple-DOS** and the **Macintosh operating system** are used on the Apple Company's microcomputers; **TRS-DOS** is used on Tandy/Radio Shack microcomputers. These disk operating systems are not generally mutually compatible.

disk utility **Applications software utility** stored on disk; used to recover files that were accidentally erased, to make backup copy of a hard disk, and to organize a hard disk by means of a **menu**-driven system.

documentation Written description of a system's or a software package's parts and procedures; can come in the form of a user's manual that tells the user how to operate a piece of hardware or run a particular software program, or it can be a large collection of volumes and printouts to be used by programmers and computer operators.

DOS *See* **disk operating system.**

dot-matrix printer **Impact printer** using pin-like hammers to strike a ribbon against paper in computer-determined patterns of dots, making possible a variety of type styles and graphics.

double-density *See* **recording density.**

double-sided disk Disk(ette) that stores data on both sides; a computer needs a **double-sided disk drive** to be able to read double-sided disks.

double-sided disk drive Disk drive with **read/write heads** for both top and bottom surfaces of a disk.

drive A (A:) Designation for the first **disk(ette)** drive in a microcomputer; the program diskette is usually inserted in this drive, which is often the left-hand or the upper drive.

drive B (B:) Designation for the second **disk(ette) drive** in a microcomputer; the data diskette is usually inserted in this drive, which is often the right-hand or the lower drive.

drive C (C:) Designation for the **hard disk** drive in a microcomputer.

editing Process of changing text—for example, inserting and deleting.

electrically erasable programmable read-only memory (EEPROM) Type of **read-only (ROM)** memory (chip) much the same as **erasable programmable read-only mem-**

ory except that changes can be made to an integrated circuit electrically—new instructions can be recorded—byte-by-byte under software control.

electroluminescent (EL) display Type of **video display screen** with light-emitting layer of phosphor and two sets of electrodes surrounding the phosphor layer—one side forming vertical columns (usually 512), the other side forming horizontal rows (usually 256). To form a **pixel** on the screen, current is sent to row-column intersection, and the combined voltages cause the phospor to glow at that point.

electronic banking Service enabling customers to access banking activities from home or private office via a terminal or personal computer connected to their telephones.

electronic bulletin board (BBS) Information service that can be reached via computer connected to telephone lines that allows user to place messages or read messages from other users.

electronic communications Movement of voice and data over short and long distances, such as by telephone or microwave, through the use of computers and communications hardware and software.

electronic mail (E-mail) Transmission and storing of messages by computers and E-mail software.

electronic shopping Service through which users can order merchandise by using microcomputers and electronic communications to browse through products listed on remote databases.

electronic spreadsheet software *See* **spreadsheet software**.

electronic surveillance The monitoring of workers' performances—often without their knowledge—through the use of computers and other electronic equipment.

emulate To operate in a manner similar to something else; for example, when the user installs software, if the make and model of the user's printer aren't listed on the software's list of supported printers but it operates similarly to one on the installation list, the user's printer has the same characteristics of, or emulates the one on the list.

encryption The encoding of data transmitted over communications lines from standard code into proprietary (secret) code to prevent eavesdropping.

Enter key Computer **keyboard** key pressed to execute a command that was entered by tapping other keys first.

erasable optical disk **Optical storage** disk whose data can be changed and erased. *Compare* **compact disk/read-only memory (CD-ROM); write once, read many (WORM)**.

erasable programmable read-only memory (EPROM) Type of **read-only memory** in which, with the help of a special device using ultraviolet light, the data or instructions on an integrated circuit (**chip**) can be erased and new data can be recorded in its place.

ergonomics The science of human comfort and health, especially as it relates to the use of computers.

Esc key Most **software applications** allow the user to press this key to back out of, or cancel, the current command procedure.

ethics A set of moral values or principles that govern the conduct of an individual or a group.

event-initiated report Computer-based report generated for **middle management** only when certain conditions exist,

such as changes requiring immediate attention (for example, equipment breakdown).

exception report Report generated for **middle management** that shows out-of-the ordinary data.

execution cycle (E-cycle) Activity in **CPU** that includes execution of instruction and subsequent storing of result in a **register**. *See also* **instruction cycle; machine cycle**.

expanded memory In a microcomputer, **main memory (RAM)** that has been added to exceed the conventional 640 K maximum; it consists of an add-on memory board and special driver software; used only in compatible 8088, 8086, 80286, and 80386 microcomputers.

expansion card *See* **add-on memory board**.

expansion slot In a microcomputer that has **open architecture,** an area within the **system cabinet** where expansion cards—such as color graphics adapter cards and expanded memory cards—can be inserted and plugged into the computer's circuitry.

expert system A computer program based on various **artificial intelligence** techniques that performs a specialized task at the level of a human expert; the expert system consists of knowledge gathered from human experts plus rules for using the system. It usually comprises: (1) a **natural language** interface with the user; (2) a knowledge base; (3) an inference machine to solve problems and make logical inferences; and (4) an explanation module to explain the conclusions to the user.

export To convert a file created by one application into a file format that can be used by another application.

Extended Binary Coded Decimal Interchange Code (EBCDIC) Pronounced *"eb*-see-dick." The most popular code used for IBM and IBM-compatible mainframe computers.

extended memory In a microcomputer, **main memory (RAM)** that has been added to exceed the conventional 640 K maximum; it consists of an **add-on memory board** and special driver software; used only in compatible 80286, 80386, and 80486 microcomputers.

external command file DOS command instructions that aren't loaded into **RAM** when you **boot** your computer. *See* **external command instructions**.

external command instructions General-purpose instructions kept in **secondary storage** for "housekeeping" tasks on microcomputers such as the sorting of files and formatting of disks; part of a computer's **systems software**. *See also* **internal command instructions**.

external modem **Modem** that is outside the microcomputer and uses its own power supply; it is connected to the computer by a cable.

facsimile *See* **fax**.

Fair Credit Reporting Act of 1970 U.S. law intended to keep mistakes out of credit bureau files; credit agencies are barred from sharing credit information with anyone but authorized customers.

fax A faxed item. *See* **fax machine**.

fax card An internal fax **modem** that differs from conventional modems in that it can send and receive both text and graphics and can typically send and receive at a faster rate.

faxing The process of transmitting a **fax**.

fax machine   Short for *facsimile machine,* a type of **scanner** that "reads" text and graphics and transmits them over telephone lines to a computer with a fax card (board) or to another fax machine.

fiber optics   Form of computer communications in which signals are converted to light form and fired by laser in bursts through thin (2,000ths of an inch) insulated glass or plastic fibers. Nearly 1 billion bits per second can be communicated through a fiber optic cable.

field   Group of related characters (bytes) of data. *See* **data storage hierarchy.**

field name   In a **database structure,** the unique name given to each field of data that is stored. A field name can be no longer than 10 characters.

field type   In a **database structure,** the specification of the kind of data that will be stored in a given **field** (character, numeric, date, logical, float, or memo).

field width   In a database structure, the width of each **field** must be defined by the user.

file   Group of related **records.** A file may contain data (data file) or software instructions (program file). *See* **data storage hierarchy.**

file management system   *See* **flat-file database management system.**

filename extension   One to three characters added to a filename to aid in file identification. The filename and the extension are separated by a dot.

filename length   Convention specified by different **operating systems**—for example, **DOS** specifies one to eight characters in filenames.

file server   A computer, usually a microcomputer, with large-capacity storage, that stores data and programs shared by a network of terminals; often the central unit in a **star network.**

file updating   A factor in **data redundancy** and **data integrity;** when an element of data in a **database** needs to be updated in *all* files that contain it.

flatbed plotter   Special-purpose output device for reproducing computer-generated drawings. Paper is placed flat and pens move horizontally and vertically across it.

flatbed scanner   Type of **scanner** that enables the user to scan text and graphics by placing each page to be scanned on a piece of glass that the scanning mechanism passes over.

flat-file database management system   **Database management system** software that can deal with data in only one **file** at a time; cannot establish relationships among data elements stored in different files.

flat screen technology   Video display screens for laptop computers; the screens are much thinner than a **cathode-ray tube (CRT).** *See* **electroluminescent display; gas plasma display; liquid crystal display.**

floppy disk   *See* **diskette.**

font   All the characters of one size in one particular typeface; includes numbers, punctuation marks, and upper- and lowercase letters.

footer   Descriptive information (such as page number and date) that appears at the bottom of each page of a document.

formatting   (1) Directing the computer to put magnetic **track** and **sector** pattern on a disk to enable the disk to store data or information. Also known as *initializing.* (2) In **word processing,** the alteration of text appearance by addition of underlining or boldface, change of margins, centering of headings, and so on. (3) In electronic **spreadsheet** processing, the alteration of numbers by the addition of dollar signs, percent signs, decimal places, and so on.

formatting commands   *See* **formatting** (2).

formula   In **electronic spreadsheets,** a mathematical expression that defines the relationships among various cells in the spreadsheet.

Freedom of Information Act of 1970   U.S. law that gives citizens the right to look at data concerning themselves that is stored by the U.S. government.

freeware   Free software that is often limited in its distribution (usually through a bulletin board service).

frequency   Number of times a signal repeats the same cycle in a second.

front-end processor   Computer used in a computer center to handle data transmission and communications from outside terminals and devices to allow the main computer to concentrate solely on processing applications as quickly as possible.

full-duplex transmission mode   Communications transmitted in both directions simultaneously.

function keys   Specialized keys on a microcomputer **keyboard** for performing specific tasks with applications software; the keys are used differently with each applications package; they are labeled F1, F2, F3, and so on.

fuzzy logic   Type of programming logic used in the development of **natural languages** and **artificial intelligence** projects; works by allowing partial membership in a set—for example, not black or white but gray, not fat or thin but a "little" fat.

gas plasma display   Used as **video display screen** in some **laptop microcomputers.** Gas plasma display uses three pieces of glass sandwiched together. The inner layer has numerous small holes drilled in it. The outer two layers are placed on both sides of the middle one, and the holes are filled with a gas mixture, usually a mixture of argon and neon. Both outer layers of glass have a thin grid of vertical and horizontal wires. A **pixel** appears at a particular intersection when the appropriate horizontal and vertical wires are electrified.

GB   *See* **gigabyte.**

general-purpose applications software   Type of applications software used in general business and professional environments; includes word processing, desktop publishing, spreadsheet, database management, graphics, communications, integrated, CAD, CAE, CAM, and utility software.

gigabyte (GB)   One billion bytes.

graphics monitor (terminal)   Screen that can display both **alphanumeric data** and graphics; different types can display one-, two-, or three-dimensional graphics. *Compare* **alphanumeric monitor (terminal).**

graphics software   Programs that allow the user to present information in pictorial form, often with text. *See* **analytical graphics; presentation graphics.**

graphic user interface   Software feature that allows user to select **menu** options by choosing **icons,** or picture, that represent particular processing functions; makes software easier to use, and typically employs a **mouse.** Macintosh microcomputers and Windows software use graphic user interfaces.

gray-scale monitor Monitor that displays different shades, or scales, of gray; the more levels of gray scale, the more realistically an image can be displayed. High-resolution gray-scale graphics files require a large amount of storage.

hacker Person who gains unauthorized access to a computer system for fun.

half-duplex transmission mode Two-way data communications in which data travels in only one direction at a time.

hand-held scanner Small input device used to scan printed documents on a limited basis to input the documents' contents to a computer.

hardcard Type of **secondary storage** device consisting of a circuit board with a disk that is plugged into a microcomputer **expansion slot.** A hard card can store up to 80 MB of data.

hardcopy Output recorded on a tangible medium (generally meaning that you can touch it) such as paper or microfilm. *Compare* **softcopy.**

hard disk **Secondary storage** device consisting of a rigid metal platter connected to a central spindle; the entire unit, including the **read/write heads,** is enclosed in a permanently sealed container. Hard disks store much more data than do **diskettes**—40 MB and up.

hardware Four categories of electronic and electromechanical computer components: input, storage, processing, and output hardware. *See also* **computer.** *Compare* **software.**

header Descriptive information (such as page number and date) that appears at the top of each page of a document.

Help facility Most **applications software** packages include a command that enables the user to display helpful information on the screen about a particular command.

Help key In many software applications, this key is used to obtain help information about the current command, a particular function key, or a particular topic.

Help screen *See* **Help facility.**

hierarchical database model The type of **database** organization in which data is arranged into related groups resembling a family tree, with **child records** subordinate to **parent records.** A parent record may have many child records, but each child record can have only one parent record. The record at the highest level is called the *root record.*

hierarchical network **Star networks** configured into a single multilevel system, with a single large computer controlling all network activity. However, a computer connected into the main computer can have a star network of devices connected to it in turn. Also known as a *tree network.*

high-level programming language Third-generation programming language designed to run on different computers with few changes—for example, **COBOL, FORTRAN,** and **BASIC.** Most high-level languages are considered to be procedure-oriented because the program instructions comprise lists of steps, or procedures, that tell the computer not only what to do but how to do it. Also known as *procedural language.*

hub Round opening in the center of a diskette, which enables the disk to fit over a spindle in the disk drive.

hypertext software Software that links basic file units called *nodes* (text, sound, and graphics) with one another in creative ways. The user typically sees index-type "cards" and "card stacks" on the screen as well as other pictorial representations of file units (nodes) and combination choices; card and stack contents can be determined by the user or supplied in an **off-the-shelf software** package (stackware).

icon Picture that represents the different application programs and processing procedures you can execute. Macintosh programs and **Microsoft Windows** use icons extensively.

impact printer Also called *character printer;* output device that makes direct contact with paper, forming the print image by pressing an inked ribbon against the paper with a hammer-like mechanism. Impact printers are of two types. *See* **letter-quality printer; dot-matrix printer.**

import To retrieve a file created by another application into the current application.

index hole Hole in protective jacket enclosing **diskette** that enables the disk to be positioned over a photoelectric sensing mechanism. Each time the disk revolves, a hole in the disk passes under the index hole in the jacket and activates a timing mechanism that determines which portion of the disk is over or under the **read/write heads.**

information Raw **data** processed into usable form by the computer. It is the basis for decision making.

information center Company department staffed by experts in hardware, software, and procedures used in the company; the experts help users in all matters relating to computer use.

information service *See* **public databank.**

initializing *See* **formatting.**

ink-jet printer **Nonimpact printer** that resembles **dot-matrix printer** in that it forms images or characters with dots. The dots are formed not by hammer-like pins but by droplets of ink fired through holes in a plate.

input hardware **Hardware** that is used to collect data and convert it into a form suitable for computer processing. The most common input device is a **keyboard.**

instruction cycle (I-cycle) In the **CPU,** the operation whereby an instruction is retrieved from **main memory (RAM)** and is decoded, alerting the circuits in the CPU to perform the specified operation.

integrated software package Software combining several applications into a single package with a common set of commands. **Word processing,** electronic **spreadsheets, database management systems, graphics,** and **data communications** have been combined in such packages.

internal command files Files that contain **DOS** command instructions that are stored in **RAM** at all times. The instructions in these files are loaded into RAM when your computer is turned on (booted).

internal command instructions Operating system software instructions loaded into **main memory (RAM)** (when the microcomputer is booted), where they direct and control applications software and hardware; they remain in main memory until the computer is turned off. *See also* **external command instructions.**

internal modem **Modem** that is inside a microcomputer; it is located on a circuit board plugged into the computer's expansion slot and draws power directly from the computer's power supply. No special cable is required. *Compare* **external modem.**

international network **Network** providing intercontinental voice and data communications, often using undersea cable or satellites.

interpreter **Language processor** that converts high-level program instructions into **machine language** one instruction statement at a time. *Compare* **compiler.**

K (KB) *See* **kilobyte.**

keyboard Device resembling typewriter keyboard for entering data and computer-related codes. Besides standard typewriter keys, it has special **function keys, cursor-movement keys, numeric keys,** and other special-purpose keys.

keyboard utility **Applications software utility,** usually **RAM-resident,** used to change the way the **cursor** appears on the screen.

kilobyte (KB) 1,024 bytes.

language processor Program that translates applications programs wirtten in **high-level programming languages** and **assembly languages** into **machine language** so that the computer can process them. Also known as a *translator.*

laptop microcomputer Microcomputer using **flat-screen technology** that is small enough to be held on a person's lap.

laser printer Output device in which a laser beam is directed across the surface of a light-sensitive drum to record an image as a pattern of tiny dots. As with a photocopying machine, the image is then transferred to the paper a page at a time.

latency period *See* **rotational delay.**

license What the user really buys when purchasing copyrighted software—that is, a license to use the software.

light pen Pen-shaped input device consisting of a light-sensitive photoelectric cell that, when touched to a video display screen, is used to signal the screen position to the computer.

line chart Shows trends over time; the angles of the line reflect variations in a trend, and the distance of the line from the horizontal axis represents quantity. *See also* **analytical graphics.**

line-of-sight System that enables users to use their eyes to point at the screen to specify screen coordinates. These systems are being used by the handicapped.

liquid crystal display (LCD) Used as a flat **video display screen** in some laptop microcomputers. LCD uses a clear liquid chemical trapped in tiny pockets between two pieces of glass. Each pocket of liquid is covered both front and back by thin wires. When current is applied to the wires, a chemical reaction turns the chemical a dark color, thereby blocking light. The point of blocked light is the **pixel.**

local area network (LAN) Communications **network** connected by wire, cable, or fiber optics link that serves parts of a company located close to one another, generally in the same building or within two miles of one another. LANs allow workers to share hardware, software, and data.

logical database design Detailed description of database structure from the user's perspective, rather than a technical perspective. It involves defining user information needs, analyzing data element requirements and logical groupings, finalizing the design, and creating the **data dictionary.** Every element of data necessary to produce required management information reports is identified, and the relationship among the records is specified. *Compare* **physical database design;** *see also* **schema, subschema.**

logical operations Operations consisting of three common comparisons: equal to, less than, and greater than. Three words used in basic logical operations are AND, OR, and NOT.

machine cycle In the **CPU** during processing, the **instruction cycle** and the **execution cycle** together, as they apply to one instruction.

machine language The language the **CPU** understands; data and instructions are represented as **binary digits.** Each type of computer responds to a unique version of machine language. Also known as **first-generation language.**

Macintosh Operating System The **operating system** designed by Apple Computers for the Apple Macintosh microcomputer.

macro Collection of procedures—a few high-level instructions that generate many machine-language instructions. Macros are created by the user and saved to disk, then used repeatedly to save time. A macro uses a few keystrokes to represent many.

magnetic tape Plastic ribbon coated with material that can be magnetized to record the **bit** patterns that represent data.

mainframe computer After the **supercomputer,** the most powerful type of computer; it is usually housed in a controlled environment and can support many powerful peripheral devices and the processing requirements of hundreds of users.

main memory The primary storage of a computer, where data and instructions are held for immediate access by the **CPU;** main memory is **volatile**—when the power is turned off, all data and instructions in memory are lost unless they have been saved to a **secondary storage** medium. Also known as *internal memory* and *RAM (random access memory).*

management Individuals responsible for providing leadership and direction in an organization's areas of planning, organizing, staffing, supervising, and controlling of business activities. Management may be low-level (operating or supervisory), middle-level (or tactical), or upper-level (strategic). *See also* **middle management, operating management, upper management.**

management information system (MIS) Computer-based processing and manual procedures within a company to provide useful and timely information to support useful and timely information to support decision making on all three levels of management.

MB *See* **megabyte.**

medium (*pl. media*) Type of material on which data is recorded—for example, paper, magnetic tape, magnetic disk, or optical disk.

megabyte (MB) 1,024 K—approximately 1 million characters.

megahertz (MHz) One million hertz; a measure of speed at which computers perform operations; **clock** speed.

memory *See* **main memory.**

menu List of options, or choices, offered to the user by the software; menus can be pulled down or popped up from the **menu bar** across the screen.

menu bar Row of on-screen **menu** options.

merging Bringing together information from two different files.

metropolitan area network (MAN) Computer-based **network** that links computer resources scattered among various office buildings in a city. *Compare* **local area network** and **wide area network.**

microcomputer Small, general-purpose computer system that uses a microprocessor chip as its **CPU.** It can usually be used by only one person at one time; can be used independently or as a **terminal.** Also known as *personal computer, desktop computer.*

microprocessor **Integrated circuit** (chip) containing the CPU circuitry for a microcomputer.

Microsoft Windows **Graphic user interface** software used with MS-DOS.

microwave system Communications technology using the atmosphere above the earth for transmitting signals point to point from tower to tower. Such systems are extensively used for high-volume as well as long-distance communication of both data and voice in the form of electromagnetic waves similar to radio waves but in a higher frequency range. Microwave signals are said to be "line-of-sight" because they cannot bend around the curvature of the earth.

middle management Level of management dealing with decisions that cover a broader range of time and are less structured than decisions made by **operating (low-level) management.** However, middle management deals with decisions that are more time-specific and more structured than decisions made by **upper-level (strategic) management.** Also called *tactical management.*

millions of instructions per second (mips) Unit of measure for speed at which a computer processes software instructions.

minicomputer Computer that is similar to but less powerful than a **mainframe computer;** it can support 2–50 users and computer professionals.

mips *See* **millions of instructions per second.**

modeling tools Program and systems design tools such as **computer-assisted software engineering (CASE), data flow diagrams, systems flowcharts,** and so on.

modem Device for translating **digital signals** from a computer into **analog signals** for transmission over wire telephone lines and then back into digital signals again for processing (a modem must be hooked up at each end of the transmission). Modem stands for MOdulate/DEModulate. (Modems are not needed for transmission over **coaxial cable** or **fiber optics cable.**

monitor Device for viewing computer output. Also known as **cathode-ray tube (CRT); screen; video display screen.**

monochrome monitor Device for viewing text and in some cases graphics in a single color, commonly green or amber. It has only one electron gun. *Compare* **RGB monitor.**

motherboard Main circuit board in a microcomputer system. It normally includes the **microprocessor chip** (or **CPU**), **main memory (RAM)** chips, all related support circuitry, and the **expansion slots** for plugging in additional components. Also known as *system board.*

mouse Hand-held input device connected to a microcomputer by a cable; when the mouse is rolled across the desktop, the pointer moves across the screen. A button on the mouse allows users to make **menu** selections, issue commands, and position the **cursor.**

MS-DOS *See* **disk operating system.**

multimedia Sophisticated software that combines basic text and graphics along with animation, video, music, and voice.

multiplexer Device that allows several terminals to share a single communications line.

multiprocessing Activity in which an **operating system** manages simultaneous execution of programs with two or more **CPUs.** This can entail processing instructions from different programs or different instructions from the same program. *Compare* **multitasking.**

multiprogramming *See* **multitasking.**

multitasking Activity in which more than one task or program is executed at a time. A small amount of each program is processed, and then the **CPU** moves to the remaining programs, one at a time, processing small parts of each. Also known as *multiprogramming.*

natural language Programming language designed to resemble human speech. Similar to **query language,** it eliminates the need for user to learn specific vocabulary, grammar, or syntax. Also known as *fifth-generation language.*

network Collection of data communications hardware, computers, communications software, communications media, and applications software connected so that users can share information and equipment. *See also* **international network; private network; public network; ring network; star network; token ring network.**

network database model Type of **database** organization similar to **hierarchical database model** but allowing multiple one-to-many relationships; each **child record** can have more than one **parent record.** Access can be from a number of points, not just the top.

network fileserver Computer to which approximately 10 other microcomputers can be connected so that data and programs can be shared.

networking The connecting of computers and other hardware peripherals so they can share hardware, software, and data resources.

nonimpact printer Output device that does not make direct contact with paper when it prints. *See* **ink-jet printer; laser printer; thermal printer.** *Compare* **impact printer.**

nonvolatile storage Type of storage that is relatively permanent—such as data saved to disk or tape; that is, computer instructions and data are not lost when the power is turned off. *Compare* **volatile storage.**

numeric data Data that can be mathematically manipulated. *Compare* **alphanumeric data.**

numeric keys (keypad) The keys labeled 0–9 on the computer **keyboard;** used to enter numbers for mathematical manipulation.

Num Lock key When a computer **keyboard** combines the **numeric keys** with the **cursor-movement keys,** the Num Lock key must be pressed before numbers can be entered via the numeric keys. Then the Num Lock key is pressed again to restore the function of the cursor-movement keys.

object code Program consisting entirely of machine-language instructions. *Compare* **source code.**

object-oriented programming A means of creating software programs by using discrete units or modules (objects) of program instructions and refining and combining them, instead of writing each single instruction from scratch every time a new software program is created.

OCR　*See* **optical character recognition**.

off-the-shelf software　**Applications software** that can be purchased in a computer store, as opposed to software that is custom-written by a programmer.

on-demand report　Report requested by **middle management** on a case-by-case basis.

open architecture　Attribute of computers that can be upgraded by the use of expansion cards, such as **expanded memory** and **VGA**; the user can open the **system cabinet** and insert expansion cards in the computer's **expansion slots**. *Compare* **closed architecture**.

operating management　The lowest level of management, which deals with **structured decisions** and daily operations. Also called *supervisory management*. *Compare* **middle management** and **upper management**.

operating system (OS)　Set of **internal command instructions** or programs to allow a computer to direct its own resources and operations and run all other progams, including **applications software**; in microcomputers, called a *disk operating system*.

Operating System/2 (OS/2)　IBM **systems software** intended to take advantage of 80286 and 80386 microprocessors (such as in the IBM PS/2 Series of microcomputers) and support multitasking and software applications requiring up to 16 MB of main memory (RAM); more powerful than **MS-DOS**.

operational decision maker　Low-level manager who typically makes **structured decisions** regarding daily business operations.

optical character recognition (OCR) software　Software used to scan characters or text from a piece of paper into the computer's memory.

optical storage　**Secondary storage** technology using a high-power laser beam to burn microscopic spots in a disk's surface coating. Data is represented by the presence and the absence of holes in the storage locations (1s and 0s). A much lower-power laser beam is used to retrieve the data. Much more data can be stored in this way than with traditional storage media, and it is faster and cheaper.

output　Computer-produced text, graphics, or sound in **hardcopy** or **softcopy** form that can be used immediately by people, or computer-produced data stored in computer-usable form for later use by computers and people.

output hardware　The purpose of output hardware is to provide the user with the means to view information produced by the computer system. Information is output in either **hardcopy** or **softcopy** form.

page description language (PDL)　Part of **desktop publishing software**; this **high-level language** defines printer output and thus allows a **laser printer** to combine text and graphics from different files on a single page. If an **applications software** program generates output in a PDL, the output can be printed on any laser printer that supports it.

parent record　In **hierarchical database**, the record higher in the structure than a **child record**. Each child can have only one parent—that is, each record may have many records below it but only one record above it, which is a *one-to-many relationship*. Deletion of a parent record automatically deletes all child records.

parity bit　An extra (ninth) **bit** attached to the end of a **byte**; it is used as part of an error-checking scheme. Computers are designed to use either an odd-parity scheme or an even-parity scheme, in which the total number of 1s in each byte, including the parity bit, must add up to an odd number or an even number.

PC-DOS　*See* **disk operating system**.

pen-based computing　Uses special software to allow user to write directly on the display screen to input data.

periodic report　Report for middle management produced at predetermined times—for example, payroll report, inventory status report.

physical database design　Hardware view of a database that identifies on what tracks, sectors, etc. various segments of the database are stored; also called the *internal view*, or *physical view*.

pixel　Picture element; a glowing phosphor on a **cathode-ray tube (CRT)** screen. Small pixels provide greatest image clarity (**resolution**).

plotter　Output device used to create **hardcopy** drawings on paper in a variety of colors. *See also* **drum plotter; electrostatic plotter; flatbed plotter**.

portable printer　Printer that is compact and typically weighs less than 5 lbs.

power supply　**Hardware** component that provides power to other hardware components; housed in the microcomputer's **system unit**.

presentation graphics　Graphic forms that go beyond simple **analytical graphics** (bar charts, line charts, pie charts); sophisticated presentation graphics software allows the user to function as an artist and combine free-form shapes and text.

primary storage　*See* **main memory**.

printer　Output device that prints characters, symbols, and sometimes graphics on paper. *See also* **impact printer; nonimpact printer**.

printer driver　File stored on a disk containing instructions that enable a software program to communicate, or print, on the user's printer.

Privacy Act of 1974　U.S. law that restricts U.S. governmental agencies in the way they share information about American citizens; it prohibits federal information collected for one purpose from being used for a different purpose.

private network　Network supporting the voice and data communications needs of a particular organization.

procedure　In an information system, specific sequence of steps performed to complete one or more information processing activities.

processing　The computer-based manipulation of **data** into **information**.

processing hardware　Hardware that is used to retrieve, interpret, and direct the execution of software instructions provided to the computer.

processing registers　In the **CPU**, the registers holding data or instructions being acted on. Their size determines the amount of data that can be processed in a single cycle.

program　Group of related instructions that perform specific processing tasks.

program independence　Attribute of programs that can be used with data files arranged in different ways—for example, some with the date first and expense items second and others with expense items first and date second. Program dependence means that a separate program has to be written to use each differently arranged data file.

programmable read-only memory (PROM) Type of **read-only memory (ROM)** chip in which data or program instructions are not prerecorded when it is manufactured; thus, users can record their own data or instructions, but once the data has been recorded, it cannot always be changed.

protocol In electronic communications, formal rules for communicating, including those for timing of message exchanges, the type of electrical connections used by the communications devices, error detection techniques, methods required to gain access to communications channels, and so on.

protocol converter Specialized intelligent **multiplexer** that facilitates effective communications between microcomputers and the main computer system.

prototyping tools Software programs used to build small-scale working models of a new system or parts of a system.

public databank Information service providing users with access, for a fee, to large databases.

public domain software Uncopyrighted software available free to users.

public network Network providing subscribers with voice and data communications over a large geographical area. Also known as *common carrier, specialized common carrier.*

pull-down menu Menu that contains options displayed down the screen rather than across a row.

quad-density *See* recording density.

query language Fourth-generation programming language that allows users to ask questions about, or retrieve information from, database files by forming requests in normal human language statements. Learning the specific grammar, vocabulary, and **syntax** is usually a simple task. The definitions for query language and for **database management systems software** are so similar that they are often considered to be the same.

QWERTY Term that designates the common computer **keyboard** layout, whereby the first six letters of the first row of lettered keys spell "QWERTY."

RAM *See* random access memory.

RAM-resident software Software always available to the user because it resides in **main memory (RAM)** at all times.

random access memory (RAM) The name given to the integrated circuits (**chips**) that make up main memory, which provides **volatile** temporary storage of data and program instructions that the **CPU** is using; data and instructions can be retrieved at random, no matter where they are located in main memory. RAM is used for storing **operating system** software instructions and for temporary storage of **applications software** instructions, input data, and output data. *See also* **internal command instructions.**

read-only memory (ROM) Type of memory in which instructions to perform operations critical to a computer are stored on integrated circuits (**chips**) in permanent, **nonvolatile** form. The instructions are usually recorded on the chips by the manufacturer. *Compare* **electrically erasable programmable read-only memory; erasable programmable read-only memory; programmable read-only memory; random access memory (RAM).**

read/write head Recording mechanism in magnetic storage devices that "reads" (accepts) the magnetic spots of data and converts them to electrical impulses and that "writes" (enters) the spots on the magnetic tape or disk. Most disk drives have two read/write heads to access the top and bottom surfaces of a disk simultaneously.

record Collection of related **fields.** *See also* **data storage hierarchy.**

recording density Number of **bits** per inch (bpi) that can be written onto the surface of a magnetic disk. Disks and drives have three kinds of recording densities: (1) single-density, (2) double-density, or (3) quad-density. The higher the density number, the more data a disk can hold.

Reduced Instruction Set Computing (RISC) **Chip** design that allows microcomputers to offer very high-speed performance by simplifying the internal chip design and reducing the number of instruction sets. The RISC design enables a computer to process data about twice as fast as one based on the **CISC** design. *See* **Complex Instruction Set Computer.**

register Temporary storage location within the **CPU** that quickly accepts, stores, and transfers data and instructions being used immediately. An instruction that needs to be executed must be retrieved from **main memory (RAM)** and placed in a register for access by the **ALU** (arithmetic/logic unit). The larger the register (the more **bits** it can carry at once), the greater the processing power.

relational database model Type of database organization in which many tables (called *relations*) store related data elements in rows (called *tuples*) and columns (called *attributes*). The structure allows complex logical relationships between records in different files to be expressed in a simple fashion. Relational databases can cross-reference data and retrieve data automatically, and data can be easily added, deleted, or modified. Data can be accessed by content, instead of address, which is the case with **hierarchical database** and **network database models.**

removable media Storage hardware media that can be removed from the computer, such as a **diskette** or a **disk cartridge.**

resolution Clarity of the image on the **video display screen;** determined by the number of **pixels** that make up the screen images.

RGB (red/green/blue) monitor Video display screen for viewing text and graphics in various colors. It has three **electron guns,** and the screen is coated with three types of phosphors: red, green, and blue. Each **pixel** is made up of three dots of phosphors, one of each color, and is capable of producing a wide range of colors. *Compare* **monochrome monitor.**

ring network Electronic communications **network** in which messages flow in one direction from a source on the loop to a destination on the loop. Computers in between act as relay stations, but if a computer fails, it can be bypassed.

Right to Financial Privacy Act of 1979 U.S. law that sets strict procedures that U.S. governmental agencies must follow when they want to examine customer records in a bank.

RISC *See* Reduced Instruction Set Computing.

robot A programmable device consisting of machinery for sensory activity and mechanical manipulation and connected to or including a computer. Typically, these machines automatically perform some task normally done by human beings.

ROM *See* **read-only memory.**

root directory In the hierarchy of the **MS-DOS directory structure** when a microcomputer program is **booted,** the first directory displayed is the root directory. This directory contains subdirectories, which can in turn contain sub-subdirectories. The root directory is similar in concept to the filing cabinet.

root record In a **hierarchical database model,** the record at the highest level, or "top" of the tree. Root records, which are the key to the structure, connect the various branches.

rotational delay In a disk drive, the time required for the disk to revolve until the correct **sector** is under or over the **read/write heads.**

satellite system In electronic communications, a system that uses solar-powered satellites in stationary orbit above the earth to receive, amplify, and retransmit signals. The satellite acts as a relay station from microwave stations on the ground (called *earth stations*).

saving Activity of permanently storing data from a microcomputer's **main memory (RAM)** (primary storage) on disk or tape (**secondary storage**).

scanhead Scanning mechanism inside a **scanner.**

scanner (scanning device) Hardware device that "reads" text and graphics and converts them to computer-usable form; scanners "read" copy on paper and transmit it to the user's computer screen for manipulation, output, and/or storage.

scanning system A microcomputer (PC), a scanner, and scanning software. These systems enable users to convert a hardcopy picture or a photograph into a computer-usable graphics file that can be understood by a desktop publishing or graphics package.

schema Describes organization of **relational database** in its entirety, including names of all data elements and ways records are linked. A **subschema** is part of the schema.

screen *See* **monitor.**

screen utility Applications software utility, **RAM-resident,** used to increase the life of the computer video screen.

scrolling Activity of moving text up or down on the **video display screen.**

script language Communications software feature that enables the user to automate communications procedures.

search and replace In **word processing,** the activity of automatically searching for and replacing text in a document.

secondary storage Any storage device designed to retain data and instructions in permanent form. Secondary storage is **nonvolatile:** data and instructions remain intact when the computer is turned off. Also called *auxiliary storage. Compare* **primary storage.**

sector One of several wedge-shaped areas on a hard disk or diskette used for storage reference purposes. The point at which a sector intersects a **track** is used to reference the data location. *See* **hard-sectored disk; soft-sectored disk.**

security Controls built into a computer system to ensure the protection of data, hardware, and software from intrusions, sabotage, and natural disasters.

seek time In a disk drive, the time required for the drive to position the **read/write heads** over the proper **track.**

semiconductor Material (often silicon) that conducts electricity with only a little ("semi") resistance; impurities are added to it to form electrical circuits. Today, the integrated circuits (**chips**) in the **main memory (RAM)** of almost all computers are based on this technology.

semistructured decision Decision typically made at the **middle management** level that, unlike **structured decisions,** must be made without a base of clearly defined informational procedures.

setting time In a disk drive, the time required to place the **read/write heads** in contact with the disks.

shareware Software distributed on request—often through an electronic bulletin board service—for which a small fee is charged if the user decides to keep the software.

sheet-feed scanner Type of **scanner** that uses mechanical rollers to move paper over the **scan head.**

Shift key Computer **keyboard** key that works in the same way that a typewriter Shift key works: when pressed in conjunction with an alphabetic key, the letter appears as uppercase.

simplex transmission mode Communications transmission in which data travels only in one direction at all times.

single-density disk *See* **recording density.**

softcopy Output produced in a seemingly intangible form such as on a video display screen or provided in voice form. *Compare* **hardcopy.**

software Electronic instructions given to the computer to tell it what to do and when and how to do it. Frequently made up of a group of related programs. The two main types of software are **applications software** and **systems software.**

software installation Process of telling an **applications software** package what the characteristics are of the hardware you will be using so that the software will run smoothly.

software package **Applications software** and **documentation** usually created by professional software writers to perform general business functions.

software piracy The illegal copying of copyrighted software onto blank disks for unauthorized use.

source code Program written in **high-level programming language.** Source code must be translated by a **language processor** into **object code** before the program instructions can be executed by the computer.

spelling checker In **word processing,** programs that check a document for spelling errors.

spreadsheet area **Spreadsheet cells** that are visible on the screen.

spreadsheet software Software program enabling user to create, manipulate, and analyze numerical data and develop personalized reports involving the use of extensive mathematical, financial, statistical, and logical processing. The user works with an electronic version of the accountant's traditional worksheet, with rows and columns, called a *spreadsheet.*

star network Electronic communications **network** with a central unit (computer or **file server**) linked to a number of smaller computers and/or terminals (called *nodes*). The central unit acts as traffic controller for all nodes and controls communications to locations outside the network.

storage hardware Devices that accept and hold computer instructions and data in a form that is relatively permanent, commonly on magnetic disk or tape or on optical disk.

string Designated sequence, or group, of text characters.

structured decision Predictable decision that can be made about daily business activities by following a well-defined set of routine procedures; typically made by **operating (low-level) management**.

subdirectory Second level in the **MS-DOS** directory hierarchy; equivalent to a file drawer in a file cabinet (**root directory**), it can contain sub-subdirectories.

subschema Part of the **schema** of a **relational database**; it refers to the way certain records are linked to be useful to the user.

summary report Report for **middle (tactical) management** that reviews, summarizes, and analyzes historical data to help plan and control operations and implement policy formulated by **upper (strategic) management**. Summary reports show totals and trends.

supercomputer The largest and most powerful computer; it is about 50,000 times more powerful than a **microcomputer** and may cost as much as $20 million. Supercomputers are housed in special rooms; the next most powerful computer is the **mainframe**.

super video graphics array (S-VGA) Expansion card plugged into **expansion slot** in **system cabinet** that allows compatible monitor to display **bit-mapped graphics** in color; must be used with appropriate software; displays up to 256 colors at a very high **resolution**.

supervisor The "captain" of the **operating system**, it remains in a microcomputer's **main memory** and calls in other parts of the operating system as needed from **secondary storage** and controls all other programs in the computer. In a **multitasking** environment, a supervisor coordinates the execution of each program. Also known as *control program*.

surge suppressor Devices into which the user plugs a microcomputer system and which, in turn, are connected to the power line. They help to protect the power supply and other sensitive circuitry in the computer system from voltage spikes.

synchronous transmission Form of transmitting groups of characters as blocks with no start and stop bits between characters. Characters are sent as blocks with header and trailer bytes (called **synch bits**) inserted as identifiers at the beginnings and ends of blocks. Synchronous transmission is used by large computers to transmit huge volumes of data at high speeds. *Compare* **asynchronous transmission**.

syntax Rules for using a command.

system board *See* **motherboard**.

system files Files that must be stored on the disk **DOS** is loaded from.

system prompt Characters that display on the screen to indicate what **disk drive** is current and what **subdirectory** is current (if the **Prompt command** has been used).

system requirements Refers to the hardware and software that is required to use a particular software application.

systems development life cycle (SDLC) Formal process by which organizations build **computer-based information systems**. Participants are users, information processing staff, management of all departments, and computer specialists. The SDLC is used as a guide in establishing a business system's requirements, developing the system, acquiring hardware and software, and controlling development costs. It is often divided into six phases: (1) analyze current system; (2) define new system requirements; (3) design new system: (4) develop new system; (5) implement new system; (6) evaluate performance of and maintain new system.

systems flowchart Systems development modeling tool used to diagram and document design of a new system and present an overview of the entire system, including data flow (points of input, output, and storage) and processing activities.

systems software Programs that are the principal interface between all hardware, the user, and applications software; comprise **internal command instructions, external command instructions,** and **language processor**. *Compare* **applications software**.

system unit Main computer system cabinet in a microcomputer, which usually houses the power supply, the **motherboard,** and some storage devices.

TB *See* **terabyte**.

teleconferencing Electronic linkage of several people who participate in a conversation and share displayed data at the same time.

terabyte (TB) One trillion bytes.

thermal printer Nonimpact printer that uses heat to produce an image. The print mechanism heats the surface of chemically treated paper, producing dots as characters. No ribbon or ink is used.

thesaurus Lists of words that have similar meaning to a given word; feature of word processing programs.

timesharing System that supports many user stations or terminals simultaneously. A **front-end processor** may be used to schedule and control all user requests entering the system from the **terminals,** enabling the main computer to concentrate solely on processing.

token ring network Electronic communications **network**, in which each computer obtains exclusive access to the communications channel by "grabbing" a "token" and altering it before attaching a message. This altered token acts as a message indicator for the receiving computer, which, in turn, generates a new token, freeing up the channel for another computer. Computers in between the sender and the receiver examine the token and regenerate the message if the token is not theirs. Thus, only one computer can transmit a message at one time.

touch screen Video display **screen** sensitized to receive input from the touch of a finger.

track (1) On **magnetic tape** a channel of magnetic spots and spaces (1s and 0s) running the length of the tape. (2) On **disks,** a track is one of the circular bands.

trackball Input hardware device that functions like a **mouse** but doesn't need to be rolled around on the desktop; the ball is held in a socket on the top of the stationary device.

track density Number of **tracks** on magnetic medium. Common track densities are 48 tracks per inch (tpi) and 96 tpi. Track density affects capacity.

transaction log Complete record of activity affecting contents of a **database** during transaction period. This log aids in rebuilding database files if they are damaged.

transaction processing system (TPS) Operating-level information system that processes a large volume of transactions in a routine and repetitive manner; supports day-to-day business operating activities, or transactions. *Compare* **decision support system (DSS)**.

translator *See* **language processor**.

tree network *See* **hierarchical network**.

uninterruptible power supply (UPS) Device used to protect hardware from the damaging effects of a power surge; also keeps the system running for about 15–30 minutes, providing the user with enough time to save work and shut the system down.

UNIX **Operating system** initially created for **minicomputers**; it provides a wide range of capabilities, including **virtual storage, multiprogramming,** and **timesharing.** Although machine independent, it is not yet widely used on microcomputers because no standards have yet been developed for it.

unstructured decision Decision rarely based on predetermined routine procedures; involves the subjective judgment of the decision maker and is mainly the kind of decision made by upper management.

upper management The level of management dealing with decisions that are broadest in scope and cover the longest time frame. A manager at this level is also known as a *strategic decision maker. Compare* **middle management; operating management**.

user Person receiving the computer's services; generally someone without much technical knowledge who makes decisions based on reports and other results that computers produce; also called *end-user. Compare* **computer professional**.

video display screen Device for viewing computer output. Two main types are **cathode-ray tube (CRT)** and **flat screen**.

video graphics array (VGA) Expansion card plugged into **expansion slot** in **system cabinet** that allows compatible monitors to display **bit-mapped graphics** in color; must be used with appropriate software; displays 16 colors at a resolution higher than **EGA**.

Video Privacy Protection Act of 1988 U.S. law that prevents retailers in the United States from selling or disclosing video-rental records without the customer's consent or a court order.

virtual memory **Operating system** element that enables the computer to process as if it contained an almost unlimited supply of **main memory**. It enables a program to be broken into modules, or small sections, that can be loaded into main memory when needed. Modules not currently in use are stored on high-speed disk and retrieved one at a time when the operating system determines that the current module has completed executing. Also known as *virtual storage*.

virtual reality A computer-simulated reality that can interact with all the senses.

virus Bugs (programming errors) created intentionally by some programmers, usually "hackers" or "crackers," that consist of pieces of computer code (either hidden or posing as legitimate code) that, when downloaded or run, attach themselves to other programs or files and cause them to malfunction.

voice input device Input device that converts spoken words into electrical signals by comparing the electrical patterns produced by the speaker's voice to a set of prerecorded patterns. If a matching pattern is found, the computer accepts it as a part of its standard "vocabulary" and then activates and manipulates displays by spoken command. Also known as *voice recognition system*.

voice mail Electronic voice-messaging system that answers callers with a recording of the user's voice and records messages. Messages can be forwarded to various locations; local telephone companies provide voice mail services; voice mail systems are also used within companies.

voice output system Synthesized or taped sound; computer output used in situations where other **softcopy** output is inappropriate, as in automotive systems.

voice recognition system *See* **voice input device**.

volatile storage Form of memory storage in which data and instructions are lost when the computer is turned off. *Compare* **nonvolatile storage**. *See also* **random access memory (RAM)**.

warm boot Loading **DOS** into **RAM** *after* the computer has been turned on.

warranty An agreement between the user and a hardware manufacturer. If something fails in the computer system within a certain period of time, the manufacturer should repair it at no cost.

wide area network (WAN) Computer-based **network** that links communications resources scattered around a country or the world. *Compare* **local area network** and **metropolitan area network**.

window Most **video display screens** allow 24–25 lines of text to be viewed at one time; this portion is called a *window*. By moving (scrolling) text up and down the screen, other windows of text become available.

Windows *See* **Microsoft Windows**.

word processing Electronic preparation of text for creating, editing, or printing documents.

word processing software Program enabling user to create and edit documents by inserting, deleting, and moving text. Some programs also offer formatting features such as variable margins and different type sizes and styles, as well as more advanced features that border on **desktop publishing**.

word wrap In **word processing,** when the **cursor** reaches the right-hand margin of a line it automatically returns (wraps around) to the left-hand margin of the line below and continues the text; the user does not have to hit a key to make the cursor move down to the next line.

write once, read many (WORM) **Optical disk** whose data and instructions are imprinted by the disk manufacturer but whose content is determined by the buyer; after the data is imprinted, it cannot be changed. *Compare* **compact disk/read-only memory (CD-ROM); erasable optical disk**.

write-protect notch On a **diskette,** a notch in the protective cover that can be covered to prevent the **read/write head** from touching the disk surface so that no data can be recorded or erased.

WYSIWYG (what you see is what you get) Page description software that allows the user to see the final version of a **desktop publishing** document on the screen before it is printed out. *Compare* **code-oriented**.

INDEX

A

Access
    to computers, 311
    to databases, 228
Access times of diskettes, 82
Accounting, computers in, 18
Accuracy
    in credit reports, 307
    of information in management
        decisions, 256–257
Actions in business decisions, 256
Ada language, 174
Adapters, video, 116
Add-on memory boards, 56–57
Add-on utilities, 146
Addressing schemes, 59
Administration in DBMS, 239–240
AFE (Apple File Exchange) utility, 167
AI (artificial intelligence), 176, 290–293
Air transportation, computer careers
    in, 266
ALT key, 26
Alternatives in business decisions,
    254–255
ALU (arithmetic/logic units), 48
American National Standards Institute
    (ANSI), 173
American Standard Code for Information
    Interchange (ASCII), 72–73
Amplitude of signals, 183
Analog signals, 183–184
Analytical graphics, 141
Animation, 37
ANSI (American National Standards
    Institute), 173
Apple File Exchange (AFE) utility, 167
Apple II computers, 12. See also
    Macintosh computers
Application generators, 175
Applications software, 6, 128
    categories of, 128–129
    common features of, 129–130
    communications, 144
    computer-aided design, 143–144
    database managers, 140
    desktop publishing, 130–138
    graphics, 141
    hypertext, 147–148
    installing, 151
    integrated, 143
    multimedia, 147
    purchasing, 149–150
    spreadsheets, 138–139
    utilities, 146
    word processing, 130–133
Arithmetic/logic units (ALU), 48
Arrow keys, 28
Art, computer careers in, 142
Artificial hearing, 316
Artificial intelligence (AI), 176, 290–293
Artificial reality, 295, 297–298
Arts, computer careers in, 37
ASCII binary code, 72–73

Assembly languages, 172
Asynchronous data transmission, 184–185
Attributes in databases, 234
Auditing, computers in, 169
AUDITOR expert system, 297
Automobiles, computer careers in, 266
Auxiliary storage. See Storage hardware

B

Back pain, 336–337
Backing up
    databases, 239
    storage hardware, 91, 312, 334–336
Baked goods, expert systems for, 296
Banking, electronic, 210
Bar codes, computers for, 202
BASIC language, 173–174
Battery-powered clocks and calendars, 15
BBS (bulletin board services), 209
Bill-paying services, 236
Bin Vision Systems, 291
Binary code, 72–73
Binary digits (bits), 49, 71, 74–75
Biometric security, 311–312
Bit-mapped displays and graphics, 114
Bits (binary digits), 49, 71, 74–75
Blocks
    data transmission, 185
    of instructions, 61
B.O.B (Brains on Board) robot, 291–292
BodyElectric software, 297
Booting, 158
Broadband channels, 187
Bulletin board services (BBS), 209
Burglary investigations, expert systems
    for, 296
Bus
    capacity of, 61
    for microprocessors, 50
Bus networks, 203
Businesses, expert systems in, 297. See also
    Management information systems
    (MIS)
Bytes, 49, 74–75, 79

C

C language, 174
Cables for data transmission, 187–188
Cache memory, 59
CAD (computer-aided design) software,
    143–144, 202
CAE (computer-aided engineering)
    software, 143–145, 202
Calendars, 15
CAM (computer-aided manufacturing)
    software, 143–145, 202
Campaigns, computers in, 113
Capacity
    of data bus, 61
    of diskettes, 79–80
    of hard disks, 83
    of storage devices, 10–11

Caps Lock key, 28
Cards
    expansion, 56
    fax, 214
    hypertext, 147
    memory, 15
    punched, 26
Careers
    in arts and entertainment, 37
    in crime fighting, 60
    in food and beverage service, 87
    in health and medicine, 295
    in information, 236
    in manufacturing, 202
    in politics and government, 113
    in science and scholarship, 142
    in transportation, 266
    in white-collar jobs, 169
Carpal tunnel syndrome, 338–339
Cartridge-tape backup units, 91
Cartridges for hard disks, 88
CASE (computer-assigned software
    engineering) tools, 276
Cash-taking software, 87
Cathode-ray tubes (CRT), 12, 111–112,
    114
CD-ROM storage devices, 89
Census, computers for, 113
Central processing units (CPU), 5, 9, 11
Century Net system, 169
CGA (color graphics adapter), 116
Channels for data transmission, 186–192
Character boxes, 114
Character-mapped displays, 114
Character printers, 102–105
Characters, 74–75
Characters per second (cps), 10
Charts, 141
Check bits, 72–73
Chief information officers (CIO), 261
Child records, 232
Chips, 9
    designing, 52
    manufacturing, 53
CIM (computer-integrated
    manufacturing), 202
CIO (chief information officers), 261
CISC (complex instruction set
    computing), 61
Civil strife, 310
Cleaning diskette drives, 334
Clip art, 89
Clocks
    for synchronizing operations, 48–49,
        61
    for time, 15
Clones, 12, 326
Closed architecture, 57
Clout language, 176
Coaxial cable, 187–188
COBOL language, 173
Code of Fair Information Practice, 309
Code-oriented page description software,
    131, 136

I2   INDEX

Coding
    of data, 71–72
    of speech, 120
Color graphics adapter (CGA), 116
Color monitors, 12, 114–115
Color printers
    dot-matrix, 104
    laser, 108
Color scanners, 31–32
Common carriers, 198
Common View language, 299
Communications, 17
    for banking and investing, 210
    data transmission characteristics,
        182–186
    electronic bulletin boards, 209
    electronic mail, 209–210
    electronic shopping, 207–208
    facsimiles, 213–215
    hardware for, 192–197
    information services, 205–207
    media for, 186–192
    networks, 198–205
    software for, 144, 197–198
    viruses from, 210–212
Comp-U-Card merchandise broker, 236
Compact disk read-only memory
    (CD-ROM) storage devices, 89
Company databases, 241
Compatibility, 12, 326
Compilers, 159–160
Complex instruction set computing
    (CISC), 61
CompuServe information service, 207
Computennis program, 37
Computer-aided design (CAD) software,
    143–144, 202
Computer-aided engineering (CAE)
    software, 143–145, 202
Computer-aided manufacturing (CAM)
    software, 143–145, 202
Computer-assigned software engineering
    (CASE) tools, 276
Computer awareness, 2
Computer-based information systems, 263
Computer competency, 2
Computer error, 72
Computer Fraud and Abuse Act of 1986,
    308
Computer-integrated manufacturing
    (CIM), 202
Computer literacy, 2
Computer Matching and Privacy
    Protection Act of 1988, 309
Computer professionals, 2
Computer Software Piracy and
    Counterfeiting Amendment of 1983,
    313
Computer systems, 2–3
    hardware in, 3–5
    software in, 5–6
    types of, 6–15
Concentrators, 194
Connectivity, 2, 144, 198–205
Control
    of desktop publishing software, 137
    by management, 249–250
    of new systems, 277–278
Control programs, 159
Control unit in microprocessors, 46–48
Controllers
    in communications, 194
    DMA, 55–56
Coordination of databases, 239

Coprocessors, 51
Copying, unauthorized, 310
Copyright Act of 1976, 313
Copyright violations, 312–314
Cost
    and computer type, 11
    and speed, 49
Courts, computers in, 60
CPU (central processing units), 5, 9, 11
Crackers, 210, 310
Crashes, disk, 85
Credit-reporting companies, checking on,
    307–308
Crime, computer, 309–310
Crime fighting
    computer careers in, 60
    expert systems for, 296
CRT (cathode-ray tubes), 12, 111–112,
    114
Ctrl key, 26, 28
Cue computers, 37
Cumulative trauma disorders, 338–339
Cursor, 28–29, 129
Cursor-movement keys, 28
Custom software, 128, 149
Cyberspace, 297

D

Daisy wheel printers, 102–103, 105
Damage from computer crime, 310
Dance, programs for, 37
Data, 2–3
    backing up, 91, 239, 312, 334–336
    entering. See Input hardware
    independence of, 226–227
    integrated, 222
    integrity of, 225–226, 228
    redundancy of, 225, 227–228
    representation of, 49, 71–74
    storing, 74–76
    verification of, 278
Data access area on disks, 76
Data bus
    capacity of, 61
    for microprocessors, 50
Data dictionaries, 230–231
Data files, 75, 334–336
Data flow diagrams (DFD), 269–270
Data manipulation language (DML),
    228, 230
Data processing, 3
Data transfer rate, 82
Data transmission
    characteristics of, 182–186
    media for, 186–192
Database administrators (DBA), 239–240
Database management systems. See
    DBMS (database management
    systems)
Databases, 17, 226
    designing, 235, 237–238
    ownership of, 241
    privacy in, 306–307, 309
DataGloves, 297
Dates, important, in information
    processing, A1–A9
DBA (database administrators), 239–240
dBASE database managers, 17
DBMS (database management systems),
    17, 140, 222–225
    administration in, 239–240
    advantages and disadvantages of,
        240–241

    data dictionaries for, 230–231
    database models for, 232–235
    designing databases in, 235, 237–238
    and file management systems, 225–226
    hardware for, 227
    ownership in, 241
    software for, 227–230
    transaction logs for, 231–232
Decision support systems (DSS), 175,
    258–260
Decisions by management, 254–257. See
    also Management information
    systems (MIS)
Decoding, 47
Dedicated backup systems, 335
Dedicated lines, 194, 199
Del key, 28
Demodulation, 183–184
DENDRAL expert system, 296
Designing
    computer-aided design for, 143–144,
        202
    databases, 235, 237–238
    digitizers for, 39
    microprocessors, 52
    new systems, 275–278
Desktop management utilities, 146
Desktop publishing (DTP) software,
    130–138, 327
Detail reports, 250
Detective work, expert systems for, 296
DFD (data flow diagrams), 269–270
Dial-back routines, 277–278
Dialog Information Service, 206
Dictionaries
    CD-ROMs for, 89
    data, 230–231
    project, 276
Digital convergence, 182, 214
Digital signals, 183–184, 191
Digitizers, 39
Digitizing tablets, 39
Dilemmas, ethical, 315
DIP switches, 194
Direct entry systems, 29–30
Direct implementation of new systems,
    280
Direct-mail, computers for, 113
Disabled people, 31, 316–318
Disaster plans, 277, 311–312
Disk cartridges, 88
Disk crashes, 85
Disk drive gates, 76
Disk drives. See also Diskettes; Hard disks
    dust in, 333–334
    operation of, 76–79
Disk operating systems
    Macintosh, 167–168
    MS-DOS, 163–166
    OS/2, 166–167
    UNIX, 167
Disk utilities, 146
Diskettes. See also Hard disks
    access times of, 82
    retrieving and storing data on, 76–79
    sectors on, 81
    size and shapes of, 81
    storage capacity of, 79–80
Distributed databases, 241
Distributing output, controls on, 277
DMA (dynamic memory access) controller,
    55–56
DML (data manipulation language),
    228, 230

Document management software, 17, 130–133
Documentation
  for clones, 326
  for software, 6, 149
Documentation libraries, 277
Doors, disk drive, 76
DOS. *See* Disk operating systems
Dot-matrix printers, 102–105
Double-density diskettes, 80
Double-sided diskettes, 79–80
Dow Jones News/Retrieval system, 207, 236
Draft quality printer mode, 103–104
Drafting, 39, 89
Drawings, 39, 143–144
DRILLING ADVISOR expert system, 296
Drives. *See also* Diskettes; Hard disks
  dust in, 333–334
  operation of, 76–79
DSS (decision support systems), 175, 258–260
DTP (desktop publishing) software, 130–138, 327
Dust, protection from, 333–334
DXplain system, 295
Dynamic file linking, 138–139
Dynamic memory access (DMA) controller, 55–56
Dyslexia, computers for, 317

E

Earth stations, 189
Ease in using software, 149
EBCDIC code, 72–73
EDP (electronic data processing) systems, 257
Education applications software, 129
EEPROM (electrically erasable programmable read-only memory), 54
EGA (enhanced graphics adapter), 116
80-DOS operating system, 163–164
EISA (Extended Industry Standard Architecture) bus system, 61
EL (electroluminescent) displays, 118–119
Elections, computers in, 113
Electrically erasable programmable read-only memory (EEPROM), 54
Electroluminescent (EL) displays, 118–119
Electromagnetic field (EMF) emissions, 337
Electronic bulletin boards services (BBS), 209
Electronic data processing (EDP) systems, 257
Electronic mail, 209–210
Electronic networks, privacy in, 308
Electronic shopping, 207–208
Electronic spreadsheet software, 18, 55, 138–139
Electronic supervision, 308, 339
E-mail, 209–210
EMF (electromagnetic field) emissions, 337
Employees, computer crime by, 310
Emulation, 151
Encryption, 277, 312
Encyclopedias, CD-ROMs for, 89
Engineering
  digitizers for, 39
  software tools for, 143–145, 202, 276
Engineering standards, CD-ROMs for, 89

Enhanced graphics adapter (EGA), 116
ENTER key, 27–28
Entering data. *See* Input hardware
Entertainment, computer careers in, 37
Entity classes, 234
Environment science, computer careers in, 142
Environmental disasters, safeguards from, 277
EPROM (erasable programmable read-only memory), 54
Erasable optical disks, 89–90
Ergonomics, 336–339
Error checking in data transmissions, 184
Error handling by software, 149–150
Esber, Edward M., 18
ESC key, 26
Ethics, 306–309, 315
E-time, 48
Europe, privacy issues in, 309
Evaluation of new systems, 281–282
Even-parity schemes, 73, 184
Event-initiated reports, 252
Exception reports, 252
Execution cycles, 48
Exoskeletal robotic devices, 317
Expanded memory, 56–57
Expansion cards, 56
Expansion slots, 15, 56
EXPERT-EASE expert system, 296
Expert systems, 176, 294, 296–297
Extended Binary Coded Decimal Interchange Code (EBCDIC), 72–73
Extended graphics array (XGA), 116
Extended Industry Standard Architecture (EISA) bus system, 61
Extended memory, 58–59
External command instructions, 159
External hard disk drives, 85–86
External modems, 194
Extra high-density diskettes, 80
Eyephones, 297
Eyescan communicator, 30
Eyestrain, 336

F

Facsimile (fax) capabilities, 17, 31, 213–215
FACTS (Facility for Accurate Case Tracking System), 60
Failures, technological, 310–311
Fair Credit Reporting Act of 1970, 308
Fans and dust, 333
FASTBACK program, 335
Fax capabilities, 17, 31, 213–215
Fax cards, 214
Fiber-optic sensors, 266
Fiber optics, 191–192
Field robots, 202
Fields, 74–75, 223
Fifth-generation languages, 175–176
File management systems, 140, 225–226
File servers, 200
File symbols in flowcharts, 270
Files
  data, 75, 334–336
  and data hierarchy, 74–75
  libraries of, 277
  linking, 138–139
  updating, 225
Finance, computers for, 18
Financial information, computer careers in, 236

Financial planning languages, 175
Fingerprint scanners, 33
First-generation languages, 172
Fishing, programs for, 37
Flat-file database management systems, 140
Flat screen technologies, 117–119
Flatbed plotters, 111
Flatbed scanners, 31–32
Floppy disks. *See* Diskettes
Flowcharts, 269–272
Flying head hard disk design, 85
FMYCIN language, 296
Follow-ups in business decisions, 256
Fonts, 110
Food services, computer careers in, 87
Formatting diskettes, 81
FORTRAN language, 173
Fourth-generation languages (4GL), 174–175
Freedom of Information Act of 1970, 308
Freeware, 212, 313–314
Frequency of signals, 183
Front-end processors
  for communications, 194, 196
  for timesharing, 162
Full-duplex data transmission, 186
Function keys, 26, 28
Future
  of information processing, A9
  of microcomputers, 18
Fuzzy logic, 293–294

G

G2 Real-Time Expert system, 296
GADS (Gate Assignment Display System), 266
Gas plasma displays, 119
GB (gigabytes), 49
General business management software, 128
General-purpose applications software, 129
Generations, programming-language, 170–176
Gigabytes (GB), 49
Government, computer careers in, 113
Graphic images, CD-ROMs for, 89
Graphic(al) user interfaces (GUI), 35, 165–166
Graphics
  scanners for, 30
  software for, 141
Gray-market computers, 328
Gray-scale monitors, 116
Gray-scale scanning, 30
Guards, 311
GUI (graphic user interfaces), 35, 165–166

H

Hackers, 210, 310
HAL retriever language, 176
Half-duplex data transmission, 185–186
Hand-held scanners, 31–32
Handicapped people, 31, 316–318
Hands, artificial, 317
Handwriting for input, 40
Hard disks, 14–15, 82–84
  backing up, 334–336
  cartridges for, 88
  retrieving and storing data on, 85–86

Hard disks (*cont.*)
  temperature changes in, 332
  as virtual memory, 59
Hard-sectored diskettes, 81
Hardcards, 85
Hardcopy output, 5, 101–111
Hardware, 2–5
  for communications, 192–197
  for DBMS, 227
  for decision support systems, 259–260
  for hard disk backups, 335–336
  input. *See* Input hardware
  for new systems, 278–279
  output. *See* Output hardware
  processing. *See* Processing hardware
  purchasing, 324–326
  storage. *See* Memory; Storage
    hardware
  for systems development projects, 264
  for virtual reality, 297
Hazards
  to data, 309–311
  to health, 336–339
Head-cleaning disks, 334
Head crashes, 85
Headaches, 336
Header bytes in data transmission, 185
Health
  computer careers in, 295
  hazards to, 336–339
Hearing, computers for, 316
Help Evaluation through Logical
    Processing (HELP) system, 295
Help screens in applications software,
    130
Hertz, 183
Hierarchical database models, 232–233
Hierarchical networks, 201
Hierarchy of data, 74–75
High-density diskettes, 80
High-level programming languages, 47,
    159–160, 170–176
History of information processing, A1–A9
Home management applications software,
    129
Home security, computer careers in, 60
Home workers, 315, 318
Hospitals, computers in, 295
Housekeeping tasks, 159
Hubs, diskette, 76
Human errors, 311
Human expertise in expert systems, 294,
    296–297
HyperTalk language, 175
Hypertext, 147–148

I

IBM PC, 12
Icons, 35, 165
I-cycles, 48
ILPRS expert system, 297
Impact printers, 102–105, 334
Implementation
  of databases, 239
  of management information systems,
    260–261
  of new systems, 279–281
Index holes on disks, 77
Individual databases, 241
Industrial robots, 202
Industry-specific software, 128–129
Industry Standard Architecture (ISA) bus
    system, 61

Information, 3
  accuracy of, 256–257
  computer careers in, 236
Information centers, 261–262
Information processing, key dates in,
    A1–A9
Information reporting systems, 257–258
Information requirements analyses for
    databases, 237
Information resellers, 306
Information resource management
    (IRM), 250
Information services, 205–207
Information systems. *See* Management
    information systems (MIS)
Initializing diskettes, 81
Ink-jet printers, 106–107
Input
  in new systems analysis, 274–275
  verification of, 278
Input hardware, 4, 12
  fax machines, 31
  keyboards, 26–29
  pen-based, 40
  pointing devices, 34–39
  scanning systems, 30–33
  voice devices, 31, 33–34
Ins key, 28
Installing applications software, 151
Instruction cycles, 48
Instruction sets, 61–62
Instructions in systems software, 158–159
Integrated data, 222
Integrated Services Digital Network
    (ISDN), 197
Integrated software, 143
Intelligent robots, 290–291
Internal command instructions, 158–159
Internal database view, 238
Internal hard disk drives, 85–86
Internal memory, 5
Internal modems, 15, 193–194
International networks, 199
International Standards Organization
    (ISO), 173, 196
Interpreters, 159–160
Inventories, computers for, 202
Investing
  computers in, 169
  electronic, 210
IPPMS expert system, 297
IRM (information resource management),
    250
ISA (Industry Standard Architecture) bus
    system, 61
ISDN (Integrated Services Digital
    Network), 197
ISO (International Standards
    Organization), 173, 196

J

Jobs, computer knowledge requirements
    for, 15–16. *See also* Careers

K

K (kilobytes), 49
KBMS (Knowledge Base Management
    System), 296
Key dates in information processing,
    A1–A9
Keyboard utilities, 146
Keyboards, 4, 12, 26–29

Kilobytes (K), 49
Knowledge Base Management System
    (KBMS), 296
Knowledge-based systems, 290
Knowledge Index service, 206

L

LAN (local area networks), 199
Language processors, 159–160, 173
Languages
  data manipulation, 228, 230
  natural, 175–176, 293–294
  page description, 108, 130
  programming, 47, 159–160, 170–176
  query, 174, 228–229
  script, 197
Laptop computers, 9
Laser printers, 108–109
Latency, 82
Laws, privacy, 308–309
LCD (liquid crystal displays), 117–118
Learning ease of software, 149
Legal libraries, CD-ROMs for, 89
Letter-quality printers, 102–103
Levels of management, 250–253
LEXIS database, 206, 236
Libraries
  documentation, 277
  legal, 89
Licenses
  for operating systems, 164
  for software, 313
Light pens, 38
Line-of-sight signals, 188
Line-of-sight systems, 34
Linking spreadsheets, 138–139
Liquid crystal displays (LCD), 117–118
LISP language, 296
Local area networks (LAN), 199
Locks, 277, 311
Loebner, Hugh, 293
Logical database design, 237–238
Logs
  for databases, 231–232
  for security, 277
Low-end mainframe computers, 8–9
Lucente, Edward, 46
Luggage handling, computers for, 266

M

Machine cycles, 48
Machine dependent operating systems, 167
Machine-independent languages, 172
Machine language, 47, 172
Macintosh computers, 12
  extended keyboards for, 29
  operating system for, 167–168
  purchasing, 326–328
Magazines
  computers listed in, 328, 331
  software listed in, 150
Magnetic tape for backups, 335–336
Magneto-optical (MO) disk drives, 90
Mail, electronic, 209–210
Mail-order purchases, 328
Main memory. *See* RAM (random access
    memory)
Mainframe computers, 8, 11
Maintaining and caring for systems
  backups for, 334–336
  dust and pollution considerations in,
    333–334

Maintaining and caring for systems (*cont.*)
new systems, 281–282
plugging in systems, 332–333
temperature considerations for, 330, 332
turning on systems, 332
and vibrations, 334
MAN (metropolitan area networks), 199
Management
of databases. *See* DBMS (database management systems)
duties of, 249–250
levels of, 250–253
Management information systems (MIS), 248
and decisions, 254–257
developing and implementing, 260–261
information centers, 261–262
and levels of management, 250–254
systems analysis and design for, 262–282
types of, 257–260
Manufacturing
computer-aided, 143–145, 202
computer careers in, 202
of microprocessors, 53
Mapmaking, 39, 113
Math, arithmetic/logic units for, 48
Math coprocessors, 51
MB (megabytes), 49
MCA (micro channel architecture) bus system, 61
Mechanical drawing, software for, 143–144
Media
for data transmission, 186–192
for storage, 75–76
Medicine, computer careers in, 295
Megabytes (MB), 49
Megahertz (MHz), 48–49
Memory
and computer type, 9, 11
main. *See* RAM (random access memory)
read-only, 51, 54
Memory boards, 56–57
Memory cards, 15
Mental health, 339
Menu bars and menus in applications software, 129–130
Meta-Virus, 210–211
Metropolitan area networks (MAN), 199
MHz (megahertz), 48–49
Michelangelo virus, 211–212
Micro channel architecture (MCA) bus system, 61
Microcomputer applications software, 175
Microcomputers, 2, 9–10
future of, 18, A9
vs. other computer types, 11
parts of, 12–15
uses of, 15–18
Microprocessors, 9
arithmetic/logic units in, 48
bus for, 50
control unit in, 46–48
coprocessors for, 51
designing, 52
manufacturing, 53
registers in, 48–50
Microsoft Windows, 164–166
Microwave systems, 188–189
Middle management, 251–252
Midsized computers, 8–9
Minicomputers, 8–9, 11

Mips (millions of instructions per second), 11
MIS. *See* Management information systems (MIS)
MO (magneto-optical) disk drives, 90
Modeling tools, 272–273
Modems, 15, 184, 193–194
Modifier keys, 28
Modula 2 language, 174
Modulation, 183–184
Money savings with desktop publishing software, 137
Monitors, 5, 12–13, 114–117, 332
Monochrome monitors, 12, 114
Motherboards, 14
Mouse, 35–36
MS-DOS operating system, 163–166
Multimedia conferences, 198
Multimedia software, 147
Multiplexers, 194
Multiprocessing, 161–162
Multiprogramming, 161
Multitasking, 59, 160–162, 166
MYCIN expert system, 294

N

Narrowband channels, 187
Natural hazards, 310
Natural language processing, 175–176, 293–294
Navigation systems, computers for, 266
Near-letter-quality (nlq) printer mode, 103–104
Neck pain, 336–337
Negotiator Pro system, 296
Networks, 17, 182, 198
bus, 203
configurations for, 199–205
in database models, 233–234
privacy in, 308
ring, 203–205
Star, 200–201
New Systems Requirements report, 275
NEXIS database, 206
NEXPRET expert system, 296
Nlq (near-letter-quality) printer mode, 103–104
Noise, 339
Nonimpact printers, 106–110
Nonprocedural languages, 174
Nonvolatile storage, 5, 71
Notebook computers, 9
Num Lock key, 28
Number of users and computer type, 11
Numeric keypad, 27–28

O

Object code, 159
Object-oriented programming, 298–300
Odd-parity schemes, 73, 184
Off-the-shelf software, 128
OIS (operations information systems), 257
On-demand reports, 252
101-key enhanced keyboards, 28
Open architecture, 57
Open Systems Interconnection (OSI), 197
Open wire lines, 187
Operating management, 250–252
Operating System 2 (OS/2) operating system, 166–167
Operating systems
Macintosh, 167–168

MS-DOS, 163–166
OS/2, 166–167
UNIX, 167
Operational decision makers, 252
Operations information systems (OIS), 257
Optical character recognition (OCR) software, 30
Optical storage devices, 88–90
Orbit Search Service, 206
Organized crime, computer crime by, 310
Organizing data. *See* DBMS (database management systems)
OS/2 (Operating System 2) operating system, 166–167
OSI (Open Systems Interconnection), 197
Output hardware, 5, 100
categories of, 101–102
cathode-ray tubes, 111–112, 114
flat screen technologies, 117–119
monitors, 114–115
printers, 102–111
speed of, 10–11
voice systems, 120
Ownership of databases, 241

P

Packets, data transmission, 185
Page description languages, 108, 130
Page description software, 131
Parallel implementation of new systems, 280
Parent records, 232
Parity bits
in data transmissions, 184
in memory, 72–73
Partitions in memory, 161
Parts for clones, 326
Pascal language, 174
Passes, 277
Passwords, 277, 309, 311
Paterson, Tim, 163
PC-DOS operating system, 164
PCs (personal computers). *See* Microcomputers
Pen-based computing, 40
Pens, light, 38
Perception robots, 290
Periodic reports, 252
Personal computers. *See* Microcomputers
Personal management applications software, 129
Personal robots, 291–293
Phased implementation of new systems, 280
Physical database design, 238
Picture elements (pixels), 35, 111–112
Pilot implementation of new systems, 281
Piracy, software, 312–313
Pixels (picture elements), 35, 111–112
PL/1 language, 173
Planning by management, 249
Plastic surgery, computers in, 295
Plotters, 102, 111
Plugging in systems, 332–333
Point-of-sales (POS) systems, computers in, 87
Pointing devices, 34
digitizers, 39
light pens, 38
mouse, 35–36
touch screens, 38
trackballs, 36
Police departments, computers in, 60
Politics, computer careers in, 113

Pollution, protection from, 333–334
Portable operating systems, 167
Portable printers, 108, 110
Porter, James, 81
Ports, 15
POS (point-of-sales) systems, computers in, 87
Post offices, natural language processing in, 293
Postimplementation evaluation of new systems, 281–282
PostScript description language, 108, 130, 327
Power of processing hardware, 59, 61–62
Power strips, 332
Power supplies, 14, 333
Presentation graphics, 141
Primary storage. See RAM (random access memory)
Printers
  drivers for, 151
  impact, 102–105, 334
  nonimpact, 106–110
  ports for, 15
  vibrations from, 334
Privacy, 306–309
Privacy Act of 1974, 308
Private networks, 198
Problem recognition and identification, 254
Procedural languages, 172–173
Procedures, 3, 248
Process symbols in flowcharts, 269
Processing, 3
Processing hardware, 5
  microprocessors, 46–53
  power of, 59, 61–62
  random access memory, 54–59
  read-only memory, 51, 54
Processing requirements in new systems analysis, 274–275
Processing speed and computer type, 11
Prodigy information service, 207
Professionals, 2
Program independence, 226
Programmable keys, 28
Programmable read-only memory (PROM), 54
Programming languages, 47, 159–160, 170–176
Programs, 6, 75
Project development teams, 261
Project dictionaries, 276
PROLOG language, 296
PROM (programmable read-only memory), 54
Proprietary databases, 241
PROSPECTOR expert system, 296
Protocols and protocol converters, 195–197
Prototyping tools, 273
Public databanks, 205–207
Public domain software, 314
Public networks, 198
Pull-down menus, 130
Punched cards, 26
Purchases
  of applications software, 149–150
  checklist for, 341–343
  of clones, 326
  guidelines for, 329–330
  of Macintosh computers, 326–328
  software and hardware considerations in, 324–326
  sources for, 328–329

Q
Q&A language, 176
Quadruple-density diskettes, 80
Query languages, 174, 223, 228–229
Queues, 248
QWERTY layout, 28

R
RAM (random access memory), 5
  chips for, 55
  and computer type, 9, 11
  function of, 54–55
  increasing, 55–59
  internal command instructions in, 158
  partitioning, 161
  requirements for, 324, 326
RAM-resident utilities, 146
Read-only memory (ROM), 51, 54
Reading machines, 316
Read/write heads, 76
Real estate, computers in, 169
REBES (Residential Burglary Expert Systems), 296
Recording density of diskettes, 80
Records, 74–75, 223, 232
Reduced instruction set computing (RISC), 61–62
Reed, Rex, 311
Reference books, CD-ROMs for, 89
Registers
  in microprocessors, 48–50
  size of, 59
Relational databases, 140, 234–235
Relationships in databases, 227
Removable media, backing up data on, 335
Repeaters, 187
Repetitive strain injury (RSI), 338–339
Report writers, 175, 229
Requests for proposal (RFP), 275
Resident commands, 158–159
Residential Burglary Expert Systems (REBES), 296
Resolution
  of CRTs, 111, 117
  of printers, 108
  of scanners, 30
Restaurant services, computer careers in, 87
RETURN key, 27–28
RFP (requests for proposal), 275
RGB monitors, 12, 114–115
Right to Financial Privacy Act of 1979, 308
Ring networks, 203–205
RISC (reduced instruction set computing), 61–62
Roadways, computers for, 266
Robots, 202, 290–293
RoleCall program, 37
ROM (read-only memory), 51, 54
Root records, 232
Rotational delay, 82
RPG language, 174
RSI (repetitive strain injury), 338–339

S
Safeguards
  for databases, 239–240
  for new systems, 277–278

Sales order entry systems, 248
Satellite systems, 189–191
Savvy Retriever language, 176
Scanheads, 31
Scanning systems, 30–33
Schema, database, 237–238
Scholarship, computer careers in, 142
Schwartz, Lillian, 142
Science, computer careers in, 142
Screen generators, 229
Screen utilities, 146
Screens, 5, 12–13, 114–117, 332
Script languages, 197
Scrolling in applications software, 129
SDLC. See Systems development life cycle (SDLC)
Second-generation languages, 172
Secondary storage. See Storage hardware
Sectors on disks, 81, 85
Security, 311–312
  for databases, 239–240
  for new systems, 277–278
  robots for, 292–293
Seek time, 82
Semiconductors, 9
Semistructured decisions, 252–253
Sensor systems, computers for, 266
Service robots, 202
Servicing of systems, 328
Shared databases, 241
Shareware, 212, 313
Sheet-fed scanners, 31
Shielded cable, 187–188
SHIFT key, 27–28
Shopping, electronic, 207–208
Signals, analog and digital, 183–184
Simplex data transmission, 185
Single-density diskettes, 80
Single-sided diskettes, 79–80
Single-user operating systems, 160–161
Sink symbols in flowcharts, 270
Size
  of CRT screens, 117
  of diskettes, 81
  of registers, 59
SLC. See Systems development life cycle (SDLC)
Smith, Robert Ellis, 307
Smoking, 333
SNA (Systems Network Architecture), 196
Soft-sectored diskettes, 81
Softcopy output, 5, 101, 111–120
Software, 2, 5–6
  applications. See Applications software
  for communications, 197–198
  for DBMS, 227–230
  for decision support systems, 260
  for hard disk backups, 335–336
  for modems, 194
  in new systems analysis, 275, 278
  pirating of, 312–313
  purchasing, 324–326
  for systems development projects, 264
  systems. See Systems software
  for virtual reality, 297
  writing, 170–176
Software Copyright Act of 1980, 313
Software packages, 6
Sound, multimedia software for, 147
Source code, 159
Source symbols in flowcharts, 270
Special discipline software, 129
Special-purpose keys, 28

Specie Select program, 37
Speech coding, 120
Speech synthesis, 120
Speed
 of clock, 49, 61
 of communications, 197
 of compilers and interpreters, 160
 and cost, 49
 of output devices, 10–11
 of printers, 102–103, 108
 of processing, 11
Spikes, voltage, 332–333
Spimaster robot, 292
Sports, computer careers in, 37
Spreadsheet software, 18, 55, 138–139
SQL (Structured Query Language), 223
Stacks, hypertext, 147
Staffing by management, 249
Standards, 12
Star networks, 200–201
Steering committees, 267
Stock market, computers in, 169
Stop-start data transmission, 184–185
Storage hardware, 5. See also Memory
 backing up, 91, 312, 334–336
 and computer type, 10–11
 for DBMS, 227
 diskettes, 76–82
 fundamentals of, 70–76
 hard disks, 82–88
 for microcomputers, 14
 in new systems analysis, 274–275
 optical devices, 88–90
Stores, purchases in, 328
Strategic decision makers, 253
Streaming-tape backup units, 91
Stress, 339
Structured decisions, 252–253
Structured Query Language (SQL), 223
Subroutines, 61
Subschema, database, 237–238
Summary reports, 252, 256
Super Video Graphics Array, 116
Supercomputers, 7–8, 11
Superdrives, 328
Supervision
 electronic, 308, 339
 by management, 249
Supervisors, 159, 250–252
Support
 for hardware, 328
 for software, 150
Surge suppressors, 332–333
Surgery, computers for teaching, 295
Surveillance, electronic, 308
Symbols, flowchart, 269–270
Synchronous data transmission, 185
Syntax, 170
System boards, 14
System units, 13–15
Systems, 2–3
 hardware in, 3–5
 software in, 5–6
 types of, 6–15
Systems analysis and design, 262–263
Systems development life cycle (SDLC),
 262–267
 analysis of current system in, 267–270
 defining new system requirements in,
 270–275
 designing new systems in, 275–278
 developing new systems in, 278–279

evaluation in, 281–282
 implementing new systems in, 279–281
Systems flowcharts, 272
Systems integration, 264
Systems Network Architecture (SNA), 196
Systems software, 6, 128, 158
 external command instructions for, 159
 internal command instructions for,
 158–159
 language processors for, 159–160
 Macintosh, 167–168
 MS-DOS, 163–166
 multiprocessing with, 161–162
 multitasking with, 160–162
 OS/2, 166–167
 timesharing with, 162–163
 UNIX, 167

T

Tactical decision makers, 252
Tape backups, 91, 335–336
Tax preparation, computers in, 169
TAXADVISOR expert system, 297
TAXMAN expert system, 297
Technical knowledge, 2
Teleconferencing services, 198
Telephone lines, 187
Television, computer careers in, 37
Temperature, importance of, 330, 332
Terragraphics guidebooks, 37
Terrorism, 310
Testing new systems, 279
Text, scanners for, 30
TheaterGame program, 37
Theft, 310
Thermal printers, 106–107
Third-generation languages, 172–174
Thompson, Kenneth, 167
TIGER system, 113
Time savings with desktop publishing
 software, 137
Time slices, 162
Timeliness of information, 257
Timesharing, 162–163
Token ring networks, 203–205
Toll-collecting systems, 307
Touch screens, 38
TPS (transaction processing systems), 257
Track densities, 80
Trackballs, 36
Tracks, 80, 85
Trailer bytes in data transmission, 185
Training for new systems, 279
Transaction logs for databases, 231–232
Transaction processing systems (TPS), 257
Translators, 159, 173
Transponders, 189
Transportation, computer careers in, 266
Tree networks, 201
Trojan horses, 212
Tuples, 234
Turing, Alan, 293
Twisted-pair cable, 187
Typewriter keys, 28

U

Unauthorized copying, 310
Unintelligent robots, 290
Uninterruptible power supplies (UPS), 333
UNIX operating system, 167

Unstructured decisions, 253
Updating files, 225
Upper management, 251–253
UPS (uninterruptible power supplies), 333
User views in databases, 237
Users, 2
 computer crime by, 310
 and computer type, 11
 in decision support systems, 260
 in systems development projects,
 263–265
Utilities, 146, 229–230

V

Vector symbols in flowcharts, 270
Versions, MS-DOS, 164
Vertical recording technology, 80
VGA (video graphics array), 116
Vibrations, 334
Video display boards, 15
Video display screen, 5, 12–13, 114–117,
 332
Video graphics array (VGA), 116
Video Privacy Protection Act of 1988, 308
Virtual memory, 59
Virtual reality, 295, 297–298
Viruses, 210–212, 314
Vision
 computers for, 316
 for robots, 291
Vocabularies for voice input systems,
 31, 34
Voice input devices, 31, 33–34
Voice output systems, 120
Voice recognition systems, 31, 33–34, 316
Voice Trader technology, 31
Voiceband channels, 187
Volatile storage, 5, 55, 70
Voltage spikes, 332–333
VP-Expert system, 296

W

Walter, Russ, 313
WAN (wide area networks), 199–200
Warranties, 326, 328
What-if analyses
 with decision support systems, 259
 with spreadsheets, 138
What-you-see-is-what-you-get
 (WYSIWYG) software, 131–132,
 134, 137
White collar computer careers, 169
Wide area networks (WAN), 199–200
Wildlife management, computer careers
 in, 142
Winchester disk drives, 85
Windows, 164–166
Word processing software, 17, 130–133
Working at home, 315, 318
WORM (Write Once, Read Many)
 technology, 89
Worms, 212
Write/protect notches, 76
WYSIWYG (what-you-see-is-what-you-
 get) software, 131–132, 134, 137

X

XCON expert system, 296
XGA (extended graphics array), 116

PHOTO CREDITS